Warfare in History

THE ENGLISH ARISTOCRACY AT WAR

FROM THE WELSH WARS OF EDWARD I
TO THE BATTLE OF BANNOCKBURN

WARFARE IN HISTORY
ISSN 1358–779X

Series editor
Matthew Bennett, Royal Military Academy, Sandhurst

This series aims to provide a wide-ranging and scholarly approach to military history, offering both individual studies of topics or wars, and volumes giving a selection of contemporary and later accounts of particular battles; its scope ranges from the early medieval to the early modern period.

New proposals for the series are welcomed; they should be sent to the publisher at the address below.

Boydell and Brewer Limited, PO Box 9, Woodbridge, Suffolk, IP12 3DF

THE ENGLISH ARISTOCRACY AT WAR

FROM THE WELSH WARS OF EDWARD I
TO THE BATTLE OF BANNOCKBURN

David Simpkin

THE BOYDELL PRESS

First published 2008
The Boydell Press, Woodbridge

ISBN 978–1–84383–388–8

The Boydell Press is an imprint of Boydell & Brewer Ltd
PO Box 9, Woodbridge, Suffolk IP12 3DF, UK
and of Boydell & Brewer Inc.
668 Mt Hope Avenue, Rochester, NY 14620, USA
website: www.boydellandbrewer.com

A CIP catalogue record for this book is available
from the British Library

This publication is printed on acid-free paper

Printed in Great Britain by
Antony Rowe Ltd, Chippenham, Wiltshire

Contents

Tables

General Editor's Preface

This volume is the most recent product of a school of research into the administrative documents of English government in the 13th and 14th centuries in search of an understanding of the composition of its armies, their recruitment, organisation leadership and activities on campaign. This is no little undertaking and might have seemed unrealisable were it not for the work of Dr Andrew Ayton of the University of Hull, who is in a way the mentor for this book, and in a more general sense the initiatives of Professor Michael Prestwich (Durham) and Professor Anne Curry (formerly Reading, now Southampton). David Simpkin is one of a generation of talented young scholars who have turned their attention the theme as a result. He is also a member of the AHRC project 'The Soldier in Late Medieval England', directed by Professor Curry.

Dr Simpkin's research has produced fascinating information on almost fifteen hundred men of knightly rank and above and some five thousand warriors of sub-knightly rank (sergeants and *valletti*) who made up the military community of Edwardian England in the late 13th and early 14th centuries. What is remarkable is that contrary to earlier views about the unwillingness of knights and others to serve in war, about eight out of ten of them and some three-quarters of the sergeants liable for service did indeed do so. This despite the evidence that the Welsh and Scottish campaigns of Edward I, and his less successful son, were far from profitable and that many soldiers of all ranks ended up seriously out of pocket as a result.

There is also plenty of evidence of long-service careers, although this can be patchy in nature. It is possible through the available materials to identify the development of a 'professional' force, hardened by regular campaigning and working together. Inevitably there is also information suggesting that warfare could be an occasional activity and that it proved difficult to keep contingents together across time. In respect of this latter point, though, it should be noted that even regiments in armies today see a change of personnel and cross-posting that make them a great deal less 'regular' in their organisation and manning than might be supposed by the bureaucratic trappings of a modern state army.

Indeed, Simpkin's work enables the reader to gain a much deeper understanding of how the Edwardian forces were recruited, organised and deployed, focussing on the Battle of Falkirk (1298) as the central point of the investigation. This requires him to deal with ideas of feudal and other forms of service in period before the indentured armies of mid-14th century. This is tricky ground but he is sure-footed amongst obstacles to understanding just how forces were put together. His view of a fusion of procedures is neatly encapsulated in this passage:

> Feudal military service, then, was perfectly compatible with the process of sub-recruitment, which was fundamental to the formation of many of the

largest campaign retinues, particularly those led by men of comital status. In fact, once the veneer of compartmentalisation presented by Crown records is removed, revealing the intricate reality of retinue recruitment and organisation at ground level, the differences between 'paid', voluntary unpaid' and 'feudal men-at-arms, and therefore between paid, gratuitous and feudal service begin to melt away. (p.176)

Finally, Simpkin's prosoprographical analysis enables him to consider the role of leadership in the military community. Too often it is glibly assumed that 'medieval' armies were led by men appointed by reason of their noble rank and no other, and that competence in command was therefore a result of random chance rather than meritocratic allocation. While it is true that there were still some cases of aristocratic amateurism, these were largely outweighed by intelligent appointments with useful outcomes. Unfortunately, the evidence does not allow us to see exactly how command was exercised in the field. However, this book gives many valuable insights, serving to educate both medievalists and historians of later periods about the professionalism which can be found in chivalric warfare.

Matthew Bennett
Royal Military Academy Sandhurst

FOR MUM, DAD AND KAREN

Preface and Acknowledgements

The idea for this book arose six years ago during conversations with Dr Andrew Ayton of the University of Hull, where I had the good fortune to be based throughout the course of my work. Possessing little idea of the immense research task involved, but keen to find out more, I decided to undertake the job of transcribing and computerising the voluminous extant records for military service from the reigns of Edward I and Edward II. The underlying objective was to push back to the late thirteenth century the boundaries of knowledge on the medieval English soldier, and the armies in which he served, thereby adding to Dr Ayton's work (and that of others) on aristocratic warriors and their activities in the period after 1327. That the journey between then and now has for the most part been a smooth one is due in large measure to Dr Ayton's unwavering enthusiasm and belief in the virtues of the project. Moreover, his suggestions on the direction of my research, and his comments on the many drafts of chapters handed to him, have on a practical level been invaluable. This book would be very different had it not been for his input; indeed, it might never have been written at all. Nor would completion of the project have been possible without the financial assistance provided by the Arts and Humanities Research Council, whose generous grant of a three-year scholarship I gladly acknowledge.

During my time at Hull I benefited from the kindness of many people, without whose assistance and support the task of researching and writing this book would have been far more difficult. The vast majority of the published materials utilised in this study were consulted in the Brynmor Jones library on the university campus, and I am grateful to the staff of that facility for responding to my many requests with alacrity and good humour. Mark Sherit, my former study companion and housemate, never failed to show an interest in what might otherwise have been a very solitary undertaking; and our conversations on matters of a non-academic nature sometimes provided a welcome distraction from the often unfathomable complexities of large-scale prosopography. My time at Hull also afforded me a few welcome opportunities to present my research and to receive feedback from some very receptive audiences. Craig Lambert was an ideal co-organiser of a conference on medieval military history, held in Hull on 12 April 2007. I would like once again to thank the contributors who presented their research on that day, many of whom travelled very long distances to share their findings. Indeed, some of the resulting discussions encouraged me to think again about various aspects of my own project on the early Edwardian soldier.

Besides Andrew Ayton, a number of people have contributed to the realisation of this monograph in very direct and practical ways. Dr Richard Gorski of the University of Hull kindly allowed me to consult his database on administrative personnel, on which many of the findings in the final part of chapter 3 are based. It has been my good fortune to work in an environment, at Hull, where data on the activities of the fourteenth-century aristocracy have been computerised for some time. Collaborative work undoubtedly holds the key to answering many of the big questions concerning the activities of the later medieval gentry. Since leaving Hull I have had the good fortune to find employment on an equally stimulating project, using similar research methods: 'The Soldier in Later Medieval England, 1369–1453'. I am much obliged to the project managers, Professor Anne Curry of the University of Southampton and Dr Adrian Bell of the University of Reading, for allowing me the time to prepare my manuscript for publication. I must also thank Dr Andrew Ayton, Dr Adrian Bell and Dr Andy King for their comments on the final drafts of some of the chapters, particularly the last-named who read through and commented on three chapters within a very short space of time as the deadline for delivery loomed. Adrian Ailes' advice on heraldic sources, made in relation to a different piece of work, has saved me from some errors of omission. Finally, Professor Michael Prestwich of the University of Durham and Dr Julian Haseldine of the University of Hull have offered some valuable suggestions and have commented at length on the text.

Throughout the duration of this project my partner Charlotte has been a source of great strength and support. I thank her for showing patience towards me during the more difficult times over the last few years.

This book is dedicated, with gratitude, to my parents and sister, who have encouraged me in all of my undertakings.

Abbreviations

Ann. Dunstaple	'Annales Prioratus de Dunstaplia (AD 1–1297), *Annales Monastici*, ed. H.R. Luard, 5 vols, Rolls Ser., xxxvi (London, 1864–9), iii
Ann. Lond.	'Annales Londonienses', *Chronicles of the Reigns of Edward I and Edward II*, ed. W. Stubbs, 2 vols, Rolls Ser., lxxvi (London, 1882–3), i
Ann. Waverley	'Annales Monasterii de Waverleia (AD 1–1291)', *Annales Monastici*, ed. H.R. Luard, 5 vols, Rolls Ser., xxxvi (London, 1864–9), ii
Ann. Wigorn.	'Annales Prioratus de Wigornia (AD 1–1377), *Annales Monastici*, ed. H.R. Luard, 5 vols, Rolls Ser., xxxvi (London, 1864–9), iv
Ann. Winton.	'Annales Monasterii de Wintonia, 519–1277', *Annales Monastici*, ed. H.R. Luard, 5 vols, Rolls Ser., xxxvi (London, 1864–9), ii
BIHR	*Bulletin of the Institute of Historical Research*
BL	British Library
Bury St Edmunds	*The Chronicle of Bury St Edmunds, 1212–1301*, ed. A. Gransden (London, 1964)
Cal. Ch. Rolls	*Calendar of the Charter Rolls*, 6 vols (London, 1903–27)
CCR	*Calendar of Close Rolls*
CCW	*Calendar of Chancery Warrants, 1244–1326* (London, 1927)
CDS	*Calendar of Documents Relating to Scotland*, ed. J. Bain, 4 vols (Edinburgh, 1881–8); v, ed. G.G. Simpson and J.D. Galbraith (Edinburgh, 1986)
CFR	*Calendar of Fine Rolls*
Chronica et Annales	*Willelmi Rishanger, quondam Monachi S. Albani, et quorundam Anonymorum, Chronica et Annales, Regnantibus Henrico Tertio et Edwardo Primo*, ed. H.T. Riley, Rolls Ser., xxviii 2 (London, 1865)
Chronica Majora	*Matthaei Parisiensis, Monachi Sancti Albani, Chronica Majora*, ed. H.R. Luard, 7 vols, Rolls Ser., lvii (London, 1872–83)
CIPM	*Calendar of Inquisitions Post Mortem and other Analogous Documents*, 23 vols (London, 1904–2004)
Complete Peerage	*The Complete Peerage*, by G.E. Cockayne, revised and edited by V. Gibbs, H.A. Doubleday, Lord Howard de Walden and G.H. White, 13 vols (London, 1910–59)
Cotton	*Bartholomaei de Cotton, Historia Anglicana (AD 449–1298)*, ed. H.R. Luard, Rolls Ser., xvi (London, 1859)
CPR	*Calendar of Patent Rolls*

CVCR	*Calendar of Various Chancery Rolls. Supplementary Close Rolls. Welsh Rolls. Scutage Rolls (AD 1277–1326)* (London, 1912)
EHR	*English Historical Review*
Feudal Aids	*Inquisitions and Assessments Relating to Feudal Aids, 1284–1431*, 6 vols (London, 1899–1920)
Flores Historiarum	*Flores Historiarum*, ed. H.R. Luard, 3 vols, Rolls Ser., xcv (London, 1890)
Foedera	*Foedera, Conventiones, Litterae etc.*, ed. T. Rymer, revised edition by A. Clarke, F. Holbrooke and J. Caley, 4 vols in 7 parts (Record Commission, 1816–69)
Guisborough	*The Chronicle of Walter of Guisborough*, Camden Society 3rd ser., lxxxix (1957)
Historical Research	*Historical Research. The Bulletin of the Institute of Historical Research*
'Lanercost'	*Chronicon de Lanercost MCCI–MCCCXLVI*, ed. J. Stevenson (Edinburgh, 1839)
Langtoft	*Pierre de Langtoft, le règne d'Édouard Ier*, ed. J.C. Thiolier (Créteil, 1989)
Liber Quotidianus	*Liber Quotidianus Contrarotulatoris Garderobae, 1299–1300*, ed. J. Topham *et al.* (London, 1787)
List of MPs	*Return of the Name of Every Member of the Lower House of the Parliaments of England, Scotland and Ireland, 1213–1874* (London, 1878)
Melsa	*Chronica Monasterii de Melsa, a Fundatione usque ad Annum 1396, Auctore Thoma de Burton, Abbate. Accedit Continuatio ad Annum 1406 a Monacho quodam ipsius Domus*, ed. E.A. Bond, 3 vols, Rolls Ser., xliii (London, 1866–8)
Parl. Roll.	*The Parliament Rolls of Medieval England, 1275–1504*, ed. C. Given-Wilson *et al.* 16 vols (London, 2005)
Parl. Writs	*Parliamentary Writs and Writs of Military Summons*, ed. F. Palgrave, 2 vols in 4 parts (London, 1827–34)
Rôles Gascons	*Rôles Gascons 1242–1307*, ed. F. Michel, C. Bemont and Y. Renouard, 5 vols (Paris, 1885–1962)
Rotuli Scotiae	*Rotuli Scotiae in Turri Londinensi et in Domo Capitulari Westmonasteriensi asservati*, ed. D. MacPherson, J. Caley, W. Illingworth and T.H. Horne, 2 vols (Record Commission, 1814–19)
Scalacronica	Sir Thomas Gray: *Scalacronica, 1272–1363*, ed. A. King, Surtees Society, ccix (2005)
Scotland in 1298	*Scotland in 1298: Documents Relating to the Campaign of Edward I in that Year*, ed. H. Gough (London, 1888)
SHR	*Scottish Historical Review*
Stevenson	*Documents Illustrative of the History of Scotland from the Death of King Alexander the Third to the Accession of Robert Bruce MCCLXXXVI–MCCCVI*, ed. J. Stevenson, 2 vols (Edinburgh, 1870)

TRHS	*Transactions of the Royal Historical Society*
Trivet	*Nicholai Triveti, de Ordine Frat. Praedicatorum, Annales (AD MCXXXVI–MCCCVII)*, ed. T. Hog, English Historical Society (London, 1845)
Trokelowe	*Johannis de Trokelowe et Henrici de Blaneforde, Monachorum S. Albani, necnon quorundam Anonymorum, Chronica et Annales*, ed. H.T. Riley, Rolls Ser., xxviii 3 (London, 1866)
WHR	*Welsh History Review*
Wykes	'Chronicon vulgo dictum Chronicon Thomae Wykes, 1066–1289', *Annales Monastici*, ed. H.R. Luard, 5 vols, Rolls Ser., xxxvi (London, 1864–9), iv

Documents cited by class number alone are taken from the National Archives, Kew.

Introduction

The military campaigns of Edward I, king of England between 1272 and 1307, were a turning-point in the history of warfare within northwestern Europe during the Middle Ages. Edward's reign did not witness any radical departures in the way that warfare was conducted and battles fought, nor were there major changes (though there *were* some significant innovations) in the methods employed to recruit mounted and foot soldiers. The era of major reform, perhaps even revolution, in the recruitment, structure and composition of English medieval armies came later, during the 1330s and 1340s, at the beginning of Edward III's French war.[1] Rather, it was the scale of Edward I's expeditions – the number of soldiers involved, the vast sums of money spent and the geographical areas affected – that contrasted sharply with the military efforts of previous reigns.[2] The heavy fighting of these decades, particularly between the outbreak of war with France in 1294 and the defeat of the army led by Edward I's son, Edward II, at the battle of Bannockburn in 1314, has left behind an extensive trail of documents recording the names of mounted armoured warriors drawn from the ranks of the English gentry and nobility. These sources far surpass, in number and detail, extant records from previous reigns relating to the performance of military service; and they enable the historian to reconstruct, if not completely than to a far greater extent than for any preceding age, the careers in arms of a large proportion of the aristocratic soldiery. The aim of this book is to incorporate such individual profiles into, and exploit them for the purposes of, a wider analysis of military recruitment, leadership, service patterns and organisation in the early Edwardian period.

The process of linking soldiers' names so as to enhance our knowledge of combatants' activities and the nature of the armies in which they served is not new. Such a methodological approach, described by Andrew Ayton as 'military service prosopography',[3] has already been employed to considerable effect in studies of English armies raised during the intermittent and drawn-out conflict with France between 1337 and 1453. Mounted armoured warriors in the years before Bannockburn, however, have been the subject of relatively little system-

---

[1] See A. Ayton, *Knights and Warhorses: Military Service and the English Aristocracy under Edward III* (Woodbridge, 1994), chapter 1; and C.J. Rogers, ' "As if a New Sun had Arisen": England's Fourteenth-Century RMA', *The Dynamics of Military Revolution 1300–2050*, ed. M. Knox and W. Murray (Cambridge, 2001), p. 23.

[2] For comment on the increase in the scale of warfare during the 1290s, see R.W. Kaeuper, *War, Justice and Public Order: England and France in the Later Middle Ages* (Oxford, 1988), pp. 3, 389.

[3] A. Ayton, 'The English Army at Crécy', A. Ayton and P. Preston, *The Battle of Crécy, 1346* (Woodbridge, 2005), p. 160. For a discussion of some of the difficulties entailed in prosopographical research, see R. Gorski, 'A Methodological Holy Grail: Nominal Record Linkage in a Medieval Context', *Medieval Prosopography*, xvii (1996), pp. 145–79.

atic study.[4] This is surprising given the extensive work that has been carried out separately by J.E. Morris,[5] Michael Powicke,[6] Michael Prestwich[7] and others on the armies of this period. Certainly, there have been influential theses or published monographs on subjects such as: the household knights of Edward I[8] and military communities[9] within the counties of Gloucestershire,[10] Cheshire[11] and Northumberland.[12] Yet, with the exception of the book by Philip Morgan on Cheshire, works on county and regional communities have tended to deal with landholding society in the round rather than with military activity in particular, soldiering constituting just one aspect of far broader investigations of local society. Moreover, the findings of such studies cannot be applied, without a good deal of caution, to the situation within the realm as a whole. There is reason to doubt, for example, whether the frequency of military service given by landholders in border counties such as Gloucestershire, Cheshire and Northumberland was matched in other parts of England. For this reason, and others besides, a wider investigation of the military activities of the English aristocracy (including a few non-English elements, such as Scots and Gascons in the Plantagenet allegiance)[13] during the reigns of Edward I and his son is long overdue.

The availability of extensive source materials naming soldiers from 1272 onwards provides an obvious and compelling reason for beginning the analysis in that year. Yet the forty-two-year period between the accession of Edward I and the battle of Bannockburn constitutes a natural phase in English medieval military history, irrespective of such considerations. The campaigns of the Plantagenets at this time can be divided, in essence, into two main categories. The conflicts that consumed most of the energies of the first two Edwards and their subjects were the wars of aggression within the British Isles. These led, in the first instance, to the conquest of the independent parts of Wales in 1282–3

---

[4]   A prosopographical study of the massed ranks of peasants serving on foot during these years is not possible, except perhaps on a very small scale, as the names of very few such men have survived in the records for military service.

[5]   J.E. Morris, *The Welsh Wars of Edward I* (Oxford, 1901).

[6]   M.R. Powicke, *Military Obligation in Medieval England: A Study in Liberty and Duty* (Oxford, 1962), chapters 6–8.

[7]   M. Prestwich, *War, Politics and Finance under Edward I* (London, 1972).

[8]   R.L. Ingamells, 'The Household Knights of Edward I', 2 vols, PhD thesis, University of Durham, 1992.

[9]   For an example of early use of the term 'military community', see P. Morgan, *War and Society in Medieval Cheshire, 1277–1403* (Manchester, 1987), pp. 149–50.

[10]   N. Saul, *Knights and Esquires: The Gloucestershire Gentry in the Fourteenth Century* (Oxford, 1981).

[11]   Morgan, *War and Society*.

[12]   A. King, 'War, Politics and Landed Society in Northumberland, *c.* 1296–*c.* 1408, PhD thesis, University of Durham, 2001.

[13]   No attempt is made in this book to focus specifically on service given by Scots, Gascons or other non-English groups in the Plantagenet allegiance. By the same token, however, not all of the mounted armoured warriors discussed, and who served in the armies of Edward I and Edward II, were of English origin. For a recent discussion of Scots who supported the English cause, see M.H. Brown, '*Scoti Anglicati*: Scots in Plantagenet Allegiance during the Fourteenth Century', *England and Scotland in the Fourteenth Century: New Perspectives*, ed. A. King and M. Penman (Woodbridge, 2007), pp. 94–115.

and, later, the near-subjugation of Scotland by 1304–5. The English defeat near Stirling in 1314 in effect brought this stage of conflict to an end; and after this reversal the initiative moved to the Scots under Robert Bruce and his brother, Edward. There was some warfare in Ireland throughout the period under investigation, but not any in which Edward I or his son took part in person.[14] Elsewhere, from 1294 through to 1298, the English fought rearguard actions on the continent to defend Edward I's ducal inheritance in Gascony.[15] Most of the time this involved sending forces to man the garrisons in southwestern France; but in 1297–8 the king led an expedition to Flanders in person, a decision that proved, ultimately, to be ineffective.[16] In total, and despite Edward I's best efforts to move continental objectives to the top of the agenda, there was only one royal-led campaign outside the British Isles between 1272 and 1314. This compares with ten such expeditions closer to home: to Wales in 1277, 1282–3 and 1294–5; and to Scotland in 1296, 1298, 1300, 1301, 1303–4, 1310–11 and 1314. By contrast, the main focus of Edward III and his successors (with the possible exceptions of Richard II and Henry IV) was the war in France. After 1337 the so-called Celtic fringe was usually a secondary concern, except in years of rebellion in Wales or border aggression in the north.

If the campaigns of Edward I and Edward II differed in key respects from those of later medieval kings of England, then so too did the structure and composition of their armies. From the 1330s onwards nearly all soldiers, from the leading duke to the lowliest archer, received Crown pay.[17] Men-at-arms fought alongside mounted archers (in roughly equal number) in 'mixed' retinues, raised by military contracts and subcontracts known as indentures of war.[18] This move towards the universal use of Crown pay is reflected in the nature of the extant documentary materials. Pay-rolls, also known as *vadia guerre* accounts, are widely available (although far from exhaustively so) for the reign of Edward III, whereas very few have survived from the reigns of Edward I and Edward II. The largest surviving pay-roll, for mounted soldiers, from the pre-Bannockburn era dates from the Welsh war of 1282–3;[19] but most of the men named in this source, as in other pay-related documents available for expeditions taking place before 1314 (such as horse inventories and wardrobe books), were household retainers and their followers. Few men from outside

[14] See R. Frame, 'Military Service in the Lordship of Ireland 1290–1360: Institutions and Society on the Anglo-Gaelic Frontier', *Medieval Frontier Societies*, ed. R. Bartlett and A. MacKay (Oxford, 1989), p. 102.

[15] For a discussion of Edward I's forces in Gascony, see M. Vale, *The Angevin Legacy and the Hundred Years War, 1250–1340* (Oxford, 1990), pp. 200–15.

[16] See N.B. Lewis, 'The English Forces in Flanders, August–November 1297', *Studies in Medieval History Presented to F.M. Powicke*, ed. R.W. Hunt, W.A. Pantin and R.W. Southern (Oxford, 1948), pp. 310–18.

[17] A. Ayton, 'English Armies in the Fourteenth Centuries', *Arms, Armies and Fortifications in the Hundred Years War*, ed. A. Curry and M. Hughes (Woodbridge, 1994), p. 22.

[18] For an overview of these developments, see Ayton, *Knights and Warhorses*, chapter 1. N.B. Lewis has analysed one of the earliest contract armies in 'The Recruitment and Organization of a Contract Army, May to November 1337', *BIHR*, xxxvii (1964), pp. 1–19.

[19] E 101/4/1.

the royal *familia* were at this time brought into Crown pay. The widespread use of paid service by Edward III and his successors also means that from the 1360s (and to some extent a little earlier) cash sums given to campaign captains can be traced on the issue rolls, which are accounts of payments made by the exchequer. More significantly, muster rolls, recording the names not only of men-at-arms serving in English armies but also of archers, crossbowmen and other, auxiliary personnel, are widely available for campaigns taking place later in the fourteenth century, especially from 1369. Historians have made effective use of this corpus of documents in order to reconstruct the activities of a large proportion of men-at-arms, and some archers, who fought for the English Crown during the Hundred Years War. These efforts have recently culminated in publications by Andrew Ayton and Anne Curry, the two main pioneers in this field of research, on the English armies at the battles of Crécy (1346) and Agincourt (1415) respectively.[20] Adrian Bell's study of the men who served on two naval expeditions during the reign of Richard II has helped to bridge the gap between these two phases in the war.[21]

The aristocratic warriors who served in English contract armies of the later Middle Ages have not, therefore, wanted for scholarly attention. By contrast, as we have seen, their ancestors, who lived during the late thirteenth and early fourteenth centuries, have been left, by and large, in the shadows. The consequences of this relative neglect may be considerable, particularly when we consider that men-at-arms of the reigns of Edward I and Edward II were recruited (at least superficially) by different means, and apparently fought in dissimilar ways, from their sons and grandsons: the elite soldiers in the armies of Edward III. In the late thirteenth and early fourteenth centuries, as has been established for some time, mounted aristocratic warriors were gathered by retinue leaders and served in companies of men-at-arms of varying size. On the other hand, the massed ranks of peasants, who fought on foot, were conscripted by commissioners of array and served separately from the mounted soldiers, in large blocks of twenty, a hundred or a thousand. Even when some attempt to combine men-at-arms with foot archers was made, as by the earl of Warwick at the battle of Maes Moydog in Wales early in 1295, the chronicle accounts make it clear, by using the word *equites*, that the men-at-arms fought on horseback.[22] Later, during the Hundred Years War, English men-at-arms customarily dismounted to fight on foot. Moreover, although all men-at-arms (as well as others) who served in English armies from the mid-fourteenth century received Crown wages, mounted soldiers in the armies of Edward I and Edward II sometimes served gratuitously or in fulfilment of feudal obligations.[23] Given, then, that the hosts of the first two Edwards

---

[20] Ayton, 'The English Army at Crécy', pp. 159–251; A. Curry, *Agincourt: A New History* (Stroud, 2005), pp. 52–72.

[21] A. Bell, *War and the Soldier in the Fourteenth Century* (Woodbridge, 2004).

[22] *Trivet*, p. 335; discussed in Morris, *Welsh Wars*, p. 256. See also Thomas Gray's account of the debacle in 1314, when the leaders of the English army 'mounted on horseback in great consternation, for they were not at all used to dismounting to fight on foot': *Scalacronica*, p. 75.

[23] Prestwich, *War, Politics and Finance*, pp. 69, 91.

differed in some fundamental ways from those of their successors, and that a great deal has been learned about later, contract armies through the study of military personnel, it is to be regretted that similar research methods have not hitherto been applied to what may be termed the pre-contract armies of an earlier epoch.

This is all the more unfortunate when we consider that the transition from the reign of Edward II to that of Edward III has been seen as a key turning-point in English medieval military history. At an overarching, structural level the differences (noted above) between the armies of Edward I and those of his grandson are clear. But no one has yet carried out the kind of in-depth research into the military service of the English aristocracy in the years before the Edwardian military reforms of the 1330s that might enable us to identify, with greater precision, aspects of change and continuity across this dividing line. If, for example, we do not understand how soldiers serving in fulfilment of feudal obligations discharged their service, then how are we to assess whether, and in what ways, the wholly paid armies of Edward III and his successors were superior to the partly 'feudal' armies of Edward I and Edward II? How, too, can we compare levels of retinue stability in the 1300s with those in the 1350s when the full range of source materials from the reigns of Edward I and Edward II that may cast light on this issue have not previously been consulted?[24] Turning our attention to issues of recruitment and frequency of service, the reign of Edward I has been seen, by some historians, as a time when the number of warriors of gentle blood increased markedly.[25] This does seem likely when one compares the relative tranquillity of the reign of Henry III with the hectic military schedule of the mid-1290s. But little attempt has hitherto been made to quantify this process, or to assess the success of Edward I's recruitment initiatives, by comparing the names of the men summoned to attend the musters with those of the men-at-arms who actually served. Furthermore, beyond the leading earls and bannerets studied by Michael Prestwich and others, very little is currently known about the relative contribution to the wars of the first two Edwards made by men from different parts of the realm.

This book seeks to address these issues by drawing on all of the extant source materials recording the names of aristocratic warriors who served in English armies between 1272 and 1314. The most useful of these documents are: horse inventories, which state the names of men-at-arms in receipt of Crown pay and the valuations of their mounts; enrolled letters of protection, of attorney and of respite of debts, which reveal the identities of individual (usually landed) warriors as they made preparations to serve in the king's armies; and proffer rolls, on which are recorded the designations of men-at-arms, both knights and *servientes*, who registered their service at feudal musters. In addition to this main body of documentary materials, this study makes use of a wide range of other,

---

[24] For the suggestion that retinue stability *may* have increased by Edward III's reign, see Ayton, 'The English Army at Crécy', p. 204.

[25] See, for example, Kaeuper, *War, Justice and Public Order*, p. 389; A. Ayton, 'Sir Thomas Ughtred and the Edwardian Military Revolution', *The Age of Edward III*, ed. J.S. Bothwell (York, 2001), pp. 111–12.

hardly subsidiary, records relating to the performance of military service. These include: wardrobe accounts, particularly the books that record payments made to (predominantly household) soldiers during the wars in Flanders and Scotland; the few extant pay-rolls recording service given by men-at-arms; garrison lists; protection warrants, which reveal the names of men who applied for letters of protection; and occasional rolls of arms, which commemorate warriors who were present on specific martial occasions. Furthermore, the analysis incorporates the full range of records drawn up in advance of the performance of military service, such as military summons lists and sheriffs' returns to orders for distraint of knighthood.

The military activities of individual men-at-arms provide a connecting thread throughout the analysis. However, with the exception, in part, of chapter 3 (where an attempt is made to reconstruct the length of mounted warriors' careers in arms, the frequency with which they joined the king's armies, and their commitment to soldiering compared with other forms of public activity), the aim is not merely to trace the contours of aristocratic military service. Prosopography can open a window into a number of broader themes. Two subjects that may benefit from such a methodological approach are military recruitment and retaining. Even the issue of leadership can be re-examined with the assistance of the records for military service. If it is not known how many times men-at-arms had served in the Crown's armies before being appointed to high office, then how can the importance attached to the quality of experience when selecting army commanders be assessed? Indeed, one of the aims of this study is to follow the aristocratic warrior through from the time when he was summoned, either directly by the king or indirectly by a sheriff or retinue leader in the counties, to the point at which he mustered and discharged his service in the armies. In chapter 5 an attempt will be made to look at how mounted aristocratic warriors serving in fulfilment of feudal obligations were integrated into the mounted part of the armies.[26] This is an appropriate theme with which to conclude as it reminds us that the armies of Edward I and his son were, in some ways, the last of their kind. Feudal military service was abandoned, in effect, following the Weardale campaign of 1327, paving the way for a new epoch in English medieval military history.

---

[26] For some preliminary work on this subject, see D. Simpkin, 'The English Army and the Scottish Campaign of 1310–1311', *England and Scotland in the Fourteenth Century: New Perspectives*, ed. A. King and M. Penman (Woodbridge, 2007), pp. 28–39.

1

Mobilisation

In medieval England the beginning of a new reign often furnished the occasion for a shift in the direction and fortunes of the realm, and the events following upon the death of King Henry III in 1272 were certainly a case in point. The accession of Henry's son, the ambitious Edward I, paved the way for an era of conflict, both within the British Isles and in France, on a scale that had never previously been witnessed during the Middle Ages. For the administrative historian T.F. Tout, writing shortly after the defeat of Kaiser Wilhelm II's armies in the First World War, the parallel with the increased military demands of his own day seemed striking. 'The magnitude of the military efforts of Edward I', he observed, 'as far transcended those of his predecessors as the war which has laid low German imperialism transcended the Napoleonic wars, or the Napoleonic wars the war of the Spanish Succession.'[1] The comparison seems particularly appropriate when we consider that both the First World War and the Napoleonic wars necessitated the extension of the obligation to military service to new social groups and classes. By stretching his manpower reserves to their limit through his wars in Wales, France and Scotland, Edward ensured that the landholding elites of late thirteenth- and early fourteenth-century England became accustomed to the martial calling to an extent that could not have been foreseen during the reign of his father.

The demands placed on the gentry and nobility were particularly exacting from the mid-1290s when the confiscation of Gascony by Philip IV of France, together with the deterioration of relations with the Scots, posed new threats to the Edwardian polity. Contemporaries were well aware of the new departure that the campaigns of these years marked in the military affairs of the realm. Above all, however, it was the steadfastness of Edward I in the face of such adversity that aroused their admiration.[2] No prince, one chronicler later reflected, had encountered so much trouble and strife as had 'sire Edward' during his time on the throne.[3] For many writers, indeed, the king personified the war effort and was the moving figure behind its most pivotal events.

The tendency of medieval commentators to focus, when discussing these wars, on the role of the Crown is understandable given the hierarchical bent of

[1] T.F. Tout, *Chapters in the Administrative History of Mediaeval England, The Wardrobe, the Chamber and the Small Seals*, 6 vols (Manchester, 1920–33), ii, p. 143.
[2] See, for example, the reaction of one chronicler to the king's successes in 1296: *Bury St Edmunds*, p. 133.
[3] *Langtoft*, p. 229.

that society. Nevertheless, Edward could not have succeeded in the conquest of Wales, or in the near-conquest of Scotland, had he not been supported by a willing and bellicose aristocracy. His achievement lay, therefore, not only in his castle-building projects at Caernarfon or Conway, or his victory in battle at Falkirk, but also in his ability to engage the energy and enthusiasm of the social elite for his ambitious campaigns. Acknowledging this, historians have customarily contrasted Edward I's campaigns with the far more modest military objectives that had characterised the fifty-six-year rule of his father, Henry III. During that long period there had been relatively little military activity.[4] In fact, had it not been for the civil war of 1264–5[5] and the Lord Edward's crusade to the Holy Land a few years later, by 1277 the landholders of medieval England would not have taken up arms for two decades. For Michael Prestwich, the signing of a peace agreement with Louis IX of France in 1259 marked an important stage in the retreat of the Crown from its military commitments, with the changing of the royal seal at that time being particularly symbolic: 'whereas the king had been depicted on the old one bearing a sword, on the new he carried a sceptre'.[6]

The infrequency of Henry's wars, and their unimpressive scale, meant that upon coming to the throne Edward had a good deal of work to do. The forces that Henry managed to muster, both overseas and within Britain, do not seem to have been particularly large. One reason for this, according to J.S. Critchley, was that while Edward sought to conquer new territories, Welsh campaigns under his father had more often been 'punitive, or attempts to establish secure footholds by constructing yet more castles'.[7] It would be facile to contrast too sharply the size of the mounted forces raised by Edward I with those gathered by his father, for Henry sometimes put into the field men-at-arms roughly equal in number to those recruited for Edward's least impressive campaigns.[8] Henry failed, nonetheless, to draw on as wide a cross-section of English landholding society for his wars as his son. Although Henry III's household force was strong,[9] he does not appear to have exploited, to any great extent, the military potential that lay dormant in the shires. In his perceptive study of the formation of the gentry, Philip Morgan saw the reign of Henry III as a time when the lesser landholders of England occupied their time primarily in non-military pursuits: 'there was simply not enough actual experience of arms to create a class of soldier career-

---

[4]   See P. Contamine, *War in the Middle Ages* (Oxford, 1984), p. 65.
[5]   The number of knights involved in the civil war does not seem to have been very large: P. Coss, *The Knight in Medieval England, 1000–1400* (Stroud, 1993), p. 70.
[6]   Prestwich, *War, Politics and Finance*, p. 14.
[7]   J.S. Critchley, 'Military Organisation in England, 1154–1254', PhD thesis, University of Nottingham, 1968, p. 173. See also, R.F. Walker, 'The Anglo-Welsh Wars, 1272–1267 with Special Reference to English Military Developments', DPhil thesis, University of Oxford, 1954, pp. 3–4.
[8]   For a comparison of the army raised by Henry in 1245 with that raised by Edward in 1277, see Walker 'Anglo-Welsh Wars', p. 510.
[9]   *Ibid.*, pp. 66, 89–90.

ists such as that which fuelled the gentry in the fourteenth century'.[10] According to Andrew Ayton, 'that experience was to be gained during the reign of Edward I, whose wars in Wales, France and Scotland provided plentiful opportunities for a real military role'.[11]

Looking back from the reign of Edward III, it is evident that the years between 1272 and 1327 represented a key stage in the gentry's development into a class of competent, hardened warriors. By the time of the French wars of Edward I's grandson the seeds sown during the 1280s and 1290s, when the Crown attempted to mobilise the gentry on a grand scale for the first time, had begun to bear fruit; but when Edward I came to the throne in 1272 he could not have predicted that the glories of Falkirk, Crécy and Poitiers lay ahead. Unlike his grandson and the Black Prince, Edward was not able to draw on a broad range of military experience among his leading subjects. J.E. Morris was undoubtedly right when he suggested that Edward 'was teaching the art of war to poor material'.[12] Indeed, the relative scarcity of experienced warriors in the armies of his early years meant that Edward was forced to act with promethean ingenuity, forging a military community out of a realm of estate dwellers.

To do this Edward acted with thoroughness and innovation, exploiting and adding to the recruitment methods that had been established by his father. The main developments in military obligation during Edward's reign have been considered by Michael Powicke and can be broken down into three stages.[13] During his early years on the throne Edward continued with the policy of distraint of knighthood: the process by which landholders of specified landed wealth were forced to become knights or pay fines for respites or exemptions. Twenty-six such writs had been issued during the reign of Henry III.[14] Despite the sums of money raised by these means, it seems that Henry's main concern had been 'to bolster his military forces' and to increase the number of knights available for other purposes, rather than merely to raise cash.[15] Under Edward I, to an even greater degree, distraint of knighthood seems to have been employed primarily as a way of enlarging the pool of military reserves within England. Three national writs of distraint were issued during the first part of Edward's reign: in 1278, 1285 and 1292. Later, around the time of Bannockburn, these writs were reintroduced, with Edward II ordering the distraint of the forty- and

---

[10] P. Morgan, 'Making the English Gentry', *Thirteenth Century England V*, ed. P.R. Coss and S.D. Lloyd (Woodbridge, 1995), p. 26.

[11] Ayton, 'Sir Thomas Ughtred', p. 112.

[12] Morris, *Welsh Wars*, p. 30.

[13] Powicke, *Military Obligation*, chapter 6; *idem*, 'The General Obligation to Cavalry Service under Edward I', *Speculum*, xxviii (1953), pp. 814–33.

[14] Powicke, *Military Obligation*, p. 71. On the decline in the number of knights within England during Henry's reign, see N. Denholm-Young, 'Feudal Society in the Thirteenth Century: The Knights', *Collected Papers of N. Denholm-Young* (Cardiff, 1969), pp. 84–5.

[15] S.L. Waugh, 'Reluctant Knights and Jurors: Respites, Exemptions, and Public Obligations in the Reign of Henry III', *Speculum*, lviii (1983), pp. 960–1. For an earlier discussion of the distraint orders of Henry III's reign, see Powicke, *Military Obligation*, chapter 4; *idem*, 'Distraint of Knighthood and Military Obligation under Henry III', *Speculum*, xxv (1950), pp. 457–70.

fifty-librate holders in 1312 and 1316 respectively. The Crown's need for greater manpower reserves was particularly acute during the mid-1290s. At that stage Edward I deviated from the policies of his father and began to seek more innovative methods of recruitment. In 1295, 1300 and 1301 he summoned forty-librate holders throughout the counties of England, whether they were knights or not. For the expedition to Flanders in 1297 he took this a step further, lowering the income bracket to include all men possessing 20 pounds or more of landed wealth per year. Finally, in his later years, Edward returned to his earlier preoccupation with knighthood. In the spring of 1306 he invited to London all men who wished to be knighted alongside his son, Edward of Caernarfon. Then, later in the same year, he drew up plans for a similar mass knighting ceremony, to be held at Carlisle.

Although the general outline of Edward's mobilisation policies is well known, the aristocratic response to these measures remains a more shadowy subject. Consequently, it is far from clear to what extent Edward was able, as a result of his efforts, to widen the manpower reserve for the mounted part of his armies. The records for military service that may cast some light on this are, for the most part, bulky, unpublished and incomplete.[16] Yet these sources – mainly letters of protection, horse inventories, proffer rolls of feudal service and pay-rolls – have survived in sufficient quantity to enable the identification of a large proportion of the mounted armoured warriors who served in the king's armies. What does comparison of these records with the records for distraint of knighthood and the summons lists mentioned above reveal about the effectiveness of the Crown's recruitment programmes?

One of Edward's first priorities as king seems to have been to increase the number of knights available for military service within England. Some historians have doubted whether this was the main objective of distraint of knighthood. David Crouch, for example, has observed that 'it may well be that the administrative and not the military problems posed by lack of knights was what eventually concerned the king more than anything else'.[17] A recent study on the fourteenth-century sheriff, however, has shown that the links between distraint of knighthood and administrative service were quite tenuous, with the ideal of knighthood represented by contemporaries being that of *miles strenuus*: the knight at war.[18] Writing a few generations later than the events that he describes, John Barbour regarded Giles de Argentein (d. 1314) as the third best knight of his time, not as a consequence of any work that he may have done in the shires, but because he had fought valiantly against the Saracens.[19] The bad or unworthy knight, by contrast, was he who failed to draw his sword, as revealed by the indictment by one chronicler of the knights who had failed to assist the earl

---

[16] Cf. Ayton, *Knights and Warhorses*, pp. 138–9.

[17] D. Crouch, *The Image of Aristocracy in Britain, 1000–1300* (London, 1992), p. 146. For a different opinion on this subject, see Saul, *Knights and Esquires*, p. 47.

[18] R. Gorski, *The Fourteenth-Century Sheriff: English Local Administration in the Late Middle Ages* (Woodbridge, 2003), p. 100.

[19] John Barbour, *The Bruce*, ed. A.A.M. Duncan (Edinburgh, 1997), p. 497.

of Gloucester when he fell at the battle of Bannockburn.[20] The association of knights with the conduct of warfare even extended to the reporting of military casualties. The chronicler Thomas Wykes noted that around 160 knights, along with numerous others who had not yet been girded with the belt of knighthood, were killed at the battle of Evesham in 1265.[21] Later, the London annalist recorded the names of thirty-seven English knights slain at Bannockburn. As for the other men-at-arms who had served in Edward II's defeated army, we are merely told that the greater part managed to flee.[22]

Whatever the king intended to achieve by issuing the distraint orders (and military requirements were almost certainly uppermost in his thoughts), many of the men forced to become knights subsequently gave service in his armies. Of the individuals who were distrained to receive knighthood in 1278, an appreciable number can be traced in the service records for the army that campaigned in Wales in 1282–3.[23] The names of around 400 men have survived in the sheriffs' returns, for 1278, from ten counties.[24] Of these individuals, at least sixty served in Edward I's second Welsh war. This is a significant figure given that many elite soldiers did not receive Crown pay and cannot, therefore, be found on the extant horse inventories and pay-rolls. Moreover, if we extrapolate from these figures to the country as a whole, it is likely that several hundred of the men distrained to knighthood in 1278 participated as mounted armoured warriors within four years of taking up knightly arms. Taking the sixty soldiers in our sample, a few, such as Laurence de Preston, Robert de Somerville, William de Say and Robert Luterel, had served in Wales as *servientes* in the war of 1277 and now returned as knightly combatants.[25] Yet the larger part would appear, from the extant evidence, to have been taking part in the king's campaigns for the first time in 1282–3. Although four of the distrainees from 1278 fought four years later as sergeants,[26] around twenty had, by the time of Edward I's second Welsh war, received the honour of knighthood (other men serving in 1282–3 took

---

20 *Vita Edwardi Secundi*, p. 93.
21 *Wykes*, p. 173.
22 *Ann. Lond.*, p. 231.
23 Comparing the names of the twenty-librate holders returned from Northumberland in 1278 with those recorded on the proffer roll for 1282, Michael Powicke drew the conclusion that little could be said about the success of the distraint order. But his analysis covered only one county and did not incorporate an analysis of the pay documents and enrolled letters of protection for Edward's army in Wales: Powicke, 'The General Obligation to Cavalry Service', p. 818.
24 For these returns, see *Parl. Writs*, i, pp. 214–18 and C 47/1/2.
25 Preston (*Parl. Writs*, i, p. 204; C 47/1/2, m. 4; E 101/4/1, m. 2); Somerville (*Parl. Writs*, i, p. 203; *ibid.*, pp. 216, 230); Say (*Parl. Writs*, i, p. 209; C 47/1/2, m. 21; *Parl. Writs*, i, p. 232); Luterel (*Parl. Writs*, i, p. 203; C 47/1/2, m. 5i; E 101/4/1, m. 1). The membranes of some of the documents utilised in this book are not accurately numbered (in the originals), with more than one membrane being accorded the same Arabic numeral. To assist the reader, in such instances a small Roman numeral has been placed, in the footnotes, beside the membrane number. Therefore, 'm. 5ii', for example, would mean the second of two or more membranes accorded the number '5'.
26 Roger le Breton (C 47/1/2, m. 5i; *Parl. Writs*, i, p. 230); William Maletake (C 47/1/2, m. 5ii; C 47/2/7, m. 10); Robert de Burgherssh (*Parl. Writs*, i, p. 216; C 47/2/7, m. 7); and Roger de Conyers (*Parl. Writs*, i, p. 216; E 101/4/1, m. 8).

out letters of protection, which do not, as a rule, reveal whether soldiers were knights). Of these new knights, several, such as William Grimbaud, Hugh de Broke, William de Audley and Laurence de St Michael, served within the paid retinues,[27] while a group of others, including Richard de Horseley, Humphrey de Cael, Richard de Harcourt and Richard Fouke, registered their service as *milites* at the feudal muster.[28]

Few sheriffs' returns have survived relating to the distraint order of 1285 when, owing to the good service given during the campaign of 1282–3, the obligation to take up knighthood was restricted to subjects possessing at least 100 pounds of landed wealth per annum. The efforts of Edward and his father meant that the number of non-knights within that wealth bracket was in any case very small. Only one man was returned from Lancashire and four from the larger county of Yorkshire.[29]

In response to the writs issued to the forty-librate holders seven years later, we have the names of thirty men distrained to receive knighthood in Lincolnshire, along with two individuals from Lancashire.[30] The returns to a general inquest into the success of the order have also survived.[31] These reveal the names of the men, from most counties, who had not received knighthood by the deadline, or who complied with the order when there was little time left to spare. Based on this corpus of evidence, the writ of 1292 would appear to have been enforced with some success. A list of men-at-arms retained in the king's service in Lincolnshire in 1297 shows that a third of the men distrained in that county five years previously had become knights.[32] Not one was named among the esquires, with the remainder probably serving in Flanders or Scotland when the list was drawn up. Of the men possessing 40 pounds or more in landed wealth in Kent, Middlesex and Rutland, every one had received knighthood by the deadline.[33] In other counties it was seldom the case that more than one or two individuals had failed to comply with the order. Given the date of the writ, Michael Powicke has suggested that the order of 1292 was probably issued with financial rather than military aims in mind.[34] That may have been the case, but many of the men returned by the sheriffs in 1292 were drafted into the war effort during the final years of the reign. Peter de Dutton, knighted on the deadline in Cheshire, obtained a letter of protection for service in the retinue of Reginald de

---

[27] Grimbaud (C 47/1/2, m. 4; C 47/2/7, m. 1); Broke (C 47/1/2, m. 21; E 101/4/1, m. 3); Audley (C 47/1/2, m. 7; C 47/2/6, m. 5; C 47/2/7, m. 7); St Michael (*Parl. Writs*, i, p. 218; C 47/2/7, m. 4).

[28] Horseley (*Parl. Writs*, i, pp. 216, 229); Cael (C 47/1/2, m. 2; *Parl. Writs*, i, p. 228); Harcourt (C 47/1/2, m. 8; *Parl. Writs*, i, p. 234); Fouke (C 47/1/2, m. 10; *Parl. Writs*, i, p. 229).

[29] C 47/1/2, mm. 14d, 20d. Seven men were returned from Wiltshire: E 198/3/3, m. 2.

[30] C 47/1/3, mm. 2, 4.

[31] E 198/3/5.

[32] C 47/2/16, m. 6. Roger de Huntingfeld, William Caus, Robert de Brakenbergh, Baldwin Pygot, William de Funtaynes, William de Diseney, Robert de Hakebech, Peter de Gipthorp, William le Breton and Ralph de Wellewyk had all probably assumed knighthood in response to the writ of 1292.

[33] E 198/3/5, mm. 10d, 12, 22.

[34] Powicke, *Military Obligation*, p. 109.

Grey in the Welsh war of 1294–5.[35] Of the men distrained to receive knighthood in Lincolnshire, Philip de Chauncy, William Fraunk of Grimsby and Peter de Gipthorp were just three of several who served in Edward I's armies during the crisis years of 1294–8.[36] Furthermore, some of the men who had not received knighthood by the deadline had done so and were fighting in the king's wars within a few years of the distraint order.[37]

The connection between distraint of knighthood and military service continued during the early years of the reign of Edward II. However, the writs of 1312 and 1316 do not appear to have been as effective as those issued during Edward I's time on the throne. The sheriffs' returns for 1312 contain around 350 names from twenty-eight counties.[38] For 1316 we have 260 names from thirty-three counties.[39] The unpopularity of the new king, and his inability to engage the martial instincts of his subjects as his father had done, may account for the fact that around seventy-two of the men distrained in 1312 were returned again four years later. Whatever the reasons for this reluctance to assume knightly arms, some of the men who were returned by the sheriffs followed the military calling much as their predecessors had done during the previous reign.

It is not always possible, owing to the nature of the sources, to know whether or not these men had received knighthood prior to embarking on their military careers, but in a few instances the pressure that was brought to bear on them probably had the desired effect. Henry de Cokefeld was distrained to receive knighthood in Suffolk in 1312.[40] Two years later he took out a letter of protection for service in the retinue of Payn de Tibetot on the Bannockburn campaign.[41] Several other distrainees returned from Suffolk in 1312 – including John de Tendring, John de St Philibert and Bartholomew de Avylers – joined Cokefeld by serving in the king's army, apparently for the first time, two years later.[42] Avylers went on to serve with the earl of Norfolk, the king's half-brother, in 1322 and on the Weardale campaign five years later.[43] In between these campaigns, he accompanied the king's other half-brother, the earl of Kent, to Gascony during the war of Saint-Sardos (1324–5).[44] Among the distrainees who later saw service in Scotland or France there were some, such as Aymer Pauncefot, who did so

[35] C 67/10, m. 3. For his service in 1282, as a *vallettus*, see C 47/2/7, m. 7.
[36] Chauncy (*Rôles Gascons*, iii, pp. 120, 126, 325, 352); Fraunk (C 67/11, m. 3); Gipthorp (C 67/11, m. 4). For the distraint of all three men, see C 47/1/3, m. 2.
[37] John de Clivedon, returned from Somerset and Dorset, had not taken up knighthood by the deadline (E 198/3/5, m. 1). However, he was summoned to Wales as a knight in 1294 and had a letter of protection for service in Gascony in the same year (*Parl. Writs*, i, p. 265; *Rôles Gascons*, iii, p. 119). For a similar example, see Roger de Thornton (E 198/3/5, m. 17d; *Rôles Gascons*, iii, p. 177; C 81/1740, m. 69).
[38] C 47/1/7.
[39] C 47/1/8.
[40] C 47/1/7, m. 33.
[41] C 71/6, m. 5.
[42] C 47/1/7, m. 33. For their service at Bannockburn, see C 71/6, mm. 1, 5.
[43] *CPR, 1321–24*, p. 187; C 71/11, m. 5.
[44] E 101/35/2, m. 7.

while retaining the rank of sergeant.[45] A few others, like Patrick de Curwen of Westmorland, had joined the king's armies prior to receiving the honour of knighthood.[46] Clearly, therefore, the assumption of knightly arms did not correlate precisely to service in the king's armies. Yet the frequent issuing of distraint orders does seem to have encouraged some individuals who had not previously been on campaign to give military service. At the very least, it ensured that military service remained at the forefront of men's minds.

The links between knighthood and military activity are further demonstrated by the martial context of many of the mass knighting ceremonies of these years. In 1264 Simon de Montfort had created a number of new knights at Lewes in an attempt to encourage his followers before the royalist onslaught.[47] In like manner, the earl Warenne apparently conferred knighthood on some of his soldiers on the morning of the battle of Stirling Bridge in 1297, many of whom fell together on that day.[48] The most extravagant mass knighting ceremony of the reign of Edward I took place at Westminster on 22 May 1306, on the occasion of the knighting of Edward of Caernarfon.[49] Several chroniclers noted at the time that the king's aim in offering *arma militaria* to young men who wished to be knighted alongside his son was to strengthen his army for Scotland in that year.[50] This is supported by the fact that a large proportion of these individuals made preparations to go to war against Robert Bruce and his adherents. Of the 297 new knights, 129 (43 per cent) appear on the Scottish roll for 1306 with letters of protection or attorney. Many of these enrolments were dated to within just four or five days of the knighting ritual.[51] Although the ceremony scheduled for Carlisle at the beginning of the following year has not received much attention from historians, it is evident, from the location specified for the conferment of knighthood, that this measure was again intended as a way of obtaining more soldiers for the king's army.[52] The issue rolls show that a sum of £1,480 15s 10d had been set aside for the purpose of equipping the new knights.[53] Unfortunately, the absence of comment in the chronicles suggests that nothing came of this proposed sequel.

Given Edward I's apparent preference for mounted forces comprising large numbers of knights, it may seem strange that between 1292 and 1306 the idea of forcing or encouraging more men to become knights was abandoned. In truth,

---

[45] C 47/1/8, m. 9d; C 71/10, m. 3, C 81/1733, m. 97. The protection warrant describes him as a sergeant and almost certainly relates to the campaign of 1319.
[46] C 47/1/7, m. 17; 1298 (C 67/13, m. 6d); 1306 (E 101/612/15, m. 1d); 1307 (E 101/612/21, m. 1i); and as a knight in 1314 (E 101/14/15, m. 5).
[47] *The Chronicle of William de Rishanger of the Barons' Wars*, ed. J.O. Halliwell, Camden Society 1st ser., xv (1840), p. 31.
[48] *Guisborough*, p. 300.
[49] For comment on this event, see, for example, *Ann. Lond.*, p. 146. For the list of men knighted, see E101/362/20, printed in C. Bullock-Davies, *Menestrellorum Multitudo: Minstrels at a Royal Feast* (Cardiff, 1978), appendix.
[50] See, for instance, *Flores Historiarum*, iii, p. 131; *Guisborough*, pp. 367–8.
[51] For example, Fulk Fitz Waryn junior's protection was enrolled on 25 May (C 67/16, m. 11); and Robert de Constable's protection is dated 24 May (C 67/16, m. 12).
[52] *CCR, 1302–07*, p. 520.
[53] E 403/134, m. 4.

there was little difference between, on the one hand, distraint of knighthood, and on the other, the summonses to the twenty- and forty-librate holders (in 1295, 1297, 1300 and 1301), which made no mention of knighthood. Distraint of knighthood was based on the same kind of economic criteria as these later writs; and by the mid-1290s Edward had reason to presume that the great majority of the individuals summoned directly from the shires would be knights.[54] Returns made in the spring of 1295 show that among the men with at least 40 pounds of landed wealth in Wiltshire, there were twelve knights compared with only six sergeants.[55] In Oxfordshire the ratio for the same year was thirty-eight knights to thirteen men who had not received knighthood, while in Berkshire there were twenty-eight knights as against just eight men of inferior status.[56] The writs to the twenty- and forty-librate holders, issued to cope with the demands of the years of crisis, signified a new stage in Edward's attempts to tap the military potential of the country gentry. Yet, as we have seen, the orders for distraint of knighthood had already been quite successful in energising that order of men during the first half of the reign.

The armies that campaigned in Wales and Gascony in 1295 are not very well documented. Nevertheless, of the 204 forty-librate holders whose names appear in the returns for that year from the counties of Wiltshire, Bedfordshire, Buckinghamshire, Berkshire and Oxfordshire, some forty-five can be traced in the said hosts.[57] Of these forty-five men, perhaps three-quarters served in direct response to the new type of writ. Fortunately, the sources for the expeditions of 1297, 1300 and 1301 are comparatively voluminous. Michael Powicke has noted that in response to the summons issued to the twenty-librate holders in 1297, around 713 names were returned from thirteen counties.[58] From this body of men, in direct response to the summons, no more than around fifty-two individuals (not including the paid company leaders) took out letters of protection for service in Flanders. Extrapolating from this, Powicke suggested that by summoning the twenty-librate holders, Edward was possibly able to add to his army around 150 mounted soldiers from all counties.[59] Powicke's calculations did not include the returns for Buckinghamshire, Bedfordshire, Essex and Hertfordshire,[60] which bring the total up to 872 names from seventeen counties. A little over 100 of these individuals took out letters of protection or attorney, or had an appraised horse for the expedition to the Low Countries.[61]

---

[54] On the success of Edward's distraint orders in stemming the decline in the number of knights within England, see P. Coss, 'Knights, Esquires and the Origins of Social Gradation in England', *TRHS*, 6th ser., v (1995), p. 155.

[55] E 198/3/6.

[56] E 198/3/8.

[57] For the returns, see *ibid.*; and E 198/3/7. The main 'record' sources for these campaigns are the enrolled letters of protection and attorney found at C 67/10 (Wales) and *Rôles Gascons*, iii, pp. 96ff (Gascony).

[58] Powicke, *Military Obligation*, pp. 111–12.

[59] *Ibid.*

[60] The additional returns can be found at C 47/1/5, mm. 1ii, 2ii.

[61] Some of these 111 men were also included in the summons to the magnates. The records for military service for the Flanders campaign are the wardrobe book (BL, Additional MS

Turning our attention to the campaigns to Scotland in 1300 and 1301, Edward's recruitment policies seem to have been more successful. Of the 1,000 or so forty-librate holders returned in 1300 from twenty-three counties,[62] some 255 (26 per cent) can be traced in the records for military service.[63] This figure does not include an additional forty men who are described, in sheriffs' returns dating from earlier in that year, as making preparations to go to Scotland.[64] Finally, for the ambitious invasion of the following year (when Edward launched two armies), of the 856 individuals who received a summons, at least 133 (16 per cent) appear to have served.[65]

We must be cautious when assessing the effectiveness of these writs. High levels of taxation and the imposition of the *maltolt* (a heavy duty on customs) meant that few members of the knightly class were willing to set out with the king towards Flanders in 1297. Edward's failure to raise a large army in that year is not in doubt.[66] Despite this, it should be remembered that we are missing, for all campaigns, the names of significant numbers of soldiers (perhaps as many as two-thirds of the men in any given army) who served neither for Crown pay nor in fulfilment of feudal obligations. Moreover, the Crown was sometimes willing to accept substitutes in place of the men whom it had summoned.[67] It is therefore likely that a few of those who did not serve in person sent sons or brothers instead.[68] Taking these factors into account, it is probable that on average at least a third, and in some cases more than a half, of the men summoned according to economic criteria took part in the campaigns, representing a mobilisation effort of some magnitude. For the expeditions to Scotland, in fact, the proportion of the forty-pounders who served may have been very much higher than this.

By issuing these summonses, what the king probably desired most of all was the service of individuals who had previously been reluctant to join his armies. In this he would appear to have been at least partly successful. Yet again, however, the incompleteness of the sources needs to be borne in mind. Edmund de la Hyde took out a letter of protection for service in the *comitiva*

7965), horse inventories (E 101/6/19, 28, 37) and letters of protection and of attorney (C 67/12).

[62] For the returns, see *Parl. Writs*, i, pp. 330–9 and C47/1/6.

[63] The sources consulted are: wardrobe book (*Liber Quotidianus*); horse inventory (E 101/8/23); letters of protection and of attorney (C 67/14, mm. 8–14); proffer roll (*Documents and Records Illustrating the History of Scotland and the Transactions between the Crowns of Scotland and England*, ed. F. Palgrave (London, 1837), pp. 209–31).

[64] C 47/1/6, mm. 3, 8, 24, 39, 57.

[65] For the returns, see *Parl. Writs*, i, pp. 349–56. The records for military service consulted are the wardrobe book (BL, Additional MS 7966a), horse inventories (E 101/9/23, 4) and letters of protection and of attorney (C 67/14).

[66] N.B. Lewis has calculated that 'the maximum cavalry force supplied by the general body of [Edward's] subjects [i.e. not including his household men, Irishmen, Scots and two of the king's 'intimates'] barely amounted to two hundred': 'The English Forces in Flanders', p. 314.

[67] See, for example, *CCR, 1296–1302*, p. 37 (Simon de Ormesby).

[68] In 1297 Ralph Perot was summoned from Essex (C 47/1/5, m. 2ii), but his son Simon may have served in his place (E 101/6/37, m. 6i).

of John de Drokensford in Flanders in 1297;[69] and in that year he seems to have been taking part in the king's wars for the first and final time. The king's summons also ensnared a twenty-pounder by the name of Peter de Suthcherch.[70] He can be traced on just one other campaign, in the following year.[71] Similarly, around twenty of the forty-pounders summoned in 1300 can be found in the records for military service for the first time in that year. This includes middling knights and sergeants, like Richard de Hywysh, Roger de Kerdeston and John de Farlington,[72] as well as young members of well-established families, such as Robert de Ufford, whose father had died a couple of years previously, and John Mauleverer.[73] Considering that the names of as many as a half to three-quarters or more of the men who served in the armies of these years are missing (there is often detailed information on the king's household force only), it is clear that this must be only the tip of the iceberg of the total body of first-time warriors. What we see, indeed, during the late thirteenth and early fourteenth centuries, is an attempt by the Crown to reach out to the country gentry and the gradual emergence of that social order as a military elite.

*

The success of Edward I's recruitment policies, in general, is indicated by the large mounted forces that he was able to raise for some of his campaigns. Although sometimes the number of aristocratic warriors that he put into the field barely exceeded the numbers mustered by his father, on other occasions he was able to mobilise the gentry and nobility on a scale that was seldom equalled during the Middle Ages.

The host that served in Wales in 1277 was one of the smallest of the reign, with perhaps 800 men-at-arms serving on what was 'a surprisingly uneventful' expedition.[74] The numbers of mounted combatants serving in the same theatre of war throughout the campaigns of 1282–3 and 1294–5 appear to have been much larger than this; but calculations are hindered by the fact that overall command was divided between Edward and his regional army captains. We are on safer ground when we come to the Scottish wars that dominated the later part of the reign. Michael Prestwich has estimated that around 3,000 mounted soldiers were put into battle against the Scots at Falkirk in 1298.[75] This seems

---

[69] For his military service, see C 67/12, m. 3. The summons can be found at *Parl. Writs*, i, p. 293.

[70] C 47/1/5, m. 4 (summons); E 101/6/37, m. 1i (service).

[71] C 67/13, m. 5.

[72] Hywysh, (E 101/8/23, m. 6); Kerdeston (C 67/14, m. 9); Farlington (E 101/8/23, m. 6). For the summonses, see C 47/1/6, m. 65; *Parl. Writs*, i, p. 334; *ibid.*, i, p. 339.

[73] Ufford (E 101/9/24, m. 2; E 101/612/11, m. 2; C 67/16, m. 7) and Mauleverer (C 67/14, m. 2; C 67/15 m. 1; C 67/16, m. 10) went on to serve in 1301, 1303–4 and 1306, as well as in other years. For their service in the army in 1300, see C 67/14, mm. 11, 14. The summonses can be found at C 47/1/6, m. 35 and *Parl. Writs*, i, p. 331.

[74] M. Prestwich, *Edward I* (London, 1988), p. 179.

[75] *Ibid.*, p. 479.

plausible given that the horse inventories name 1,350 men in the king's pay.[76] The majority of the earls and bannerets who served in the army in that year did not receive Crown wages. A similar number of elite soldiers assembled in Scotland in the spring of 1303 for the expedition that culminated, during the summer of the following year, in the siege and capture by the English of Stirling castle.[77] Finally, in 1314, for the Bannockburn campaign, Edward II perhaps had around 2,500 aristocratic warriors in his service.[78] When we take into account that there were at most around 9–10,000 families of gentle blood within England at this time, including the 'marginal' parish gentry,[79] it can be seen that a very sizeable proportion of the landholding community took part, at one stage or another, in these wars.

Unfortunately, gaining insights into the mentality of the aristocracy is rather more difficult than providing estimates for the number of men who served in royal and baronial armies. Even more problematic is the task of trying to discern subtle variations in the way that the landholding classes perceived themselves, and their role within society, regionally and over time. One way of overcoming this problem is by analysing the concerns that occupied the thoughts of the gentry and nobility as they neared their deaths. Wills provide a rare insight into the minds of the leading men of the age; and a number that have survived from the late thirteenth and early fourteenth centuries reveal that martial considerations were often uppermost in their thoughts. In September 1296, when preparing for his death, the earl of Warwick requested that two great horses be provided to carry his armour at his funeral.[80] The northern lord William le Vavasur expressed a similar desire when he composed his will fifteen years later.[81] It is interesting that these men wished to be remembered, above all, for their military prowess. Equally revealing in these wills is the preoccupation with the conferment of military equipment.[82] William le Vavasur bequeathed armour to two of his sons, Walter and Henry.[83] Both of these men gave military service: Walter with his

---

[76] *Scotland in 1298*, pp. 160–237; E 101/6/39, 40. There were also around nine hundred enrolled letters of protection for the army of 1298: C 67/13.

[77] M. Haskell, 'Breaking the Stalemate: The Scottish Campaign of Edward I, 1303–4', *Thirteenth Century England VII*, ed. M. Prestwich, R. Britnell and R. Frame (Woodbridge, 1999), p. 229.

[78] J.E. Morris, *Bannockburn* (Cambridge, 1914), p. 41.

[79] C. Given-Wilson, *The English Nobility in the Late Middle Ages: The Fourteenth-Century Political Community* (London, 1987), pp. 72–3.

[80] *Testamenta Vetusta: Being Illustrations from Wills, of Manners, Customs etc. as well as of the Descents and Possessions of many Distinguished Families*, ed. N.H. Nicolas, 2 vols (London, 1826), i, pp. 50–2.

[81] *Wills and Inventories Illustrative of the History, Manners, Language and Statistics, etc. of the Northern Counties of England from the Eleventh Century Downwards*, Part 1, ed. J. Raine, Surtees Society, ii (1835), no. 14. Vavasur had fought in Wales in 1277 and 1282 (*Parl. Writs*, i, p. 199; C 67/8, m. 8) and in Gascony in 1294 and 1295 (*Rôles Gascons*, iii, pp. 161, 294). He also served on many campaigns to Scotland, including in 1298, 1300 and 1306 (C 67/13, m. 7; C 47/2/13, m. 8; C 67/16, m. 10).

[82] For comment on these kinds of bequest and their wider significance, see Ayton, 'Sir Thomas Ughtred', p. 113.

[83] *Wills and Inventories*, no. 14.

father in 1306, and Henry on the Weardale campaign in the first year of the reign of Edward III.[84] In 1325 Fulk de Penebrigg left military equipment to all four of his male descendants.[85] Strangely for a man with such an array of armour to bequeath, Penebrigg does not appear in the extant records for military service. Yet he was summoned, as a forty-librate holder, in 1300 and 1301.[86] It is likely that he was one of the many landholders with estates on the Welsh March who served without Crown pay.

Unfortunately, wills are a far from perfect guide to the mindset of the English aristocracy during the reigns of Edward I and Edward II. Besides not having survived in sufficient quantity to enable anything beyond a superficial analysis, they also reveal little about changing attitudes to warfare over time. It can be shown that the gentry and nobility were actively engaged in the promotion of military culture and the dispersal of armour, but we lack the continuity in evidence that would enable profitable comparisons to be made with earlier and later decades. For insights into the mentality of the aristocracy during these years of heavy campaigning, therefore, we must turn to evidence of a different kind: heraldry.

Heraldry emerged gradually during the mid-twelfth century following a period of 'proto-heraldry' in the 1120s and 1130s. Initially lords had placed symbols on their banners and shields to aid the process of identification on the battlefield and tourney ground. True heraldry developed only once these designs had become hereditary within particular families. Use of the face visor, which led to greater concealment, may have provided an important stimulus to the adoption of these images; but Adrian Ailes has convincingly argued that changes in military accoutrements, most notably the development of the smooth shield, surcoat and lance pennon, facilitated the use and spread of heraldic designs.[87] The practical origins of the science of heraldry are further demonstrated by the phrase 'coat of arms', for 'it was the practice of painting arms on the linen surcoats worn by knights over their mail which gave rise to the term "cote armure"'.[88] Once armorial imagery had become established on the battlefield its use spread rapidly into other areas of aristocratic life. As early as the mid-twelfth century, equestrian seals bearing heraldic images were being used in private correspondence.[89] Such designs eventually filtered down from the nobility to

---

[84] C 67/16, m. 10; E 101/18/6.
[85] BL, Stowe Charter 622; M. Prestwich, *Armies and Warfare in the Middle Ages: The English Experience* (London, 1996), pp. 26–7.
[86] C 47/1/6, m. 45; *Parl. Writs*, i, p. 351.
[87] A. Ailes, 'The Knight, Heraldry and Armour: The Role of Recognition and the Origins of Heraldry', *Medieval Knighthood IV*, ed. C. Harper-Bill and R. Harvey (Woodbridge, 1992), p. 16. For a more traditional version of the practical origins of heraldry, see M. Keen, *Chivalry* (London, 1984), p. 125.
[88] A. Payne, 'Medieval Heraldry', *Age of Chivalry: Art in Plantagenet England 1200–1400*, ed. J. Alexander and P. Binski (London, 1987), p. 55.
[89] J. Cherry, 'Heraldry as Decoration in the Thirteenth Century', *England in the Thirteenth Century*, ed. W.M. Ormrod (Stamford, 1991), p. 124. See also T.A. Heslop, 'English Seals in the Thirteenth and Fourteenth Centuries', *Age of Chivalry: Art in Plantagenet England 1200–1400*, ed. J. Alexander and P. Binski (London, 1987), p. 116. On the rise in the use of the

ordinary knights. By the early fourteenth century, even men of sub-knightly status were beginning to seal with their own coats of arms.[90] The diffusion of heraldry took place, therefore, over several centuries, and it was already well advanced by the time that Edward I succeeded to the throne.

Be that as it may, the heavy campaigning demands of the late thirteenth and early fourteenth centuries instilled this visual culture with renewed martial meaning at a time when heraldry had become detached from its origins in the practicalities of war. Put another way, 'the Edwardian wars transformed an adopted military culture into a more vibrant one underpinned by collective experience and a shared mentality'.[91] Although the reign of Henry III had provided the gentry with few opportunities to share in the military pursuits of their lords, the increased frequency and scale of warfare under Edward I meant that lesser landholders were once again serving in large numbers in the king's hosts. In this environment it was only natural that they should wish to adopt the martial trappings that were so celebrated by their social superiors. This desire manifested itself in the large number of military effigies and brasses that were erected throughout the realm during these years.[92]

It was partly as a consequence of the need to keep track of the growing number of armigerous families within England that herald-minstrels began to compile rolls of arms that listed, in heraldic paintings or blazon, the arms borne by a large number of the militarily active knights of the age (few men of sub-knightly status were at this stage included on such rolls). The first extant roll of arms, Glover's roll, contains around 200 names and dates from the 1250s;[93] but it was not until the 1270s that rolls of arms began to proliferate and the number of men recorded on them markedly increased. This growth in heraldic activity may be attributed, to some extent, to Edward I's predilection for all

---

shield-of-arms on seals by the late thirteenth century, see P.D.A. Harvey and A. McGuiness, *A Guide to British Medieval Seals* (London, 1996), p. 50.

[90] A. Ailes, 'Up in Arms: The Rise of the Armigerous *Vallettus, c.* 1300', *The Coat of Arms*, new ser., xii (1997), pp. 10–16. During the 1290s squires had still been expected to bear the arms of their lords: *The Statutes of the Realm, 1101–1713*, ed. A. Luders *et al.* (Record Commission, 1810–28), i, p. 230. By contrast, 'by 1410 a non-armigerous gentleman was a rarity needing explanation': A.R. Wagner, *Historic Heraldry of Britain* (London, 1939), p. 20.

[91] Ayton, 'Sir Thomas Ughtred', p. 112.

[92] See, for example, M. Clayton, *Catalogue of Rubbings of Brasses and Incised Slabs* (London, 1979); and, for some revised dates of brasses, see J. Coales ed., *The Earliest English Brasses: Patronage, Style and Workshops 1270–1350* (London, 1987). For details relating to effigies dating from this period, see H. Lawrance, *Heraldry from Military Monuments before 1350 in England and Wales*, Harleian Society, xcviii (1946). For comment on the image presented by the aristocracy in death, see J. Alexander and P. Binski, eds., *Age of Chivalry: Art in Plantagenet England 1200–1400* (London, 1987), p. 246. During these years heraldic images were also 'to be found on dress, on domestic plate, on caskets and chests, on wall paintings and on tiled pavements': P. Coss, 'Knighthood, Heraldry and Social Exclusion in Edwardian England', *Heraldry, Pageantry and Social Display in Medieval England*, ed. P. Coss and M. Keen (Woodbridge, 2002), p. 39.

[93] *Aspilogia II: Rolls of Arms, Henry III*, ed. A.R. Wagner, Harleian Society, cxiii, cxiv (1961–2), pp. 115–66.

things chivalric and his employment of heralds at the royal court.[94] Eighteen armorials have survived, either in the original or as copies, from the years 1272 to 1307.[95] The largest and most impressive English heraldic roll of the period, the Parliamentary roll of arms, dates from early in the reign of Edward II. Four of the armorials from the reign of Edward I – the Falkirk, Caerlaverock, Galloway and Stirling rolls – were compiled to commemorate specific martial events; and these armorials are known, consequently, as 'occasional rolls'. The remainder were 'general rolls', which were probably put together by heralds or other men with knowledge of heraldry, to serve as works of reference. These rolls of arms, when considered together, 'were the product of an intense, varied and continuous heraldic activity that would never be exceeded or even rivalled in any other time or place during the Middle Ages'.[96]

Given the unprecedented military demands of Edward I's reign, it seems likely that many of the lesser knights named on these armorials came from newly armigerous families that had sent representatives to war during the king's campaigns in Wales, France and Scotland. The only way to test this theory is to turn to the records for military service and to compare the names of the men-at-arms found there with those of the knights listed on the rolls of arms.

One of the largest armorials of this period was the Lord Marshal's roll, which dates from 1295.[97] The sole surviving version of this roll, a seventeenth-century copy, contains 588 charges;[98] but when kings, earls, Welshmen and Scots are subtracted, together with the numerous unidentifiable blazons, we are left with 499 Englishmen of the status of knight banneret or knight bachelor. Of these, around 405, or 81 per cent, served as mounted combatants at some point between 1277 and 1314. For a number of reasons, however, this figure is likely to under-estimate the true total. As we have seen, large numbers of men-at-arms did not serve for Crown pay or in fulfilment of feudal obligations. Unless they took out letters of protection, appointed attorneys or benefited from respite of debts, such men simply do not appear in the campaign records compiled by royal clerks. An equally serious problem is that the seventeenth-century copy of the roll appears to be riddled with transcription errors. Some of the captions 'are garbled';[99] and it has been shown that the William Ughtred named on the armorial, a man who does not seem to have existed, was a transcription error for Robert Ughtred who

---

[94] For comment on Edward I's knightly interests, including his participation in tournaments and holding of Round Tables, see J.R.V. Barker, *The Tournament in England, 1100–1400* (Woodbridge, 1986), pp. 12–13. See also: N. Saul, ed. *Age of Chivalry: Art and Society in Late Medieval England* (London, 1992), p. 16; *Flores Historiarum*, iii, p. 62; *Ann. Lond.*, p. 104; 'Lanercost', p. 180. For discussion of Edward's employment of heralds, see A.R. Wagner, *Heralds and Heraldry in the Middle Ages: An Inquiry into the Growth of the Armorial Function of Heralds*, 2nd edition (Oxford, 1956), p. 50.

[95] *Aspilogia III: Rolls of Arms, Edward I (1272–1307)*, ed. G.J. Brault, 2 vols (Woodbridge, 2007), i, p. 39.

[96] *Ibid.*, i, p. 41.

[97] G.J. Brault, 'A French Source of the Lord Marshal's Roll (1295–6)', *The Antiquaries Journal*, lxxiii (1993), pp. 27–8.

[98] *Rolls of Arms, Edward I*, i, pp. 323–59.

[99] Brault, 'A French Source of the Lord Marshal's Roll', p. 27.

did take part in the king's wars.[100] Of the ninety or so men named on the Lord
Marshal's roll who do not appear to have given military service, Gerard Brault
has been unable to identify fifteen. The most likely reason for this is that there
were a few mistaken identities.

The largest armorial of the period was the Parliamentary roll of arms, of
c. 1312.[101] This heraldic record contains the names and arms of around 1,100
knights, including some 850 knights bachelor arranged, albeit imperfectly, by
county.[102] Maurice Keen has remarked that it was 'the nearest that medieval
England ever produced to a national armorial'.[103] Consequently, by comparing
the names found on this roll of arms with those listed in the records for military
service dating from 1277 to 1314, it is possible to assess the contribution to the
English war effort made by knights bachelor from all parts of the realm. Table
1.1 shows how large a proportion of the men named on the Parliamentary roll
appear in the records for military service drawn up between Edward I's first
Welsh war and the Bannockburn campaign.

**Table 1.1: Numbers of knights bachelor on the Parliamentary roll of arms who
gave military service (1277–1314)**

County	Total knights	Number who served
Bedfordshire	21	14 (67%)
Berkshire	13	13 (100%)
Bucks.	29	22 (76%)
Cambs.	29	20 (69%)
Cheshire	10	8 (80%)
Corn./Devon	14	9 (64%)
Cumb./Northu.	28	26 (93%)
Derb./Notts.	22	19 (86%)
Dorset/Som.	20	17 (85%)
Essex	58	49 (84%)
Gloucestershire	54	47 (87%)
Herefordshire	20	20 (100%)
Hertfordshire	12	9 (75%)
Huntingdon.	12	8 (67%)
Kent	41	39 (95%)
Leicestershire	40	32 (80%)

100 Ayton, 'Sir Thomas Ughtred ', p. 115, n. 36.
101 For a printed copy of the armorial, see *Parl. Writs*, i, pp. 410–20.
102 Nigel Saul has noted that 'of the fifty-five knights in the Gloucestershire list, as many as
twenty-four seem to have held no land in the county at all': *Knights and Esquires*, p. 30.
103 M. Keen, 'Heraldry and Hierarchy: Esquires and Gentlemen', *Orders and Hierarchies in
Late Medieval and Renaissance Europe*, ed. J. Denton (London, 1999), p. 97. See also Coss,
Knight in Medieval England, pp. 82–4.

Lincolnshire	58	48 (83%)
Middlesex	5	3 (60%)
Norfolk	59	46 (78%)
Northants./Rut.	36	29 (81%)
Oxfordshire	23	20 (87%)
Shropshire	17	17 (100%)
Staffordshire	12	11 (92%)
Suffolk	60	47 (78%)
Sussex/Surrey	26	22 (85%)
Warwickshire	31	26 (84%)
Westm./Lancs.	17	13 (76%)
Wilts./Hants.	33	32 (97%)
Worcestershire	11	10 (91%)
Yorkshire	43	38 (88%)
Total	854	714 (84%)

Remarkably, a total of 714, or 84 per cent, of the knights bachelor whom it has been possible to identify within the county section of the Parliamentary roll of arms appear to have given military service in at least one year between 1277 and 1314. Prosopography on such a large scale is a difficult and imprecise exercise, but the margin of error is unlikely to be great. Furthermore, when assessing the aristocratic response to the king's recruitment efforts, the service provided by aristocratic families can be just as revealing as that given by individual knights. As such, the possibility that one or two knights have been mistaken for others of the same name need not detract from the general impression conveyed by the figures presented in table 1.1. These show that military service among the knightly class was more widespread than has been perceived. Noel Denholm-Young's suggestion, that 'there were, including earls and barons, some 1,250 actual knights in England, as against some five hundred fighting knights',[104] has to be revised, not least because the figure of 714 men noted above as having performed military service excludes 100 or so earls and bannerets who are also named on the Parliamentary roll. These men were, almost without exception, the most active campaigners of their day.

The commitment to military service in some counties should not occasion surprise. Cheshire and Shropshire, along with other shires on the Welsh border, had become highly militarised during the Welsh wars. Many of the knights listed on the Parliamentary roll under these counties gave regular service in the retinues of Marcher lords and other border magnates. John Pichard took out letters of protection with John Tregoz and Fulk Fitz Waryn on separate occasions;[105] John de Orreby rode in the *comitiva* of Reginald de Grey in Wales in 1294

---

104 Denholm-Young, 'Feudal Society in the Thirteenth Century: The Knights', p. 87.
105 1296 (C 67/11, m. 1); 1297 (C 67/12, m. 9).

and later in Scotland in 1301 and 1303;[106] and Roger de Chandos served in the retinue of the earl of Gloucester in 1306 before joining the company of the earl of Hereford for the Bannockburn campaign.[107] The results for other counties, with far less geographical connection with Edwardian theatres of war, are more unexpected. Table 1.2 provides a breakdown of the data for the knights listed on the Parliamentary roll of arms under the heading of Berkshire, where the proportion of militarily active knights bachelor was surprisingly high.

Table 1.2: Military service given by Berkshire knights on the Parliamentary roll of arms (1277–1314)[108]

Name	Place and year of service
Thomas de Coudray	Gascony (1294), Flanders (1297), Scotland (x 7, 1298–1314)
Robert Achard	Scotland (1300, 1303, 1306, 1314)
Richard Fokeram	Wales (1294)
Robert de Sindlesham	Wales (1282), Scotland (1298)
John de la Ryvere	Wales (1294), Flanders (1297), Scotland (x 8, 1298–1314)
John de la Huse	Wales (1294), Scotland (1303, 1306)
John de Lenham	Wales (1277), Gascony (1294), Scotland (1304, 1310)
Adam Martel	Scotland (1314)
Roger de Ingelfeld	Scotland (1306)
William Videlou	Flanders (1297), Scotland (1303)
John de la Beche	Scotland (1297, 1301, 1303, 1306, 1310, 1314)
Richard de Wyndesore	Flanders (1297), Scotland (1300)
John de Foxley	Wales (1294)

That so many of the knights listed under counties like Berkshire, Oxfordshire and Kent appear to have served as men-at-arms in the king's armies demonstrates just how widespread military service was among the gentry during this time.

---

[106] 1294 (*CCW*, p. 46); 1301 (BL, Additional MS 7966a, fol. 84r); 1303 (C 67/15, m. 4).
[107] 1306 (C 67/16, m. 11); 1314 (C 71/6, m. 5).
[108] Coudray (*Rôles Gascons*, iii, p. 166; C 67/12, m. 3d; *Scotland in 1298*, p. 187; C 67/14, m. 11d; C 67/14, m. 3; C 67/15, m. 11; C 47/5/7, m. 1; *CDS*, v, p. 446; C 71/6, m. 5); Achard (C 67/14, m. 11; C 67/15, m. 12; C 67/16, m. 6; C 71/6, m. 3. Another Robert Achard died *c.* 1298, so only the service after that date has been ascribed to this individual: *Knights of Edward I*, ed. C. Moor, 5 vols, Harleian Society, lxxx–lxxxiv (1929–32), i, pp. 3–4); Fokeram (C 67/10, m. 4); Sindlesham (SC 1/10, no. 99; C 67/13, m. 8); de la Ryvere (C 67/10, m. 5d; E 101/6/28, m. 2i; *Scotland in 1298*, p. 216; C 67/14, m. 10; C 67/14, m. 2; E 101/612/10, m. 1; *CDS*, v, p. 445; J.R.S. Phillips, *Aymer de Valence, Earl of Pembroke 1307–1324: Baronial Politics in the Reign of Edward II* (Oxford, 1972), appendix 2; C 71/5, m. 4; C 71/6, m. 5); de la Huse (C 67/10, m. 5; C 67/15, m. 15; C 67/16, m. 10. This individual has been distinguished, as far as possible, from a man named John de Huse); Lenham (*Parl. Writs*, i, p. 207; *Rôles Gascons*, iii, p. 125; *CVCR*, p. 93; *Parl. Writs*, II ii, p. 408. It is probably correct to ascribe this service to the father rather than to the son, who inherited his father's lands in 1316: *Knights of Edward I*, iii, pp. 29–30); Martel (C 71/6, m. 5); Ingelfeld (C 67/16, m. 6); Videlou (C 67/12, m. 2; C 67/15, m. 9); de la Beche (E 101/6/30, m. 1; E 101/9/23, m. 3; E 101/612/11, m. 3d; E 101/13/16, fol. 17r; C 71/4, m. 13; C 71/6, m. 3), Wyndesore (C 67/12, m. 3; C 67/14, m. 9); Foxley (C 67/10, m. 4).

The evidence provided separately by the Lord Marshal's roll and the Parliamentary roll also indicates that the rolls of arms of Edward I and Edward II should be understood in a military context.[109] Once it is accepted that the individuals named on the armorials of this period are primarily, if not exclusively, men who served as mounted warriors in the king's armies, we can begin to compare the information contained in the heraldic rolls with the extant records for military service. This may provide some valuable insights into the wider cultural and social impact of the Crown's heavy recruitment demands.

Given what has been said about the connection, during these years, between martial display and martial reality, it is probably not by chance that the first appearance of some knights on the rolls of arms coincided with the onset of their military careers. Ingelram de Berenger, for example, is named on the Lord Marshal's roll of 1295.[110] This is the earliest surviving armorial on which he appears. In the previous year he had given military service, apparently for the first time, in the king's army in Wales.[111] Other men whose military careers began around 1295 and whose coats of arms were listed, as far as we can tell, for the first time on the Lord's Marshal's roll include Adam de Welles, John de Ralegh and Adam de Huddleston.[112] Herald-minstrels were evidently very diligent in the modification of their records; and they seem to have been well informed about the identities of a large proportion of the up-and-coming warriors of the day. Given that very few men of sub-knightly status at this stage appear on rolls of arms, it is also interesting to find, on these armorials, the names of individuals who had only recently received the honour of knighthood. For example, no fewer than seventeen of the men knighted at the Feast of Swans in 1306 are named on the Nativity roll, which was probably composed in the following year or, at the latest, in 1308.[113] Bearing these points in mind, the rolls of arms of Edward I and Edward II furnish a fascinating corpus of evidence with which to compare the more commonplace source materials recording the names of the Edwardian aristocratic soldiery.

The appearance in the heraldic records of men who had only recently taken up knighthood means that it is possible to use the rolls of arms to trace individual responses to the distraint process. Thirty-three of the men who were distrained to receive knighthood in 1278 appear on the Heralds' roll of *c.* 1279.[114] It is difficult to be sure just how many (if any) of the families thus represented were receiving coats of arms for the first time. John d'Abernon, whose arms *azure, a chevron or* can be found on a monumental brass in the parish church that bears

109 Maurice Keen has remarked on 'the strong association of heraldic insignia with battle and tournament in this age': 'Heraldry and Hierarchy', p. 94.
110 *Rolls of Arms, Edward I*, ii, 46.
111 C 67/10, m. 5.
112 Welles (C 67/10, m. 3); Ralegh (*Rôles Gascons*, iii, p. 170); Huddleston (*Rôles Gascons*, iii, p. 161). For their heraldic biographies, see *Rolls of Arms, Edward I*, ii, pp. 233, 355 and 451.
113 N. Denholm-Young, *History and Heraldry 1254 to 1310: A Study of the Historical Value of the Rolls of Arms* (Oxford, 1965), p. 117.
114 For the returns, see *Parl. Writs*, i, pp. 214–18 and C47/1/2; and for the Heralds' roll, see *Rolls of Arms, Edward I*, i, pp. 79–142.

his name, was clearly assuming the charge that had been borne by his ancestors.[115] Nevertheless, there were other, more obscure figures – such as Richard de Ashburnham, Roger le Covert and Hamo Bovet, each of whom was returned by the sheriff of Sussex[116] – who were possibly the first members of their families to bear coats of arms. Similarly, a minimum of eleven of the men who were distrained to knighthood in 1292 first appear on surviving rolls of arms dating from 1295 to 1300. Alexander de Botheby of Lincolnshire, who is listed on the Lord Marshal's roll of 1295, seems to have been the first man of that surname to bear the arms *gules, two chevrons within a bordure argent*, or, for that matter, any coat of arms.[117] Robert de Flixthorp, a distrainee from Leicestershire,[118] was also probably the first member of his family to bear a coat of arms. He appears on just one surviving armorial, dating from 1295.[119] This influx of new men and families into the social and military elite continued into the reign of Edward II. A few of the men distrained to receive knighthood in 1312 or 1316 were later named on rolls of arms dating from the reign of Edward III. Gilbert de Cokerington, distrained in Yorkshire in 1316,[120] was perhaps the 'G. de Cokerington' listed on the Ashmolean roll of 1334.[121] Likewise, the 'Monsieur de Metstede' who is named on both the Ashmolean roll and Cotgrave's Ordinary (*c.* 1340) may have been the Andrew de Medestede who, like Cokerington, had been distrained to receive knighthood in 1316.[122] No knights with these surnames can be found in the records for military service or on the rolls of arms of the reign of Edward I.

Thus, the combined testimony of the military and armorial records reveals a

---

[115] Clayton, *Catalogue of Rubbings of Brasses*, Plate 1. For his distraint, see *Parl. Writs*, i, p. 218.

[116] For the returns, see *Parl. Writs*, i, pp. 216–17. There is no extant heraldic evidence, on rolls of arms or on seals, for any men with these surnames before 1279. The following collections of rolls of arms and seal catalogues have been consulted: *Rolls of Arms, Henry III*; *Eight Thirteenth-Century Rolls of Arms in French and Anglo-Norman Blazon*, ed. G. J. Brault (London, 1973); *Rolls of Arms, Edward I*; W. de Gray Birch, *Catalogue of Seals in the Department of Manuscripts in the British Museum*, 6 vols, (London, 1887–1900), ii, iii (Equestrian and Heraldic Seals); R. H. Ellis, *Catalogue of Seals in the Public Record Office: Personal Seals*, 2 vols (London, 1978–81); The National Archive card index, located in the Map Room. The same catalogues and collections have been consulted in all subsequent cases, in this chapter, where it is suggested that particular individuals or families may have been bearing coats of arms for the first time. Although it seems that no heraldic evidence survives for the Ashburnham family before 1279, a Reginald de Ashburnham does appear on an equestrian seal dating from the twelfth century: *Catalogue of Seals: Brit. Mus.*, ii, no. 5625.

[117] *Rolls of Arms, Edward I*, ii, p. 66. For his distraint to knighthood, see C 47/1/3, m. 2.

[118] He did not receive knighthood by the deadline in 1292 (E 198/3/5, m. 106d), but this pressure seems to have persuaded him to accept knighthood during the intervening years before the Lord Marshal's roll was composed in 1295.

[119] *Knights of Edward I*, ii, p. 74; *Rolls of Arms, Edward I*, ii, p. 178.

[120] C 47/1/8, m. 31.

[121] *English Mediaeval Rolls of Arms: Volume 1, 1244–1334*, ed. R.W. Mitchell (Peebles, 1983), p. 482. Gilbert de Cokerington should not be confused with members of the Cokington family, who bore different heraldic designs.

[122] C 47/1/8, m. 26d; *English Mediaeval Rolls of Arms*, p. 483; *Rolls of Arms of the Reigns of Henry III and Edward III*, ed. N.H. Nicolas (London, 1829), p. 38.

process of heraldic diffusion that was driven by, and reflective of, the heightened military demands of the late thirteenth and early fourteenth centuries. Warfare during this period changed the outlook not of the leading magnates and nobility, whose predilection for military service probably never waned even during the relatively peaceful reign of Henry III, but of the men who lay on the fringe of the social elite and whose previous experience of campaigning is likely to have been minimal.[123] Moreover, by adapting the coats of arms of their tenurial lords and military leaders, these warriors of relatively modest status gradually became assimilated to a martial culture that had traditionally been the preserve of their social superiors.

Roger le Bret was just such a warrior. In 1292 he was distrained to receive knighthood in Lincolnshire;[124] and three years later his name was recorded on the Lord Marshal's roll, where he appears with the arms *gules billety and a fess dancetty or*.[125] The explanation for Bret's adoption of these arms, which were the arms of Edmund Deyncurt differenced, is not difficult to find. He had appeared as a *serviens* on Deyncurt's behalf at the feudal musters of 1277 and 1282.[126] He therefore had a natural desire, like so many other newly armigerous knights, to base the design of his own coat of arms on that of his feudal lord and military leader. But why did Deyncurt allow Bret to copy his coat of arms in this way? Some light is shed on this by an unusual entry on the patent rolls dated February 1314. Although he was to live on until 1327, Deyncurt was already concerned, thirteen years earlier, that his surname and arms would die out as his immediate heir was his daughter Isabella. He therefore begged Edward II to allow him to enfeoff whomsoever he wished of the lands that he held in chief, so that the persons whom he so enfeoffed might bear his surname and arms in his memory and honour.[127] This concern to ensure that his name and arms, *azure billety and a fess dancetty or*, survived beyond his death, demonstrates the strong link between heraldry and lineage that, as David Crouch has shown, obtained in the Middle Ages.[128] Given the pride and honour that was invested in such images, it is, perhaps, understandable that leading members of the aristocracy were keen for their military retainers and followers to bear coats of arms similar to their own.

Through combined study of the military and heraldic records it is possible to trace a number of men, like Roger le Bret, who adopted differenced versions of the arms of their retinue leaders. The years from 1295 to 1300, when Edward I's recruitment demands reached new heights, were important in this respect. Robert

---

[123] This is a modification of the view expressed in J. France, *Western Warfare in the Age of the Crusades, 1000–1300* (London, 1999), pp. 58–9.

[124] C 47/1/3, m. 2.

[125] *Rolls of Arms, Edward I*, ii, p. 73.

[126] *Parl. Writs*, i, pp. 204, 230.

[127] *CPR, 1313–17*, p. 89; M. Prestwich, *Plantagenet England, 1225–1360* (Oxford, 2005), p. 408.

[128] D. Crouch, 'The Historian, Lineage and Heraldry, 1050–1250', *Heraldry, Pageantry and Social Display in Medieval England*, ed. P. Coss and M. Keen (Woodbridge, 2002), pp. 17–37.

de Haustede senior, who had been a household knight by 1289–90,[129] appears on the Lord Marshal's roll of 1295 with an erroneous tincture.[130] On Collins' roll of the following year the correct blazon is given as *gules, a chief checky or and azure.*[131] The charge in the chief was that of Robert de Clifford,[132] whom Haustede accompanied to Scotland in 1296 and during the winter of 1297–8.[133] The arms of a large number of knights bachelor were recorded for the first time on the Galloway roll of 1300, which commemorates the knights who were present during a skirmish at the river Cree in southwestern Scotland.[134] Some of these men, too, were bearing more complex versions of the arms of their military leaders. Adam de Welles' former knight Robert de Bavent, who had been with Welles in Flanders in 1297,[135] appears to have differenced the Welles arms *or, a lion rampant with a forked tail sable.*[136] Edmund Bacon, who followed the St John family to Flanders in 1297 and then to Scotland in 1298, 1299, 1302 and 1303,[137] carried on his shield the charge *gules, on a chief argent two mullets sable*, which were the arms of St John with different tinctures.[138] Finally, Hugh de Paunton,[139] John le Moyne[140] and William de Beaumont[141] each incorporated

---

[129] E 101/4/27.

[130] *Rolls of Arms, Edward I*, ii, p. 221.

[131] *Ibid.*, ii, p. 221. During the later years of the reign of Henry III a Peter de Haustede had sealed with a completely different coat of arms ('apparently ermine, two chevronels, or a chevron ermine') from the one borne by Robert: *Catalogue of Seals: Brit. Mus.*, iii, no. 10,431. This suggests that Robert may have abandoned his family coat of arms in favour of one based on the design borne by his retinue leader.

[132] Clifford's coat of arms was *checky or and azure, a fess gules*: *Rolls of Arms, Edward I*, ii, p. 109.

[133] E 101/5/23, m. 1i; E 101/6/30, m. 1iv.

[134] On the Galloway roll, see N. Denholm-Young, *The Country Gentry in the Fourteenth Century, with Special Reference to the Heraldic Rolls of Arms* (Oxford, 1969), pp. 151–2; *idem*, 'The Galloway Roll', *Collected Papers of N. Denholm-Young* (Cardiff, 1969), pp. 131–2.

[135] E 101/6/37, m. 4.

[136] For Welles' arms, see *Rolls of Arms, Edward I*, ii, p. 451. Bavent bore *or, a lion rampant with a forked tail sable surmounted by a bend compony argent and gules*: *ibid.*, ii, p. 37.

[137] C 67/12, m. 1; E 101/8/26, m. 3; E 101/612/12, m. 6; C 67/15, m. 14.

[138] *Rolls of Arms, Edward I*, ii, p. 23. St John bore *argent, on a chief gules two mullets or*: *ibid.*, ii, p. 372.

[139] He served with Antony Bek, bishop of Durham in Scotland in 1296 (C 67/11, m. 2) and Flanders in 1297–8 (C 67/12, m. 3d). Paunton bore the arms *gules, two bars and in dexter chief a cross moline ermine*, the chief containing the arms of Bek: *Rolls of Arms, Edward I*, ii, pp. 44, 330. Paunton also witnessed a notarial authentication for Antony Bek in 1303: *Records of Antony Bek, Bishop and Patriarch 1283–1311*, ed. C.M. Fraser, Surtees Society, clxii (1953), no. 84.

[140] He served with Robert de Tibetot in Gascony in 1296 (*Rôles Gascons*, iii, p. 349) and with Robert's son, Payn, in Scotland in 1306 and 1307 (E 101/13/7, m. 1; E 101/14/15, m. 9). Moyne's coat of arms was *or, a saltire indented gules*, and both Robert and Payn de Tibetot bore the similar coat, *argent, a saltire indented gules*: *Rolls of Arms, Edward I*, ii, pp. 295, 415.

[141] He served with William de Ryther in 1300 (E 101/8/23, m. 5) and 1301 (E 101/9/24, m. 1). It seems that he incorporated Ryther's crescent design into his arms: *Rolls of Arms, Edward I*, ii, pp. 42, 369.

aspects of the arms of their military leaders, namely Antony Bek, bishop of Durham, Payn de Tibetot and William de Ryther respectively.

The personal relations that led to this process of dissemination can often be traced back to landholding, marital and friendship ties.[142] There is no need to contrast heraldic links arising from social connections with those resulting from shared military experience, for the one kind of bond reinforced and strengthened the other. A good example of this is provided by the heraldic trail left by John de Crumwell. He seems originally to have differenced the arms of his military leader Roger de Mohaut, *azure, a lion rampant argent*, with whom he served on the Welsh expedition of 1294–5,[143] by adding a forked tail and a crown of gold.[144] Following Mohaut's death and Crumwell's marriage, in 1301, into the Vepont family, Crumwell changed his arms to *gules, six annulets or*, which were the arms of his new patrons with tinctures reversed.[145] Before this marriage he had already begun to forge connections with landed families on the western March towards Scotland, the area where the Vepont family held their main estates. In the opening years of the Scottish war he had served alongside Thomas de Hellebek and Hugh de Louther in the retinue of one of the leading magnates from the northwestern counties, Robert de Clifford.[146] Louther bore the arms *or, six annulets sable*, while Hellebek bore *gules, six annulets or, a label argent*.[147] Although Crumwell first appears with his new coat of arms on the Stirling roll of arms of 1304, after his marriage, it is likely that his betrothal followed his entry into the northwestern military community.[148] By marrying into the Vepont family he therefore strengthened social and military bonds that he had already begun to build in that region, bonds that gained expression through the distinctive six annulets charge.

Coats of arms were disseminated not only between retinue leaders and their followers, but also between men who fought alongside one another or who shared the same locality. This has been demonstrated by Andrew Ayton in his study of the Ughtred family of Yorkshire. They shared the cross patonce design with other families in the East Riding.[149] Many similar heraldic links can be detected in other parts of the realm. Giles de Trumpeton, a knight who served

---

142 See, for example, R. Norton, 'The Arms of Eustace Hatch and Others', *The Coat of Arms*, new ser., v (1982), pp. 18–19.

143 *CCW*, p. 51.

144 *Rolls of Arms, Edward I*, ii, pp. 128, 294. The lion rampant emblem was not that of his father Ralph, who had borne *argent, a chief gules surmounted by a bend azure*.

145 For Crumwell's new heraldic design, see *ibid.*, ii, p. 128. The Vepont coat of arms, as borne by Nicholas de Vepont, was *or, six annulets gules*: *ibid.*, ii, p. 439.

146 Crumwell: 1297 (E 101/6/30, m. 1iv); 1298 (*Scotland in 1298*, p. 196); 1300 (*Liber Quotidianus*, p. 176). Hellebek: 1298 (*Scotland in 1298*, p. 196); 1300 (E 101/8/23, m. 5). Louther: 1297 (E 101/6/30, m. 1iv); 1298 (C 67/13, m. 7); 1300 (E 101/8/23, m. 5).

147 *Rolls of Arms, Edward I*, ii, pp. 224, 268.

148 Crumwell was still using the lion rampant charge in 1300, so the adoption of the new coat was clearly a consequence of his marriage to Idonea de Vepont in 1301: *ibid.*, ii, p. 128. John de Vepont served with Crumwell in Scotland in 1301 (E 101/9/23, m. 1), 1303 (E 101/612/7, m. 3) and 1306 (E 101/612/15, m. 1).

149 Ayton, 'Sir Thomas Ughtred', pp. 115–18.

regularly with the earl of Lincoln between 1294 and 1306,[150] used a canting device in the form of *azure crusily and two trumpets pilewise or*.[151] Given the distinctiveness of this charge, it seems likely that James de Neville, who served under the earl during the same years and who bore the trumpets while changing the tincture of the field, adopted his coat (whether during the wars of Edward I or at some earlier date) from the Trumpeton family.[152] These men may have served together in the earl of Lincoln's retinue during the Welsh wars of 1277 and 1282, as Neville had sealed with the trumpets design as early as 1285.[153] However, a Laurence de Neville appears on the Dering roll of *c.* 1280 bearing the same coat.[154] This suggests that the heraldic link between the two families may have arisen from an older, tenurial connection. This seems to have been true also of the shared pattern borne by the Echingham and St Leger families. Robert de Echingham, Thomas de St Leger and Edmund de St Leger served together, as sergeants in the company of William de Leyburn, in Flanders in 1297.[155] At Bannockburn in 1314 Robert de Echingham could again be found alongside Thomas de St Leger, but this time in the retinue of the earl of Gloucester.[156] The camaraderie that such shared endeavours must have forged between these families was proudly displayed in the common charge of *azure fretty argent*, which appears to have been differenced by the St Leger family.[157] The fretty motif had been used by the St Leger family since at least *c.* 1210;[158] and a William de Echingham appears on the Heralds' roll (*c.* 1279) with the aforesaid arms.[159] In this case, then, as possibly with the Trumpeton–Neville connection, the wars of Edward I seem to have reactivated, in a martial context, heraldic ties that had existed for some time.

When we reflect on the evidence presented in this chapter, it is evident that the late thirteenth and early fourteenth centuries bore witness to a fundamental shift in the activities and lifestyle of the English aristocracy. For the gentry, in particular, the reigns of the first two Edwards must have come as a shock to

---

[150] 1294 (*Rôles Gascons*, iii, p. 161); 1295 (*ibid.*, iii, 294); 1298 (C 67/13, m. 6d); 1300 (C 47/2/13, m. 8); 1303 (C 67/15, m. 5d); 1306 (C 67/16, m. 10).

[151] *Rolls of Arms, Edward I*, ii, p. 423.

[152] *Ibid.*, ii, p. 319. Trumpeton and Neville were with the earl of Lincoln in Gascony in 1294 and 1295 (*Rôles Gascons*, iii, pp. 161, 294). They were also with the earl in Scotland in 1300 (C 47/2/13, m. 8; C 67/14, m. 11) and 1306 (C 67/16, m. 10).

[153] *Catalogue of Seals: Brit. Mus.*, iii, no. 12,109. Neville was proffered (as a knight) by the earl at the feudal muster in 1282 (*Parl. Writs*, i, p. 229). There is no evidence that Giles de Trumpeton served in Edward I's army in that year, but a Roger de Trumpeton did take out a letter of protection independently: C 67/8, m. 2.

[154] *Rolls of Arms, Edward I*, i, p. 155.

[155] E 101/6/37, m. 4.

[156] C 71/6, m. 5; C 81/1727, m. 11.

[157] *Rolls of Arms, Edward I*, ii, pp. 157, 374; *Parl. Writs*, i, p. 412. William de Echingham's inquisition *post mortem* in 1294 shows that he had held land from John de St Leger in Sussex: *CIPM*, iii, no. 191. The two families may have been connected by additional tenurial bonds.

[158] C.L. Kingsford, 'On Some Ancient Deeds and Seals belonging to Lord de L'Isle and Dudley', *Archaeologia, or Miscellaneous Tracts Relating to Antiquity*, lxv (1914), p. 263.

[159] *Rolls of Arms, Edward I*, i, p. 96.

the system as the demands of the Crown's wars placed unanticipated strains on their resources, both human and financial. It may be unwise to write about the creation of a socio-professional elite; but it is clear that, during this era, the number of families and individuals who were involved in warfare at some stage in their lives increased dramatically. Edward I had gone a long way towards expanding the reserve of mounted armoured warriors for his wars. It was now the responsibility of the nobility and baronage to provide the leadership with which to exploit these resources to the full.

2

Captains, Retinue Leaders and Command

Edward I's achievement in recruiting large numbers of the gentry for his wars should not obscure the fact that the responsibility for conducting the king's campaigns still lay primarily with the upper ranks of the aristocracy. The scale of the Crown's ambitions led to the enlistment of many families that had never previously seen active service; but it was the traditional warrior elite who provided the human and financial resources that made this mobilisation programme possible. The earls, barons and bannerets of the realm were Edward's chief henchmen in his attempts to conquer and colonise Wales and Scotland; and it was their assistance that he and his son relied upon most heavily when attempting to defend their ducal inheritance in southwestern France. Indeed, without the support of the large retinues brought to war by their magnates, the kings of England would have been powerless to meet their enemies in open battle. Before proceeding to look at the identities of this elite, their careers in arms and the duties that they performed, this chapter will begin with two preliminary and closely related questions: how did contemporaries refer to men who held positions of military command, and what can these terms tell us about the different kinds of military leadership exercised by the aristocracy in Edwardian England?

Rank and Title in Edwardian Armies

The terminology of military rank was at this time dominated by nouns that tell us little about the details of military command. *Miles*, meaning 'knight', is a word of ancient origin that initially meant 'soldier'. Following the barbarian invasions of the fourth and fifth centuries the word gradually became associated, on the continent, with mounted warfare; but in England it was only after the Norman Conquest that *milites* become synonymous with mounted soldiers or *equites*.[1] The warriors who came to England with the Conqueror were men of varying status.[2] Towards the late twelfth and early thirteenth centuries, however, knighthood began to acquire the more elite status that it had finally attained by the

---

[1] S. Morillo, *Warfare under the Anglo-Norman Kings, 1066–1135* (Woodbridge, 1994), p. 11.
[2] See S. Harvey, 'The Knight and the Knight's Fee in England', *Past and Present*, il (1970), pp. 3–43; but, for a different interpretation of the evidence, see D.F. Fleming, 'Landholding by *Milites* in Domesday Book: A Revision', *Anglo-Norman Studies XIII*, ed. M. Chibnall (Woodbridge, 1991), p. 97.

reign of Edward I. This was due, in part, to its association with the Church and the crusading movement.[3] As Nigel Saul has demonstrated, crystallisation at the top of the military hierarchy led in turn to the appearance of other military ranks below the level of knight. The terms *serviens*, *scutifer*, *armiger* and *vallettus* were used interchangeably by the late thirteenth century to describe men-at-arms who continued to fight on barded horses, but could no longer afford the costly trappings of knighthood.[4] Such men were ultimately to become known as 'esquires', a term of humble origin that by the time of the sumptuary legislation of 1363 had come to denote 'those who were on the same level economically as knights' as well as others who ranked alongside 'all manner of gentle men below the estate of knight'.[5] Neither 'knight' nor 'esquire' had direct associations with leadership on the battlefield: this was reserved primarily for bannerets. Men of this status received twice the pay of ordinary knights and bore rectangular banners rather than simple pennons. Unlike knights bachelor[6] and esquires (for whom command over other soldiers was incidental to their status), bannerets were expected to lead troops of men to war. The rectangular banner was a status symbol reflecting the wealth and social precedence of the man who bore it; but, unlike the other terms already discussed, 'banneret' did not survive as a mark of social or military status much beyond the chivalrous age.[7]

'Banneret', 'knight' and 'esquire' are the socio-military terms most familiar to students of medieval warfare; but, these words tell us little about the details of military command at its highest levels. The status of 'banneret' is also of limited value for an understanding of military leadership at a lower level, for many of the men who led retinues to war during this period were not bannerets. The problem, therefore, is one of definition. According to Peter Coss, 'if we look for terminological exactitude in medieval sources we are likely, as often as not, to be disappointed'.[8] This is largely true of the military records as elsewhere; but how do we account for this general imprecision in usage? One possible explanation is that the armies of Edward I and Edward II were social organisms knitted together from the communities and localities of the realm. This meant that in practice a variety of terms was used to describe soldiers who led other men to war. This interpretation is partly borne out, albeit for a slightly later period, by

---

3 Crouch, *Image of Aristocracy*, p. 139; K. Faulkner, 'The Transformation of Knighthood in Early Thirteenth-Century England', *EHR*, cxi (1996), pp. 20–1. Peter Coss has seen 'the rising cost of knighthood, at least at the end of the twelfth century', as one of the developments helping 'to turn the knight into an aristocratic figure': *Lordship, Knighthood and Locality: A Study in English Society c. 1180–c. 1280* (Cambridge, 1991), pp. 15–16.

4 Saul, *Knights and Esquires*, pp. 12–14.

5 P. Coss, *The Origins of the English Gentry* (Cambridge, 2003), pp. 228–9.

6 T.F. Tout has argued that by the mid-thirteenth century the term 'bachelor' still meant 'simply young novices': 'The *Communitas Bacheleriae Angliae*', *EHR*, xvii (1902), pp. 94–5. However, the term 'knight bachelor' also has a more general meaning, denoting knights below the status of banneret. For a detailed discussion of the origins and use of the term 'bachelor', see J.M.W. Bean '"Bachelor" and "Retainer"', *Medievalia et Humanistica: Studies in Medieval and Renaissance Culture*, new ser., iii (1972), pp. 117–31.

7 Coss, *Origins of the English Gentry*, pp. 241–2; Prestwich, *Armies and Warfare*, pp. 13–15.

8 Coss, *Origins of the English Gentry*, p. 218.

the ordinances of war drawn up at Durham for Richard II's Scottish expedition of 1385.[9] In clause four of these ordinances it was ordered that 'no one be so hardy as to go before, or otherwise than in the battle to which he belongs, under the banner or pennon of his lord or master' (*qe nul soit si hardys daler devant, si noun en son bataille desouz le baner ou penon le son seignur ou mestre*).[10] In clause sixteen, likewise, we find that every soldier was obliged to give a third of his booty 'to his lord or master' (*a son seignur, ou mestre*).[11] It is true that military nomenclature may have changed considerably between the early and late fourteenth centuries, but it is likely to have become more precise rather than less so as the century wore on.

'Captain' is the term most traditionally used by military historians when referring to troop commanders in medieval armies. Indeed, the words 'chevytaigne' and 'capitaigne' were employed alongside 'lord' and 'master' in the army ordinances of 1385.[12] Yet it is not always clear how the word 'captain' was understood by contemporaries. For example, in 1282 the Marcher lord Roger de Mortimer was granted permission to accept the Welshmen of Builth into the king's peace, but the gesture of conciliation was not extended to their captains and lords (*exceptis Capitaneis et dominis eorundem*).[13] It is now impossible to discern whether 'captains' and 'lords' were here simply different words used to refer to the same men. Nevertheless, some attempt at greater precision is necessary so as to distinguish between the two main types of military leadership exercised in the armies of Edward I and Edward II: on the one hand, the command of armies, garrisons and conquered territories, and on the other, the leadership of retinues of men-at-arms.

Generally speaking, 'captain' was used in the government sources of the late thirteenth and early fourteenth centuries to denote the superior type of leader. When war broke out in Wales towards the end of 1276, the king appointed two *capitaneii* to defend the March and to organise the armed forces in that part of the country. By late November of that year, the earl of Warwick was placed in command of the king's men-at-arms in Lancashire and Cheshire.[14] Meanwhile, Roger de Mortimer kept guard of the central Marches from his position as 'captain' of Shropshire, Staffordshire, Herefordshire and the surrounding areas.[15] Chroniclers, too, tended to employ the word *capitaneus* when referring to regional army and garrison commanders. Narrative accounts are a far less

---

[9] For a full discussion of these ordinances, see M. Keen, 'Richard II's Ordinances of War of 1385', *Rulers and Ruled in Late Medieval England: Essays presented to Gerald Harriss*, ed. R.E. Archer and S. Walker (London, 1995), pp. 33–48. Further details on the structure of the army in 1385 can be found in S. Armitage-Smith, *John of Gaunt. King of Castile and Leon, Duke of Aquitaine and Lancaster, Earl of Derby, Lincoln and Leicester, Seneschal of England* (London, 1964), appendix 2.

[10] *Monumenta Juridica: The Black Book of the Admiralty*, ed. T. Twiss, 4 vols, Rolls Ser., lv (London, 1871–76), i, p. 453.

[11] Keen, 'Ordinances of War', p. 38; *Monumenta Juridica*, p. 456.

[12] See, for example, *Monumenta Juridica*, p. 456 (clause 17).

[13] C 77/3, m. 8; *CVCR*, p. 221.

[14] *Parl. Writs*, i, p. 193.

[15] *Ibid.*, i, p. 193; Morris, *Welsh Wars*, p. 115.

reliable guide to terminological usage at this time than the government records, but their testimony should not be discounted out of hand. When writing about the appointment of Hugh de Vere as commander of the English garrison at St Sever in Gascony in 1295, the chronicler Nicholas Trivet felt it appropriate to describe him as a *capitaneus*.[16] Chroniclers also tended to use the word *capitaneus* (or its derivatives) when referring to commanders who led the major divisions or battles within royal and baronial armies. According to Thomas Wykes, the earl of Gloucester was the captain of a battle (*aciei ... capitaneus*) when he fought on the royalist side at Evesham in 1265.[17] Similar terminological usage can also be found in the rolls of arms. The Falkirk roll of 1298, for example, refers to the earl of Lincoln as the *cheveteyn de la premiere batayle* and the earl Warenne as *cheveteyn de la quarte batayle*.[18]

Of the various types of military command within Edwardian England, the word *capitaneus* was most commonly associated with the leadership of regional armies, or of hosts that were gathered when the king could not be present in person. During the first Welsh war (1277) Payn de Chaworth was active as a captain in west Wales while the main army was being assembled in the north.[19] Later, in the 1290s, the earls of Lancaster and Lincoln were employed separately in a similar capacity in Aquitaine at a time when Edward was distracted by rebellions in Wales and Scotland.[20] Such captaincies became increasingly common during the later years of Edward I's reign, when the king was often too feeble to venture north in person. In 1306 the English force was divided, for strategic purposes, into smaller hosts. The main leaders of these armies – Aymer de Valence and Henry de Percy – were described as *capitaneii* in writs, announcing their appointments, sent by the king to the men of the north.[21] In some years, even though large royal armies ventured north of the border, it was necessary to appoint captains to control the areas where the king could not be present in person. The host that campaigned in Scotland in 1303 spent much of its time in the north of the country, which left the south and the border counties of England open to enemy incursions. To reduce this threat, Edward appointed Aymer de Valence as captain south of the Firth of Forth.[22] During his tenure of that office Valence referred to himself in his correspondence with the Crown as 'captain of the host and lieutenant of our lord the king' (*cheventeyn del ost et lui tenaunt nostre seignur le Roi*).[23] In 1311, when the army of Edward II spent many months inactive in the vicinity of Berwick upon Tweed, the earl of Angus was made captain in the north of Scotland. Although he was joined by a small group of barons headed by Payn de Tibetot, only the earl was accorded the official title of *capitaneus*.[24] Finally, following the breakdown of order on

---

[16] *Trivet*, p. 336.
[17] *Wykes*, p. 172.
[18] *Rolls of Arms, Edward I*, i, pp. 406, 415.
[19] *Trivet*, p. 296.
[20] *Rôles Gascons*, iii, p. 300.
[21] C 66/127, m. 28; *CDS*, ii, no. 1754; *CPR, 1301–07*, p. 426.
[22] *CCR, 1302–07*, p. 59.
[23] SC 1/31, no. 33.
[24] Bodleian Library, Tanner MS 197, fol. 52r.

the northern border after Bannockburn, the positions of captain and warden (*custos*) were combined, as they had been, on occasion, at an earlier stage of the war.[25] In 1315 Edward II and his council reacted to the threat of a Scottish invasion of northern England by making Aymer de Valence captain and warden of the March (*capitaneus et custos Marchie*). Again, although Valence was joined by the powerful lords Mohaut and Badlesmere, it was made clear that overall command lay in the hands of the earl.[26]

'Captain' was not the only word used to designate military commanders during the wars of Edward I and Edward II. Walter of Guisborough employed *duces* to refer to John Giffard and Roger de Mortimer junior, two of the chief officers during the Welsh war of 1282.[27] The same author felt that *custodes* was the most appropriate usage for the three main army leaders in 1307.[28] The word *dux* seldom appears in official records at this time, but *custos*, usually translated as 'warden' or 'keeper', frequently does. Alan Harding has observed that during the civil war of 1264–5 the duties of the *capitaneus* and the *custos* (later, in this context, the *custos pacis*) were closely linked, becoming separated only once the civil war was over.[29] A similar situation obtained in Scotland and the northern counties of England, where the functions of the *capitaneus* and *custos* were often indistinguishable. As we have seen, the two roles were sometimes combined under the same man. Fluctuating fortunes on the northern March meant that there was often little to distinguish aggressor from victim, with raids from both sides being a common hazard of border life. The first appointment of a *custos* in disputed territories came in 1201 when Hubert de Burgh was named keeper of the border between England and Wales (*custodem finium Angliae et Walliae*).[30] During the early stages of the Anglo-Scottish wars of the late thirteenth century such appointments became increasingly common until, by 1309, they finally evolved into the permanent institution of Warden of the March.[31] Rebellions following the English victory at Dunbar meant that all of Scotland was regarded as an area requiring the attention of a permanent official. Consequently, the earl Warenne was named in 1296 as keeper of Edward I's realm and land of Scotland (*custodem nostrum regni et terre Scotie*).[32] Then, in the following year, Brian Fitz Alan was offered the same position.[33] The wording of these appointments suggests that the *custos* was primarily a territorial official.

---

[25] See *CPR, 1292–1301*, p. 185.

[26] E 101/376/7, fol. 60r. For a discussion of captaincies in the years after Bannockburn, see C. McNamee, *The Wars of the Bruces: Scotland, England and Ireland 1306–1328* (East Linton, 1997), pp. 147–52.

[27] *Guisborough*, p. 220.

[28] *Ibid.*, p. 378.

[29] A. Harding, 'The Origins and Early History of the Keeper of the Peace', *TRHS*, 5th ser., x (1960), p. 97.

[30] F.C. Suppe, *Military Institutions on the Welsh Marches: Shropshire, AD 1066–1300* (Woodbridge, 1994), p. 102.

[31] R.R. Reid, 'The Office of Warden of the Marches; Its Origin and Early History', *EHR*, xxxii (1917), pp. 481–2.

[32] *Rotuli Scotiae*, i, p. 27.

[33] *Ibid.*, i, p. 45.

However, it would be unwise to make too much of this distinction. Wardens also commanded men-at-arms, just as captains patrolled regional zones.

The captains and wardens of government record evidently possessed considerable authority, wielding powers that had been conferred on them by the king and his council. In other contexts the term 'captain' could be understood in a more pluralistic sense, sometimes referring, as in the later fourteenth century, to the lesser company leaders within the armies; but, it is relatively unusual to find *capitaneus* employed in this way in the chancery and exchequer accounts of the reigns of Edward I and Edward II.[34] Contemporaries were aware of the need to distinguish between the different levels of military command within Edwardian hosts and sought, where necessary, to make such distinctions clear. This is shown by a list that has survived from 1315 containing the names of northern lords summoned by the archbishop of York to do military service.[35] The archbishop wished to convene a meeting of the region's most influential landowners for the purpose of defending the north of England against Scottish invasion. Some fifty men were summoned by name but only ten of these were described as 'chief captains' (*principales capitanei*). This group included Robert de Clifford, Henry de Percy, Ralph Fitz William and Peter de Mauley: the elite of the northern soldiery. The remaining list ended with the word *milites*. Some prominent names can be found among this second group of 'knights', such as Twenge, Furnivall, Meynill and Constable. These were all men who led armed companies on royal campaigns in the hosts of Edward I and his son, but the distinction between the 'chief captains' and 'knights' is significant. It reflects the presence within medieval armies of different levels of power and authority, as well as the tendency to use social or quasi-social terms, such as *barones* or *milites*, for the lower rung of leaders. In this context it should be remembered that the ordinances drawn up for Richard II's campaign of 1385 referred to retinue leaders not only as captains (*capitaignes*) but also, more frequently, as lords or masters (*seignurs ou mestres*). Such usage was reflective of the fundamentally social nature of these companies.

If, under Edward I and Edward II, the word 'captain' usually referred to individuals appointed by royal commission to command hosts or defend territorial zones, the question remains as to how we should style the leaders of the armies' constituent companies. As we have seen, such men were sometimes simply referred to as 'lords' or 'masters', but there were other alternatives. One method was to refer to the banner that each lord carried on campaign. According to David Crouch, 'men who had banners were great men, for the practical reason that only a man with the resources to lead a company of troops would need such an item to distinguish himself from others'.[36] The army that the Lord Edward led towards London in 1267 consisted, we are told, of 109 banners (*vexilla*).[37] Bartholomew Cotton entered into greater detail on the English army

---

34 For a rare instance of such usage, see C 54/123, m. 8d; *CCR, 1302–07*, p. 455.
35 *Historical Papers and Letters from the Northern Registers*, ed. J. Raine, Rolls Ser., lxi (London, 1873), pp. 246–7.
36 Crouch, *Image of Aristocracy*, p. 114.
37 *Ann. Winton.*, p. 105.

at Falkirk. The host was divided into four 'battles', the first consisting of twenty-three 'banners, of earls and magnates' (*vexilla comitum et magnatum*).[38] He put the count for the second battle under the bishop of Durham at twenty-three banners, but Guisborough gave a higher figure of thirty-six bannerets (*vexillarii*).[39] Cotton's account would appear to have been the more accurate of the two, for the Falkirk roll of arms names twenty-seven bannerets in Bek's division.[40] The significance of bannerets and banner-bearers at this level of military organisation is further suggested by the canon of Bridlington, who described the rebel baronial army of 1322 as comprising 'a large number of barons and bannerets' (*multi ... barones et baneretti*).[41] Indeed, this kind of division into battles and banners matched continental practice. J.F. Verbruggen has noted that the French royal army that fought against the Flemings at Cassel in 1328 consisted of a dozen battles comprising a total of 196 banners.[42] Most narrative depictions of English royal hosts tend, however, to be less precise than this. The army that fought in Wales in 1277 consisted, we are told, of 'earls and barons' (*comitibus et baronibus*).[43] Similarly, the host that the earl of Cornwall led into Wales against Rhys ap Maredudd in 1287 was led by the earl, as keeper of England, along with other 'earls, barons, knights, and all the army of England' (*comitibus, baronibus, militibus et totu exercitu Angliae*).[44] It is to be regretted that few chroniclers entered into much detail concerning the composition of the king's forces.

Despite the general imprecision of the military terminology found in contemporary sources, some useful distinctions can be made. Military captains and wardens, as revealed in the records of chancery and exchequer, were usually men who occupied specific positions of command, whether that was over garrisons in the Welsh borderlands or regional armies in the north of Scotland. For the most part (though by no means always), the contingents that comprised royal hosts were led not by 'captains' of this kind, but by 'earls', 'barons' and 'knights': terms of a social origin. Bannerets appear to have formed the crucial tactical link between battle (or divisional) commanders and the lesser company leaders, but such precise ranks were rare below the level of captain or warden. For the purposes of simplification, therefore, the words 'captain' and 'warden' will be used in the remainder of this chapter, as appropriate, to refer to men who held high command, whereas 'retinue leaders' or similar terms will designate

---

[38] *Cotton*, pp. 343–4.
[39] *Ibid.*, pp. 343–4; *Guisborough*, p. 327.
[40] *Rolls of Arms, Edward I*, i, pp. 408–11.
[41] 'Gesta Edwardi de Carnarvon, Auctore Canonico Bridlingtoniensi, cum Continuatione ad AD 1377', *Chronicles of the Reigns of Edward I and Edward II*, ed. W. Stubbs, 2 vols, Rolls Ser., lxxvi (London, 1882–3), ii, p. 74.
[42] J.F. Verbruggen, *The Art of Warfare in Western Europe during the Middle Ages: From the Eighth Century to 1340*, 2nd edition (Woodbridge, 1997), p. 81.
[43] *Annales Cestrienses; or, Chronicle of the Abbey of St Werburg, at Chester*, ed. R.C. Christie, The Record Society for the Publication of Original Documents Relating to Lancashire and Cheshire, xiv (1886), p. 104.
[44] *Ann. Lond.*, p. 96.

men who led their own companies to war, however large or small their companies happened to be.

High Command: Powers and Responsibilities

In the summer of 1297 Hugh de Cressingham, Edward I's much-maligned appointee as treasurer of Scotland, sent a letter to the king concerning the state of affairs north of the border. Policing the country was proving difficult and, to make matters worse, a crisis had arisen among the leaders of the English force. Brian Fitz Alan's reluctance to assume responsibility for the government of Scotland, in the wake of the earl Warenne's attempts to resign the post of keeper, had created uncertainty within the army as day by day the strength of the enemy continued to grow. In his report Cressingham urged the king to appoint a new commander-in-chief with all haste, 'for, in proportion as the matter is pressed onwards with good thought and good deliberation, so much the better for you'.[45] On 7 September the earl was ordered to continue as leader of the expedition;[46] but just four days later, at a time when both he and his men were coming to terms with the new command structure, the occupying army was routed by the Scots at Stirling Bridge. The treasurer was among those killed, his warning having been heeded too late to save his life and the lives of many others.

The defeat at Stirling Bridge demonstrates the importance of strong and decisive leadership in medieval warfare. Although a number of errors, including tactical decisions made on the day of the battle, led to the catastrophe in 1297, the confusion over command of the army, together with the slow resolution of that problem, probably contributed to the reversal. Medieval military theorists, like modern historians, were able to discern the implications of such events. Writing early in the fifteenth century, Christine de Pizan observed that in war, 'nothing has greater importance than the selection of military leaders'.[47] As military men themselves, medieval kings were aware of the need to select captains whose good service and prestige would set an example to others. A problem that they faced, as in all ages, was to discern who the most able men were, for the numerous administrative and military qualities that were required in a leader were rarely found in one man. The processes by which military commanders were selected are now hidden from view; but, by considering the characteristics of the soldiers who were entrusted with such responsibilities it may be possible to reconstruct the criteria according to which captaincy commissions were issued.

Experience was perhaps the most important qualification that a candidate for military leadership could possess. It was the strong war record of the earl Warenne that made him such a promising choice for the custodianship of

---

45 *Stevenson*, ii, p. 226. This letter was dated 5 August.
46 *Ibid.*, ii, p. 230.
47 Christine de Pizan, *The Book of Deeds of Arms and of Chivalry*, trans. S. Willard and ed. C.C. Willard (Philadelphia, Pa., 1999), p. 23.

Scotland in 1297. The composer of a contemporary song on the Scottish wars observed that the king had appointed 'a worthy man to the government of the kingdom, John de Warenne, whom he had often proved'.[48] The earl had enjoyed a suitably active military career for a man of his status. A veteran of the reign of Henry III, he had fought alongside the Lord Edward at Lewes[49] before going on to serve with distinction throughout the Welsh wars. In 1287 he had helped to put down the rising of Rhys ap Maredudd while the king was in France.[50] Although a sexagenarian by 1297, Warenne had shown sufficient ability in leading a force to victory over the Scottish feudal army at Dunbar in the previous year to suggest that his age need not be a bar to success.[51] For the greater part of his reign Edward placed his trust in those, like the earl, who were soldiers of his own generation.[52] A number of knights who had been on crusade with the prince during 1270–2, including Robert de Tibetot, Payn de Chaworth, William de Valence and the king's brother, Edmund of Lancaster, held positions of command during the Welsh wars of 1277 and 1282–3.[53] Other veterans of the expedition to the east, most notably John de St John,[54] later gave prominent service in Gascony and Scotland, providing the king with an experienced and able leadership corps during the years of crisis. Despite the arrival of a new generation of commanders in the late 1290s, the majority of the men employed as wardens on the Scottish March had cut their teeth as retinue leaders during the wars against Llywelyn ap Gruffydd. Brian Fitz Alan was offered the position of *custos* of Scotland in 1297, twenty years after first campaigning against the Welsh;[55] and William le Latimer,[56] Robert Fitz Roger[57]

---

[48] *Thomas Wright's Political Songs of England: From the Reign of John to that of Edward II*, with introduction by P. Coss (Cambridge, 1996), p. 168.

[49] *Chronica et Annales*, p. 26.

[50] He received a prest in 1287 (E 372/132, m. 1) and obtained letters of protection for his men in 1277 (*CPR, 1272–81*, p. 222), 1282–3 (C 67/8, mm. 3–4) and 1294–5 (C 67/10, m. 7).

[51] The earl was born 'in or after August 1231': *Complete Peerage*, xii (i), 503. On the battle of Dunbar, see G.W.S. Barrow, *Robert Bruce and the Community of the Realm of Scotland*, 3rd edition (Edinburgh, 1988), p. 72. The earl's grandson, another John, earl Warenne, later held command (in 1326) in the northern counties of England: F. Royston Fairbank, 'The Last Earl of Warenne and Surrey, and the Distribution of his Possessions', *Yorkshire Archaeological Journal*, xix (1907), p. 225.

[52] Prestwich, *War, Politics and Finance*, p. 49. Most of the men who had served as commanders under Henry III had died before Edward came to the throne: Walker, 'Anglo-Welsh Wars', p. 97.

[53] For their participation in the crusade, see S. Lloyd, *English Society and the Crusade 1216–1307* (Oxford, 1988), appendix 4; B. Beebe, 'The English Baronage and the Crusade of 1270', *BIHR*, xlviii (1975), appendix. For their appointments to captaincies in Wales, see: Tibetot (*Parl. Writs*, i, p. 222); Chaworth (*CCR, 1272–79*, p. 366); Valence (*Parl. Writs*, i, p. 227); and Lancaster (*CPR, 1272–81*, p. 213).

[54] His service as a captain is discussed at length, in the main text, below.

[55] For his service in Wales, see *CPR, 1272–81*, p. 190. For his appointment in 1297, see *Rotuli Scotiae*, i, p. 45.

[56] For his captaincy, see *Parl. Writs*, i, p. 319. He had served in Wales in 1282–3 (E 101/4/1, m. 2) and was also a member of the king's household during the 1280s: E 101/4/9; E 101/351/26, m. 1.

[57] See *Parl. Writs*, i, p. 301. He had fought in Wales in 1277 (E 101/3/12), 1282 (C 67/8, m.

and John de Segrave[58] were just three of the many men for whom command in the Scottish wars was reward for a lifetime of military activity on behalf of the Crown.

From the mid-1290s, when the scale of warfare increased due to the outbreak of hostilities in France and Scotland, military experience was less difficult to come by than it had been during the relatively peaceful period following Edward I's accession. When the earl of Pembroke was appointed as captain and keeper in Scotland in 1314, it was observed that he had been selected because of the industry and diligence that he had shown in the past.[59] In the seventeen years since first serving as a retinue leader on the Flanders campaign in 1297, he had fought, not uncommonly for those coming of age at that time, on at least eight different expeditions, seven of which had been conducted north of the border.[60] Following a successful apprenticeship as captain in southern Scotland in 1303, Valence went on to lead small armies north of the border in the last two years of Edward I's reign. During that time he confronted Robert Bruce in battle on two occasions, defeating his adversary at Methven (1306) but suffering a reversal the following year at Loudon Hill. When the northern counties of England were faced with repeated Scottish raids in the months following Bannockburn, he was the commander to whom Edward II turned to stem the tide. Reappointments of this kind were common as an elite band of warriors was repeatedly drawn on to occupy the most important military positions. Robert Fitz Roger served as a commander on the eastern March in 1297, then again in 1300, before leading a group of Northumbrian stipendiaries in 1306.[61] John de Segrave was employed as a captain on the northern March throughout much of the opening decade of the fourteenth century.[62] Earlier, both William de Valence and Reginald de Grey had provided an important thread of continuity throughout the Welsh campaigns of the first two decades of the reign.[63]

Not all of the men appointed by the Crown to important positions of command were experienced war veterans. Robert de Clifford was in his early twenties and had only recently begun to serve as a retinue leader when he was named keeper of the western March towards Scotland in 1296.[64] In this instance geographical proximity to the theatre of war appears to have been decisive, as the Cliffords were the largest landowning family in the affected area. It has been suggested

---

8d), 1287 (E 372/132, m. 1) and 1294–5 (C 67/10, m. 6). He had served in Scotland in 1296 (C 67/11, m. 3).

[58] See *Foedera*, II, i, 70; and for his service in Wales in 1277 and 1282–3, see *Parl. Writs*, i, pp. 206, 233.

[59] *Foedera*, II, i, p. 252.

[60] He had served in Flanders in 1297 (BL, Additional MS 7965, fol. 68r) and in Scotland in 1298 (*Scotland in 1298*, p. 216), 1300 (C 67/14, m. 11), 1301 (E 101/9/24, m. 1d), 1302 (C 67/15, m. 16), 1303–4 (E 101/612/8, m. 1), 1306 (E 101/13/16) and 1307 (C 67/16, m. 3). He could also be found on the Scottish March in the winter of 1311–12: C 71/5, m. 4.

[61] *Parl. Writs*, i, p. 301, 340; *CDS*, ii, no. 1760.

[62] In 1302–3, 1305 and 1309–10: *Knights of Edward I*, iv, pp. 236–7.

[63] Valence: 1277 (*CPR, 1272–81*, p. 211); 1282–3 (C 67/8, m. 8); 1294–5 (C 67/10, m. 7). Grey: 1277 (*CPR, 1272–81*, p. 189); 1282–3 (C 67/8, m. 5); 1287 (E 372/132, m. 1d); 1294–5 (E 101/5/18, m. 14).

[64] *Complete Peerage*, iii, pp. 290–1; *CDS*, ii, no. 734.

that 'lack of money' sometimes forced the king 'to engage as his captains the men who had a personal interest in keeping the Marches safe'.[65] Such men as these would not have wanted for motivation to perform their military duties. During the Welsh wars the comital families of Clare and Bohun, as well as the baronial dynasties of Mortimer, Grey and Lestrange, played prominent roles in the conflicts fought close to their own lands. Scottish landowners, such as the earl of March, the earl of Angus, and Alexander d'Abernethy,[66] were not infrequently called upon to serve as captains north of the border. Membership of the king's household might also be a factor in the selection of officers as men in receipt of fees could be supervised with less difficulty than comital warriors, who liked to remind the king of their rights and privileges. Authority in the Welsh and Scottish Marches was often committed to household knights. Four of the king's bannerets – Robert de Clifford, John de St John, John Botetourt, and Richard de Siward – acted as wardens of the Scottish March between 1296 and 1307.[67] Likewise, both Roger de Mortimer of Wigmore and Roger Lestrange had been members of the household during their spells as captains in the second Welsh war (1282–3).[68] Despite this, the role of the household knights as military leaders should not be exaggerated. For all their reliability, 'the major military commands were rarely entrusted to them';[69] and, owing to the objections that the king would have faced from the nobility, 'no household knight was ever made commander-in-chief of a battalion in a major campaign'.[70]

Alongside experience, ability was the most sought-after quality in a war captain. Yet, as J.R. Maddicott has reminded us, 'one of our chief difficulties in writing about medieval nobles is our lack of the means to judge their capabilities'.[71] The captains on whom the Crown most frequently relied, such as Aymer de Valence, were probably the ones who possessed the greatest ability in the field. Unfortunately, however, detailed descriptions of commanders in action, such as that of the earl of Warwick at the battle of Maes Moydog in 1295, are rare.[72] In any case, ability counted for little without the accompanying advantages of social status and material wealth. Without these, even the most competent soldier would find it difficult to exercise his authority. When offered the position of keeper of Scotland in August 1297, Brian Fitz Alan declined the post, explaining to the king that 'the goods which I have would be too small,

---

[65] Reid, 'Office of the Warden of the Marches', p. 490.

[66] On d'Abernethy, see Brown, 'Scots in Plantagenet Allegiance', pp. 97, 100, 108.

[67] Ingamells, 'Household Knights of Edward I', i, p. 105, ii, pp. 51–2.

[68] *Ibid.*, i, p. 105, ii, pp. 48. Edward I also entrusted members of his *familia* with important positions of command in Ireland. He appointed 'no fewer than five former household knights as justiciar': B. Hartland, 'The Household Knights of Edward I in Ireland', *Historical Research*, lxxvii (2004), pp. 161–2.

[69] Prestwich, *War, Politics and Finance*, p. 60. However, R.F. Walker has noted that during the reign of Henry III commanders were 'drawn from two principal sources, the Marcher lords, and the knights of his household': Walker, 'Anglo-Welsh Wars', p. 96.

[70] Ingamells, 'Household Knights of Edward I', i, p. 102.

[71] J.R, Maddicott, *Simon de Montfort* (Cambridge, 1994), p. 358.

[72] *Trivet*, p. 335.

as far as I can stretch them, to keep that land well to your honour'.[73] The earl Warenne had struggled to perform his duties owing to insufficient resources; and Fitz Alan claimed that with an annual income of just 1,000 pounds he would find it difficult to keep fifty armed horses in the field as befitted the status of the commander-in-chief.[74] In the thirteenth and early fourteenth centuries social eminence was still regarded, for the most part, as a necessary precondition for the exercise of high command. The Scottish force that invaded Weardale in 1327 was led by 'the most high-ranking barons of all the realm of Scotland' (*les plus haults barons de tout le royaume d'Escoce*).[75] In England, too, the leading positions of command were almost invariably given to men drawn from the upper echelons of noble society. Combatants of comital rank disliked the notion of serving under men of inferior status. In 1277 Payn de Chaworth, who had been a captain in west Wales since the end of the previous year, was placed under the higher authority of the earl of Lancaster, the king's lieutenant in the area.[76] Five years later, Robert de Tibetot was replaced as captain in south Wales by the earl of Gloucester after only two weeks in the office.[77] It was not easy to reconcile the king's wish to appoint the most able soldiers with the traditional precedence afforded in such matters to men of comital status.

One way around this problem was to issue joint commands so that young men of high social standing could learn their trade in the company of more experienced baronial leaders. On 1 July 1294 John de St John was made seneschal of Gascony.[78] At the same time, Jean de Bretagne, the future earl of Richmond,[79] was appointed as captain of the king's forces there.[80] According to the chronicler Nicholas Trivet, St John and another knight, Robert de Tibetot, had been specially chosen, owing to their skill and experience in war, to act as advisors to the young captain.[81] This made perfect sense as St John was Jean de Bretagne's senior by some twenty years.[82] Joint commissions of this kind were not uncommon. In October 1294 the earl of Arundel, who was in his late twenties at the time, was sent on an expedition to Bere castle in Wales along with Robert Fitz Walter, a veteran of the first and second Welsh wars. Although the earl was made captain, in recognition of his high social standing, it was understood that he was 'to succour and furnish the said castle' according to the recommendations given to him by Fitz Walter. The earl was assisted not only by Fitz Walter but also by a number of experienced Marcher lords, including

---

73 *Stevenson*, ii, p. 223.
74 *Ibid.*
75 *Chronique de Jean le Bel*, ed. J. Viard and E. Déprez, 2 vols (Paris, 1904–5), i, p. 52.
76 *CPR, 1272–81*, p. 213.
77 *CVCR*, p. 213.
78 *Rôles Gascons*, iii, p. 172.
79 Although Jean de Bretagne only became earl of Richmond in 1306, his hereditary claim to the title means that, in essence, he possessed comital status at this earlier date.
80 *Rôles Gascons*, iii, p. 172.
81 *Trivet*, p. 331; Morris, *Welsh Wars*, p. 241.
82 I. Lubimenko, *Jean de Bretagne, Comte de Richmond: Sa Vie et son Activité en Angleterre, en Éscosse et en France (1266–1334)* (Paris, 1908), pp. 6–7.

Roger Lestrange and Peter Corbet.[83] Similarly, the earl of Gloucester was only seventeen when he was made captain of an expeditionary force to Rutherglen in Scotland in 1308. While the earl was appointed captain of the expedition (*capitaneus nostrum expeditionis*), John de Crumwell was made leader of the knights, *valletti*, sergeants and footmen.[84] Crumwell and the men serving under him were officially subordinated to the young earl's command. However, given the earl's inexperience and the fact that Crumwell had served with distinction as a retinue leader on several previous campaigns, it is likely that Crumwell was expected to act in an advisory capacity to the future tragic hero of Bannockburn.

The man responsible for the appointments of the earl of Gloucester and John de Crumwell in 1308, Edward II, had undergone a similar period of tutelage in the art of military command as a teenage prince. Like the young Gilbert de Clare, Edward had acquired little military experience prior to his appointment as leader of an army in western Scotland in 1301. On that occasion he was accompanied by a number of elder bannerets, including William de Leyburn and Reginald de Grey, who were trusted associates of the prince's father.[85] Members of the royal family shared with sons of the higher nobility the need to obtain training in war from an early age. Indeed, many of the commissions that were given to young men can be explained in this light. However, not all joint commissions were granted because of the need to combine status with experience, or wealth with ability. In August 1315, in response to an attack by Robert Bruce on the border fortification of Carlisle, the earl of Lancaster was made commander-in-chief (*superiorem capitaneum*) over all men-at-arms and foot between the River Trent and Roxburgh.[86] The earl of Pembroke had already been appointed as captain in that area in July and would appear to have been a more able and trustworthy commander than the king's irascible cousin. J.R.S. Phillips has suggested that 'the major reason for putting Pembroke under Lancaster's orders on 8 August may have been because the immediate Scottish threat to Carlisle was close to Lancaster's home base and also because Pembroke's forces happened to be in the area at the time'.[87] If this were so, it may be that captaincies were sometimes conferred in recognition of a noble's claim to territorial supremacy rather than for the sole purpose of strengthening national defence. 'In effect', Phillips pointed out, 'Pembroke and his men were doing Lancaster's job for him'.[88]

Several considerations, then, influenced the selection of military captains, not least experience, ability, wealth and social status; but what of the processes by which these captains were chosen? Comparison with the situation across the Channel, where the extant sources for the selection process are more detailed, may supply some clues. In mid-fourteenth-century France, at a time of national

---

[83] *CVCR*, p. 360. The earl was born in 1266 or 1267 (*Complete Peerage*, i, p. 240) and seems to have had his first experience of war in 1287 (*Parl. Writs*, i, p. 253). For Fitz Walter's service in 1277 and 1282–3, see *CPR, 1272–81*, p. 220 and E 101/4/1, m. 1 respectively. He had also fought during the Barons' War.
[84] *Rotuli Scotiae*, i, p. 60.
[85] BL, Additional MS 7966a, fol. 84r.
[86] *Rotuli Scotiae*, i, p. 148.
[87] Phillips, *Aymer de Valence*, p. 90.
[88] *Ibid.*, p. 90.

crisis following the capture of John II at the battle of Poitiers, a series of ordinances were issued aimed at regulating the process by which military captains were appointed. In May 1358 it was announced that, owing to the way that many captains had been appointed in various parts of the country without due consideration of their merits and had spent a great deal of the king's money for no apparent profit, all captains were to be chosen in future in full council.[89] The method of appointing military captains only after deliberation by the king and his counsellors seems to have been adopted in England from a relatively early date. Following the death of John de St John in 1302, some thought was given to who should replace him as warden on the western March towards Scotland. The treasurer, Walter de Langton, informed the king that he believed John Botetourt to be a suitable man for the position; but Edward, despite being aware that the latter was a 'good man, both wise and sufficient' (*bon homme et sage et suffisant*), declared that he was not willing to make a decision until he had had the opportunity to talk with his council at the next parliament.[90] In the event Botetourt was appointed as *cheventain* on the western March by 4 January 1303.[91] The discussion of such issues in council was not confined to this one occasion. Captaincy commissions were often made by the king and his council (*per regem et consilium suum*), as demonstrated by the terms of the appointments of the earl of Angus in 1311 and the earl of Pembroke in 1315.[92] This is as one would expect given that defence of the country was a matter of concern not only for the king, but for the community of the realm at large.

Following the selection process the captain or warden was invested with wide-ranging powers, which he exercised in the name of the Crown. Royal support was essential if the king's captains were to retain control over the hundreds and sometimes thousands of soldiers placed under their authority. The more powerful these soldiers were, the more carefully the king's officials had to tread in their dealings with them. This was especially the case during the Welsh wars, when the traditionally independent and very powerful Marcher lords had to be cajoled into cooperating with the captains placed over them. For this reason, the men appointed to command over the Marcher lords tended to be Marchers themselves. In 1282 Roger de Mortimer of Wigmore was placed in command not only of the lesser men-at-arms of the central Welsh Marches, but also over ten leading border magnates, including Ralph de Tony, Peter Corbet and Roger Lestrange. Each of the same ten men was sent an individual summons by the chancery clerks, informing him of Mortimer's appointment.[93] Following Mortimer's death in October 1282, one of these men, Lestrange, was given the captaincy in his stead. The magnates who had previously served under

[89] *Ordonnances des Roys de France de la troisième race*, ed. D.F. Secousse *et al.*, 21 vols (Paris, 1723–1849, repr., 1967–8), iii, p. 224.

[90] SC 1/13, no. 110. This document has been printed in 'Notes and Communications', *SHR*, xxiv (1927), pp. 325–6.

[91] *Parl. Writs*, i, p. 368.

[92] Bodleian Library, Tanner MS 197, fol. 52r; E 101/376/7, fol. 60r.

[93] *CVCR*, p. 212.

Mortimer were now bound to Lestrange's leadership.[94] Such local appointments made practical sense. They would certainly have been far less objectionable to the Marcher lords than the appointment of outsiders, who probably knew little about Marcher customs and privileges.

The parameters of a captain's powers were determined by not only the number and quality of men under his command but also the geographical areas over which he exercised control. During the second Welsh war, leadership of the king's armies was divided between several regional captains. Reginald de Grey was given command of Cheshire and Flint; Roger de Mortimer, as we have seen, possessed control on the central Marches; and Robert de Tibetot held sway in west Wales.[95] Operations in Gwynedd were left primarily to the king and his household force. When John de St John was made captain on the western March towards Scotland in 1300, his authority extended over a large area to include 'Cumberland, Westmorland, Lancaster, Annandale and the whole Marches to the bounds of Roxburgh'.[96] Later, in the summer of 1310, Alexander d'Abernethy was given authority over the area between the Firth of Forth and the Scottish Highlands (*inter aquam de Forth et montes Scocie*).[97] Within these regions, captains were empowered to call on the services of all men fit to bear arms. To facilitate the smooth transition to wartime government, orders were sent out to the men of the towns and counties, via sheriffs and other royal officials, ordering them to be responsive and obedient to the commanders placed over them.[98] Such men might be called on to serve under the captains; but, in advance of their service, captains would usually contract to serve with a more compact, full-time troop. An indenture drawn up in 1296 stipulated that Robert de Clifford was to have in his service 140 men-at-arms and 500 foot to assist him in his defence of the western March towards Scotland.[99] The earl of Richmond and John de Segrave each had sixty mounted warriors in their *comitivae* when serving as keepers of Scotland in 1307 and 1309 respectively.[100]

The above terms of service provided a basic framework upon which captains and other royal officials could build their authority, but the powers that they exercised did not stop there. Just how far a captain's powers might range is vividly demonstrated by a commission issued early in the reign of Edward I's grandson, Edward III. On 25 April 1338 Richard Fitz Alan, earl of Arundel was appointed as captain and leader of the English forces in Scotland. The powers conferred on him by the king were extensive. He was given full powers to punish transgressions and felonies committed by all men within the army; to elect as many men-at-arms, hobelars and archers as he required between the March of Scotland and the river Trent; to meet with the keepers of the various castles and

---

94 *Ibid.*, p. 244. For a discussion of these appointments, see Suppe, *Military Institutions on the Welsh Marches*, pp. 120–1.
95 *Parl. Writs*, i, p. 222.
96 *CDS*, ii, no. 1134.
97 *Foedera*, II, i, p. 108.
98 See, for example, *Parl. Writs*, i, p. 193.
99 *CDS*, ii, no. 734.
100 *Foedera*, II, i, pp. 6, 70. Aymer de Valence had sixty men in his retinue, too, when serving in Scotland in a similar capacity during the reign of Edward II: E 101/373/23.

garrisons within Scotland to arrange for their better defence; to supervise the armaments at the said garrisons; to raise all men between the ages of sixteen and sixty within the northern counties, placing them into infantry troops of thousands, hundreds and twenties; and to imprison all soldiers who disobeyed his orders.[101] Although such a long list of powers and responsibilities was quite exceptional, the terms of this commission give some idea as to the measure of control that English war captains might possess. It is unusual to find all of these powers bestowed upon one man; but various aspects of the command exercised by the earl of Arundel in 1338 were possessed by English war captains during the reigns of Edward I and Edward II.

Of the powers conferred by Edward III on Richard Fitz Alan, perhaps the most useful were those concerning judicial and punitive rights. Although military captains and keepers were granted authority over large numbers of soldiers, they had no way of enforcing their will unless the king gave them the freedom to use coercion and punishment. One problem (though probably not the main one) facing the Crown's agents in Scotland, Wales and Gascony was desertion. An entry on the close rolls dated 13 December 1295 reveals that William Fitz Waryn had left the king's service in Gascony and returned to England without the permission of the captain of the king's men in those parts.[102] It is unlikely that such actions were commonplace; and it is only when large numbers of aristocratic warriors deserted simultaneously, as they did during the Scottish campaign of 1306, that any particular motives or groupings can be discerned among the men involved.[103] To deal with such offences, captains were given powers to punish and discipline men who disobeyed their orders, or who rebelled against their authority.[104] This enabled them to deal with such malefactors without having to resort to the king's courts. On 10 December 1297 the earl Warenne, as keeper in Scotland, was given authority to arrest, imprison and punish the men under his command if he deemed it necessary for the better pursuance of the king's business and the defence of the realm.[105] Six years later, both John Botetourt and John de Segrave, captains on the western and eastern Marches of Scotland respectively, were given full powers to arrest anyone who disobeyed their orders.[106] Although such powers may have been conferred with the eternal problem of desertion among footsoldiers in mind, it seems likely that they were also used, whenever necessary, to deal with socially elevated offenders.

The prerogatives to punish and distrain were sorely needed if the king's captains were to emerge victorious from their struggles against disobedience and apathy. Such powers, moreover, enabled them to exercise control over the castles

---

[101] *Rotuli Scotiae*, i, pp. 524–5.

[102] *CCR, 1288–96*, p. 502.

[103] J.S. Hamilton, 'Desertion from the Army of Edward I, 1306–7', a paper presented at the Leeds International Medieval Congress, July 2006.

[104] They might also be called on by civilian authorities to prevent escalations in crime and disorder within areas affected by war. See, for example, *Calendar of Ancient Correspondence Concerning Wales*, ed. J.G. Edwards (Cardiff, 1935), p. 40.

[105] *Parl. Writs*, i, p. 307.

[106] *Ibid.*, i, p. 368.

and garrisons within their spheres of influence. Indeed, the management of fortifications within conquered territories was one of the Edwardian war captain's principal duties. In 1300 the king gave to John de St John full powers to garrison and victual all castles that were surrendered to him or that he had taken by force, except for fortresses that the king had already granted to his other magnates as reward for their services.[107] Captains such as St John appear to have enjoyed some independence in the methods that they used to obtain strongholds from the enemy. During the second Welsh war William de Valence and Roger Lestrange promised the sum of 80 pounds to the Welsh garrison at Bere if they would surrender the castle there.[108] Once they had acquired a fortification, the king's commanders were expected to hold on to it, occupying it as they saw fit, unless another member of the landholding elite had a prior claim on the castle. In June 1282 Edward ordered the earl of Gloucester, his captain in south Wales, to give seisin of the castle of Llandovery to John Giffard of Brimpsfield.[109] Giffard had occupied that fort during the war of 1277 and had since laid claim to it through his wife; but his designs in that part of Wales had been thwarted due to a legal dispute with a native lord, Rhys Fychan.[110] The conquest of Gwynedd enabled Giffard, and many more men like him, to take a more secure hold on disputed possessions. Castle supervision in the northern counties of England took on added significance in the years following the English defeat at Bannockburn. John de Crumwell and the earl of Angus, wardens of the March of Northumberland in 1319, were obliged, according to the terms of their contracts with the Crown, to defend Newcastle upon Tyne and to supervise and supply the garrisons in the county. Any shortcomings in the defence of the region were their responsibility; and many of the fine details, such as the number of men to be stationed in the garrisons, were left to the wardens' discretion.[111]

More mundane than castle supervision, but just as significant, were the many policing duties that captains had to perform. One of these was the reception of enemy soldiers into the king's peace. In 1306 Aymer de Valence, as captain in Scotland, was empowered to absolve the lesser men (*mediocres homines*) of that country who wished to surrender to him.[112] This offer was later extended to all of the king's former enemies, except for those who had participated in, or assented to, the murder of John Comyn.[113] Other duties involved the captains in organisational tasks. During the second Welsh war, for example, the king ordered all soldiers on the central Marches and in the south to perform their service under the regional commanders rather than with his own army in the north.[114] Consequently, captains like William de Valence were called on to testify

---

[107] *CCR, 1296–1302*, p. 334.
[108] *Littere Wallie*, ed. J.G. Edwards (Cardiff, 1940), no. 325.
[109] *CVCR*, p. 222.
[110] Morris, *Welsh Wars*, pp. 117, 125, 147.
[111] E 101/15/26. For the powers enjoyed by these officers, see M.L. Boyle, 'Early History of the Wardens of the Marches of England towards Scotland, 1296–1377', MA thesis, University of Hull, 1980, pp. 103–4.
[112] E 101/331/17.
[113] E 39/95/10.
[114] *CVCR*, p. 254.

to the performance of feudal service throughout the course of that campaign.[115] William's son, Aymer, performed a similar function during his spell as captain in southern Scotland twenty years later.[116] Captains were also responsible, wholly or in part, for a wide range of administrative duties, such as the payment of wages (or declaring when such payment should begin);[117] the receipt of attorneys for their men;[118] the provision of horse compensation in the event of losses suffered by their men-at-arms;[119] and the distribution to other prominent men in their hosts of orders issued by the king.[120] In addition to such responsibilities captains might be required to oversee the building of bridges;[121] to send for warhorses from abroad;[122] or to raise revenues from vacant sees within occupied territories.[123] Each of these duties added to the overall power wielded by the captains, but the many obligations that were incumbent on them may indicate why military leadership was not to everyone's taste.

The king's commanders within the British Isles possessed extensive powers. Compared to their counterparts in Gascony, however, the scope of their authority was somewhat limited. Despite spending many years at war in Wales and Scotland, Edward I would have preferred to have committed more of his time to the pursuit of his ambitions on the continent. His attempts to concentrate on his interests in France were held back by rebellions closer to home. This perhaps explains why he was willing to give free rein to the seneschals, captains and lieutenants who represented him in Gascony. Two such officials, John de St John and Jean de Bretagne, were empowered in 1294 to make agreements of friendship with the king of Castile and with powerful local lords such as the count of Foix.[124] Writs of commission of the following year, appointing the earls of Lancaster and Lincoln, separately, as lieutenants in Aquitaine, demonstrate even more clearly the extraordinary independence of action enjoyed by the king's representatives in southwestern France. Not only was each earl, in turn, given full powers to make agreements with kings and princes whomsoever they may be (*amicicias et confederaciones cum quibuscumque regibus vel principibus*), but they were also granted special authority to appoint lieutenants, captains, seneschals, sub-seneschals, castellans, mayors and other ministers as they saw fit throughout the duchy.[125] In effect, the king's captains and seneschals in Gascony were empowered to act almost as petty kings. This freedom of action gave men like John de St John and the earl of Richmond much of the experience that they were later able to draw on as leaders in the war against the Scots.

The king's willingness to alienate so much of his power to his representatives

---

[115] See, for example, *Ancient Correspondence Concerning Wales*, pp. 46, 132–3.
[116] SC 1/31, no. 33.
[117] E 159/71, m. 106d.
[118] *CCR, 1272–79*, p. 358.
[119] *Littere Wallie*, nos 329, 332.
[120] *Foedera*, I, ii, p. 889.
[121] *Littere Wallie*, no. 323.
[122] *CPR, 1272–81*, p. 194.
[123] *Foedera*, I, ii, p. 877.
[124] *Rôles Gascons*, iii, p. 172.
[125] *Ibid.*, iii, p. 300.

in Gascony throws into sharp relief the more restrictive nature of his relations with his commanders in northern England, Scotland and Wales. In these theatres of war Edward attempted to retain in his own hands as much of the responsibility for the conduct of the campaigns as possible. Indeed, commanders in the field were expected to correspond with the king on a regular basis about a wide range of subjects. Payn de Chaworth and the earl of Warwick, captains in Wales, wrote to Edward in the spring of 1277 informing him that their men had come to the end of their periods of service.[126] Both commanders were aware of the need to keep these soldiers in the field, but they appear to have been powerless to act without first obtaining Edward's consent. Captains were also expected to inform the king whenever a castle came into their possession, supplying details of its location and features as well as of how they had maintained the fortress. Prince Edward, leader of the army in western Scotland, wrote to his father in 1301 with news of the condition of Turnberry castle and details of how it was being guarded and provisioned.[127] Generally, the king wished to be notified of all movements in the field, regardless of how far removed he might be from the theatre of war in which they were taking place. In the summer of 1297, when Edward was busily making preparations for his expedition to Flanders, the earl Warenne and Henry de Percy maintained regular contact with the king about their activities in the north. Percy ended one letter, dated 27 July, by assuring Edward that as soon as their circumstances changed they would let him know 'with all the haste possible'.[128]

Correspondence of this kind flowed in both directions. On some occasions, the news that Edward sent to his captains could prove vital for their safety and the security of the lands under their control. A good example of this dates from the spring of 1300, when the king warned John de St John that the Scots were planning to surround him as soon as he had crossed the border into enemy territory.[129] Edward had been updated, by John de Clavering, about the Scots' movements in southwestern Scotland, and his position as commander of all armed forces enabled him to relay news from one war zone to another with relative ease. In the following year, Edward wrote to Alexander de Balliol (we know this because of Balliol's response to the king, written on 21 September 1301), reporting that John de Soules was active in the passes of Galloway with a large company of Scots. Balliol was ordered to inform the wardens of the March immediately and to employ spies to keep abreast of the enemy's activities.[130] How effective Edward was in trying to manage the war effort in this way cannot be determined with any certainty. Yet it is likely that his subordinates welcomed any information that he was able to offer about the activities of the Welsh and

---

126 *Ancient Correspondence Concerning Wales*, pp. 67, 71–2.
127 SC 1/16, no. 148.
128 *Stevenson*, ii, pp. 183–4, 215–16.
129 *CCR, 1296–1302*, pp. 334–5.
130 SC 1/15, no. 2.

the Scots, just as the king sought his magnates' assistance when, following his long absences overseas, they briefed him about recent events at the front.[131]

Although Edward sometimes wrote to his captains and other military leaders warning them of enemy movements or requesting their counsel, it seems that his main concern was to ensure that his captains were acting in accordance with his wishes. Early in 1298 he ordered his captain and keeper in Scotland, the earl Warenne, not to wait until the arrival of levies of footmen coming from Wales but to proceed towards the Scottish March immediately.[132] Edward was in Flanders at the time of writing. His interference in the earl's decisions suggests, therefore, that he did not have complete confidence in the wisdom of his subordinate. This was possibly a consequence of Warenne's failings in the previous year at Stirling Bridge; but it seems likely that Edward was generally inclined to meddle in the affairs of his captains. For example, in the autumn of 1302 the king ordered John de Segrave and the cofferer Ralph de Manton to ride by Stirling and Kirkintilloch, keeping in close contact with the enemy without straying too far from English-held lands, before dispatching a special messenger to report on how they had fared.[133] Segrave, an experienced soldier, probably found the king's close supervision of his activities unnecessary and infuriating. Early in 1307 the lines of communication broke down completely as the king's captains in Scotland neglected to inform him of the problems that they were experiencing in the field. Edward concluded that things must have gone so badly that they did not wish him to know, but it is possible that Aymer de Valence and Henry de Percy were venting their frustration at the king's persistent demands for information.[134]

War captains had to maintain regular contact not only with the Crown but also with other officials who had been appointed by the government. In the autumn of 1298, for example, the earl of March was chosen as captain of the king's men-at-arms in the garrisons of southern Scotland. This created a series of overlapping areas of jurisdiction as the earl's powers threatened to clash with the authority exercised by the garrison constables. To resolve this situation it was set out in the terms of the earl's commission that should it be necessary for them to assemble, the earl would be captain of all and each constable would be captain of his own men.[135] Captains and wardens also had to forge relationships with the bureaucrats sent to assist them in organising and supplying their armies. Most of these administrators were, or had been, barons of the exchequer. Edward was aware that tensions might arise between his military captains and the clerks sent to assist them. To deal with this, in the spring of 1300 he explained to John de St John why he had employed the clerk Richard de Abingdon to work alongside him, making it clear that Abingdon was there to assist him, not to

---

[131] See, for example, the arrangements that Edward I made on returning to England from Flanders in 1298: *CCR, 1296–1302*, p. 201.
[132] *Foedera*, I, ii, pp. 884–5.
[133] *Stevenson*, ii, p. 448.
[134] *CDS*, ii, no. 1895.
[135] *CPR, 1292–1301*, p. 372.

interfere in his decisions.[136] In the following year St John complained to Ralph de Manton that payments had fallen into arrears and that the poor people in his area of jurisdiction were suffering for want of victuals;[137] but for the most part the system of employing the king's administrators to assist military officials in their duties appears to have worked tolerably well.

Given the numerous duties that military leaders in this age were expected to perform, and the potentially grave consequences should they fail to carry them out successfully, the onus was on the king to provide sufficient rewards to his captains for their services. K.B. McFarlane believed that under Edward I 'life-long and devoted service was too often inadequately rewarded'.[138] However, the situation was a little more complex than that. It is true that the king did not create any new earldoms, but he did try to reward his captains in other ways. Following the campaign of 1282–3, Edward divided the central Welsh lands among the leading men of the realm while keeping the coastal castles for himself.[139] So extensive were his grants that 'the Edwardian endowments ... transformed the March in terms both of its political geography and of the personnel of its lords'.[140] The earls of Gloucester and Hereford, as well as William de Valence, may have felt poorly rewarded; but a number of lords and captains – including the Mortimers, Reginald de Grey, and the earls of Lincoln and Warenne – had much reason to be pleased with the lands granted to them.[141] Edward adopted a similar policy during the Scottish wars. Following the victory at Falkirk in 1298, the king announced that his earls and barons were to be rewarded with property in the conquered territories.[142] The shifting political situation north of the border meant that he was not always able to fulfil his promises. Neverthe-less, lords who were frustrated in their attempts to occupy the lands conferred on them in Scotland were sometimes compensated with grants or wardships in England.[143] The final windfall of the reign came following Bruce's rebellion in 1306. His titles and estates were distributed among some of Edward's most faithful servants, including Robert de Clifford and Henry de Percy;[144] but such opportunities for largesse were few and far between at a time when the Crown's financial reserves were being stretched to their limit. Bearing these problems in mind, it seems that the scarcity of rewards noted by McFarlane was probably, for the most part, a consequence of necessity rather than of choice.

So far we have examined the powers and responsibilities incumbent on military captains and commanders-in-chief, but these were not the only men who exer-

---

136 *CCR, 1296–1302*, p. 334; *CDS*, ii, no. 1133.

137 *CDS*, ii, no. 1218.

138 K.B. McFarlane, *The Nobility of Later Medieval England* (Oxford, 1973), pp. 266–7.

139 *Polychronicon Ranulphi Higden Monachi Cestrensis*, ed. C. Babington and J.R. Lumby, 9 vols, Rolls Ser., xli (London, 1865–86), viii, p. 264.

140 R.R. Davies, *Lordship and Society in the March of Wales, 1282–1400* (Oxford, 1978), p. 37.

141 See Prestwich, *Edward I*, p. 204.

142 *Guisborough*, pp. 328–9.

143 M. Prestwich, 'Colonial Scotland: The English in Scotland under Edward I', *Scotland and England 1286–1815*, ed. R.A. Mason (Edinburgh, 1987), p. 10.

144 *Guisborough*, pp. 369–70.

cised military authority within Edwardian England. The most important officers responsible for the organisation and discipline of the Crown's armies were the marshal and constable. Richard II's ordinances for the Scottish expedition of 1385 reveal that, by the late fourteenth century, these individuals possessed extensive powers over all soldiers within the army. All men who broke ranks, robbed, caused disturbances within the host, or committed any other offences while in battle array, were referred to the marshal and constable for punishment. These officials were also responsible for the guarding of prisoners and the distribution of ransoms, as well as for all matters relating to discipline and order.[145] A plea roll for Edward I's host in Scotland in 1296 shows that they had discharged similar duties in the armies of Edward I. All manner of transgressions, ranging from neglect of watch and ward through to trespass and robbery, were dealt with and recorded on the deputy marshal's roll.[146] In addition to such judicial responsibilities, the marshal and constable fulfilled an organisational function in the build-up to royal campaigns. Writing in the 1380s, the French military theorist Honoré Bonet noted how medieval armies were divided into 'battles', 'which each marshal of the host makes large or small at pleasure'.[147] Although it is difficult to be sure how much influence the marshal and constable possessed over tactical dispositions within the armies of Edward I and Edward II, it seems likely that they were the king's main supporters (along with the captains) in ensuring that operations ran smoothly.

Under Edward I the constable, the earl of Hereford, and the marshal, the earl of Norfolk, each held their positions by hereditary privilege. Yet these were not merely honorific titles devoid of any significance in the field. On the contrary, it was necessary for practical purposes that these officials, or associates representing them, were with the armies. When the earl of Hereford could not be present at the start of a campaign during the Welsh wars he appointed his uncle, John de Bohun, to take his place until his arrival.[148] In like manner, the king sent a letter to the earl of Norfolk in 1301 requesting that if, due to bodily weakness, he was unable to serve in person, he should appoint another good and sufficient man to take his place as marshal of the host.[149] Not only was it essential to have a marshal and constable with the main army led by the king, but it was sometimes deemed advantageous to assign men to these positions within the regional armies under noble captains. During the Welsh uprising of 1294–5, the king sent the earl of Norfolk to south Wales to serve in the host under William de Valence. To fill the gap in his own army, Edward appointed the banneret Roger de Molis as temporary marshal in the north.[150] Similarly, when the earl of Hereford was assigned to the Prince of Wales' army in the west of Scotland in 1301, the king demanded that the earl send somebody else to act as constable with the main

---

[145] *Monumenta Juridica*, pp. 453–8; Keen, 'Richard II's Ordinances of War', pp. 40–2.
[146] 'A Plea Roll of Edward I's Army in Scotland, 1296', ed. C.J. Neville, *Miscellany XI*, Scottish History Society, 5th ser., iii (1990), pp. 7–133.
[147] *The Tree of Battles of Honoré Bonet*, ed. G.W. Coopland (Liverpool, 1949), p. 130.
[148] SC 1/22, no. 117.
[149] *Foedera*, I, ii, p. 927.
[150] *CPR, 1292–1301*, p. 126.

force setting out from Berwick upon Tweed.[151] The capabilities of the men who succeeded the earls of Hereford and Norfolk following their deaths, or who took their places in their absence, further attest to the value attached to the marshalcy and constableship. Following the demise of the earl of Norfolk in 1306 the rank of marshal was bestowed upon Robert de Clifford, who was one of the king's ablest soldiers.[152] Humphrey de Bohun's refusal to perform his duties on the Scottish campaign of 1310–11 meant that Bartholomew de Badlesmere was called upon to act as his lieutenant.[153] By then Badlesmere had seen extensive service in the kings' armies over the previous sixteen years.[154]

Besides captains, constables and marshals, 'battle commanders' held the most elevated rank within Edwardian armies. Although the men who occupied these positions enjoyed disciplinary rights over the men-at-arms under their control, their most important function was as leaders of tactical units in combat. Contemporary battle narratives often place these sub-commanders in the forefront of the action. Walter of Guisborough's version of the battle of Falkirk shows that they were responsible for the movements of the massed ranks of men-at-arms under their authority.[155] The English defeat at Bannockburn may have been due, in part, to the ineffective functioning of these divisions at the start of the battle. The chronicler Thomas Gray noted (possibly on the testimony of his father, who had served in Edward II's army in 1314) that the English had been unable to fight effectively because the main divisions of the army had been jammed together.[156] There is no evidence for the activities of battle commanders during Edward I's Welsh wars, but we do possess the names of the soldiers who led the English battles during the war against the Scots. Experience in this role, as in the main positions of command, was essential, for three of the battle commanders at Falkirk – the earl of Lincoln, earl Warenne and the king himself – were also employed in the same capacity two years later at Caerlaverock.[157] The only alteration came when the young Prince Edward replaced the bishop of Durham.[158] Edward was expected to earn his spurs as a sub-commander within his father's army before going on to lead his own forces on later campaigns. The author of the heraldic *Song of Caerlaverock* noted how six barons were placed

---

[151] *CCR, 1296–1302*, p. 487.

[152] Clifford could draw on a wealth of experience from his time as leader on the Marches. He had served there, for example, during the winter of 1298–9: *Parl. Writs*, i, p. 318; E 101/7/19, m. 2.

[153] See *Parl. Writs*, II, ii, p. 401.

[154] Badlesmere had served in Gascony in 1294 (*Rôles Gascons*, iii, p. 97), Flanders (C 67/12, m. 1), and Scotland in 1298 (*Scotland in 1298*, p. 190), 1300 (*Rolls of Arms, Edward I*, i, p. 443), 1301 (E 101/9/23, m. 2), 1303–4 (BL, Additional MS 8835, fol. 59v), 1306 (E 101/612/15, m. 1), 1307 (*CDS*, v, p. 445) and 1308 (*CDS*, v, p. 447).

[155] *Guisborough*, pp. 327–8.

[156] *Scalacronica*, p. 75.

[157] *Rolls of Arms, Edward I*, i, pp. 406–17, 434–43.

[158] The bishop's leadership at Falkirk had been opposed by at least one of the knights under his command: *Guisborough*, p. 327.

alongside the prince as his 'conductors and guardians', with John de St John and William le Latimer being set aside 'to array his squadron'.[159]

Below this there were a number of other officers within Edwardian armies, such as millenars, centenars and vintenars. The men who occupied such positions tended, however, to be drawn from lower down the social scale than the leading members of the aristocracy discussed above.[160] To be a captain required a combination of wealth, status and ability, as well as a capacity to exercise leadership over large numbers of independently minded men. Despite possessing a wide range of military and judicial powers, these commanders were agents of the Crown who were expected to conform to the terms of service by which they had been employed. To ensure that they were performing their duties, the Crown kept a careful watch over all of their activities. Nevertheless, some captains, such as the king's lieutenants in Gascony, benefited from considerable freedom of action. Although the rewards for leading the king's armies and garrisons could at times be considerable, the responsibilities of high command probably outweighed any perquisites that might have been on offer. Only the king's most dedicated soldiers and trusted confidants, like John de St John, Robert de Clifford and Aymer de Valence, were charged with such commissions. If a military elite existed within England at this time, then it was surely personified by these men.

Retinue Leaders

The tenor of the discussion so far suggests that military leadership in Edwardian armies issued outwards from the centre. Appointments to captaincies, custodianships and other positions of high command were the prerogative of the king and his council. The pool of men employed in this way was not very large. As such, an important distinction has to be made between, on the one hand, the command exercised by men chosen to lead armies, hold castles and defend border areas, and on the other, the very different kind of authority enjoyed by soldiers who led companies to war as part of royal or baronial hosts. The former were government agents whose influence rested on the political power conferred on them by the Crown, whereas the latter derived their pre-eminence solely from the social prestige arising from the lands that they held at a local and regional level. Many of these company commanders served at their own expense and equipped their men from their own resources. Indeed, each retinue leader was master of his own *comitiva*, in much the same way as the king was lord of the whole. Consequently, although Edward I was a strong centralising monarch, his ability to enforce his will through armed struggle would have been seriously curtailed had it not been for the cooperation of the leading representatives of local and regional society.

---

[159] *The Roll of Arms of the Princes, Barons, and Knights who attended King Edward I to the Siege of Caerlaverock, in 1300*, ed. T. Wright (London, 1864), pp. 19–20.
[160] Men of knightly rank did sometimes perform such roles, as in 1296: E 101/5/23, m. 1ii.

The companies that combined to form royal armies during these years existed independently of Crown control. One symptom of this self-sufficiency was the tendency of the leading men of the realm to resort to private warfare. This remained a threat to internal peace and stability throughout the late thirteenth and early fourteenth centuries, as demonstrated by the actions, in 1273, of Hugh de Turberville and Reginald Fitz Peter, who together wasted the earl of Hereford's lands in Wales.[161] Recurring violence was also a major problem among the gentry of south Lancashire in the months and years leading up to the battle of Boroughbridge (1322).[162] Despite the legal distinction that was made between criminal and legitimate acts of violence,[163] public and private warfare had many features in common.[164] The banner was raised in feuds just as it was in royal hosts. Moreover, when a lord's men pillaged the lands of his neighbour, he took a share of the booty as was his right under the king.[165] Essentially, the war *comitiva* served much the same function in royal armies as it did in private disputes, resembling a miniature army dependent on its lord. Just as prominent landholders employed receivers and attorneys to manage their financial and judicial affairs in peacetime, so they needed men with military and administrative expertise to assist them when summoned to arms by the king. We have seen how the marshal of England performed a key judicial and organisational role throughout the wars of Edward I. Perhaps in imitation of this, the earls and leading magnates had their own marshals with them on campaign. Gilbert de Lyndeseye served as marshal for the earl of Hereford in Scotland in 1296, finding lodgings for his lord's men at the end of each day.[166] John de Morley performed a similar function for Robert de Tateshale on the same expedition.[167] Some retinue leaders even took their own secretariats with them to war. Edward II's favourite, Piers Gaveston, had at least five clerks in his company as earl of Cornwall during the Scottish campaign of 1310–11.[168] Men like Gaveston probably had little time, when on campaign, to carry out all the administrative tasks that were required of them, so clerks such as these had a crucial role to perform.

Taken as a whole, the hundreds of soldiers who served as retinue leaders during the reigns of Edward I and Edward II constituted a most diverse group of men. The sheer weight of numbers gives some idea as to the variety of their backgrounds and connections. To possess command over other men-at-arms, even at the very lowest level, required some degree of influence within the royal household or in the localities; but ability, wealth and military experience varied considerably from one individual to the next. Some soldiers served in the retinues of other men for several campaigns prior to becoming company

---

161 *CCR, 1272–79*, p. 56.
162 *South Lancashire in the Reign of Edward II*, ed. G.H. Tupling, Chetham Society 3rd ser., i (1949), *passim*.
163 See, for example, Kaeuper, *War, Justice and Public Order*, p. 264.
164 This point has been made by Helen Nicholson, among others: *Medieval Warfare: Theory and Practice of War in Europe 300–1500* (Basingstoke, 2004), p. 1.
165 For evidence of these practices, see *CVCR*, pp. 337–8.
166 'Plea Roll, 1296', no. 160.
167 *Ibid.*, no. 168.
168 C 71/4, mm. 8, 10.

leaders in their own right. Henry de Appelby accompanied Robert de Tateshale in the war against Madog ap Llywelyn in 1294, on the opening campaign of the Scottish war and to the siege of Caerlaverock in 1300,[169] before establishing himself as a valued member of the Prince of Wales' household.[170] He served the prince as a retinue leader in 1306 and 1307 and continued to act in that capacity once Edward had become king.[171] Appelby was not alone in finding himself elevated into the royal household following a spell of service among the rank and file. John de Usflete joined the retinue of John de Eyville for the second Welsh war.[172] Later, during the Welsh rebellion of 1294–5, he served under Peter de Champayne.[173] His first experience as a retinue leader came on the Scottish expedition of 1296; and in the years that followed he led companies of men-at-arms on the Flanders, Falkirk and Caerlaverock campaigns.[174] Usflete appears to have ended his career as a company leader in 1301.[175] There was no more prestigious aristocratic household in which to obtain military experience than that of the much-praised Robert de Clifford. John de Crumwell fought under Clifford's banner at Falkirk in 1298 as well as on other occasions.[176] No doubt benefiting from that experience, three years later he began a long period of service as a household retinue leader in his own right.[177]

Although the normal pattern of progression was for soldiers to move up through the ranks before establishing themselves at the head of a group of soldiers, some lords led troops of men to war from the beginning of their military careers. Lineage could qualify certain individuals for military leadership even when experience in the field was lacking. Bartholomew de Badlesmere began his military career at the head of a small troop of men-at-arms in Gascony in 1294.[178] He later served independently at Falkirk and Caerlaverock before being absorbed into the affinities of firstly Robert de Clifford and secondly the earl of Gloucester.[179] His father, Guncelin, had fought during the Welsh wars, having at one point held the position of Justiciar of Chester,[180] and it is likely that Bartholomew was encouraged from an early age to follow his example. Likewise, Payn de Tibetot probably owed his place at court to the reputation of his father Robert, who had been one of Edward I's captains during the Welsh

---

[169] 1294–5 (C 67/10, m. 7), 1296 (C 67/11, m. 5) and 1300 (C 67/14, m. 10).
[170] BL, Additional MS 8835, fol. 58r; *Documents and Records of Scotland*, p. 271.
[171] 1306 (E 101/13/7, m. 2), 1307 (E 101/14/15, m. 9; *CDS*, v, p. 445) and 1310–11 (BL, Cotton Nero C VIII, fol. 4r).
[172] C 47/2/7, m. 8.
[173] C 67/10, m. 2.
[174] 1296 (E 101/5/23, m. 1ii); 1297 (E 101/6/37, m. 6i); 1298 (*Scotland in 1298*, p. 176); 1300 (*Liber Quotidianus*, p. 234).
[175] E 101/9/24, m. 2.
[176] See above, p. 29, n. 146.
[177] E 101/9/23, m. 1.
[178] See above, p. 54, n. 154.
[179] For his service up to and including 1308, see above, p. 54, n. 154. Having served under the earl of Gloucester in 1307 and 1308, Badlesmere joined the retinue of the same lord in 1310 (C 71/4, m. 13) and 1314 (C 71/6, m. 5; C 81/1727, m. 18). He served as the earl's sub-leader on the Bannockburn campaign.
[180] Morris, *Welsh Wars*, pp. 119, 130, 144, 174.

wars. Prior to serving as one of Edward of Caernarfon's sub-leaders in Scotland in 1303, Payn had only been giving military service for two or three years.[181]

Earls and bannerets stood at the top of the military hierarchy. These men invariably led the largest retinues; and it was not uncommon for a man of the status and wealth of the earl of Gloucester or the earl of Pembroke to lead in excess of 100 men-at-arms to war. Still, at the opposite end of the spectrum, even the lowliest sergeants might occasionally go to war with small troops of one or two men-at-arms under their command. In one of the many petitions that were sent to the Crown from the northern counties during the Scottish wars, a certain John de Bilton, valet-at-arms, petitioned Edward II for the arrears of 153 pounds that he was owed for service in war. He claimed to have served north of the border with three men-at-arms, adding further, for good measure, that two of his brothers had died at the hands of the king's enemies.[182] Bilton and many other lesser men from the northern counties no doubt felt aggrieved at the Crown's lack of urgency in meeting their costs and expenses despite the sacrifices that they and their families were making, and the hardship they were suffering daily. Small companies such as Bilton's can often be detected in the pay-rolls and horse inventories of this period; but troops consisting of two or three men-at-arms were usually led by knights bachelor rather than by men of inferior status.

Not only do the horse inventories highlight the diverse leadership of the military retinues that were led to war during the reigns of Edward I and his son, but they also provide an opportunity to compare the status and wealth of the retinue leaders with those of their men. As Andrew Ayton has noted, 'by associating named individuals with warhorses of specified quality, they [the horse inventories] offer a unique insight into the character and attitudes of the military aristocracy in fourteenth-century England'.[183] Ayton has also observed, drawing again on the evidence of the horse inventories, that the horse of each retinue leader 'would generally be more valuable than those of his retainers and often of higher quality than those employed by others of comparable military rank'.[184] If this were true for the reign of Edward III, it was also true for the reigns of that king's father and grandfather. Table 2.1 compares the horse-valuation data for retinue leaders in the armies of Edward I and Edward II with the same kind of information for their men. It also distinguishes between, on the one hand, the values of the horses belonging to knights within the retinues and, on the other, those of the mounts possessed by men of lesser status.

---

181 For his service in 1303, see E 101/612/11, m. 2d. Payn appears first to have served on the expedition of 1300: C 67/14, m. 11.
182 *Ancient Petitions Relating to Northumberland*, ed. C.M. Fraser, Surtees Society, clxxvi (1966), no. 143.
183 Ayton, *Knights and Warhorses*, p. 138.
184 *Ibid.*, p. 229.

**Table 2.1: Mean warhorse values (£) for retinue leaders
and their men (1282–1314)**[185]

Year	Retinue leaders	Knightly followers	All followers
1282	17.5 (67 men)	12.3 (70 men)	7.3 (476 men)
1296	16.9 (47)	14.3 (16)	8.3 (190)
1297–8	23.6 (89)	21.4 (64)	10.5 (690)
1298	20.8 (131)	18.6 (130)	9.7 (941)
1300	26.5 (67)	19.8 (51)	11.6 (385)
1301	24.1 (96)	21.1 (64)	10.7 (553)
1303–4	24.9 (107)	19.9 (57)	10.2 (634)
1306	24.2 (53)	19.7 (37)	10.1 (245)
1307	17.2 (36)	15.3 (17)	7.8 (154)
1311–14	19.3 (10)	8.6 (7)	6.8 (184)

It was normal during the reigns of Edward I and Edward II for company leaders to possess chargers worth around 10 pounds more than that of an average follower. In some years, such as 1297, 1300 and 1301, the difference was even greater. Most of the men who led retinues to war in the late thirteenth and early fourteenth centuries were knights; and there was a great gulf, for the most part, separating such men from the lowliest sergeants in their companies. In 1296 Hugh le Despenser served in Scotland with a horse valued at 70 marks. However, thirteen of the twenty-four men in his company, twenty-one of whom were *valletti*, had mounts worth less than 10 pounds.[186] In most years over 75 per cent of men-at-arms in an Edwardian army were of sub-knightly status,[187] so comparison of the mounts of retinue leaders with those of the average man-at-arms in their companies will always reveal a marked divergence in values. Nevertheless, lords also tended to serve with horses of higher quality than those of the knights who were with them. In 1282, during the second Welsh war, William le Latimer served on a mount valued at 50 marks; but the other six knights in his *comitiva* campaigned on horses worth 35 marks or less.[188] Over two decades later, in 1306, Robert de Clifford's steed was appraised at 30 marks more than the most valuable mount among his knightly companions.[189]

The horse inventories enable us to quantify the varying status and wealth of the men in the retinues in a way that is not possible with any other source. Yet,

---

185 Sources: Wales in 1282 (C 47/2/7); Scotland in 1296 (E 101/5/23); Flanders in 1297–8 (E 101/6/19, 28, 37); and Scotland in 1298 (*Scotland in 1298*, pp. 160–237); 1300 (E 101/8/23); 1301 (E 101/9/23, 4); 1303–4 (E 101/612/7, 8, 9, 11); 1306 (E 101/13/7; E 101/612/15, 19); 1307 (E 101/612/20, 21; E 101/14/15 m. 9); 1311–14 (E 101/14/15, mm. 1–5). Besides knights and *valletti*, the section headed 'all followers' includes clerks, 'masters' and men to whom no status is ascribed in the sources. However, it does not include men-at-arms serving independently. Many archers had horses appraised in 1313–14, which may explain the low valuations in that year. Not all men-at-arms had appraised horses, hence the slight difference between some of these figures and those presented below in table 2.2.

186 E 101/5/23, m. 1i.

187 Ayton, *Knights and Warhorses*, p. 5.

188 C 47/2/7, mm. 4, 6.

189 E 101/612/15, mm. 1, 2.

the value of a man's mount was probably less important as an indicator of his status in the eyes of his contemporaries than the number of men whom he was able to lead to war. K.B. McFarlane has pointed out that 'a man's worship, his standing among his fellow noblemen, and his influence in his own county, were measured by the number and consequence of those who were enrolled in his *meinie*'.[190] This is superbly demonstrated by the contents of a petition sent to the king by Walter de Huntercombe, a leading banneret, during the first decade of the fourteenth century. Since the beginning of the Scottish war, Huntercombe proudly claimed, he had served at the siege of Berwick (in 1296) with twenty mailed horse, at Stirling Bridge (1297) with thirty-two horse and at Falkirk (1298) with a troop of thirty men-at-arms, as well as in Galloway two years later.[191] It was the ability to lead such large troops of men-at-arms to war that placed certain individuals in the forefront of the military community. Yet few retinue leaders were able to command followings as powerful as those of Walter de Huntercombe. This is demonstrated by the evidence of the horse inventories drawn up between the second Welsh war and the battle of Bannockburn, which indicate that companies of much smaller size were common.

Table 2.2: Average retinue sizes based on the horse inventories (1282–1314)[192]

Year	Leaders	Knight followers	Average per leader	Other followers	Average per leader	Total followers	Average per leader
1282	87	71	0.8	409	4.7	480	5.5
1296	51	16	0.3	176	3.5	192	3.8
1297–8	114	64	0.6	648	5.7	712	6.2
1298	151	136	0.9	835	5.5	969	6.4
1300	90	51	0.6	336	3.7	387	4.3
1301	113	64	0.6	495	4.4	559	4.9
1303–4	143	58	0.4	594	4.2	652	4.6
1306	60	37	0.6	210	3.5	247	4.1
1307	61	18	0.3	141	2.3	159	2.6
1311–14	12	7	0.6	224	18.7	231	19.3
Total	882	522	0.6	4068	4.6	4588	5.2

The average aristocratic contingent as revealed on the horse inventories consisted of only five men-at-arms, the majority if not all of whom were soldiers of sub-knightly status. (In this respect the figures for the retinues on the Scottish March during the years 1311–14 should be regarded as an anomaly, caused by the exceptional circumstances of the war on the border and the small number of retinues contained within that sample). It is striking, particularly considering

[190] McFarlane, *The Nobility of Later Medieval England*, p. 106.
[191] *Parl. Roll.*, ii, p. 475. In 1282–3 he served at wages with two knights and seven sergeants (C 47/2/7, m. 7). On the horse list of 1300 he had twenty-one men-at-arms: E 101/8/23, m. 7.
[192] The information in this table has been compiled from the same sources used in table 2.1.

that the vast majority of the company commanders recorded in table 2.2 were knights, that most of these units did not contain a single follower who had been girded with the belt of knighthood. Although these figures do not encompass the companies led to war by the earls and leading barons who did not accept Crown pay, or the unpaid parts of other retinues, they do highlight the significant contribution made by a large number of small companies. Retinues like those of Thomas Paynel and John Fitz Simon, who were followed to war by just a few *valletti* in 1297 and 1300 respectively,[193] were a common phenomenon, and for every man who led a large company of more than a dozen men-at-arms there were likely to be several with less impressive followings. Of some ninety retinues and sub-companies on the horse inventory for the second Welsh war (1282–3), around fifty appear to have contained fewer than five mounted soldiers. Only one unit (the one under William le Latimer) comprised more than twenty men-at-arms.[194] Furthermore, analysis of the horse inventories compiled for the army that campaigned in Scotland in 1303 shows that on that occasion just three companies – those of Robert de Clifford, John de Drokensford and John de Benstede[195] – were staffed by more than a score of mounted combatants, whereas about ninety consisted of four men-at-arms or fewer.

Many of the most prominent magnates, and the men in their companies, are not named on the horse inventories, either because they did not receive Crown pay or because the said inventories are incomplete. Urian de St Peter is named on the main pay-roll of 1282 with a company of nine knights and thirty-one sergeants,[196] but the values of the horses in his retinue are not given. As a rule, it is only possible to estimate (from enrolled letters of protection, of attorney or of respite of debts) the size of the companies that were led to war by the earls. Unusually, however, twenty-seven of the earl of Warwick's men had their horses appraised in 1297 before the earl withdrew from the Flanders campaign (his son Guy led his retinue in that year).[197] This was eighteen men fewer than Thomas, earl of Lancaster had in his paid retinue for the Falkirk campaign in the following year.[198]

Fortunately, the royal wardrobe books for 1297, 1300, 1301 and 1303 offer fairly precise figures for the company strengths of knights bachelor and banneret. These sources distinguish, unlike the horse inventories, between the two types of knight. Table 2.3 shows, using the wardrobe books, how the retinues led to

---

193 E 101/6/37, m. 2ii; E 101/8/23, m. 1.

194 C 47/2/7 *passim*; *ibid.*, mm. 4, 6.

195 E 101/612/11, mm. 2, 3, 5. The wardrobe book for 1303–4 shows that payments were made to Drokensford's three knights rather than to the keeper of the wardrobe himself. Two of these knights had been in Drokensford's retinue in 1301: BL, Additional MS 8835, fol. 58r; BL, Additional MS 7966a, fol. 85v.

196 E 101/4/1, m. 13.

197 E 101/6/37, m. 6i. I am grateful to Andrew Spencer for pointing out to me that Guy led his father's retinue to Flanders.

198 *Scotland in 1298*, pp. 179–81. Earls did occasionally accept pay. The earl of Lincoln served at the king's wages with six knights and twenty-three sergeants in 1277 (E 101/3/12), and the earl of Arundel was paid for a company of thirty-nine men-at-arms in 1298 (E 101/6/35, fol. 12r).

war by bannerets differed markedly in size from those led to war by knights bachelor.

Table 2.3: Company strengths of knights bachelor and knights banneret[199]

	1297		1300		1301		1303–4	
	Banneret	Bachelor	Banneret	Bachelor	Banneret	Bachelor	Banneret	Bachelor
Number of leaders	22	49	25	39	31	41	20	28
Knights	55	7	66	6	60	4	35	1
Average	2.5	0.1	2.6	0.2	1.9	0.1	1.8	0.04
Sergeants	230	151	267	108	293	102	182	68
Average	10.5	3.1	10.7	2.8	9.5	2.5	9.1	2.4
Total average	13	3.2	13.3	3.0	11.4	2.6	10.9	2.44

Michael Prestwich has observed, based on information contained in the early thirteenth-century *Histoire* of William Marshal, that each banneret was responsible for an average of around thirteen men-at-arms.[200] The figures presented in table 2.3, though based on evidence that does not lend itself easily to statistical analysis, seem to bear that statement out. Although knights bachelor seldom received pay for other belted soldiers, bannerets could usually count two or three men of knightly status among their followers. Moreover, bannerets tended to lead around ten men more than knights of inferior status. Bachelors, indeed, were generally accompanied on campaign by no more than two or three sergeants.[201] Given the difference between the armed strengths of companies led by knights bachelor and those under bannerets, it seems likely that promotion to the status of banneret brought with it greater expectations and responsibilities. When the English army sailed for Flanders in 1297, John Botetourt had one knight and seven sergeants in his *comitiva*.[202] He was promoted to the status of banneret on 23 August in that year;[203] and for the Scottish campaign of the following summer, he can be found on the household horse inventory with a larger retinue of three knights and thirteen sergeants.[204] This was a reflection,

---

[199] The figures in this table have been compiled from the following wardrobe books: 25 Edward I (BL, Additional MS 7965); 28 Edward I (*Liber Quotidianus*); 29 Edward I (BL, Additional MS 7966a); and 32 Edward I (BL, Additional MS 8835). One or two exceptionally large retinues brought from overseas, such as that of the earl of Ulster in 1301, have been left out of the analysis so as not to distort the figures. Companies frequently changed size and composition, so optimum retinue numbers have been used.

[200] Prestwich, *Armies and Warfare*, p. 14.

[201] These figures conceal considerable variations between the retinues of individual bachelors and bannerets. On the Flanders campaign of 1297–8, for example, Geoffrey de Geneville led a company of four knights and twenty-two sergeants, but another banneret, Simon Fraser, had a contingent of only one knight and two sergeants: BL, Additional MS 7965, fols 64r, 68r.

[202] BL, Additional MS 7965, fol. 64r.

[203] *Ibid.*, fol. 64r.

[204] *Scotland in 1298*, pp. 166–7.

no doubt, of his newly won status. The special position of the knights banneret within Edwardian England is demonstrated by the layout of the Parliamentary roll of arms of *c.* 1312. Following a section devoted to the king, the earls and the bishop of Durham, the armorial lists around 150 bannerets with their arms, recorded in blazon. These are then followed, as we have seen, by the other knights of England divided into the counties in which they held their principal lands.[205] The significance of bannerets on a practical level is further suggested by Jean le Bel's account of the Weardale campaign of 1327. Le Bel recalled how as soon as the men-at-arms awoke, they would arrange themselves under the appropriate banners.[206] Besides the earls and the king himself, bannerets were the most highly valued members of the military community.

Many of the most prominent retinue leaders served at some stage in their careers as bannerets within the *familia Regis*. Robert de Clifford, John de Crumwell and John de St John each received the king's fees and robes during the Scottish wars.[207] Family groups such as the Badlesmeres, Latimers and Beauchamps supplied a thread of continuity within the royal household throughout most of the reign.[208] R.L. Ingamells has shown how many of the household bannerets in the 1270s and 1280s were soldiers who had previously served as *familiares* of either Henry III or the Lord Edward.[209] A large number of household retainers during the Scottish wars of the later part of Edward I's reign were the sons of these men.[210] The wealth of documentation on the king's household makes it possible to follow the careers of the king's knights and bannerets in greater detail than the careers of other men, who fell outside the purview of the wardrobe clerks. Some of these household men worked their way up the military hierarchy from relatively humble origins to become trusted members of the king's personal following. Aymer de la Bret was a king's sergeant in 1286 and still held that rank three years later.[211] By 1300 he was receiving pay as a banneret.[212] In this instance persistent service was rewarded with gradual recognition; but for other men the rewards might come far more rapidly. In 1304 Payn de Tibetot was made a banneret even though he had never been knighted.[213] Such a double promotion was highly unusual. Edward I was perhaps keen to create a new leadership corps capable of supporting his son. Whatever the reason for this exceptional measure, it seems that special favour could accomplish in one moment what it took others many years to achieve.

Bannerets like Tibetot feature strongly on the occasional rolls of arms of the reigns of the first two Edwards. As we have seen, these armorials were compiled

205 *Parl. Writs*, i, pp. 410–20.
206 *Chronique de Jean le Bel*, i, p. 55.
207 See, for example, *Liber Quotidianus*, p. 189; BL, Cotton Nero C VIII, fol. 91v; Ingamells, 'Household Knights of Edward I', i, p. 105.
208 Compare, for example, E 101/4/8, *Liber Quotidianus*, p. 189, and E 101/369/11, fol. 107r.
209 Ingamells, 'Household Knights of Edward I', i, p. 36.
210 Prestwich, *Edward I*, pp. 150–1.
211 E 101/351/26, m. 1; E 101/352/31, m. 1.
212 *Liber Quotidianus*, p. 200.
213 BL, Additional MS 8835, fols 55v, 114r.

to commemorate specific martial events, such as battles or tournaments. One of these rolls of arms, the Falkirk roll (1298), has been considered in some detail by J.E. Morris and Michael Prestwich, both of whom have noted that only forty-eight of the 115 men named on that armorial also appear on the horse inventories for Edward I's campaign to Scotland in 1298.[214] Building on this discovery, Prestwich went on to show that large numbers of earls and bannerets in Edward I's armies must have served gratuitously.[215] This observation has greatly improved our understanding of late thirteenth- and early fourteenth-century armies, providing an insight into the independence retained by many baronial warriors during their military service to the Crown. Conversely, however, it should also be noted that 107 company leaders who are not named on the roll of arms appear on the horse inventories for the Falkirk campaign.[216] In addition to this, a further twenty-eight retinue leaders obtained letters of protection for their men but appear on neither the roll of arms nor the horse inventories.[217] Evidently, either the leaders of these companies were serving independently of the bannerets whose names are recorded on the armorial (which would suggest an extremely atomised structure), or they were incorporated into the larger companies for the duration of the campaign.

Comparison of the three main sources at our disposal, the roll of arms, the horse inventories and the letters of protection, shows that many of the smaller units were attached to larger retinues led by bannerets. Richard de Herthill, Fulk Lestrange and Hugh de St John each obtained letters of protection in 1298 for compact companies of men-at-arms; but all three leaders also had letters of protection or attorney enrolled for service in the company of Ralph de Monthermer, earl of Gloucester.[218] Both John de Heselarton and Gerard Salveyn led small troops of armoured warriors within the larger *comitiva* of William le Latimer senior, while John de Kyngeston and Gilbert Talebot served as small company leaders under the household steward Walter de Beauchamp.[219] It appears, therefore, that the smallest companies fused with the larger retinues led by bannerets, thereby increasing the organisational cohesion of the army. Viewed from this perspective, the bannerets appear not only as leaders of large troops under their own command; they were also focal points around which other, smaller units would assemble. Furthermore, this process of integration seems to have taken place independently of any central planning. The initiative came from the bannerets, who applied for letters of protection for the sub-leaders in their retinues. Although the marshal and constable seem to have performed a valuable organisational role, it is likely that most companies, large or small, arrived at the muster fully formed.

---

[214] Morris, *Welsh Wars*, p. 314; Prestwich, *War, Politics and Finance*, p. 68; *Rolls of Arms, Edward I*, i, pp. 406–417.

[215] Prestwich, *War, Politics and Finance*, p. 91.

[216] For the horse inventories, see *Scotland in 1298*, pp. 160–237.

[217] For the letters of protection, see C67/13.

[218] C 67/13, mm. 5, 6d, 8 and 9.

[219] C 67/13, m. 5; *Scotland in 1298*, p. 185; C 67/13, m. 8.

The processes by which numerous small companies joined together to create larger retinues are generally hidden from view in the pay accounts drawn up by the household clerks. Yet, as Andrew Ayton has shown, there is a corpus of documents that enables us to examine this phenomenon more closely.[220] Enrolled letters of protection provide neat summaries of the main company leaders and the men-at-arms in their service; but, as a rule, they offer little insight into any subdivisions that may have existed within these units. By contrast, the *fiat* warrants for protection, which were 'the product of an earlier stage in the process of retinue recruitment',[221] sometimes enable us to see more clearly the way that aristocratic companies were constructed in the build-up to royal campaigns. The earl of Gloucester's retinue in Scotland in 1310 is a particular case in point. The Scottish roll shows that in that year, forty-five men had letters of protection enrolled in the earl's company.[222] Presented in this way, it seems that all of these men were recruited by the earl directly. Yet a warrant drawn up prior to the enrolment of these protections indicates that at least one sub-unit existed within this larger whole. The banneret Geoffrey de Say is listed at the head of a small contingent, consisting of two knights and three sergeants.[223] Each of these men-at-arms is identified as a member of Say's retinue; but a note written on the warrant makes it clear that they were also part of the larger *comitiva* of the earl of Gloucester. When we look again at the letters of protection on the Scottish roll, we find the same six soldiers listed as they appear on the warrant; but now no indication is given that Say was a sub-leader, or, indeed, that these men formed a separate group of companions at all.[224] Such sub-units can be traced within comital retinues on other occasions during the wars of Edward I and his son.[225] The evidence suggests that the largest retinues of this period (as with those of later periods) were raised by subcontracts, even if at this stage such contracts were not necessarily drawn up in written form.

Careful scrutiny of the record sources reveals a great deal about the disposition of military retinues within the armies of the first two Edwards that would otherwise be concealed from view. But what of the experience of the men who led these retinues? Analysis of the bannerets named on the Falkirk roll of arms of 1298, which offers a manageable sample of an elite band of warriors, shows that English armies at the beginning of the Scottish wars were led by a large number of veterans of the Welsh campaigns of the 1270s and 1280s. Of the 115 bannerets whose names are recorded on the armorial, some fifty (43 per cent) had given service on either one or both of the expeditions against Llywelyn ap Gruffydd: those of 1277 and 1282. Reginald de Grey,[226] Walter de Hunter-

---

[220] Ayton, *Knights and Warhorses*, pp. 160–2.

[221] *Ibid.*, p. 161.

[222] C 71/4, *passim*.

[223] C 81/1738, m. 66.

[224] C 71/4, m. 13.

[225] See, for example, C 81/1727, m. 18 and C 81/1728, m. 55.

[226] See above, p. 41, n. 63.

combe,[227] Peter de Mauley[228] and Hugh Pointz[229] were among several lords who had fought in every major army raised against the Welsh, including the hosts gathered to put down the risings of 1287 and 1294–5. These men were joined at Falkirk by numerous other veterans of the first two Welsh wars, such as Peter Corbet,[230] Ralph Fitz William,[231] Walter de Beauchamp[232] and Thomas de Berkeley.[233] A further twenty bannerets (17 per cent) appear to have gained their first experience of war during the later Welsh conflicts, against Rhys ap Maredudd and Madog ap Llywelyn. Adam de Welles, Hugh le Despenser, Henry de Percy and John Wake should be counted among this number.[234] In total, a minimum of around two-thirds of the bannerets named on the Falkirk roll had seen some action in Wales before the focus of attention moved to the north and the war with the Scots. Of the remainder, many were the sons of soldiers who had died during the 1290s after giving many years of military service on behalf of the Crown. The fathers of Hugh de Courtenay, Philip Darcy, John de Engayne and Thomas de Furnivall all died between 1291 and 1297, leaving their offspring to lead their retinues on the Falkirk campaign.[235]

This kind of continuity from father to son helped to ensure an element of stability within the leadership corps of these armies. Some soldiers were fortunate in having several sons, who were able to carry the leadership baton that was handed down to them. James de Audley, the Justiciar of Chester who accompanied the Lord Edward on the crusade of 1270, had one son, William de Audley, who gave service in Wales before his death there in 1282.[236] His youngest son, Hugh, later led small bands of men-at-arms during the wars in Scotland.[237] Not all magnates were so lucky, however. The destruction of the English army at Bannockburn, and the deaths there of a large number of prominent warriors, should remind us that the fortunes of war did not always favour the men of highest status. Many of the magnates who succumbed to the Scottish pikemen in 1314 had either no children or descendants who were too young to supply their places immediately. When it was found that the earl of Gloucester's wife had not conceived, his lands were divided among his sisters.[238] Although Payn de Tibetot did have a son of just over one year old, it would be some time before he would be able to occupy the boots that had previously been filled by his father.[239] The deaths of these leaders seriously depleted the forces available to

---

227 *Parl. Writs*, i, p. 201; C 47/2/7, m. 7; *CPR, 1281–92*, p. 272; C 67/10, m. 7d.

228 *Parl. Writs*, i, p. 199; C 67/8, m. 7; *CPR, 1281–92*, p. 274; C 67/10, m. 7d.

229 E 101/3/13; C 67/8, m. 7; *CPR, 1281–92*, p. 272; C 67/10, m. 7.

230 *Parl. Writs*, i, p. 204; C 67/8, m. 7.

231 *Parl. Writs*, i, p. 204; C 47/2/7, m. 6.

232 *Parl. Writs*, i, p. 199; C 67/8, m. 4d.

233 *Parl. Writs*, i, p. 204; C 67/8, m. 6d.

234 For their service in 1294–5, see C 67/10, mm. 5, 5d, 6, 7.

235 *Knights of Edward I*, i, pp. 243, 266, 307; ii, pp. 92–3.

236 For James' service, see Lloyd, *English Society and the Crusade*, appendix 4. His second son William is named in the annals of Chester as one of sixteen knights drowned in the crossing from Anglesey in 1282: *Annales Cestrienses*, pp. 110–11.

237 See, for example, E 101/9/9, fol. 4r.

238 *CIPM*, v, no. 538.

239 *Ibid.*, v, no. 519.

Edward II during the difficult years following the defeat at Bannockburn. The failure of the king to respond effectively to the Scottish threat demonstrates, yet again, how important such company commanders were to the military fortunes of the Edwardian kings.

3

The Military Community

Although of central importance to the Edwardian war effort and to the organisation of English hosts in this period, captains, wardens and retinue leaders were in a minority when set against the total number of landowners and non-landed gentry who took up arms in the late thirteenth and early fourteenth centuries. Attempts to calculate the size of this pool of men-at-arms, consisting of both regular and occasional campaigners, have hitherto been hindered by the sheer bulk of the source materials and the interpretative problems associated with their use. However, such a quantitative approach is necessary if we are to gauge the extent of the English aristocracy's involvement in war during the reigns of the first two Edwards. By analysing the service records that provide information relating to military status (primarily the horse inventories, but also pay-rolls, proffer rolls and others), it has been possible to identify some 1,350 knights and 4,900 men of sub-knightly status, or sergeants, who took part in campaigns in Wales, Scotland and on the continent between 1272 and 1314.[1] It should be noted, however, that the said records are far from complete, that sources not providing information relating to status (such as letters of protection, of attorney and of respite of debts) have not been included in this calculation, and that between a half and two-thirds of mounted soldiers tended to serve without Crown pay. Consequently, it may be estimated, very roughly, that around 1,700 knights and 6,000 sergeants acquired some experience of war between the accession of Edward I and the battle of Bannockburn.[2] For the historian, attempting

---

[1]   These figures have been extracted from a database created by the author containing some 38,000 records relating to the performance of military service. This figure does not include data which have also been computerised by the author concerning distraint of knighthood and military summonses.

[2]   To arrive at this estimation the figures of 1,350 knights and 4,900 sergeants were originally increased by 50 per cent. This was done to account for soldiers who served on particular campaigns without appearing in the records for military service, or who do appear in the service records but not with specified ranks. It seems that on most campaigns at least a half of bannerets and other lords who led retinues to war, and on some occasions a larger proportion, did not serve for Crown pay. Such men as these tend not appear in the type of document, such as horse inventories, that provide information relating to soldiers' status. However, as it is likely that the ranks of some of the men not in receipt of Crown pay on specific occasions were recorded in the service records for other campaigns, the figures of 1,350 and 4,900 have been increased by only 25 per cent. Such calculations are necessarily imperfect. The fact that there are over 18,000 enrolled letters of protection, of attorney and of respite of debts, including duplicates, which do not normally specify soldiers' status, highlights the potential shortfall in the figures given here.

to interpret and summarise the broad range of experience encompassed by these figures is a most difficult task. The aim of this chapter is to trace the aspects of war that were common to these men-at-arms, while acknowledging the unique details that made many of their careers so remarkable.

Men-at-Arms and the Fortunes of War

During times of war, ordinary men were capable of performing extraordinary feats. In the winter of 1282 the last native Prince of Wales, Llywelyn ap Gruffydd, was killed near Builth as he struggled with a regional English army under the command of the Marcher lord Roger Lestrange. His death was one of the most significant events of the Edwardian wars, depriving the men of Gwynedd of their natural leader and thereby accelerating the English conquest of Wales. Such an important historical figure deserved a fitting end; yet, of the man responsible for Llywelyn's demise, identified by the chronicler Walter of Guisborough as Stephen de Frankton,[3] we know relatively little. Although J.E. Morris was able to identify him as an associate of Lestrange who later served as an infantry commander in the war of 1287,[4] Frankton has left few other traces in the military sources. It is not until 1314 that we again find a man of that name preparing to go to war, and there is no way of knowing whether the Stephen de Frankton who obtained a letter of protection for service with Theobald de Verdon on the Bannockburn campaign was the man who had played so singular a role in the events of thirty-two years earlier.[5] Frankton's story demonstrates the important contribution that the more obscure members of the Edwardian military community made to the English war effort. However, it also highlights the difficulties that are involved in trying to reconstruct the military careers of such men. In this respect it is not difficult to empathise with Edward II, who in *c.* 1320 received a petition from a certain William de Cranbergh requesting some reward for seven years of service in Scotland. Evidently finding it impossible to retain a personal knowledge of all of his soldiers and their activities, the king wished to know 'qi il est et de son service'.[6]

Although it is not always possible to know who men like Cranbergh were and what service they had performed, there can be little doubt that the attempts of Edward I to establish his supremacy throughout the British Isles and in southwestern France placed great demands on the lesser landowners of England. 'Fighting war on an unprecedented scale', Scott Waugh has noted, 'demanded more out of communities in terms of both money and men than they had been

---

3   *Guisborough*, pp. 220–1.
4   Morris, *Welsh Wars*, p. 210.
5   C 71/6, m. 3. For the names of other men who may have been responsible for Llywelyn's death, see L.B. Smith, 'The Death of Llywelyn ap Gruffydd: The Narratives Reconsidered', *WHR*, xi (1982), pp. 200–13.
6   SC 8/82, no. 4083. The king's reply is written on the dorse of the petition.

accustomed to providing.'[7] Indeed, few gentry families could avoid the burdens imposed by the king's wars completely. The pressure placed by the Crown on its subjects was particularly intense between the outbreak of war with France in 1294 and the victory over the Scots at Falkirk in 1298. Fighting wars in Wales, France and Scotland imposed a heavy burden on the community of the realm. In the closing months of 1294 Edward I wrote to John Giffard of Brimpsfield, ordering that in addition to the men that he had sent to Gascony to serve under the earl of Lancaster he must now dispatch more soldiers to Wales.[8] In the following year similar orders were sent to the earl of Cornwall, demanding that he raise a troop of men to go to Scotland despite the fact that some of his tenants were already fighting on his behalf in France.[9] The knights and sergeants who shouldered the burden of these orders sometimes found themselves being required to serve in several theatres of war at once; and they might even be accused of trying to avoid giving military service even though they were performing it elsewhere. In the summer of 1297 an anonymous writer sent word to Edward informing him that James de Multon could not be present at a forthcoming muster as he was staying 'in the company of Henry de Percy and Robert de Clifford, as a mounted warrior, in the war in Scotland'.[10] That August the king also received a letter from the bishop of Durham, explaining that John de Greystoke had not been able to attend the muster arranged by Henry de Percy for a raid into Scotland because he was already riding with the bishop elsewhere north of the border. Greystoke had wrongly been accused of non-service, on account of which his lands had been taken into the king's hand.[11]

Unfortunately, it is very difficult to reconstruct the campaigning experiences of men like Multon and Greystoke beyond the recruitment stage. If it is sometimes possible to trace the daily activities of captains like Robert de Tibetot and John de St John as they corresponded with the Crown and issued orders to their subordinates, then it is still the case that the everyday routines of most ordinary men-at-arms remain shrouded in mystery. Many of the less wealthy knights and sergeants may have hoped for nothing more than to perform their service without suffering any personal damage or losses, for war could be both a risky and expensive business. One major concern was the protection of military equipment. The warhorse, in particular, was frequently at the centre of disputes between men-at-arms on campaign. In a case brought before the king's council in 1295, Ralph Saunsaver complained that the warhorses provided for him by William de Breouse for his service in Gascony had not been of sufficient quality. He had covenanted to serve for Breouse in return for 100 pounds. The latter met this by giving him 60 pounds and two horses; but, as the horses did not

---

[7] S.L. Waugh, 'The Third Century of English Feudalism', *Thirteenth Century England VII*, ed M. Prestwich, R. Britnell and R. Frame (Woodbridge, 1999), p. 54.

[8] *Parl. Writs*, i, p. 266.

[9] *Ibid.*, i, p. 277.

[10] SC 1/21, no. 167: '*en la compaignie monsieur Henri de Perci e monsieur Robert de Clifford en ceste guerre Descoce as chevaux e armes*'. Multon was in Gascony in 1294 (*Rôles Gascons*, iii, p. 120) and 1295 (*ibid.*, iii, p. 318) before switching to Scotland in 1297, 1298 (C 67/13, m. 5d), 1300 (C 67/14, m. 14) and 1304 (C 67/15, m. 4d).

[11] SC 1/21, no. 123.

meet his expectations, Saunsaver demanded 10 marks more.[12] Arguments over military equipment and the rightful ownership of horses can also be traced on the plea roll for the army that served in Scotland in 1296. Laurence de Preston complained that Matthew de Forneys was withholding a grey horse of his valued at 8 marks, which had run away from its groom.[13] In a similar incident, Alan Fitz Waryn launched a suit against Robert de St Paul for the theft of his mount.[14] Such material concerns are hardly surprising given that 'the horse represented a very major investment for a knight, perhaps in many cases equivalent to a year's income'.[15]

The misfortunes of war often amounted to much more than the loss of a horse. For many men the experience of war was a savage and brutal one, leading to personal disfigurement, the loss of property or even death. Fatalities and heavy casualties were encountered with sufficient regularity by the English throughout this period to ensure that men-at-arms could not take military service lightly. In addition to the heavy losses suffered at the bridge of boats (1282), Belle-garde (1297), Stirling Bridge (1297), Roslin (1303) and Bannockburn (1314), there were a few lesser battles and skirmishes in which English soldiers were discomfited. Men also frequently found themselves in financial difficulties as a consequence of their service in royal hosts. The author of the *Song of Trail-baston* probably spoke for many when he bemoaned the fact that despite many years of activity in Gascony, Flanders and Scotland he had made little gain.[16] One man who may have empathised with the author of this poem was William de Weston, a northern sergeant. Notwithstanding his lengthy service in Flanders, Scotland and in the garrison at Berwick, he claimed, in a petition to Edward II in 1318, that he was some 600 pounds out of pocket in owed wages and lost horses.[17] Weston's petition was typical of many that were sent to the king and his council by ordinary men-at-arms who had suffered loss and damage during their service to the Crown. Particularly common were petitions for financial assistance by men who had been captured by the enemy and forced to pay ransoms for their release. John le Frcunceys wrote to the Crown in 1307 of how he had been taken by the Scots at the battle of Roslin and had been detained north of the border for fifty-seven weeks until he had found the 40 marks that he needed to secure his freedom.[18] The Northumbrian men-at-arms John de Heselrigg and Robert de la Vale were each imprisoned following the debacle at Bannockburn.

[12] *Select Cases Before the King's Council, 1243–1482*, ed. I.S. Leadam and J.F. Baldwin, Selden Society, xxxv (1918), p. 16.
[13] 'Plea Roll, 1296', no 38.
[14] *Ibid.*, no 63.
[15] M. Prestwich, *'Miles in Armis Strenuus:* The Knight at War', *TRHS*, 6th ser., v (1995), p. 211.
[16] *Thomas Wright's Political Songs*, p. 232.
[17] *Northern Petitions Illustrative of Life in Berwick, Cumbria and Durham in the Fourteenth Century*, ed. C.M. Fraser, Surtees Society, cxciv (1981), no. 33. A William de Weston was in garrison at Berwick in 1298 (E 101/7/5, m. 1 – there is a slight doubt over the date of this document), 1301 (E 101/9/9, fol. 2v), 1303 (E 101/612/9, m. 2), and 1310 (BL, Cotton Nero C VIII, fol. 5r).
[18] *Parl. Roll.*, ii, p. 449.

They were later forced to pay 200 marks and 500 marks respectively before they could return to their war-torn lands.[19] A further petition highlights how the pitfalls of war affected not only the men who served but also their families. During the reign of Edward II a certain Simon de Rosse wrote of how his father Wadyn, who had served the king and his father in Gascony, Wales and Scotland for thirty years and more, had been taken prisoner at Berwick and decapitated, leaving Simon and his four siblings in a state of destitution.[20] Evidently, military service under Edward I and his son was no guarantee of prosperity or even financial security.

The risks involved in warfare led many men-at-arms to seek the patronage of more prominent figures within the military community. This meant entering the service of a retinue leader of high social standing. As we have seen, military service was strewn with potential hazards; and it could prove difficult for obscure sergeants and lesser knights, acting on their own behalf, to obtain redress for losses. By entering the service of men of comital and baronial status such individuals were able to find some insurance against the worst that military campaigning had to offer. Retinue leaders would sometimes write to the king on behalf of men in their service to ask that they be released from the debts that they owed to the Crown.[21] Alternatively, such patronage was used by some men to obtain writs excusing them from the performance of military service. This is how Gilbert Sikelfont benefited from his relationship with the earl Warenne in 1312, the year that he was distrained to knighthood.[22] In return for such favour, men-at-arms were expected to perform reliable service for their lords whenever and wherever it was required. Besides fighting (the most fundamental obligation discharged by ordinary soldiers), such individuals might be employed on logistical missions on behalf of their lords. The yeoman John le Bret was sent to Ireland in 1282 to purchase victuals for Robert Fitz Walter and the members of his retinue in Anglesey.[23] Similarly, a number of leaders in Gascony in 1294 and 1295 dispatched sergeants from their retinues to obtain much-needed supplies from within the British Isles.[24] In 1297 the earl Warenne employed two of his knights, Elias d'Aubeny and Saer de Huntingfeld, on a special mission to inspect the castles of Scotland.[25] Later, in 1310, two of the earl of Richmond's *valletti*

---

[19] *Ancient Petitions Relating to Northumberland*, nos 115, 122. See also A. King, ' "According to the Custom used in French and Scottish Wars": Prisoners and Casualties on the Scottish Marches in the Fourteenth Century', *Journal of Medieval History* xxviii (2002), pp. 263–90. In this article King argues that 'capture by the Scots was not nearly as disastrous as is often supposed' (p. 286). Be that as it may, it is unlikely that English soldiers enjoyed being taken prisoner, under any circumstances.

[20] SC 8/87, no. 4309: '*a Berewik fust pris e decole en vostre service pur sa Lewte*'. For evidence of Wadyn's military service, see E 101/10/5, m. 9.

[21] See, for example, *Ancient Correspondence Concerning Wales*, p. 148.

[22] *Parl. Writs*, II, ii, p. 419; C 47/1/7, m. 3.

[23] *CVCR*, p. 241.

[24] *Rôles Gascons*, iii, pp. 173, 214.

[25] *Stevenson*, ii, pp. 175–6.

acted as the eyes and ears of their lord, relaying news to him from the Scottish campaign while he was engaged on diplomatic business in France.[26]

In addition to such 'vertical' relationships, men-at-arms could usually find support among soldiers of equal status residing within their own counties and localities. Although there has been much debate about the importance of the 'county community' within medieval England, and indeed over whether such communities existed at all,[27] men would tend to find themselves operating in close proximity to their landed neighbours when on campaign.[28] During the second Welsh war of 1282–3 the men of Somerset, Dorset, Devon and Cornwall were ordered to perform their feudal service together in west Wales.[29] Meanwhile, landholders from Herefordshire, Shropshire and Staffordshire were commanded to serve at Montgomery under Roger de Mortimer.[30] Evidence of men-at-arms from the same county serving together also survives from the years of the war with France. The sheriff of Essex claimed in 1295 that the knights and free tenants of the county were unable to attest a proof of age because too many of them were guarding the coast against French invasion.[31] When war broke out with Scotland in 1296, the focus of attention shifted to the north of England. In the following year, Henry de Percy and Robert de Clifford launched a raid into Scotland with the men-at-arms of Cumberland and Westmorland. A chancery warrant confirms that the men of those counties served north of the border in 1297 without Crown pay.[32] Six years later the men of Northumberland also gave gratuitous service in Scotland for a short time.[33] During the reigns of Edward I and Edward II, the men of the eastern March towards Scotland were heavily engaged in military activity. A contemporary song indicates that many of the soldiers killed at Stirling Bridge in 1297 were landowners from the northeast;[34] and Edward I employed a group of Northumbrians to garrison Stirling castle in

26 *CDS*, iii, no. 166.

27 For different views on this subject, see, for example, J.R. Maddicott, 'The County Community and the Making of Public Opinion in Fourteenth-Century England', *TRHS*, 5th ser., xxviii (1978), p. 43; M. Prestwich, *English Politics in the Thirteenth Century* (London, 1990), pp. 58–9; C. Carpenter, 'Gentry and Community in Medieval England', *Journal of British Studies*, xxxiii (1994), pp. 345–52; D. Crouch, 'From Stenton to McFarlane: Models of Societies of the Twelfth and Thirteenth Centuries', *TRHS*, 6th ser., v (1995), pp. 192–3.

28 For some late fourteenth-century evidence of men from the same locality serving together on campaign, see Bell, *War and the Soldier*, pp. 117–25.

29 *CVCR*, p. 254.

30 *Ibid.*, p. 254. Cf. Walker, 'Anglo-Welsh Wars', p. 169.

31 *Select Cases in the Court of King's Bench under Edward I*, ed. G.O. Sayles, 3 vols, Selden Society, lv–lviii (1936–9), iii, no. 20.

32 *CCW*, p. 98. Percy and Clifford 'were obliged to sign a declaration that' the voluntary service given by the men of Cumberland and Westmorland 'should not be made a precedent against them': Reid, 'Office of the Warden of the Marches', p. 489. See also *Chronica et Annales*, p. 171.

33 *CPR, 1301–07*, p. 101. However, in the years following Bannockburn it became customary for the gentry of Northumberland to accept Crown pay even for service within their own county: A. King, '"Pur Salvation du Roiaume": Military Service and Obligation in Fourteenth-Century Northumberland', *Fourteenth Century England II*, ed. C. Given-Wilson (Woodbridge, 2002), p. 19.

34 *Thomas Wright's Political Songs*, p. 173.

the following year.[35] For the gentry of the eastern March towards Scotland, in fact, war was an inescapable feature of everyday life, a point that has been eluci-dated in recent research by Andy King.[36] For men-at-arms residing in highly militarised regions such as these, 'horizontal' ties with soldiers of relatively modest status were often of greater import than the patronage offered by a leading earl or banneret.[37]

Middling landowners from the Welsh and Scottish Marches were well placed to take advantage of office-holding opportunities in the conquered territories. Soldiering during these years was not as profitable as it was later to prove for many during the Hundred Years War,[38] but gainful employment was to be had by men willing to reside in hostile regions for prolonged spells. Although the major captaincies and custodianships were offered to earls and other magnates, lesser positions were available to men-at-arms of relatively modest means. Following the war of 1282–3, leading native Welsh families were excluded from the positions that they had formerly held.[39] In the words of R.R. Davies, 'the personnel of the new governmental dispensation in Wales was ... "colonial" in its recruitment'.[40] The new governing class included 'English' families who had held lands in Wales since before the conquest, such as the Camvilles of Llan-stephan. During the second Welsh war Geoffrey de Camville served at his own expense in the garrisons of west Wales.[41] Perhaps in recognition of this, William de Camville was later appointed as the king's keeper of Carmarthenshire and Cardiganshire.[42] Roger de Springehose, the sheriff of Shropshire, was placed in charge of the garrison at Oswestry in 1282 during the absence of Roger de Mortimer. He was rewarded, for his service, with the lands of a Welsh rebel.[43] Another family that came to prominence in the office-holding community of

[35] *Chronica et Annales*, p. 388.

[36] A. King, 'Englishmen, Scots and Marchers: National and Local Identities in Thomas Gray's *Scalacronica*', *Northern History*, xxxvi (2000), pp. 225–8; *idem*, '"Pur Salvation du Roiaume"', pp. 13–31.

[37] Adrian Bell has uncovered a number of 'horizontal' links among the men of Shropshire who served on the earl of Arundel's expeditions of 1387 and 1388: Bell, *War and the Soldier*, pp. 159–62.

[38] Discussing the campaigns of Edward I's reign, Anthony Tuck has stated that 'war in Scot-land offered the nobility little opportunity for either profit or glory': *Crown and Nobility, 1272–1461: Political Conflict in Late Medieval England* (Oxford, 1985), p. 46. Andy King has provided a more nuanced interpretation of the evidence by showing that the North-umbrian gentry did quite well, financially, from the war with the Scots: 'War, Politics and Landed Society', pp. 129–30; but overall, especially as many lords did not serve for Crown pay during the reigns of Edward I and Edward II, it is doubtful that great profits were made, by the aristocracy at large, from the wars in Scotland in the years before Bannockburn.

[39] A.D. Carr, 'An Aristocracy in Decline: The Native Welsh Lords after the Edwardian Conquest', *WHR*, v (1970), pp. 119–20.

[40] R.R. Davies, *Conquest, Coexistence, and Change: Wales 1063–1415* (Oxford, 1987), p. 366.

[41] *CVCR*, p. 229.

[42] *Ibid.*, p. 354.

[43] *Ibid.*, pp. 222, 265. A sergeant of that name later served under John de Havering at Falkirk: *Scotland in 1298*, p. 229.

post-conquest Wales was the Stauntons of Staffordshire. Robert de Staunton was appointed as sheriff of Merioneth in March 1284; and his son Vivian later found employment as constable of Harlech castle, where he was serving by the time of the revolt of 1294–5.[44] Some of the men who were elevated to office in post-conquest Wales held relatively little land. Hugh de Wlonkeslowe, granted the constableship of Harlech in October 1284,[45] held only half a knight's fee in the vill of Longslow, Shropshire, at the time of Kirkby's Inquest (an inquiry into the knights' fees held of the Crown) of 1285.[46] He probably relied on the annual stipend of 100 pounds that he received from that office to maintain his family in the status of knighthood to which they aspired.[47]

Similar office-holding opportunities were available to the men of the northern counties during the war with Scotland. Although the major captaincies were given, as in Wales, to prominent figures of a national standing, such as Robert de Clifford and the earl of Pembroke, auxiliary posts were sometimes granted to knights bachelor whose interests were restricted to one county or region. In 1302 Richard le Brun and Hugh de Multon were employed as keepers of Cumberland and Westmorland.[48] Five years later Brun was employed on the western March in a similar capacity along with a fellow Cumbrian knight, John de Wigeton.[49] Meanwhile, Roger Heron and Simon Warde, of Northumberland and Yorkshire respectively, were made keepers of the peace on the eastern March.[50] Many opportunities for employment were created in the towns and castles north of the border following the English victory at Dunbar in 1296. Initially Edward had allowed many Scots to retain possession of their castles.[51] However, this policy changed in the wake of Wallace's revolt. As the Scottish chronicler Andrew de Wyntoun later ruefully reflected, Edward took possession of all the Scottish castles 'and stuffit thaim with Inglismen'.[52] Some of the newly appointed constables and sheriffs in Scotland were drawn from the northern counties of England. Robert de Joneby and John de Huddleston of Cumberland, for example, found service in Dumfries and Galloway.[53] But other positions in

---

[44] *CVCR*, p. 283; *Calendar of Ancient Petitions Relating to Wales (Thirteenth to Sixteenth Century)*, ed. W. Rees (Cardiff, 1975), p. 507; E 101/5/17, m. 5.

[45] *CVCR*, p. 291.

[46] *Feudal Aids*, iv, p. 221.

[47] It is not clear whether this Hugh de Wlonkeslowe was a knight, but his son later appears, bearing arms, on Collins' roll: *Rolls of Arms, Edward I*, ii, p. 264.

[48] *Parl. Writs*, i, p. 364.

[49] *Ibid.*, II, ii, p. 369.

[50] *Ibid.*, II, ii, p. 369.

[51] *Scotichronicon by Walter Bower*, ed. D.E.R. Watt *et al.*, 9 vols (Aberdeen and Edinburgh, 1987–98), vi, p. 81.

[52] *The Original Chronicle of Andrew of Wyntoun*, ed. F.J. Amours, 6 vols, The Scottish Text Society, l–lxiii (Edinburgh, 1903–14), v, p. 346. See also *Scotichronicon*, vi, p. 293; and *Johannis de Fordun Chronica Gentis Scotorum*, ed. W.F. Skene, The Historians of Scotland Series, i (Edinburgh, 1871), p. 335.

[53] S.J.P. Howarth, 'King, Government and Community in Cumberland and Westmorland *c.* 1200–*c.* 1400, PhD thesis, University of Liverpool, 1988, p. 230.

Scotland were granted to household knights,[54] to pro-English Scots,[55] and to veterans from other parts of the country who had already obtained experience of colonial government elsewhere.[56] Among the last-mentioned group was the Staffordshire knight Robert de Hastang senior, who had been employed in Ireland prior to his appointment as constable of Roxburgh castle.[57]

The establishment of an English hegemony throughout the British Isles created opportunities for advancement that might to some extent have offset the hazards of war. Yet, the path to promotion was available to relatively few of the thousands of knights and sergeants who engaged in warfare; and it would be a mistake to assume that those who held constableships and other offices in conquered territories made rich pickings during their periods of tenure. On the contrary, castle constables and other royal officers residing within enemy territory had to be constantly vigilant. Robert de Hastang, for one, frequently found it necessary to draw his sword during his time as constable at Roxburgh.[58] He and men like William Biset, the sheriff of Clackmannan and Stirling, employed spies and scouts in their service because of the constant threat of enemy attack.[59] Far from being a route to prosperity, service for the Crown in Scotland, aptly described by Fiona Watson as the 'Siberia of English office-holding', was a dangerous and energy-sapping task.[60] Similar dangers and burdens confronted men holding office in Wales. In *c.* 1308–9 the former constable of Haverford, Hugh de Paunton, claimed that despite having spent large amounts of his own money on restoring and maintaining the castle there, he was now unable to recover his outlay because the fort had been granted to the earl of Pembroke. He had received no assistance from the Crown, financial or otherwise, and was being forced from office without having anything to show for his efforts.[61] Seven years later John de Scudemor, the king's yeoman, wrote to Edward II of how he lived in fear of reprisals by his enemies, who sought revenge for the judicial punishments that he had carried out during his time as constable of the castle at Llanbadarn Fawr.[62] Such occupations as these were not for the faint-hearted.

The men-at-arms who served under these constables in the garrisons of Wales and Scotland made a most significant contribution to the English war effort. Garrison service tended to be dominated by soldiers of fairly lowly origins. Few bachelors, and even fewer bannerets and earls, ever warmed to this kind of activity. At Roxburgh in 1301, for example, there were just three knights

---

[54] Prestwich, 'Colonial Scotland', p. 12.

[55] M. Brown, 'War, Allegiance, and Community in the Anglo-Scottish Marches: Teviotdale in the Fourteenth Century', *Northern History*, xli (2004), pp. 226, 236.

[56] F.J. Watson, *Under the Hammer: Edward I and Scotland, 1286–1306* (East Linton, 1998), p. 99.

[57] For his service in Ireland, see *Documents Illustrative of English History in the Thirteenth and Fourteenth Centuries*, ed. H. Cole (London, 1844), p. 73; and for his garrison service in Scotland, see, for example, E 101/7/7, m. 2 and E 101/9/9, fol. 2r.

[58] *Scalacronica*, p. 45.

[59] *CDS*, ii, no. 1221; SC 1/12, no. 71.

[60] Watson, *Under the Hammer*, p. 209.

[61] *Ancient Petitions Relating to Wales*, p. 100.

[62] *Ibid.*, p. 285.

compared to twenty-seven men-at-arms of inferior status.[63] This distinction even stretched to the royal household. The king's *servientes ad arma* formed an important sub-group within the garrisons of Wales and Scotland; but their knightly counterparts, for the most part, preferred to remain at home until major expeditions were launched. During the reign of Henry III the king's sergeants-at-arms had sometimes received pay for service at castles such as Carmarthen and Montgomery.[64] When Edward I came to the throne they were able to continue with such activities across a broader geographical range. Following the outbreak of war with Scotland in 1296, large numbers of the king's sergeants were employed in the garrisons north of the border. Richard de Chaumbre, John de Enefeld, William de Hulle and several others formed the core of the garrison at Linlithgow in 1302.[65] Later, around the time of Edward II's first expedition as king, eight of the king's sergeants-at-arms were employed in the garrison at Dundee.[66] When a raiding force from Berwick castle was ambushed by the Scots in the years following Bannockburn, the majority of the men captured or killed in the attack were sergeants drawn from the royal household.[67]

The king's sergeants-at-arms were not alone in giving repeated service in these hazardous theatres of war. Although most men-at-arms were keen to avoid garrison service, others seem to have carried it out willingly for a number of years. Their motives for doing so, however, are difficult to discern. During the course of their prolonged service in enemy territory some soldiers formed strong bonds with their fellow garrison members. In 1305 the men of the Linlithgow garrison petitioned as a group for the arrears of their pay.[68] Indeed some soldiers spent most of their time walled up in strongholds and fortified towns, thereby forming part of a well-defined garrison community. A typical member of this group was John de Untank. He resided in the garrison at Carstairs in 1302 before going on to serve at Kirkintilloch and Linlithgow.[69] Hugh de la Mare was employed at Berwick between 1298 and 1301 and could be found there again at the time of the Scottish campaign of 1310–11. In the intervening period he gave service, for part of the time, at Edinburgh castle.[70] Given the close quarters in which soldiers in the garrisons were forced to live, it is understandable that some men-at-arms chose to serve alongside their kinsmen. In 1302 the garrison at Carstairs contained no fewer than four members of the Bilton family.[71] Else-

---

63 E 101/9/9, fol. 3v.

64 *Calendar of the Liberate Rolls*, 6 vols (London, 1916–64), iii, p. 7. For information relating to the numbers of, and payments made to, the king's sergeants-at-arms during the reigns of Edward I and Edward II, see C. Given-Wilson, *The Royal Household and the King's Affinity: Service, Politics and Finance in England 1360–1413* (London, 1986), pp. 21–2.

65 E 101/10/5, m. 9.

66 Bodleian Library, Tanner MS 197, fols 30r–v.

67 *CDS*, iii, nos 470, 477.

68 *Memorando de Parliamento, or, Records of the Parliament holden at Westminster on the Twenty-Eighth Day of February, in the Thirty-Third Year of the Reign of King Edward the First (AD 1305)*, ed. F.W. Maitland, Rolls Ser., xcviii (London, 1893), p. 170.

69 E 101/10/5, m. 9; E 101/12/18, fol. 4r; E 101/12/38.

70 E 101/7/1, m. 9; E 101/7/7, m. 1; E 101/9/9, fol. 2v; E 101/10/5, m. 9; BL, Cotton Nero C VIII, fol. 5r.

71 E 101/10/5, m. 9.

where, the brothers John and William de Cotes fought alongside one another for a number of years at Roxburgh;[72] and Hugh, John and Robert de Herley served together in the garrison at Linlithgow.[73] The presence of family groups such as these probably made life in the fortresses of Scotland more bearable than it would otherwise have been.

Nevertheless, garrison service remained a risky business, both for the men-at-arms employed in them and the castle constables. Gerald of Wales had written in the twelfth century of the bloodthirsty nature of the struggles between the English garrisons and the native populations in Wales;[74] and the situation at the time of the Edwardian conquest was no different from this. The author of the *Brut y Tywysogyon* noted that Gruffudd ap Maredudd and Rhys Fychan had spared the lives of the men of the Aberystwyth garrison in 1282 because of the approach of Easter.[75] On other occasions, and in other parts of the Edwardian empire, the English were not so fortunate. One former garrison member, Geoffrey de Ampelford, noted that he had been maimed in the right eye during his service at Carstairs.[76] His injury could perhaps be overcome, but it is likely that other soldiers were forced to retire from military service because of the wounds that they had sustained. This kind of damage to life and limb might have been worthwhile had garrison service offered much prospect of material gain; but it is more likely that the reverse was the case, particularly during the years following Bannockburn. The experience of Robert de Blakeburn of the Berwick garrison supports this theory, for by 1320 his long military career had left him with nothing to live off following the fall of that town to the Scots.[77] Such stories give some idea of the reality of warfare for many ordinary English soldiers and remind us that warfare in the age of chivalry was not all about glory and material gain.

The Mounted Armoured Warrior at Falkirk

Evocative as the above evidence may be, the snapshots of military service provided by petitions and other personal testimonies shed light on the activities of only a small proportion of the men-at-arms of the late thirteenth and early fourteenth centuries. The historian who wishes to know more about the experiences of mounted soldiers who gave service for the Crown must rely on more prosaic materials, such as horse inventories, pay-rolls and enrolled letters of protection. These sources, when taken together, supply the names of thousands of warriors, drawn from the social elite, who fought for Edward I and his son.

---

[72] E 101/9/9, fol. 3v; E 101/12/18, fols 1v–2v.

[73] E 101/12/18, fol. 4v; E 101/12/38.

[74] *Giraldi Cambrensis Itinerarium Kambriae, et Descriptio Kambriae*, ed. J.F. Dimock, Rolls Ser., xxi 6 (London, 1868), pp. 49–50.

[75] *Brut y Tywysogyon or The Chronicle of the Princes, Peniarth MS. 20 Version*, trans. T. Jones (Cardiff, 1952), p. 120.

[76] SC 8/9, no. 443.

[77] *Northern Petitions*, no. 35.

They also offer the most accurate impression of the size and composition of the military community. Moreover, by linking the names found in these sources it is possible to reconstruct some portion of the careers in arms of many of the mounted soldiers who went to war during these years. The difficulty, when dealing with such a large and amorphous body of men, is to know how to sample the group in such a way as to facilitate meaningful analysis and discussion while retaining the diversity of the whole. Most historians whose research has focused on the later medieval gentry have sought to solve this problem by adopting a land-centric approach, thereby rooting knights and esquires in the counties and localities where they resided.[78] This method, while enabling detailed scrutiny of the military commitments of the men of particular localities, is less suitable for a study such as this, which aims to look at the military service given by the aristocracy at a national level.

Consequently, a different sampling technique has been employed here. Ideally one would seek a group of soldiers both large enough to encompass a wide range of military experience and sufficiently diverse in terms of rank, status and geographical origin to justify the claim to universality. For this purpose the most appropriate type of source, offering 'a slice through the military community' as many of its constituent members prepared for war, are the horse inventories.[79] As Andrew Ayton has noted, 'the greatest yield of detailed nominal data on the "ordinary" men-at-arms in Edwardian armies is to be had from the horse inventories, where the modestly priced mounts of these men are listed alongside the destriers and coursers of their wealthier or more celebrated comrades-in-arms'.[80] By providing the names of hundreds of men-at-arms of both knightly and sub-knightly status as they had their horses appraised at the beginning of royal campaigns, these lists offer the ideal starting point for a discussion of the military service of the aristocracy. From this corpus of documents, the most suitable sample is provided by the horse inventories drawn up for the Falkirk campaign of 1298.[81] These lists contain the names of a larger number of men-at-arms than any of the other horse inventories of the period. Furthermore, the Falkirk campaign took place just twenty-one years after Edward I's first Welsh war, of 1277, and sixteen years before the battle of Bannockburn. Thus it falls conveniently at an approximate mid-point within the temporal parameters set for this book.

Knights

22 July 1298 was a momentous date in the Anglo-Scottish wars. On that day a royal-led English host of around 3,000 mounted warriors and 25,000 foot routed

---

[78] For the aims of such studies, see M.J. Bennett, *Community, Class and Careerism: Cheshire and Lancashire Society in the Age of* Sir Gawain and the Green Knight (Cambridge, 1983), p. 3. Bennett drew inspiration from R.H. Hilton, *A Medieval Society: The West Midlands at the End of the Thirteenth Century* (London, 1966). For studies of military service within particular localities, see, for example, Morgan, *War and Society*, and Saul, *Knights and Esquires*, pp. 36–59.

[79] Ayton, *Knights and Warhorses*, p. 5.

[80] *Ibid.*, p. 5.

[81] For the horse inventories, see *Scotland in 1298*, pp. 160–237.

a Scottish force under the command of William Wallace at Falkirk. Although the victory was not decisive, either politically or militarily, it did ensure that the English regained the initiative north of the border following the Scottish resurgence under Wallace and Andrew Moray. As G.W.S. Barrow has noted, 'not for another sixteen years did the Scots attempt a full-scale pitched battle against the English'.[82] Success no doubt tasted all the sweeter given the dismal defeat that had been suffered by the earl Warenne at Stirling Bridge in the previous year, and the devastation caused by Scottish raids into northern England throughout the winter months that had followed.[83]

It is to be regretted, therefore, that the names of only a proportion of the English men-at-arms who took part in the Falkirk campaign can now be recovered. The two extant horse inventories for Edward I's army reveal the identities of 136 knights who served within the retinues as well as four knights who seem to have joined the army independently.[84] It is these 140 lesser knights (that is, not including the retinue leaders)[85] who will form the subject of our case study. These men, who represent around 10 per cent of the total number of knights in England at this time,[86] were distributed throughout forty-eight retinues. Over 100 of the companies recorded on the horse inventories contained not a single knight. Eighty-nine knights served in the king's household division; the other fifty-one, meanwhile, were brought into pay for the duration of the campaign. Around forty of the retinues that contained knights were manned by three belted warriors or fewer, whereas only two companies, those of Hugh le Despenser and Thomas of Lancaster, contained ten knights or more.[87] At this point a note of caution must be sounded. As we have seen, of the 115 earls and bannerets named on the Falkirk roll of arms, only forty-eight also appear on the extant horse inventories for the campaign.[88] The men in our sample, therefore, probably represent no more than 40 per cent of the total number of knights serving in the English retinues in 1298. In fact, given that only two lords of comital status, Thomas of Lancaster and Aymer de Valence,[89] are named on both the roll of

---

[82] Barrow, *Robert Bruce*, p. 103.

[83] C.J. McNamee, 'William Wallace's Invasion of Northern England in 1297', *Northern History*, xxvi (1990), pp. 40–58.

[84] No status was recorded for 283 of the men named on the Falkirk horse inventories, and it is possible that a few of these individuals were knights. The sample group has been confined to men who are clearly identified, on the horse inventories for 1298, as knights. The four knights who served independently were Robert de Bures, John de Luda, Adam de Blida and John Kirkpatrick: *Scotland in 1298*, pp. 161, 163, 175, 228.

[85] The service given by the retinue leaders is likely to have been exceptional in terms of both frequency and length. Their careers in arms are not, therefore, representative of the service performed by most ordinary members of the military community, with which this chapter is concerned. For discussion of the service given by retinue leaders, see above pp. 55–67 and below pp. 121–2.

[86] There seem to have been around 1,250 knights within England *c.* 1312: Keen, 'Heraldry and Hierarchy', p. 97.

[87] For the retinues of Despenser and Lancaster, see *Scotland in 1298*, pp. 187–9 and 179–81

[88] See above, p. 64.

[89] Lancaster had recently become an earl, whereas Valence was heir to an earldom.

arms and the horse inventories, the proportion of the knightly mounted force represented by the men in our sample is probably nearer 30 per cent. Nevertheless, a thorough analysis of the backgrounds, age, status and military experience of these men should provide us with some idea as to the general composition of the mounted armoured element of Edward I's armies during the early years of the war in Scotland.

A few of the knights who served at Falkirk had been in possession of their estates since the Hundred roll enquiries of the mid-1270s. Robert Barry, who served in 1298 in the retinue of Ralph Pipard, had been accused in 1276 of withholding a suit concerning the lands that he held in chief in Billing, Northamptonshire.[90] This may explain why it seems to have taken some time before he was willing to lend his support to the war effort.[91] William de Scalebroke, another knight of Ralph Pipard, had likewise held his lands since at least the opening decade of the reign, as had John de Blakeford, who was with Simon de Montacute at Falkirk.[92] By contrast, William de Horkesley, who inherited from his father Robert in December 1295, joined the landed elite just a few years before serving in Scotland.[93] Still others, like Robert de Haustede junior, had to wait until the reign of Edward II to receive their patrimonies.[94] To contrast the contribution made by landed knights to the Falkirk campaign with that of their non-landed counterparts would be to miss the point. In 1298 military service attracted both those whose landholding status carried a concomitant military obligation as well as others for whom a lack of land may have acted as a stimulus for adventure. The same principle applies to service given by older and younger sons, for examples of both can be found among our sample of knights.[95]

During the late Middle Ages most members of the knightly class held land in more than one county. An inquisition into the men-at-arms available for coastal defence in Essex in 1295–6 showed that of 102 knights holding land in that county, only around twenty-four were actually resident there.[96] Some of the others may have been away on military service; but the majority probably possessed estates in several shires, as did most of the knights at Falkirk. Thomas de Scales, who was with Fulk Fitz Waryn in Scotland in 1298, had landed inter-

---

[90] *Rotuli Hundredorum temp. Hen. III. and Edw. I. in Turr' Lond' et in Curia Receptae Scaccarii Westm. asservati*, ed. W. Illingworth and J. Caley, 2 vols (Record Commission, 1812–18) ii, p. 13.

[91] See below, p. 87.

[92] *Rotuli Hundredorum*, ii, pp. 714, 764–5; i, pp. 65, 86–7.

[93] *CIPM*, iii, no. 345.

[94] *Ibid.*, vi, no. 316.

[95] For comment on the prospects for older and younger sons within medieval society, see G. Duby, 'Youth in Aristocratic Society: Northwestern France in the Twelfth Century', *The Chivalrous Society* (London, 1977), pp. 117–18. Edmund Foliot, Fulk Peyforer and Henry de Segrave were three of the younger sons among the knights at Falkirk. Ingelram de Berenger and Nicholas Pointz, for example, were the eldest sons in their families.

[96] *Parl. Writs*, i, pp. 273–4. J.C. Ward has noted that 'the knights and gentry of fourteenth-century Essex were connected with wider networks covering far more than the county': *The Essex Gentry and the County Community in the Fourteenth Century*, (Essex Record Office, 1991), p. 20.

ests in Cambridgeshire, Hertfordshire and Norfolk.[97] William de Hardreshull held numerous lands in Lincolnshire, in addition to the manor of Hartshill in Warwickshire.[98] That said, most middling knights, as opposed to the earls and bannerets, tended to hold their estates in one part of the country.[99] This means that it is possible to divide the 140 knights in our sample into the counties and regions from which they came. One product of this enquiry is that relatively few northerners, defined as those who held their estates in Cumberland, Westmorland, Lancashire, Yorkshire, Durham or Northumberland, can be found among the knights named on the horse inventories. This is contrary to what one would expect given that this was a campaign to Scotland and that knights from the northern counties resided closest to the border. Comparison with the Falkirk roll of arms shows that the reason for this is that a relatively large number of northern bannerets did not serve for Crown pay. Of the bannerets who appear on both the roll of arms and the horse inventories, only five – Robert de Clifford, Thomas de Furnivall, William de Ryther, William de Cantilupe and Nicholas de Meynill – held their main estates in the north.[100] By contrast, seventeen of the bannerets named on the roll of arms who *do not* appear in pay on the horse inventories were northerners. What one finds in the group of knights in our sample, therefore, is a picture of the military community largely dominated by men-at-arms who held lands in the Midlands or the southern counties. A sizeable group of around thirty-two knights came from the southwest under lords like Robert Fitz Payn, Hugh de Courtenay, John de Beauchamp of Somerset and Simon de Montacute. The next largest body of knights (around twenty) was drawn from the southeast.

The ages of the knights who served in the mounted retinues at Falkirk varied widely. The Statute of Winchester of 1285 had specified that all men between the ages of fifteen and sixty were to be assessed and sworn to armour.[101] In November 1298, just a few months after the battle of Falkirk, Thomas de Furnivall was ordered to raise men-at-arms between the ages of twenty and sixty from the counties of Derbyshire and Nottinghamshire.[102] An Edwardian soldier's career was potentially a very long one. Nicholas Orme has noted how late medieval writers encouraged young men to undertake military training from their mid-teens;[103] and men of roughly that age seem to have featured in large

---

97   *CIPM*, ii, no. 520.

98   *Ibid.*, ii, nos 185, 807.

99   See Hilton, *A Medieval Society*, pp. 58–9. In his study of the gentry of Gloucestershire, Nigel Saul observed that 'the horizons of most of the knights [seem to have been] surprisingly narrow': *Knights and Esquires*, p. 82.

100 For a fuller list of knights from the northern counties of England who served at Falkirk, see C.H. Hunter Blair, 'Northern Knights at Falkirk, 1298', *Archaeologia Aeliana, or Miscellaneous Tracts Relating to Antiquity*, ed. C.H. Hunter Blair, 4th ser., xxv (1947), pp. 68–114.

101 *Statutes of the Realm*, i, p. 97.

102 *CPR, 1292–1301*, p. 387.

103 N. Orme, *From Childhood to Chivalry: The Education of the English Kings and Aristocracy 1066–1530* (London, 1984), p. 182.

numbers in Simon de Montfort's army at Lewes in 1264.[104] The same seems to have been true of Edward I's army in 1298. John de Claron, who was with Henry de Beaumont in that year, was said to be forty years old in 1324.[105] This would have made him just fourteen in 1298. Although there is every reason to doubt the accuracy of inquisitions *post mortem* as a source for age,[106] it seems likely that Claron was in his teens when he served at Falkirk. Other youngsters in Edward I's army included Robert de Haustede junior, who was 'thirty-six and more' when he inherited his father's lands in 1323,[107] placing him roughly in his mid-teens at the time of Falkirk, and Maurice de Berkeley, who was perhaps seventeen when he accompanied his father to Scotland.[108] At the opposite end of the age spectrum was the Staffordshire knight William de Mere, who claimed at a proof of age in 1323 that he was eighty.[109] This would have made him about fifty-five in 1298. Of the same generation was Thomas de Berkeley senior, who was aged about fifty-three in that year.[110] Most knights, as one would expect, were aged somewhere between these two extremes. Thomas de St Loe, aged around twenty-nine in 1298, Geoffrey de Aubermarle, who was perhaps thirty-one, and Nicholas de St Maur, in his mid- to late-twenties, were all very much in the prime of life when they confronted the Scots at Falkirk.[111]

The broad range in age, wealth and experience among these knights was reflected in the varying quality of their warhorses in 1298. To some extent the horse valuations serve as a convenient indicator of the status of the men-at-arms at Falkirk. At the lower end of the scale were two knights, Stephen de Depham and Nicholas de la Launde, whose horses were valued at just 8 marks.[112] Knights who had been in possession of their estates since the 1270s not surprisingly had higher value mounts. Robert Barry's *equus*, for example, was appraised at 24 marks.[113] But the most expensive chargers were reserved for regular campaigners like Roger de Bilney (50 marks) and William de Hardreshull (80 marks); men who were bannerets or led sub-retinues, such as Thomas de Berkeley senior (60 marks) and William de Ferrers (70 marks); and the sons of the retinue

---

104 *The Song of Lewes*, ed. C.L. Kingsford (Oxford, 1890), p. 4.

105 *CIPM*, vi, no. 422.

106 See J.T. Rosenthal, *Old Age in Late Medieval England* (Philadelphia, Pa., 1996), chapter 1. For a discussion of some of the methods used to calculate age, see J. Bedell, 'Memory and Proof of Age in England 1272–1327', *Past and Present*, clxii (1999), pp. 3–27.

107 *CIPM*, vi, no. 316.

108 *Complete Peerage*, ii, p. 128. For evidence of teenage soldiers, see A. Ayton, 'Knights, Esquires and Military Service: The Evidence of the Armorial Cases before the Court of Chivalry', *The Medieval Military Revolution: State, Society and Military Change in Medieval and Early Modern Europe*, ed. A. Ayton and J.L. Price (London, 1995), p. 92; M. Keen, 'English Military Experience and the Court of Chivalry: The Case of Grey v. Hastings', *Guerre et Société en France, en Angleterre et en Bourgogne XIVe-XVe siècle*, ed. P. Contamine, C. Giry-Deloison and M. Keen (Lille, 1992), p. 131; and Bell, *War and the Soldier*, p. 144.

109 *CIPM*, vi, no. 354.

110 *Complete Peerage*, ii, p. 127.

111 *CIPM*, v, no. 157; *ibid.*, ii, no. 720; *ibid.*, iii, no. 386.

112 *Scotland in 1298*, pp. 169, 226.

113 *Ibid.*, p. 220.

leaders, like Thomas de Leyburn (100 marks).[114] Judged by the concentration of highly valued horses in his retinue, Hugh le Despenser led the most impressive company to Scotland.[115] Knights like Berkeley senior, John ap Adam and William de Ferrers led small companies of their own within the *comitivae* of their patrons. Thomas de Berkeley senior had, in fact, been the constable of Edward I's army in Flanders during the previous year.[116] Even some relatively obscure knights, like Reginald de St Martin and Robert de Bures, had led small troops of two or three men-at-arms on campaign in the past.[117] The knights who served in the retinues at Falkirk were, therefore, of varied social and military standing. This point should be borne in mind as we now consider their careers in arms in greater detail.

The first thing that needs to be discovered about the military service of our knights is the number of years that they had been participating in the king's wars before the Falkirk campaign. By discerning how long these men had been giving military service by 1298, we can obtain some idea of the collective experience of Edward I's mounted armoured force at the battle of Falkirk. Based on the extant material for the years between the Lord Edward's crusade of 1270–2 and the expedition of 1298, table 3.1 shows the years in which the knights in our sample appear to have taken up arms for the first time.

Table 3.1: First recorded military service of the 'lesser' knights at Falkirk

	1270	1277	1282	1287	1294	1295	1296	1297	1298
Holy Land	2	–	–	–	–	–	–	–	–
Wales	–	6	12	3	21*	–	–	–	–
Gascony	–	–	–	–	15	1	–	2	–
Flanders	–	–	–	–	–	–	–	20	–
Scotland	–	–	–	–	–	–	20	4	34
Total	2	6	12	3	36	1	20	26	34

* Includes those who served in Wales in both 1294 and 1295

Before we attempt to analyse these figures a word of caution is due. The sources that contain the names of English soldiers for this period are incomplete. Furthermore, on all campaigns there were large numbers of knights who did not receive Crown pay; and such men as these do not appear on the pay-rolls and horse inventories. Maurice le Brun is first mentioned in the service records in 1298.[118] However, the plea roll for the army that campaigned in Scotland in 1296 shows that he had been militarily active at least two years before that time.[119] Some of the knights in our sample were summoned by the king before they appear to

---

114 *Ibid.*, pp. 209, 191, 216, 189 and 194. Thomas de Leyburn served in the retinue of his father, William.
115 *Ibid.*, pp. 187–9.
116 *Chronica et Annales*, p. 173.
117 BL, Additional MS 7965, fol. 79r; E 101/6/37, m. 1i.
118 *Scotland in 1298*, p. 176.
119 'Plea Roll, 1296', no. 127.

have begun their military service. Simon de Ralegh was ordered to go to Wales in 1294, but he does not appear in the army records as a soldier until the Scottish campaign of two years later.[120] It cannot now be said with certainty whether he had previously gone to Wales. Nicholas de Carru, who was in the retinue of Aymer de Valence at Falkirk, spent a large part of his military career in Ireland away from the purview of the king's paymasters.[121] Consequently, his military record contains larger gaps than most. The figures presented in table 3.1 are, therefore, biased towards more recent military activity and service given for Crown pay. Nevertheless, the data as presented do point towards some general trends. Although at least twenty-three knights (16 per cent of the total in the sample) had fought in the Welsh wars of 1277 to 1287 or earlier, most of the knights (117, or 84 per cent) appear to have taken up the sword during the years of crisis between 1294 and 1298. This was the time when military commitments placed the greatest strain on the Crown's resources: the year 1294–5 witnessed the highest royal expenditure of the reign and some of the highest levels of taxation.[122] The figures given above add weight to the general impression that the outbreak of war with France in 1294, and with Scotland two years later, placed unprecedented demands on the services of the gentry.

Table 3.1 gives some idea as to when the knights at Falkirk first took up arms, but it does not reveal the full extent to which they had participated in Edward I's campaigns prior to 1298. This information is presented in table 3.2.

Table 3.2: Previous military service of the 'lesser' knights at Falkirk

	1270	1277	1282	1287	1294	1295	1296	1297	1298
Holy Land	2	–	–	–	–	–	–	–	–
Wales	–	7	17	5	38*	–	–	–	–
Gascony	–	–	–	–	18	7	1	6	–
Flanders	–	–	–	–	–	–	–	68	–
Scotland	–	–	–	–	–	–	34	8	140
Total	2	7	17	5	56	7**	35	82	140

* Includes those who served in Wales in both 1294 and 1295
** Not including those continuing their service from Wales in the previous year

A substantial minority of the knights on the Falkirk campaign fall into the veteran category. At least two knights, William Wyther and William de Detling, had journeyed to the Holy Land with the Lord Edward and his brother Edmund at the beginning of the 1270s.[123] Detling was proffered as a knight in the Welsh war of 1277 before campaigning in France; and he appears to have served for

120 *Parl. Writs*, i, p. 265; E 101/5/23, m. 2.
121 *Siege of Caerlaverock*, p. 7.
122 *Book of Prests of the King's Wardrobe for 1294–5*, ed. E.B. Fryde (Oxford, 1962), p. lii; W.M. Ormrod, 'The Domestic Response to the Hundred Years War', *Arms, Armies and Fortifications in the Hundred Years War*, ed. A. Curry and M. Hughes (Woodbridge, 1994), pp. 88, 90–1 (figures 5.2 and 5.3).
123 Lloyd, *English Society and the Crusade*, appendix 4.

the final time in Scotland in 1301, three years before his death.[124] Thomas de Eyville was another who registered his service at the feudal muster in 1277, as was Thomas de Berkeley senior, who had fought, as a teenager, during the civil war of 1264–5.[125] Some men in the veteran category had begun their military careers as *servientes* during the first two Welsh wars. William de Wygebere, who was with Robert Fitz Payn at Falkirk, had registered his service as a sergeant in 1277.[126] Stephen de la More, John de Bracebridge and Robert de Bavent were probably all very young men when they fought as *servientes* five years later in the great war of 1282–3.[127] But a few of the other old hands at Falkirk who had served in these earlier wars had already been fairly established figures during the 1270s and 1280s. This is borne out by their appearance on early rolls of arms. Ralph le Bygod, Humphrey de Beauchamp and Robert Fitz Nigel each took out letters of protection for service in Wales in 1282–3.[128] Detling and Fitz Nigel are named on the Heralds' roll of *c.* 1279, and Bygod appears on Charles' roll of *c.* 1285.[129] Such men as these formed the backbone of Edward I's expeditionary forces throughout the 1280s and 1290s. Indeed, they probably led the charge against the Scots at Falkirk.

Despite the presence of such veterans in Edward I's army, tables 3.1 and 3.2 suggest that the majority of the knights at Falkirk were relative novices in war. By 1298 several of these knights had been girded with the belt of knighthood for no more than a year or two. We know this because the extant horse inventories and wardrobe books, concerned as they were with practical matters of pay,[130] indicate the days on which soldiers were knighted. One relative newcomer to the chivalric order was Waleran de Rocheford. He had been knighted in Scotland on 25 March 1296 while serving in the retinue of John de Engayne, the

---

124 1277 (*Parl. Writs*, i, p. 207); 1294 (*Rôles Gascons*, iii, p. 179); 1298 (*Scotland in 1298*, p. 194); 1301 (E 101/9/24, m. 1d).

125 Eyville served in 1277 (*Parl. Writs*, i, p. 197), 1282 (C 67/8, m. 5), 1297 (C 67/12, m. 3d) and for the final time, it seems, in 1298 (*Scotland in 1298*, p. 211). In addition to his service during the Barons' War (*Complete Peerage*, ii, pp. 127–8), Berkeley had fought in 1277, 1282 (for his service in both years, see above, p. 66, n. 233), 1294–5 (C 67/10, m. 4) and 1297 (E 101/6/28, m. 2i).

126 He was in Wales in 1277 (*Parl. Writs*, i, p. 206), 1282 (C 47/2/4, m. 8) and 1294 (C 67/10, m. 7).

127 De la More was in Wales in 1282 (*Parl. Writs*, i, p. 234) and 1295 (C 67/10, m. 3). He was in Flanders in 1297 (E 101/6/37, m. 1ii). Bracebridge served in 1282 (C 47/2/7, m. 2), 1295 (C 67/10, m. 5d; *Rôles Gascons*, iii, p. 298) and 1297 (C 67/12, m. 2). Finally, Bavent fought in Wales 1282 (E 101/4/1, m. 9) and 1294 (*Book of Prests*, p. 51), and he served as a knight in Scotland in 1296 (E 101/5/23, m. 3). There were two men, a father and his son, named John de Bracebridge. The sergeant in 1282 was the junior man of that name, as the father had been a knight by 1273. See M. Jones, 'An Indenture between Robert, Lord Mohaut, and Sir John de Bracebridge for Life Service in Peace and War, 1310', *Journal of the Society of Archivists*, iv (1972), p. 387; and *CCR, 1272–79*, p. 41.

128 Bygod (C 67/8, m. 7); Beauchamp (C 67/8, m. 4d); Fitz Nigel (C 67/8, m. 4).

129 *Rolls of Arms, Edward I*, i, pp. 139, 294.

130 Knights received 2 shillings per day, whereas sergeants received only 1 shilling. This means that changes in status, within the retinue, had a direct effect on the payments made to each lord. Clerks recorded the reasons for such modifications in the wardrobe books.

man whom he again followed north of the border two years later.[131] The wardrobe book for the twenty-fifth year of Edward I's reign contains a number of entries relating to knightings carried out in Flanders. These were conducted on 1 November 1297, probably as part of a mass knighting ceremony. Among the men who were knighted on that day and who also served in Scotland a few months later were: Adam de la Forde; William de Chabenore; Philip de Welles; Philip Paynel; Simon le Chamberleyn; Simon de Asshton; Nicholas Pointz; and Ralph de Seccheville.[132] Two other knights in the retinues at Falkirk – Bartholomew de Somerton and John de Vaux – served as sergeants in Flanders and may, therefore, have been two of the young men who were knighted (according to Guisborough) at the beginning of the Falkirk campaign.[133] As one would expect, many of these new *milites* were among the forty-six men, from the overall sample of 140, who seem to have begun their military careers in 1296 or 1297 (see table 3.1). However, a few of the knights who appear to have joined the king's armies for the first time in 1297 or 1298, like John de Blakeford and Robert Barry, had been in possession of their lands for many years. It may be that they had previously served without Crown pay and thereby avoided the attention of the wardrobe clerks; but it is likely, given that the Falkirk host was the largest of the reign, that many established knights were forced from their country idylls for the first time in 1298.

For most up-and-coming knights, as well as for some of the veterans who were not yet ready to hang up their swords, the Falkirk campaign marked only the beginning of many more years of military service in Scotland. An attempt has been made to summarise this post-Falkirk activity in table 3.3, which indicates whether the service was given independently, in the retinue of another man or as a retinue leader.

Table 3.3: Service given by the Falkirk knights in Scotland (1298–1314)

	1298	1300	1301	1302	1303	1306	1307	1309	1310	1314
Independent	4	19	7	–	7	12	2	1	2	5
Retainer	136	51	38	1	42	27	10	3	15	13
Retinue leader	–	5	15	3	18	9	9	1	1	4
Total	140	75	60	4	67	48	21	5	18	22

Many of the knights in Edward I's army embarked on their military careers, as far as we can tell, only three or four years before 1298. However, it was precisely these individuals, for the most part, who formed the core of the mounted forces raised for the Scottish expeditions that followed. That is not to say that the veterans of the Welsh wars all died or stopped fighting within a few years of Falkirk, for a few – such as Robert de Bures, Henry de Glastingbury,

[131] E 101/5/23, m. 1i; *Scotland in 1298*, p. 190.
[132] BL, Additional MS 7965, fols 64v, 68r, 69r, 78r.
[133] E 101/6/37, mm. 1i, 2i; *Guisborough*, p. 325.

Edmund Foliot and Stephen de la More[134] – gave repeated service in Scotland. It is merely to observe that the long-term future lay with those soldiers, like the men who were knighted in 1296 or 1297, whose military careers coincided with the onset of the Scottish wars. Table 3.3 shows that continuity of service beyond 1298 was very high; and we should remember that these are minimum figures, that some of the later armies, such as those of 1306 and 1307, were relatively small, and that source survival for several campaigns, particularly that of 1314, is poor. Among the knights whose careers seem to have begun at Falkirk, but who featured prominently in the campaigns that followed, was the Hampshire knight John de Scures. He served in 1300, 1301, 1303, 1306 and 1314.[135] Scures was one of the twenty-one knights in our sample who later had letters of protection enrolled for the Bannockburn campaign, thereby appearing to have taken part in the two great battles of the era.[136] A few of the youngest knights at Falkirk, like Robert de Haustede junior and Nicholas de Meynill junior,[137] continued to serve beyond Bannockburn into the later stages of the reign of Edward II. Their records were surpassed, however, by that of Robert Fitz Nigel, a veteran of the war of 1282 who was still active thirty-seven years later when he served at the siege of Berwick.[138]

Although men like Fitz Nigel were evidently very active campaigners, not all men-at-arms possessed the same appetite for the king's wars. There were some who took up arms far more frequently, and over a longer period of time, than others. Some indication as to the varying commitment to military service among the knights in our sample is given in table 3.4.

---

[134] Bures appears in the records for military service for the final time in 1307: C 67/16, m. 3. Glastingbury, Foliot and de la More, who each (like Bures) seem to have begun their military careers in 1282–3, can still be traced serving in the armies of 1306, 1307 and 1310 respectively: E 101/13/7, m. 1; E 101/612/21, m. 1; C 71/4 m. 10.

[135] 1300 (*Liber Quotidianus*, pp. 202–3); 1301 (BL, Additional MS 7966a, fol. 71v); 1303 (E 101/612/11, m. 5); 1306 (C 67/16, m. 9); 1314 (C 71/6, m. 3).

[136] Those present in 1314 included: Ingelram de Berenger (C 71/6, m. 3); John de Scures (C 71/6, m. 3); Maurice le Brun (C 71/6, m. 4); Walter de Beauchamp junior (C 71/6, m. 4); Simon le Chamberleyn (C 71/6, m. 1); Henry de Segrave (C 71/6, m. 3); Walter Haket (C 71/6, m. 5).

[137] Haustede served in 1300 (E 101/8/23, m. 1), 1301 (BL, Additional MS 7966a fol. 87r), 1303 (BL, Additional MS 8835, fol. 58v), 1314 (C 71/6, m. 3), 1319 (C 71/10, m. 4) and 1322 (BL, Stowe MS 553, fol. 60r). Meynill gave military service in 1300 (C 67/14, m. 12), 1301 (C 67/14, m. 2), 1303 (E 101/612/10, m. 1), 1314 (C 71/6, m. 1) and 1319 (C 71/10, m. 9).

[138] For his service in 1319, see C 71/10, m. 5.

Table 3.4: Number of campaigns fought by the Falkirk knights (1270–1314)[139]

Hosts served in	Number of knights	% of total	Total number of hosts
1	19	13.6	19
2	17	12.1	34
3	15	10.7	45
4	15	10.7	60
5	17	12.1	85
6	18	12.9	108
7	15	10.7	105
8	9	6.4	72
9	9	6.4	81
10	5	3.6	50
11	0	0	0
12	1	0.7	12
Total	140		671
(Mean average)			(4.79 hosts per knight)

Nineteen of these 140 knights seem to have given military service on no other occasion. Included among this group of men were ten foreigners who had been drawn from Edward's territories in the southwest of France.[140] This means that the vast majority of the English knights in the army of 1298 served on at least one further campaign. Indeed, thirty-nine knights served on seven occasions or more. This group included: Maurice le Brun, who took up arms eight times between 1296 and 1314;[141] Stephen de la More and Thomas de Coudray, who can each be located in nine different hosts;[142] and Henry de Segrave, who wielded the sword a further nine times following his debut alongside his father, Nicholas, in Wales in 1295.[143] These figures are very impressive given that we are only considering service given up to 1314. Yet the prize for the most bellicose record would be taken by John de Crumwell. He can be traced in twelve

---

[139] Statistically speaking, the average of 4.79, with a standard deviation of 2.68, shows that there is not much variance around the mean in this sample of 140 knights' service records. Therefore, the average of just under five campaigns per knight (a minimum based on the extant evidence) would be statistically representative for this particular sample. I would like to thank Dr Adrian Bell of the University of Reading for his advice on this table.

[140] The origins of some of these knights, such as Ebles de Lignan, have been traced (for a different purpose) by Malcolm Vale in 'The Gascon Nobility and the Anglo-French War 1294–98', *War and Government in the Middle Ages: Essays in Honour of J.O. Prestwich*, ed. J. Gillingham and J.C. Holt (Woodbridge, 1984), pp. 135–6.

[141] 1296 ('Plea roll, 1296', no. 127); 1298 (*Scotland in 1298*, p. 176); 1300 (C 47/2/13, m. 8), 1301 (C 67/14, m. 4), 1303 (E 101/612/11, m. 2), 1306 (C 67/16, m. 10), 1307 (*CDS*, v, p. 446), 1314 (C 71/6, m. 4).

[142] De la More: before 1298 (see above, p. 86, n. 127), 1298 (*Scotland in 1298*, p. 183); 1300 (E 101/8/23, m. 2); 1301 (E 101/9/24, m. 2); 1303 (E 101/612/8, m. 1d); 1307 (E 101/14/15, m. 9); 1310 (C 71/4, m. 10). Coudray: see above, p. 24, n. 108.

[143] 1294 (C 67/10, m. 6); 1296 (E 101/5/23, m. 3); 1297 (C 67/12, m. 9); 1298 (*Scotland in 1298*, p. 187); 1301 (C 67/14, m. 6); 1303 (C 67/15, m. 15); 1306 (C 67/16, m. 6); 1307 (*CDS*, v, p. 445); 1311 (C 71/4, m. 6); 1314 (C 71/6, m. 3).

armies between 1294, when he took out a letter of protection for service in Wales, and 1314.[144] The careers of these knights seem to test the theory that a professional soldiery did not emerge until a later era in English history, but warriors like Segrave and Crumwell were quite exceptional in their apparent lust for war. Table 3.4 shows that it was more usual for knights to participate in royal campaigns on between four and seven occasions. Indeed the mean average, from the extant evidence, is 4.79 campaigns per knight. This supports Maurice Keen's observation that 'a very common pattern of service ... is one that lies somewhere between the professional and the occasional'.[145] Representative of this tendency were the careers of Adam de la Forde, who took part in four expeditions between 1297 and 1301, and John de Caltoft, who appears in the extant records the same number of times between 1294 and 1306.[146]

Such varied commitment to military service produced careers that differed markedly in length. Given that landholders were obliged to possess arms between the ages of fifteen and sixty, it is not surprising to find that the martial activities of some of the knights at Falkirk spanned many years. Although not one of these knights was able to match the extensive experience later acquired by John Sully and Thomas de Rokeby, who claimed during the Scrope-Grosvenor dispute of 1385 to have served for eighty and sixty years respectively,[147] quite a few can be shown to have been militarily active for at least two or three decades. Nine knights (including John de Bracebridge, Thomas de Berkeley junior, William de Detling, John ap Adam and Robert Fitz Nigel) bore arms for over thirty years,[148] while a further twenty-nine engaged in military service for two decades or more. When we bear in mind that the records for military service are incomplete, it seems likely that most militarily active knights under Edward I and Edward II bore arms for at least fifteen years, even if there were a substantial minority who took part in only one or two campaigns during their lives. This is in accordance with the depositions given at the Court of Chivalry case between Thomas, Lord Morley and John, Lord Lovel during the reign of

---

[144] For his service on five expeditions between 1294 and 1301, see above, p. 29, nn. 143, 146 and p. 57, n. 177. He also fought in 1303 (E 101/612/7, m. 3), 1306 (E 101/612/15, m. 1), 1307 (E 101/14/15, m. 9), 1308 (*CDS*, v, p. 446), 1309 (*CDS*, v, p. 448), 1310 (BL, Cotton Nero C VIII, fol. 2r) and 1314 (C 71/6, m. 5).

[145] M. Keen, *Origins of the English Gentleman: Heraldry, Chivalry and Gentility in Medieval England, c. 1300–c. 1500* (Stroud, 2002), p. 62.

[146] Forde: 1297 (BL, Additional MS 7965, fol. 64v); 1298 (*Scotland in 1298*, p. 164); 1300 (E 101/8/23, m. 5); 1301 (E 101/9/23, m. 1). Caltoft: 1294 (C 67/10, m. 4); 1298 (*Scotland in 1298*, p. 172); 1303 (E 101/612/11, m. 2); 1306 (C 67/16, m. 11).

[147] *The Controversy between Sir Richard Scrope and Sir Robert Grosvenor in the Court of Chivalry, AD MCCCLXXXV–MCCCXC*, ed. N.H. Nicolas, 2 vols (London, 1832), i, pp. 74, 116. On the tendency, during the Middle Ages, of old people to exaggerate their age and experience, see S. Shahar, *Growing Old in the Middle Ages: 'Winter Clothes Us in Shadow and Pain'* (London, 1997), p. 30.

[148] The start and end dates for the men mentioned in the text were: Bracebridge 1282–1315 (C 47/2/7, m. 2; E 101/15/6, m. 2); Berkeley junior 1294–1335 (C 67/10, m. 7; C 71/15, m. 26); Detling 1270 (and before that the Barons' War)-1301 (Lloyd, *English Society and the Crusade*, appendix 4; E 101/9/24, m. 1d); ap Adam 1277–1307 (*CPR, 1272–81*, p. 217; *CDS*, v, p. 446); Fitz Nigel 1282–1319 (C 67/8, m. 4; C 71/10, m. 5).

Richard II, which show that careers spanning thirty or forty years were at that stage not uncommon.[149] From the evidence presented here, it would seem that the knights who served in English armies during the reigns of Edward I and Edward II were no less martially inclined than their more celebrated descendants: the men who lived later in the fourteenth century during the period of sustained conflict with France.

Sergeants

Throughout the late thirteenth and early fourteenth centuries, then, knights continued to perform an important military role. What a study of the knights at Falkirk does not reveal is that this was also a time when the proportional contribution of these elite soldiers to the English war effort was gradually decreasing. This shift was due not to any decline in the number of knights performing military service, for quite the reverse was true. Rather it was reflective of the heightened demands being placed on the lesser tenants and rear-vassals of the shires and localities, requirements that saw the 'squire', or 'sergeant', gradually replace the knight as the mainstay of the Crown's forces. Some indication of the extent of this shift is given by comparing the armies raised by Henry III with those of his son. For example, in 1223 at least 387 knights and 145 sergeants appeared at the feudal muster to oppose Llywelyn the Great; and for the Deganwy campaign twenty-two years later, there were around 354 knights as against 306 mounted soldiers of inferior status.[150] Under Edward I, by contrast, mounted forces were weighted far more heavily towards soldiers who had not received knighthood. Figures for the Flanders campaign of 1297–8 reveal that the army of that year, at its peak, contained 140 knights and bannerets compared to 755 sergeants.[151] At Falkirk, the men described on the extant horse inventories as *valletti* represented approximately 74 per cent of the total number of men-at-arms in receipt of Crown pay.

The Crown's increased dependence on its sub-knightly combatants explains, in part, why the knightly class in its widest sense has attracted so much attention among historians. A great deal has been written about the shifting boundaries between knights and those below them in the social hierarchy. Much ink has also been spilled on the extent to which, over time, such dividing lines became more or less difficult to cross.[152] Social and economic theories of growth and crisis have naturally contributed much to this debate.[153] Even the problem of

---

149 Ayton, 'Knights, Esquires and Military Service', p. 88.
150 Walker, 'Anglo-Welsh Wars', pp. 182, 510.
151 Lewis, 'The English Forces in Flanders', pp. 312–13.
152 See, for example, Coss, 'Knights, Esquires and the Origins of Social Gradation', *passim*; M. Bennett, 'The Status of the Squire: The Northern Evidence', *The Ideals and Practice of Medieval Knighthood I*, ed. C. Harper-Bill and R. Harvey (Woodbridge, 1986), pp. 1–11; J. Scammell, 'The Formation of the English Social Structure: Freedom, Knights, and Gentry, 1066–1300', *Speculum*, lxviii (1993), p. 613. For some examples of terms used to denote men of sub-knightly status in the twelfth century, see D. Crouch, *The Birth of Nobility: Constructing Aristocracy in England and France 900–1300* (Harlow, 2005), pp. 249–50.
153 P. Coss, 'Sir Geoffrey de Langley and the Crisis of the Knightly Class in Thirteenth-Century England', *Past and Present*, lxviii (1975), pp. 26–7; D.A. Carpenter, 'Was there a

definition has proved difficult to resolve: for David Crouch at least, 'to talk of squires as *potential*, rather than actual, aristocrats would be safest before 1300'.[154] Although that may be the case, the consensus is that the status of the squire was rising, inexorably so, and that the thirteenth and fourteenth centuries lay at the heart of this process. Where disagreement *has* arisen is between, on the one hand, historians who have traced the new-found confidence of the squires to their control over lands in the shires and localities, and on the other, those to whom the military nexus seems to have been more pertinent. For Peter Coss, 'territoriality is crucial to the understanding of the gentry as a social formation'.[155] Maurice Keen has argued, however, that the squires came of age as a social group due to their frequent and lengthy campaigning, this experience of military service encouraging them, later in the fourteenth century, to aspire to their own coats of arms.[156]

Both points of view find support in late medieval sources. Nevertheless, the gradual emergence of 'esquire' as a mark of high social status should not obscure the fact that the mounted soldiers of sub-knightly status from the reign of Edward I were a heterogeneous group. In fact the focus on the 'esquire' or 'squire' is misleading, for 'there was no stratification of landed society below the rank of knight in 1300'.[157] For this reason it is more accurate to talk of 'sergeants' rather than 'esquires' when discussing the lesser men-at-arms who served in early Edwardian armies. These men were defined less by a unity of status and wealth than by a process whereby, as non-knights, they came to share a common identity as mounted soldiers of the secondary order. The sergeants of the reigns of Edward I and Edward II were drawn from a wide variety of backgrounds. Some were 'the descendants of landed families who could count knights in their ancestry', but others were 'of non genteel, urban or even peasant origins'.[158] Thus, the requirements of warfare bound together large numbers of men who otherwise would have had very little in common. Indeed, it was their position as mounted combatants that distinguished the lesser sergeants from the massed ranks of peasant footsoldiers and that, for military purposes at least, brought them into contact with the mores of the social elite. This was not an equal relationship: at the feudal muster the service of two sergeants was still regarded as equivalent to that of one knight.[159] Nevertheless, Edward I's heavy recruitment of lesser men-at-arms appears to have led to a greater appreciation of their military role. It is perhaps significant that by the time of the Weardale campaign of 1327, Jean le Bel was seeing fit to place 'chevaliers et escuiers' at

---

Crisis of the Knightly Class in the Thirteenth Century? The Oxfordshire Evidence', *EHR*, xcv (1980), pp. 748–52.

[154] Crouch, *Image of Aristocracy*, p. 171.

[155] Coss, *Origins of the English Gentry*, p. 9.

[156] Keen, *Origins of the English Gentleman*, p. 81.

[157] Saul, *Knights and Esquires*, p. 16.

[158] Keen, *Origins of the English Gentleman*, p. 73.

[159] As shown by the preparations made by the abbot of Ramsey for his 'feudal' contingent, to serve in Gascony, in 1294: *Select Pleas in Manorial and other Seignorial Courts Volume One: Reigns of Henry III and Edward I*, ed. F.W. Maitland, Selden Society, ii (1888), p. 80.

the heart of Edward III's army, contrasting them with other mounted soldiers serving 'on small hackneys' (*sur petites hageneez*).[160]

However great may have been the social gulf separating the sergeants of the reign of Edward I from the esquires of the reign of Edward III, from a military perspective the two groups had a good deal in common. Many of the sergeants who took part in the Falkirk campaign were just as committed to the calling of arms as their more celebrated scions during the Hundred Years War. One of the sergeants who served at Falkirk was William de Walhope. In a petition to the Crown, he later claimed to have witnessed the fall of Berwick in 1296, the battle of Dunbar which followed and the battle of Falkirk (*la baille de la Vere Chapele*) two years later.[161] Walhope's name does not appear on the extant horse inventories for the Falkirk campaign. It therefore seems likely that he (like so many others) served in the army without Crown pay.[162] A name that *does* appear on one of the horse inventories is that of Alan de Walingford. Later, a man of that name wrote to Edward II stating that he had served the king and his father for 'thirty years and more in Wales, Gascony and Scotland' (*trente aunz et plus en totes vos guerres de Gales, Gasconie e Escoce*).[163] The most extraordinary account to have come down to us, however, is that relating to a certain John de Thirlewall. This man's son claimed, in the 1380s, that his father had witnessed the knighting of Richard de Scrope's grandfather during the Falkirk campaign. He also claimed that his father had been 145 years old at the time of his death, making him the oldest esquire in the north of England.[164] The veracity of much of this story has rightly been questioned. Nevertheless, two men named John de Thirlewall did have their horses appraised in the English army in 1298.[165] The deposition, fantastical as it was, did have some grounding in truth.[166]

As already noted, to analyse the sergeants at Falkirk as if they constituted a single body of men would be to run the risk of conflating two very different groups. J.E. Morris noted this dichotomy many years ago when he commented on the presence amid the sergeants of this period of 'both the young aspir-

---

160 *Chronique de Jean le Bel*, i, p. 53. The hackney was 'a horse for the march rather than the battlefield': Ayton, *Knights and Warhorses*, p. 57.

161 *CDS*, ii, no. 1969.

162 A sergeant of that name had served in Scotland earlier in 1298 (E 101/6/35, fol. 11v) and was drawn, as a man-at-arms, from the county levy in Northumberland in 1301: BL, Additional MS 7966a, fol. 95r; E 101/9/15.

163 SC 8/152, no. 7563. Walingford served in the armies of 1298 (*Scotland in 1298*, p. 210) and 1301 (BL, Additional MS 7966a, fol. 96r) before staying in the Edinburgh garrison between 1302 and 1304 (E 101/10/5, m. 9; E 101/12/11; E 101/12/20). Following the Falkirk campaign he had entered the garrison at Berwick: E 101/7/1, m. 9.

164 *Scrope-Grosvenor Controversy*, i, pp. 181–3.

165 *Scotland in 1298*, pp. 195, 210.

166 For additional information on a John de Thirlewall living during the reign of Edward I, see A. Rushworth and R. Carlton, *Thirlwall Castle: History of a Northumberland Border Stronghold*, Northumberland National Park Documentary Survey (Northumberland National Park Authority, 2001), p. 17.

ants to knighthood and the plebeian troopers who never rose higher'.[167] Some of the former can be detected among the sergeants who served in Edward I's mounted force at Falkirk. Economically, the elite of the *valletti* in 1298 were the twenty- and forty-librate holders, who were summoned from the counties for royal campaigns. Such men as these could hold their own against the lesser knights in terms of annual income. William de Launceleyn, summoned from Northamptonshire as a twenty-pounder in 1297,[168] and Benedict de Blakenham, also recruited from the counties for the Flanders expedition,[169] would certainly have been among the more affluent sergeants to venture north of the border in 1298. Giles de Argentein, one of the most acclaimed knights of the early four-teenth century, served as a *vallettus* at Falkirk;[170] but his high social standing is demonstrated by his appearance on Collins' roll of *c.* 1296.[171] Interestingly, Argentein does not appear as a knight in the records for military service until five years later, in 1301.[172] It was highly unusual in the reign of Edward I for a man of sub-knightly status to be named on a roll of arms. Argentein's appearance on Collins' roll probably owed more to the fact that he came from a knightly family than to anything that he might have achieved while serving among the rank and file.

As we have seen, some of the knights who served in the retinues at Falkirk appear to have been knighted quite early in their military careers. Yet this should not lead us to conclude that those sergeants prosperous enough to aspire to knighthood, or who came from knightly families, were always quickly promoted to that honour. On the contrary, quite a few of the sergeants at Falkirk served for several years among the sub-knightly ranks before being accepted into the exclusive club of the chivalrous elite. William Botetourt fought as a sergeant for at least six years, between 1297 and 1302, before appearing as a knight at the siege of Stirling castle in 1304.[173] Thomas de Monteny, a member of another prominent knightly family, served as a *vallettus* on the Scottish expedition of 1296.[174] He continued to possess that status during the expeditions of 1300, 1303 and 1306 before finally gaining promotion at some point before 1311, when he gave service as a knight in the retinue of Robert de Clifford.[175] A lack of financial resources may have placed limits on the social aspirations of most mounted combatants of sub-knightly status. One way around this problem was

[167] J.E. Morris, 'Cumberland and Westmorland Military Levies in the Time of Edward I and Edward II', *Transactions of the Cumberland and Westmorland Antiquarian and Archaeological Society*, new ser., iii (1903), p. 310.

[168] *Parl. Writs*, i, p. 289; *Scotland in 1298*, p. 191.

[169] *Parl. Writs*, i, p. 290; *Scotland in 1298*, p. 175.

[170] *Scotland in 1298*, p. 189.

[171] *Rolls of Arms, Edward I*, ii, p. 16.

[172] E 101/9/23, m. 1.

[173] 1297 (E 101/6/37, m. 1i), 1298 (*Scotland in 1298*, p. 166), 1300 (E 101/8/23, m. 3), 1302 (E 101/612/12, m. 6), and 1304 (*Documents and Records of Scotland*, p. 272).

[174] E 101/5/23, m. 1i.

[175] 1297 (E 101/6/30, m. 1iv); 1298 (*Scotland in 1298*, p. 197); 1300 (*Liber Quotidianus*, p. 176); 1303 (E 101/612/11, m. 2); 1306 (E 101/612/15, m. 1); 1311 (BL, Cotton Nero C VIII, fol. 20r).

to find service in the royal household. Ralph de Kerdiff's military career appears to have begun when he fought as a *vallettus* at Falkirk in 1298. He is listed on the *forinsec* horse inventory for that year as Raulinus de Kerdife.[176] Thirteen years later, on the Scottish campaign of Edward II, he was receiving pay as a household sergeant until, on 23 June 1311, he was knighted. On the following day he began to receive fees and robes as a *miles simplex de hospicio Regis*.[177] Had it not been for his household connections, Kerdiff may never have attained the status of knight.

In effect, sergeants such as William Botetourt and Thomas de Monteny must have known, or least expected, that they would one day become knights. By contrast, mounted soldiers at the other end of the sub-knightly spectrum were very much the finished product. They had no reason to hope to make further progress, either socially or militarily. Some of these men, 'squires who were descended from squires rather than knights' as Helen Nicholson has put it,[178] could lay claim to a degree of gentility; but, there were also others, 'members of modestly endowed families "hovering perilously close to the level of the richer peasantry"', who were not aristocratic by even the most admissive standards.[179] These were possibly the kind of men that the author of the *Anonimalle Chronicle* had in mind when he wrote of the 'fraunkleyns' who had been captured by Edward II's supporters during the baronial uprising of 1322.[180] Nigel Saul has depicted such individuals as the sub-gentle parvenus of the later fourteenth century.[181] There were certainly a large number of less wealthy sergeants among the rank and file in Edward I's mounted force in 1298; yet it is far from easy to distinguish between those who had their feet on the lowest rungs of the gentle ladder and those who were rummaging around at its base for scraps. The most obvious place to look for evidence of the latter is among the body of soldiers who turned up for the Falkirk campaign with mounts of poor quality. Around 23 per cent of the 700 or so soldiers listed on the horse inventories as *valletti* had horses valued at 100 shillings or less. Such men as these, including William Howel, whose horse was appraised at just 60 shillings,[182] probably relied on military service as their main source of income. Nevertheless, we must be cautious about generalising from evidence such as this. Even members of prominent knightly families might sometimes serve on mounts of modest quality.[183]

More profitable subjects of enquiry are the middling sergeants who took part in the Falkirk campaign: those owners of fractional fees and landholders in small

---

176 *Scotland in 1298*, p. 209.
177 Bodleian Library, Tanner MS 197, fols 8v, 26v, 33r.
178 Nicholson, *Medieval Warfare*, p. 56.
179 Ayton, *Knights and Warhorses*, p. 5, quoting C. Carpenter, *Locality and Polity. A Study of Warwickshire Landed Society, 1401–1499* (Cambridge, 1992), p. 38.
180 *The Anonimalle Chronicle 1307–1334, From Brotherton Collection MS 29*, ed. W.R. Childs and J. Taylor, The Yorkshire Archaeological Society Record Ser., cxlvii (1991), p. 110.
181 N. Saul, 'The Social Status of Chaucer's Franklin: A Reconsideration', *Medium Aevum*, lii (1983), p. 22.
182 *Scotland in 1298*, p. 170.
183 Geoffrey de Bracebridge, for example, had a horse valued at just 5 marks: *ibid.*, p. 209.

vills who constituted the emerging squirearchy in its truest sense. The names of around a third of the sergeants who served at Falkirk can be located in the various landholding enquiries carried out between 1284–5 and 1316.[184] Soldiers such as John de Rothewell, who held the third part of a fee in Orby, Lincolnshire, in 1303,[185] and John de Cary, a landowner of modest means in Dorset during the reign of Edward II,[186] seem to have been representative of the kind of men who formed the bulk of the *valletti* in Edward I's army in 1298. Although neither wealthy nor perhaps ambitious enough to take up the status of knight or find service in the royal household, many of these middling landholders served quite happily for many years as sergeants. Ralph de Worteley was probably one of the oldest of these men in the army at Falkirk. An individual of that name had had his horse appraised as a lesser man-at-arms during the second Welsh war (1282–3); and he appears to have served for the final time, still as a *vallettus*, on the campaign of 1300.[187] Reconstructing military careers inevitably becomes more difficult as one goes further down the military hierarchy; but one would expect there to have been a large number of veterans of the Welsh wars, like Worteley, among the sergeants who served at Falkirk. The Henry de Curzon who rode to Scotland in 1298 was perhaps the man of that name who had earlier gone to war, in the retinue of Roger de Mortimer, in 1282.[188] Roger de Bray, with Thomas of Lancaster at Falkirk, appears previously to have served in Wales in 1277 and 1294–5.[189] Looking forward to later campaigns, William le Skirmissour, who seems to have taken up arms during the mid-1290s, was still serving as a sub-knightly man-at-arms in Scotland in 1314.[190] Furthermore, of the *valletti* who served under Aymer de Valence in 1298, three – William Symeon, John de Stodley and John de Gacelyn – continued to be summoned to war as sub-knightly men-at-arms (*armigeri*) into the 1320s.[191] There was therefore no guarantee that repeated and lengthy service would lead to social elevation.

Over 100 of the mounted soldiers listed on the extant horse inventories for 1298 are described as having come from particular counties. These men, of whom the majority did not serve within the constituent retinues, seem to have been raised by shire levies conducted by sheriffs and other Crown officials. We find, for example, a *Johannes Sampson de comitatu Eboracum* and a *Nicholaus de Leeke de comitatu Notingham*.[192] Similar county arrays were carried out for other campaigns, including those of 1297, 1300 and 1301. Marginal comments on the horse inventories show that many of these men were sent to serve in the

---

[184] *Feudal Aids, passim.*

[185] *Ibid.*, iii, p. 161.

[186] *Ibid.*, ii, p. 39. See also *The Dorset Lay Subsidy Roll of 1327*, ed. A.R. Rumble, Dorset Record Society, vi (1980), p. 91.

[187] Worteley served under William le Latimer in Wales in 1282: C 47/2/7, m. 4. He later fought in Gascony (*Rôles Gascons*, iii, p. 156) before heading north of the border in Edward I's armies of 1298 (*Scotland in 1298*, p. 178) and 1300 (E 101/8/23, m. 2).

[188] C 67/8, m. 4; *Scotland in 1298*, p. 189.

[189] *Parl. Writs*, i, p. 208; C 67/10, m. 4; *Scotland in 1298*, p. 181.

[190] C 67/10, m. 2; *Scotland in 1298*, p. 183; E 101/14/15, m. 5d.

[191] *Scotland in 1298*, p. 217; *Parl. Writs*, II, ii, p. 588.

[192] *Scotland in 1298*, p. 206.

garrisons of Berwick and Roxburgh. As such, it is unlikely that they took part in the battle of Falkirk. The remainder possibly served independently or alongside one another in small groups. Overall, these appear to have been individuals of quite humble status. Table 3.5 shows the number of men-at-arms who were raised in this way in each of the represented shires.

Table 3.5: County of origin of the men-at-arms recruited from the shires (1298)

County	Number of men
Berkshire	2
Buckinghamshire	1
Cheshire	3
Derbyshire	1
Essex	1
Hampshire	1
Herefordshire	3
Lancashire	2
Leicestershire	2
Lincolnshire	5
London	2
Middlesex	1
Norfolk	2
Northants.	7
Northumberland	9
Nottinghamshire	3
Oxfordshire	1
Shropshire	5
Somerset	2
Staffordshire	2
Suffolk	1
Warwickshire	1
Westmorland	6
Wiltshire	1
Worcestershire	1
Yorkshire	48
Total: 26 counties	113 men-at arms

Most of the men-at-arms raised by county levy in 1298 were northerners: 42 per cent came from Yorkshire alone. This contrasts with the origins of the men who served in the magnate retinues. Most of these, as we have seen, rode under retinue leaders from the Midlands and the southern counties. Comparison with other military sources suggests that nearly all of the 113 men raised from the counties were sergeants, the one exception being John de Boys of Lincolnshire.[193] A few of these sergeants, like Adam de Dokesford of Northumberland,[194] may have been reasonably wealthy individuals at a local level. Most, however, if not all, were figures of relatively little consequence socially. According to the

---

[193] *Ibid.*, p. 206.
[194] *Ibid.*, p. 214; *The Northumberland Lay Subsidy Roll of 1296*, ed. C.M. Fraser (Newcastle upon Tyne, 1968), p. 160.

feudal survey of 1303, Robert de Essington held three bovates of land (a bovate varied in extent between seven and thirty-two acres) in Nunburnholme in the East Riding of Yorkshire.[195] His fellow Yorkshireman Hugh de la Mare possessed four bovates in the North Riding vill of Yafforth;[196] and he was assessed at 4*s*. 4*d*. for a fifteenth on his moveable goods in the thirtieth year of Edward I's reign.[197] Such relatively lowly origins did not prevent many of these soldiers from taking part in the king's expeditions on a regular basis. Indeed, the prospect of the king's pay must have had a special allure for such men. John de Ixinynge of Essex later served in the retinue of Robert de Scales in Scotland in 1301.[198] In the same year, Nicholas Lenginneur of Cheshire joined the company of his fellow Cestrian, Hamo de Mascy.[199] Other men sent to Scotland in 1298 remained there once the army had returned to England and continued to receive pay in the garrisons. The *forinsec* horse inventory for the Falkirk campaign records that John de Hedlegh joined the garrison at Roxburgh.[200] He later entered the fort at Linlithgow, where he served under his fellow Northumbrian William de Felton.[201] Adam de Chetewynde served at Jedburgh for a few years from the autumn of 1298, having been apportioned to the garrison at Berwick or Roxburgh (the horse inventory does not make it clear which) that summer.[202] Both he and the constable at Jedburgh, Richard de Hastang, came from Staffordshire. Based on this admittedly far from comprehensive evidence, it would appear that the composition of the garrisons in Scotland was not random, and that men-at-arms were sometimes placed under constables with whom they were probably acquainted.

The vast majority of the *valletti* in Scotland in 1298 were serving not in the garrisons but in the retinues of the earls and bannerets. Thomas, earl of Lancaster's *comitiva* in that year included thirty-one men of sub-knightly status, excluding clerks.[203] Simon Walker has observed how, later in the fourteenth century, John of Gaunt, as duke of Lancaster, was able to recruit followers from twenty-two different counties where he exercised some seigneurial control.[204] This thorough system of recruitment was already in place, to some extent, under the earlier earls of Lancaster. Thomas of Lancaster's knightly retainers were drawn from several regions: the north Midlands; the south Midlands and East Anglia; Yorkshire; the far north; Lancashire; and the Welsh March.[205] Although

---

[195] *Scotland in 1298*, p. 211; *Feudal Aids*, vi, p. 147.

[196] *Scotland in 1298*, p. 214; *Feudal Aids*, vi, p. 100.

[197] *Yorkshire Lay Subsidy being a Fifteenth, collected 30 Edward I (1301)*, ed. W. Brown, The Yorkshire Archaeological Society Record Ser., xxi (1897), p. 11.

[198] *Scotland in 1298*, p. 214; E 101/9/24, m. 2.

[199] *Scotland in 1298*, p. 211; E 101/9/23, m. 2.

[200] *Scotland in 1298*, p. 214.

[201] E 101/10/12, m. 2; E 101/12/38.

[202] *Scotland in 1298*, p. 215; E 101/7/7, m. 2d; E 101/8/7, m. 1d; E 101/9/9, fol. 4r; E 101/12/18, fol. 2v.

[203] *Scotland in 1298*, pp. 179–81.

[204] S. Walker, *The Lancastrian Affinity 1361–1399* (Oxford, 1990), p. 32.

[205] J.R. Maddicott, *Thomas of Lancaster 1307–1322: A Study in the Reign of Edward II* (Oxford, 1970), pp. 54–5.

the geographical origins of the sergeants with him at Falkirk are less easy to ascertain, there seems to have been a similar spread. By all appearances, Robert de Jorz and William de Basing later became fairly established figures in the north and east Midlands.[206] John de Kenilworth and Richard de Melbourne derived their surnames from important Lancastrian estates in Warwickshire and Derbyshire respectively. There was also a smattering of Yorkshiremen and Lancastrians, as one would expect. The most notable example of the latter was Robert de Holland, who later betrayed his lord in his hour of greatest need before the battle of Boroughbridge in 1322. In the years after 1298 Holland became, in effect, Lancaster's 'junior partner'.[207] The closeness of the relationship between these men made Holland's betrayal of his lord in 1322 all the more despicable in the eyes of his contemporaries.

Few men, if any below the king, could match Thomas of Lancaster's resources. Nevertheless, other regional magnates possessed widespread influence that enabled them to recruit sergeants from outside the main areas under their control. Robert de Clifford's retinue in 1298 contained a few *valletti* whose demesne lands lay far from the concentration of his own estates in the northwest.[208] If most sergeants with Clifford at Falkirk were Cumbrians and Westmorlanders such as Robert de Whiterugg, Thomas de Hauteclou and William de Boyville,[209] he could also call on the services of Gilbert and John de Ellesfeld, Thomas de Monteny, and Gilbert Mauduyt, men who had significant landed interests in other parts of the country.[210] The last-named was later hanged, in 1306, for his adherence to Robert Bruce.[211] Men like Robert de Holland and Thomas de Monteny occupied the uppermost strata of men-at-arms below the rank of knight; but the average sergeant serving in the retinues on the Falkirk campaign was a man of more modest wealth and status than those discussed so far. Nicholas de Audley's retinue included one or two prominent Shropshire lords such as William and Ralph le Botiller of Wem; but men like Richard de Cleobury and Simon de Madeley would be difficult to place were it not for toponymical evidence linking them to areas close to where Audley and the Botillers held their estates.[212] At the core of Hugh de Courtenay's retinue were three fellow Devonshire men, Robert Beaupel, Ralph Beaupel and John de Chevreston, figures of some standing locally but who had little influence outside their own county.[213] Surrounding this nucleus were more obscure individuals like Richard de Wastehose, Eustace de Eyville and Alan de Roseles. Creating

206 *Knights of Edward I*, ii, p. 274; *CIPM*, v, no. 566.
207 J.R. Maddicott, 'Thomas of Lancaster and Sir Robert Holland: A Study in Noble Patronage', *EHR*, lxxxvi (1971), p. 450.
208 For the names of the *valletti* who served with Clifford in 1298, see *Scotland in 1298*, pp. 196–8.
209 *CIPM*, iv, no. 264; *CIPM*, v, no. 533, p. 303; *CIPM*, vi, no. 238, pp. 143–4.
210 *Knights of Edward I*, i, 303–4, iii, pp. 129, 194.
211 *CPR, 1301–07*, p. 482.
212 *Scotland in 1298*, pp. 219–20.
213 *Ibid.*, p. 208; *Feudal Aids*, i, pp. 351, 359–62; *The Tax Roll for Devon 31 Edward I*, ed. T.M. Whale, *Transactions of the Devonshire Association for the Advancement of Science, Literature, and Art*, xxxi (1899), pp. 383, 389, 407–13; *The Devonshire Lay Subsidy of 1332*,

profiles of such men as these can be an impossible task, particularly when the extant landholding sources do not yield any information about them. The most that one can say is that they were probably younger sons on the lookout for adventure.

Given that the geographical origins and social standing of the sergeants on the Falkirk campaign were extremely varied, one may also expect to find a similar lack of uniformity in their military activities. Unfortunately, the evidence available for the military service of men of sub-knightly status is less complete than that for their knightly counterparts. This, combined with the prosopographical pitfalls of working with a group of men for whom landholding records and reliable reference guides are largely unavailable, means that the large-scale reconstruction carried out for the military service of the knights at Falkirk cannot be repeated for the *valletti*. Nevertheless, a closer examination of the military activities of the sergeants in one retinue, that of the banneret Hugh de Courtenay, may serve as a convenient indicator as to some of the more general trends arising from the evidence.

Table 3.6: Military service given by the *valletti* with Hugh de Courtenay in 1298

Name of *vallettus*	Years of military service to 1314
John de Chevreston	1298, 1303, 1306
Richard de Wastehose	1298, 1310
William de Sully	1296, 1298, 1303, 1307, 1310
Auger Joce	1298
Alan de Roseles	1298
Eustace de Eyville	1282, 1296, 1297, 1298, 1303, 1311
Robert Beaupel	1295, 1296, 1298, 1300, 1306, 1314
Ralph Beaupel	1295, 1298
Nicholas de Romesey	1298, 1299, 1300

Courtenay's retinue at Falkirk contained a mixture of regular campaigners, such as Eustace de Eyville and Robert Beaupel, occasional soldiers, exemplified by John de Chevreston, and men who do not appear in the service records at any point before or after 1298, like Alan de Roseles and Auger Joce.[214] Still, such are the gaps in the evidence for the military service of sergeants that all nine *valletti* in Courtenay's *comitiva* may have been regular campaigners. It is impossible to know for certain whether the Eustace de Eyville who served at Falkirk was the man of that name who had earlier fought in the second Welsh war. Yet it would

ed. A.M. Erskine, *Devon and Cornwall Record Society*, new ser., xiv (1969), pp. 6–8, 25–8, 55, 62, 76, 83, 122.
[214] Eyville: Wales in 1282 (C 67/8, m. 6d); Scotland in 1296 (E 101/5/23, m. 3); Flanders in 1297 (E 101/6/37, m. 6i); Scotland in 1298 (*Scotland in 1298*, p. 208); 1303 (C 67/15, m. 6); 1311 (C 71/4, m. 6). Robert Beaupel: Gascony in 1295 (*Rôles Gascons*, iii, p. 326); Scotland in 1296 (E 101/5/23, m. 2); 1298 (*Scotland in 1298*, p. 208); 1300 (C 67/14, m. 10); 1306 (C 67/16, m. 10); 1314 (C 71/6, m. 5). Chevreston: 1298 (*Scotland in 1298*, p. 208); 1303 (C67/15, m. 8); 1306 (C 67/16, m. 5).

be surprising if there were not a few seasoned campaigners spread among the sergeants in Scotland in 1298, as was the case with the knights. One apparent veteran of the Welsh wars to whom some scholarly attention has been devoted was Peter de Ros, a *vallettus* of William de Echingham. Nigel Saul has compared him to 'those protean administrators ... who could turn their hand equally to land management, man management, and soldiering'.[215] Tracing the service of such men back to Edward I's early campaigns is made a little easier when there were long-term connections linking sergeants to particular retinue leaders or their families, but even in such instances a degree of caution is required. The Roger le Burgilloun who served in the retinue of Nicholas de Audley at Falkirk was most probably the man of that name who had previously served, in 1282, with William de Audley.[216] However, it is equally plausible that the man who served in 1298 was the son of the man who had fought in Wales. Most of the time, the greater problem is simply a lack of information on the activities of men of sub-knightly status. Of the *valletti* who were with Hugh Bardolf in 1298, a few, such as Warin de Bassingburn,[217] William de Calveley[218] and Alexander de Montfort,[219] can be found in the records for military service on four or more campaigns. More typical, however, is the lack of evidence for the men in the retinue of John Tregoz. Of the ten sergeants who were with him at Falkirk, six do not appear in the extant service records on any other occasion. The same can be said to a greater or lesser degree of most of the retinues in the army.

Although there were sergeants, therefore, who can be shown to have been just as prolific in their military activities as the bachelors and bannerets whose orders they obeyed and by whose martial culture they were imbued, there were probably many more who have escaped the attention of the historian completely. Not only do the surviving records leave an image that distorts the contribution of knights and sergeants to the English war effort in favour of the former, but the sergeants on whom we are more fully informed are generally those, like Giles de Argentein and Thomas de Monteny, who went on to become knights. If it is true that the military activities of English men-at-arms during this period can only ever be partially reconstructed, then it is just as important to stress that those of sub-knightly status are the ones for whom the process of reconstruction tends to be least satisfactory. These reflections should serve to remind us that many of the sergeants whose names appear on the Falkirk inventories and

---

215 C 47/2/5, m. 2; N. Saul, *Scenes from Provincial Life: Knightly Families in Sussex 1280–1400* (Oxford, 1986), pp. 65–6.

216 *Scotland in 1298*, p. 219; C 47/2/7 m. 7.

217 1298 (*Scotland in 1298*, p. 221); 1300 (*Documents and Records of Scotland*, p. 224); 1301 (C 67/14, m. 3); 1303 (E 101/612/8, m. 1). He may have served on additional campaigns. However, as there was more than one man of this name alive during the reign of Edward I, the references given in this footnote relate only to instances when a Warin de Bassingburn served in the retinue of Hugh Bardolf.

218 1294 (*Rôles Gascons*, iii, p. 156); 1298 (*Scotland in 1298*, p. 221); 1301 (C 67/14, m. 3); 1303 (E 101/612/8, m. 1).

219 1294 (*Rôles Gascons*, iii, p. 156); 1298 (*Scotland in 1298*, p. 221); 1300 (*Documents and Records of Scotland*, p. 224); 1301 (C 67/14, m. 3); 1303 (E 101/612/8, m. 1); 1306 (C 67/16, m. 12).

for whom no other trace of military service has survived may in fact have been some of the most dedicated soldiers of their day. It is at least worth bearing in mind that were it not for the testimony of his son during the reign of Richard II, John de Thirlewall, the 'oldest squire in the north' and veteran of numerous martial adventures, would have been, like so many others, nothing more than a name on parchment.

War and public service: The wider context
Many of the knights and sergeants who took part in the Falkirk campaign of 1298 were regular campaigners. The heavy involvement of the gentry in the wars of Edward I and his son attests to a continued predilection among the landholding elites for the heat of the battlefield and camaraderie of the march, a disposition that was doubtless enhanced by the successes achieved against the Welsh. The kinds of service pattern noted above were all the more impressive given that this was a time of increased aristocratic involvement in the affairs of local government. During the first twenty years of Edward I's reign campaigns had been waged against corruption and the alienation of royal rights. These undertakings placed a significant strain on the king's subjects.[220] Several of the knights in the English army in 1298 had served on juries during the *Quo Warranto* proceedings, while others had been summoned to testify before the king's justices.[221] The growing number of commissions issued by the Crown added to these responsibilities. In 1287 keepers of the peace were appointed to enforce the articles of the Statute of Winchester. These appointments, in effect, marked the arrival of these officials in local government.[222] The wars in Wales, France and Scotland also necessitated the employment of commissioners of array, while still more men were needed to collect the subsidies granted by parliament to pay for these wars.[223] War, indeed, was the prime catalyst behind most of these developments, not least the process by which representatives from the shires came to be summoned with increased regularity from the mid-1290s to give assent to the Crown's tax-raising initiatives.[224] For G.L. Harriss, 'the need for representatives to come with full powers and participate in common counsel

---

[220] For an idea of the number of men involved in the hundred enquiries, see H.M. Cam, 'Studies in the Hundred Rolls: Some Aspects of Thirteenth-Century Administration', *Oxford Studies in Social and Legal History*, ed. P. Vinogradoff, vi (Oxford, 1921), p. 131, where evidence is given relating to Norfolk.

[221] The jurors were John de Blakeford, Richard de Kirkebride, William de Mere and William Wyther: *Placita de Quo Warranto temporibus Edw. I. II. and III. in Curia Receptae Scaccarii Westm. asservata*, ed. W. Illingworth (Record Commission, 1818), pp. 701, 119, 713, 708. For comment on the intensity of the proceedings, see D.W. Sutherland, *Quo Warranto Proceedings in the Reign of Edward I 1278–1294* (Oxford, 1963), p. 2.

[222] H.M. Jewell, *English Local Administration in the Middle Ages* (Newton Abbot, 1972), p. 167.

[223] On the subject of taxation, see, for example, G.O. Sayles, 'Parliamentary Representation in 1294, 1295 and 1307', *The English Parliament in the Middle Ages*, ed. H.G. Richardson and G.O. Sayles (London, 1981), XI, p. 110.

[224] See D. Pasquet, *An Essay on the Origins of the House of Commons* (London, 1964), p. 197; and D.A. Carpenter, 'The Beginnings of Parliament', *The Reign of Henry III* (London, 1996), pp. 393–4.

was an inescapable concomitant of the demand for the war taxation of these years of emergency'.[225] On many levels, therefore, and not only in war, the reign of Edward I required a great effort on the part of the gentry, placing constant demands on their services and binding them more firmly to the king.

The intensification of local government inevitably added to the pressure placed on the middling landowners of medieval England to contribute to public life. During times of peace the gentry would have been able to shoulder such burdens with ease; but, the heavy recruitment demands created by the wars in Wales, France and Scotland meant that from the mid-1290s the Crown's manpower reserves were becoming increasingly stretched. This was not a time when the military service of English landholders 'was being transformed into the exercise of territorial authority in the name of a developing state',[226] as had perhaps been the case during the reign of Henry III, for under Edward I the proliferation of commissions and the extension of the obligation to serve in the king's armies ran along parallel lines. Rather, the service of the gentry, as in the later fourteenth century, was becoming more complex, producing 'a lifestyle in which military and civilian responsibilities, family interests and private passions competed for precedence while becoming interwoven'.[227]

The requirements of war did not always sit easily alongside the business of local administration. Although it may be true that there were enough knights and squires within the country to keep the cogs of government turning when armies were put into the field,[228] the military expeditions that took place almost annually from 1294 removed from the equation many of the individuals who were most qualified for office. In 1295 Osbert de Spaldington had to be replaced as the justice of gaol delivery in Nottinghamshire and Derbyshire because he was with the king's army in Wales.[229] Twelve years later, John de Hotham was too busy serving with Henry de Percy north of the border to fulfil his duties as a coroner in Yorkshire.[230] Evidently, one could not be a soldier and at the same time contribute fully to local administration. Many men may therefore have followed the example of John de Swyneford, who in 1306 surrendered his office as a coroner in Huntingdonshire and committed himself to the calling of arms.[231] This kind of dilemma can only occasionally be glimpsed in the govern-

---

[225] G.L. Harriss, *King, Parliament, and Public Finance in Medieval England to 1369* (Oxford, 1975), p. 52.
[226] A. Harding, *England in the Thirteenth Century* (Cambridge, 1993), p. 180.
[227] A. Ayton, 'Edward III and the English Aristocracy at the Beginning of the Hundred Years War', *Armies, Chivalry and Warfare in Medieval Britain and France* (Stamford, 1998), p. 175.
[228] See Saul, *Knights and Esquires*, pp. 57–9. The evidence from Lincolnshire suggests that the campaign of 1298 did not leave a major imprint on the affairs of local government, but the Welsh expedition of 1277 affected the hearing of pleas: *A Lincolnshire Assize Roll for 1298*, ed. W.S. Thomson, Lincoln Record Society, xxxvi (1944), p. xxxiv; *Select Cases in the Court of King's Bench*, i, no. 21.
[229] *CCW*, p. 55.
[230] *CCR, 1302–07*, p. 487. For similar examples, relating to Northumberland, see King, 'War, Politics and Landed Society', pp. 68–9.
[231] *CCR, 1302–07*, p. 389.

ment sources, but it is likely to have confronted a large number of individuals at work in all parts of the country.

The experiences of the knights and sergeants who took part in the Falkirk campaign can tell us much about the way that the gentry responded to these dual pressures. As soldiers they encompassed a broad range of military experience: from those who appear to have served in the king's armies only once or twice during their careers, to others who campaigned relentlessly over two or three decades. Yet these men, particularly the knights, were also leaders of local society whose importance to the smooth functioning of regional government was just as crucial as their military role. Specialisation was one way of reconciling these conflicting duties. In his study of the military community of Cheshire, Philip Morgan noted that 'many of its members found only a somewhat truncated role in county society as a consequence of their military careers'.[232] The evidence relating to the knights at Falkirk, for whom the record is more complete than the sergeants, to some extent supports this conclusion. If we discount the nineteen non-English knights who rode north of the border in 1298 we are left with 121 men in our sample, of whom fifty-two appear never to have served in any of the five major capacities of sheriff, knight of the shire, arrayer, keeper of the peace and tax assessor.[233] Some of these were almost certainly the less active men of their day, preferring to manage their estates rather than trouble themselves with local or national affairs. Such perhaps were Ralph de Picheford and William de Horkesley. The former appears in the extant military records on just two occasions, in 1294 and 1298, and the latter seems to have served only at Falkirk.[234] Neither of these men, as far as we can tell, made a contribution to the running of local government. Others in this group of fifty-two knights, however, served regularly in the king's armies, thereby putting their military responsibilities before all other commitments. Edmund Foliot served in nine different hosts;[235] Thomas de St Loe was present on eight campaigns between 1296 and 1307;[236] and Hugh Godard, despite his lack of administrative service, was an enthusiastic campaigner throughout the war in Scotland.[237]

Even if such a group of specialist soldiers did exist, it would be a mistake to suggest that there was a division between, on the one hand, the most bellicose knights, and on the other, those responsible for maintaining law and order in the

[232] Morgan, *War and Society*, p. 168.

[233] I am grateful to Dr Richard Gorski of the University of Hull for allowing me to consult his database on administrative personnel. Most of the 'record' references relating to the performance of administrative service, utilised in the remainder of this chapter, have been extracted from this database.

[234] Picheford: Wales in 1294 (C 67/10, m. 5); and on the Falkirk campaign (*Scotland in 1298*, p. 192). Horkesley: *Scotland in 1298*, p. 203.

[235] 1282 (C 67/8, m. 7d); 1296 (C 67/11, m. 4); 1298 (*Scotland in 1298*, p. 211); 1300 (C 67/14, m. 9); 1301 (C 67/14, m. 1); 1302 (E 101/10/12, m. 3); 1303 (C 67/15, m. 10); 1306 (E 101/612/19, m. 1); 1307 (E 101/612/21, m. 1).

[236] Flanders in 1297 (E 101/6/28, m. 3i); Scotland in 1296 (E 101/5/23, m. 1i); 1298 (*Scotland in 1298*, p. 224); 1300 (*Liber Quotidianus*, p. 196); 1301 (E 101/9/24, m. 1); 1303 (E 101/612/11, m. 2); 1306 (C 67/16, m. 11); 1309 (*CDS*, v, p. 448).

[237] 1298 (*Scotland in 1298*, p. 224); 1301 (E 101/9/23, m. 2); 1303 (C 67/15, m. 11); 1306 (C 67/16, m. 8); 1310 (C 71/4, m. 13); 1314 (C 71/7, m. 9).

localities. At least sixty-nine of the knights in our sample, or some 57 per cent when we exclude the foreigners, served in some form of administrative capacity during their careers. Table 3.7 compares the different forms of public service given by these men up to 1335.

**Table 3.7: Forms and frequency of service given by
the Falkirk knights (1270–1335)**

		Service given by the knights at Falkirk as:					
		Soldier	MP	Sheriff	Arrayer	Keeper of the peace	Taxer
Frequency (number of occasions)	1	3	18	8	16	13	9
	2	6	7	4	5	7	6
	3	5	8	1	3	3	3
	4	5	2	–	2	2	1
	5	9	3	–	2	2	–
	6	8	1	–	1	2	–
	7	9	3	–	1	1	–
	8	10	–	–	–	–	–
	9	7	–	–	–	–	–
	10 or more	7	–	–	–	–	–
	Total	69	42	13	30	30	19

Given that the activities of over half of the knights at Falkirk extended beyond the purely military sphere, it cannot be said without some qualification that these men were professional soldiers. Nevertheless, it would be equally misleading to draw too sharp a distinction between military and civilian duties, for it was precisely their experience of warfare that qualified many of these men for office. An acquaintance with arms was certainly advantageous for anyone appointed as a commissioner of array or keeper of the peace as both of these posts required the use of strong-arm tactics to discipline troops and restore order.[238] Moreover, the election of experienced soldiers as knights of the shire to some extent mirrored the prevailing practice among the peerage, who were summoned both to military assemblies and to parliament.[239] The one position for which a strong campaigning record was perhaps less necessary was that of sheriff, whose military duties, it has been argued, had become 'purely auxiliary' by the late thirteenth century.[240] Even so, both Nigel Saul and Richard Gorski

[238] See A. Verduyn, 'The Selection and Appointment of Justices of the Peace in 1338', *Historical Research*, lxviii (1995), p. 7; Gorski, *Fourteenth-Century Sheriff*, pp. 145–6.
[239] P.W. Smith, 'A Study of the Lists of Military and Parliamentary Summons in the Reign of Edward I: The Families of Lists and their Significance', PhD thesis, University of Iowa, 1967, 2 parts, ii, pp. 544–5.
[240] W.A. Morris, *The Medieval English Sheriff to 1300* (Manchester, 1927), p. 237. See also B. Breslow, 'The English Sheriff during the Reign of King Edward I', PhD thesis, University of Ohio, 1968, p. 136; and H.M. Cam, *The Hundred and the Hundred Rolls: An Outline of Local Government in Medieval England* (London, 1930), pp. 85–7.

have demonstrated that many of the men appointed as sheriffs during the fourteenth century did have some military experience.[241]

A few of the knights in our sample appear to have served in administrative capacities far more frequently than they did as soldiers. One such knight was William Trumwyn. In 1298 he went to war, in the retinue of James de la Plaunche, for what appears to have been the only time in his career.[242] By contrast, his name regularly appears on lists of men appointed to office in local government and shire administration. He was knight of the shire for Staffordshire on four occasions, keeper of the peace the same number of times, tax assessor thrice and commissioner of array on two occasions.[243] Another man in this mould was Robert Barry. He served in the royal host on at least three campaigns, in 1298, 1300 and 1301,[244] but this pales in comparison with the number of times that he gained appointment to local office. He was knight of the shire for Buckinghamshire three times and for Northamptonshire twice, in addition to receiving several other commissions.[245] Such overt commitment to administrative rather than to military service was unusual among the knights serving in Edward I's army in 1298. The fact these individuals were recruited to the army in that year is a measure of how extensive Edward I's mobilisation policies were at that time.

One of the most striking details to emerge from the figures presented in table 3.7, despite the presence of leading players in local government like Trumwyn and Barry, is the preponderance of military service over other forms of public service given by the knights at Falkirk. To some extent this is to be expected given that the sample has been taken from a military source. Nevertheless, the sheer frequency with which these men took part in royal expeditions in comparison with other forms of public service indicates that most knights spent far more time at war than they did attending parliament or keeping the peace in the shires. War did not exercise a monopoly over their activities, but it did take up enough of their time to prevent them, at least for a large part of their careers, from taking part in local government on anything more than an intermittent basis. As Nigel Saul noted in his study of fourteenth-century Gloucestershire, 'the *strenui milites* ... cannot be identified exclusively with the men who shouldered the burden of local administration'.[246] Of the sixty-nine knights in our sample who were employed in an administrative capacity at some point in their lives, around a quarter gave military service on at least five occasions more than they did all other major forms of public service when taken together.[247]

241 Saul, *Knights and Esquires*, pp. 55–6; Gorski, *Fourteenth-Century Sheriff*, p. 144.
242 *Scotland in 1298*, p. 199.
243 *List of MPs*, pp. 15, 18, 49 and 51; *CPR, 1307–13*, pp. 31, 53; *CPR, 1313–17*, pp. 107, 123; *CPR, 1307–13*, p. 23; *CPR, 1313–17*, pp. 474, 530; *Rotuli Scotiae*, i, p. 97; *CPR, 1313–17*, p. 461.
244 *Scotland in 1298*, p. 220; C 47/1/6, m. 3; E 101/9/23, m. 1.
245 *List of MPs*, pp. 5, 25, 35, 42, 53; *CPR, 1281–92*, p. 265; *CPR, 1292–1301*, p. 104; *CPR, 1307–13*, p. 185; *CFR*, iii, p. 31.
246 Saul, *Knights and Esquires*, p. 55.
247 The other 'major' forms of public service (as elsewhere in this analysis) are: knight of the shire; sheriff; commissioner of array; keeper of the peace; tax assessor.

Characteristic of this group were men like Nicholas de St Maur, a follower of Thomas of Lancaster, who rode in eight different hosts between 1294 and 1306, but whose sole contribution to peacetime affairs was as knight of the shire for Gloucestershire in 1313;[248] and Robert Fitz Nigel, a frequent campaigner whose involvement in local government was limited to one spell as an arrayer and one as a peace commissioner in Buckinghamshire in the 1320s.[249]

For most of the knights at Falkirk, then, participation in expeditions to Wales, France and Scotland provided a far more regular focus of activity than work in the shires. Yet even the most frequent campaigners tended to give some additional form of public service at one point or another. Some idea as to how the sixty-nine soldier-administrators in our sample were able to combine such activities can be obtained from table 3.8, which compares the decades in which these knights began to undertake different forms of public service.

Table 3.8: Decades in which the Falkirk knights began different forms of service

	Soldier	MP	Sheriff	Arrayer	Keeper of the peace	Taxer
1270–79	5	–	–	–	–	–
1280–89	9	–	–	1	3	–
1290–99	55	6	1	1	–	4
1300–09	–	17	5	4	9	6
1310–19	–	17	3	12	6	7
1320–29	–	1	3	10	8	–
1330–39	–	1	1	2	4	2

The figures presented in table 3.8 show that few of the knights at Falkirk had served in an administrative capacity before riding north of the border in 1298. Most in fact did not commence their activities as knights of the shire and in local government until the closing years of the reign of Edward I or later. To some extent, this can be explained by the problems of documentary survival for the final years of the reign of Henry III and the first half of the reign of his son. Representatives from the shires participated in a number of parliaments during the 1260s, 1270s and 1280s, but the names of the knights present at those assemblies have been lost.[250] In like manner, the lack of service given by the knights as keepers of the peace before 1298 is due in large measure to the

---

248 Military service: 1294 (C 67/10, m. 3); 1295 (*Rôles Gascons*, iii, p. 296); 1297 (E 101/6/19, m. 1); 1298 (*Scotland in 1298*, p. 179); 1300 (C 67/14, m. 9); 1301 (C 67/14, m. 7d); 1303 (C 67/15, m. 12); 1306 (C 67/7, m. 3). For his appointment as a knight of the shire, see *List of MPs*, p. 37.

249 For his military service, see p. 86, n. 128 and p. 137, n. 152. He also served in: 1294 (*Rôles Gascons*, iii, p. 161); 1297 (*Rôles Gascons*, iii, p. 346); 1298 (*Scotland in 1298*, p. 221). For his other duties, see *CPR, 1324–27*, p. 221; *CPR, 1327–30*, p. 89.

250 See J.G. Edwards, 'The Personnel of the Commons in Parliament under Edward I and Edward II', *Essays in Medieval History presented to T.F. Tout*, ed. A.G. Little and F.M. Powicke (Manchester, 1925), p. 198; J.R. Maddicott, 'Edward I and the Lessons of Baronial Reform: Local Government, 1258–80', *Thirteenth Century England I*, ed. P.R. Coss and S.D. Lloyd (Woodbridge, 1986), pp. 16–17; and *idem*, 'The Crusade Taxation of 1268–1270 and

fact that those officials were not appointed on a regular basis until the reign of Edward II.[251]

Some men may, then, have given administrative service before they appear to have done so. Nevertheless, the lack of evidence for the administrative service of the knights in our sample before the opening decades of the fourteenth century is probably (in most cases) a consequence of a deliberate division of labour between the earlier and later stages in their careers. In her study of the men appointed to office in Yorkshire between the mid-thirteenth and mid-fourteenth centuries, Helen Jewell noted that 'men became most active in administration around the age of forty'.[252] A similar trend has been discerned by J.S. Illsley in his study of the knights of the shire returned from Essex during the reign of Edward I.[253] Not all individuals conformed to this pattern; and there were certainly many veteran soldiers and young administrators at work within Edwardian England.[254] Yet the careers of the knights who served at Falkirk add weight to the theory that regular campaigners did not usually turn their hands to shire administration until later in life. John de Scures gave military service on six occasions between 1298 and 1314, and he was first returned as a knight of the shire during a year of relative peace in 1309. He then went on to serve as a parliamentary representative for Hampshire in 1314 and 1322, sheriff of that county in 1321, arrayer on seven occasions during the 1320s and 1330s and peace commissioner three times.[255] Stephen de Haccombe took part in six military ventures between 1294 and 1306 before being returned as knight of the shire for Devon twice, keeper of the peace once and commissioner of array five times over the following twenty years.[256] Finally, Thomas de Coudray campaigned regularly from the mid-1290s up to and including the Bannockburn

the Development of Parliament', *Thirteenth Century England II*, ed. P.R. Coss and S.D. Lloyd (Woodbridge, 1988), p. 113.

[251] B.H. Putnam, 'The Transformation of the Keepers of the Peace into the Justices of the Peace, 1327–1380', *TRHS*, 4th ser., xii (1929), p. 23.

[252] H.M. Jewell, 'Local Administration and Administrators in Yorkshire, 1258–1348', *Northern History*, xvi (1980), pp. 12–13.

[253] J.S. Illsley, 'Parliamentary Elections in the Reign of Edward I', *BIHR*, xlix (1976), p. 37. See also, for knights of the shire from Somerset, A.R.J. Juřica, 'The Knights of Edward I: An Investigation of the Social Significance of Knightly Rank in the Period 1272–1307 based on a Study of the Knights of Somerset', PhD thesis, University of Birmingham, 1976, p. 223.

[254] Gorski, *Fourteenth-Century Sheriff*, pp. 142–3. It should be noted that in border counties the duties of local government and defence were far more intertwined than elsewhere. Andy King has observed, for example, that 'by sheer force of circumstance, the same men who ran the Crown's local administration in Northumberland bore much of the responsibility for defending the county on a day-to-day basis': 'War, Politics and Landed Society', p. 60.

[255] For his military service, see above, p. 88, n. 135. See also: *List of MPs*, pp. 29, 45, 16; *List of Sheriffs for England and Wales, From the Earliest Times to AD 1831*, PRO Lists and Indexes, ix (London, 1893), p. 54; *CPR, 1321–24*, pp. 96, 213, 267; *CPR, 1324–27*, p. 220; *Rotuli Scotiae*, i, pp. 249, 370; *Foedera*, II, ii, p. 1071; *CPR, 1324–27*, pp. 228, 285; and *CPR, 1330–34*, p. 293.

[256] He campaigned in Wales in 1294 (C 67/10, m. 7) and in Scotland in 1296 (E 101/5/23, m. 1i), 1298 (*Scotland in 1298*, p. 208), 1300 (C 67/14, m. 9), 1303 (C 67/15, m. 8) and 1306 (C 67/16, m. 9). See also: *List of MPs*, pp. 30, 33; *CPR, 1317–21*, p. 459; *CPR 1321–24*, pp. 213, 267, 274; and *CPR, 1324–27*, pp. 8, 218.

expedition.[257] He then began an equally intensive administrative career in the southern counties in 1318.[258] For individuals such as these, the most active men of their day, a division of duties according to different stages in the life cycle was the most appropriate way of reconciling the pressures of military service with the need to participate fully in the affairs of the shire.

The proliferation of commissions during these years meant that the king could not rely solely on the service of men of knightly status. Lesser men, too, had an important role to perform in local government. Among the sergeants at Falkirk who later gave administrative service in the localities, however, a large proportion did not do so until they had already been knighted. John de Haustede served as a lesser man-at-arms in the company of his father, Robert, in the king's household division in Scotland in 1298.[259] During his career he benefited extensively from royal patronage, progressing from a yeoman in the household of Prince Edward during the opening years of the fourteenth century to the ranks of the parliamentary peerage in the 1330s.[260] Following a long period of military service, which began in Flanders in 1297 and appears to have ended with the war of Saint-Sardos of 1324–5, he was appointed as a justice of the peace for Buckinghamshire in 1332 and returned as a knight of the shire for the same county three years later.[261] His career closely resembled those of the knights already discussed. Indeed, this progression from sub-knightly man-at-arms to warrior-knight and finally to respected figure in local government was matched by several others among the more prominent sergeants in Edward I's army at Falkirk. Reginald de Paveley went on to serve in Scotland in 1300, 1301, 1306 and on the Bannockburn campaign before receiving his first commission as a keeper of the peace for Wiltshire in 1320.[262] John de Twyford, with Ralph Pipard at Falkirk, was first returned to parliament in 1315, five years after appearing in the extant records for military service for the final time.[263]

'Lesser' or 'permanent' sergeants made an appreciable contribution to public

---

257 See above, p. 24, n. 108.
258 *List of MPs*, pp. 54, 67; *CPR, 1327–30*, p. 429; *CPR, 1330–34*, p. 295; *CPR, 1334–38*, pp. 210, 357, 368; *CPR, 1324–27*, p. 8; *CPR, 1327–30*, p. 571; *Rotuli Scotiae*, i, p. 249; *CPR, 1334–38*, p. 138; *Rotuli Scotiae*, i, pp. 329, 370. His only administrative work before 1314 was as a commissioner of array for Hampshire in 1311: *Rotuli Scotiae*, i, p. 97.
259 *Scotland in 1298*, p. 170.
260 J.S. Bothwell, *Edward III and the English Peerage: Royal Patronage, Social Mobility and Political Control in Fourteenth-Century England* (Woodbridge, 2004), p. 17.
261 He served in Flanders in 1297 (E 101/6/37, m. 2ii), in Scotland in 1298 (*Scotland in 1298*, p. 170), 1300 (E 101/8/23, m. 1), 1301 (E 101/9/23, m. 1), 1303 (E 101/612/11, m. 3d), 1306 (E 101/13/7, m. 2), 1319 (E 101/378/4, fol. 26v) and 1322 (*CPR, 1321–24*, p. 188), and in Gascony in 1324–5 (BL, Additional MS 7967, fol. 33v). For his administrative service, see *CPR, 1330–34*, p. 293 and *List of MPs*, p. 90.
262 1298 (*Scotland in 1298*, p. 171); 1300 (*Documents and Records of Scotland*, p. 229); 1301 (E 101/9/24, m. 1d); 1306 (C 67/16, m. 10); 1314 (C 71/6, m. 5). For his other work, see: *CPR, 1317–21*, p. 462; *CPR, 1327–30*, p. 429; *CPR, 1330–34*, pp. 137, 286; *List of MPs*, p. 77; *CPR, 1321–24*, pp. 124, 268; *CPR, 1324–27*, pp. 8, 221; and *List of Sheriffs*, p. 152.
263 He served in Scotland in 1298 (*Scotland in 1298*, p. 220); 1306 (C 67/16, m. 11); 1310 (*Parl. Writs* II, ii, p. 406). See also *List of MPs*, pp. 46, 52, 55 and *CPR, 1330–34*, pp. 137, 295, 401, 445.

life; but they did not occupy the leading positions of sheriff and knight of the shire as frequently as their sons and grandsons were to do later in the four-teenth century. Of the sergeants at Falkirk who never became knights, only a few appear to have served in either of those capacities during their careers. Adam de Skelton was returned as knight of the shire for Cumberland in 1318.[264] This may have been the man of that name who had served as a *vallettus* under Thomas of Lancaster in 1298 and had still not become a knight when he accompanied Andrew de Harcla on the Scottish March sixteen years later.[265] Inevitably, the activities of such men are more difficult to trace than those of their knightly counterparts. For example, it is impossible to know whether the John de Staf-ford who joined the retinue of Thomas of Lancaster in 1298 was the man of that name returned as a man-at-arms from Staffordshire in 1324, let alone whether either of these was the John de Stafford who served as a knight of the shire for the same county in 1339.[266] As a rule we are probably right to err on the side of caution. When men who had served as sergeants in 1298 appear on lists of appointees to local office, it is usually as holders of the lesser posi-tions of arrayer, tax assessor or keeper of the peace. Robert de Whiterugg, a *vallettus* with Robert de Clifford at Falkirk, was appointed as a commissioner of array in Cumberland in 1307;[267] and in 1311 William Hathewy and William de Colebroke, veterans of the campaign of 1298, were employed as arrayers in Gloucestershire and Middlesex respectively.[268] Such men as these appear to have contributed relatively little as individuals to the running of the shires, but collectively their service was of vital importance to the Crown.

As with their military service, so with their administrative service, there is perhaps a tendency to underestimate the contribution made by men of sub-knightly status to the Edwardian polity. If A.J. Musson is right that most sub-keepers of the peace in the hundreds 'were perhaps minor gentry and included some who were substantial peasants', then it may be that many of the sergeants at Falkirk carried out activities of this kind that are sometimes difficult to trace in the public records.[269] Others may have been employed as coroners, who assisted the sheriffs in much of their work in the provinces.[270] But given that almost half of the knights in our sample appear to have given no major admin-istrative service at all, and that most of those who did served far more regularly as soldiers than in any other capacity, it might simply be the case that most of the sergeants who campaigned in Scotland in 1298 had also chosen to follow the military calling and therefore had little opportunity to carry out other duties. For

264 *List of MPs*, p. 52.

265 For his military service, see: 1295 (*Rôles Gascons*, iii, p. 298); 1298 (*Scotland in 1298*, p. 180); 1300 (C 67/14, m. 10); 1303 (C 67/15, m. 8); 1306 (C 67/16, m. 10); 1311 (E 101/14/15, m. 3); and 1314 (E 101/14/15, m. 2).

266 *Scotland in 1298*, p. 181; *Parl. Writs*, II, ii, p. 647; *List of MPs*, p. 107.

267 *CPR, 1301–07*, p. 498; *Scotland in 1298*, p. 197.

268 Hathewy: *Scotland in 1298*, p. 192; *Rotuli Scotiae*, i, p. 100. Colebroke: *Scotland in 1298*, p. 178; *Rotuli Scotiae*, i, p. 98.

269 A.J. Musson, 'Sub-Keepers and Constables: The Role of Local Officials in Keeping the Peace in Fourteenth-Century England', *EHR*, cxvii (2002), p. 20.

270 See R.F. Hunnisett, *The Medieval Coroner* (Cambridge, 1961), p. 173.

both types of man-at-arms, military service in the late thirteenth and early fourteenth centuries constituted far more than an occasional break from the daily routine of shire administration. On the contrary, between 1294 and 1314 the demands of war were almost incessant; and, for the first time in several generations, a career in arms had become a viable alternative to the more mundane business of estate management.[271] Many of the men who took part in Edward I's campaign to Scotland in 1298 evidently saw some wisdom in pursuing the life of the soldier. In doing so they helped to forge a military tradition that was to serve the kings of England well in the years to come.

[271] For a similar view, see M. Bennett, 'Careerism in Late Medieval England', *People, Politics and Community in the Later Middle Ages*, ed. J. Rosenthal and C. Richmond (Gloucester, 1987), p. 21.

4

Recruitment Networks

A cautionary note must always be struck when attempting to apply abstract concepts and phrases to complex historical phenomena. Nevertheless, if we understand the term to mean a large society of frequent campaigners who were connected to one another through an extensive web of personal relationships, it does not seem inappropriate to suggest that there was a military community in late thirteenth- and early fourteenth-century England. Given its scale and the variety in rank and social status of its members, a full comprehension of the dynamics of that community is probably beyond the capacity of any historian working independently. Yet the evidence examined in chapter 3 demonstrates that there are sufficient data available to reach some informed conclusions about the patterns of service, length of careers and frequency of employment of a large number of men (particularly those of knightly status) who went to war under Edward I and his son. To gain a greater appreciation of the social bonds and personal networks that brought such men into the Crown's service, and to understand why so many individuals were prepared to risk life and limb on an almost annual basis throughout the years of heaviest campaigning from 1294 to 1314, it is now necessary to consider in greater detail the relations between the military leaders and the soldiers who followed them to war.

Lords, Retainers and Followers

Few forms of social relationship were as pervasive and adaptable within medieval England as that involving lords and their men. Scratch their surface and the *comitivae* of the earls and barons who went to war under Edward I do not appear so very different from the warbands that were so prominent a feature of the military landscape in the Anglo-Saxon age, or the retinues that accompanied the duke of Normandy and his followers on their fateful expedition in 1066. Indeed 'lordship and hierarchy were present in Germanic society from the very beginning of the Middle Ages'.[1] Such was the ubiquity of the military retinue that Robert Bartlett has seen fit to describe it as 'one of the basic social organisms of medieval Europe'.[2] The war *comitiva* was certainly a unit of considerable signif-

---

[1] R.P. Abels, *Lordship and Military Obligation in Anglo-Saxon England* (London, 1988), p. 22.
[2] R. Bartlett, *The Making of Europe: Conquest, Colonization and Cultural Change 950–1350* (London, 1993), p. 45.

icance within Plantagenet England. Yet before we go on to look in greater detail at the service patterns of the men who staffed these retinues during the reigns of Edward I and Edward II, some preliminary questions need to be answered. For example, what were the chief components of such retinues? And how did lords ensure that they had sufficient reserves of men ready and willing to follow them to war whenever they were summoned to arms by the king?

It is important to recognise that most military retinues in the late thirteenth and early fourteenth centuries comprised two main elements: on the one hand, the corpus of the lord's permanent retainers, represented primarily through the institution of the household or *familia*, and on the other, his wider circle of associates. When Henry III's baronial opponents put their case before Louis IX of France in 1264, one of their complaints was that Roger de Mortimer had disturbed the peace by allowing his men and members of his household (*homines ... et familiares ipsius Rogeri*) to attack one of the earl of Leicester's castles and its constable.[3] The distinction between Mortimer's 'men' and the members of his *familia* was a common one, reflecting contemporary perceptions about the dual nature of magnate affinities.[4] In a similar example, dating from 1312, the constable of Dublin castle was accused of appropriating the money given to him for the purpose of retaining twelve additional soldiers and of using it to pay the members of his own household.[5] Thus, despite considerable overlap between the two, the *familia* and the expanded retinue of men-at-arms did not amount to the same thing. Nigel Saul has inferred from this that by the fourteenth century it was perhaps the looser, less stable element of magnate affinities that performed the most important military role. By then, 'magnates kept their corps of household knights and esquires with a view to peacetime, not wartime, conditions'.[6] This may have been true in the later part of the fourteenth century, but during the reigns of the first two Edwards the members of a lord's household seem to have performed an appreciable military role.[7]

The most fundamental concept to have arisen from this division between the two main parts of the magnate retinue is 'bastard feudalism', the 'quintessence' of which, according to K.B. McFarlane, 'was payment for service'.[8] In his seminal study of this perceived phenomenon, McFarlane traced the origins of 'bastard feudalism' back to the Welsh wars of the 1280s and 1290s, but dated its full blossoming to 'the two centuries following the death of Edward I'.[9] No discussion of military lordship in the thirteenth and fourteenth centuries would be complete without reference to 'bastard feudalism', not least because McFarlane's arguments have influenced a large number of subsequent debates. Yet

---

[3] *Documents of the Baronial Movement of Reform and Rebellion 1258–1267*, selected by R.F. Treharne and edited by I.J. Sanders (Oxford, 1973), p. 266.
[4] See also *CCR, 1272–79*, p. 315. For more general comment on this division, see M. Hicks, *Bastard Feudalism* (London, 1995), p. 68.
[5] *Historical and Municipal Documents of Ireland AD 1172–1320*, ed. J.T. Gilbert, Rolls Ser., liii (London, 1870), pp. 304–8.
[6] Saul, *Knights and Esquires*, p. 84. See also Walker, *The Lancastrian Affinity*, p. 10.
[7] For some examples, see below, p. 136.
[8] K.B. McFarlane, 'Bastard Feudalism', *BIHR*, xx (1943–5), p. 162.
[9] *Ibid.*, pp. 161–2.

there is no consensus among historians as to the extent to which retaining practices under Edward I and Edward II differed from those of previous reigns. G.A. Holmes long ago described 'bastard feudalism' as 'a misnomer'.[10] Other critics of the concept have included J.M.W. Bean and David Crouch, both of whom have detected a considerable degree of continuity in lordship practices.[11] Indeed, as we have seen, even McFarlane was of the opinion that 'bastard feudalism' did not take full hold within English society until after 1307. Although the debate will continue to rage, it is reassuring to note that lordship, and in particular military lordship, retained many of its older features.

The household was the single most constant element of magnate retinues throughout the Middle Ages, and its central place within medieval society has long been recognised.[12] Much of this chapter will deal with the military role performed by the households of the lords of the late thirteenth and early fourteenth centuries; but the *familia* was much more than a collection of men organised for war. Viewed in its widest sense, a lord's household would consist of 'a body of knights, esquires and men-at-arms involved in the fulfilment of his quota of military service, the nucleus of officials who carried out the administration of his estates, and other officials who handled the routines of everyday life'.[13] In essence the magnate retinue provided a form of cement that held together the different strata of medieval society under powerful leaders. The binding nature of the *familia* in particular is demonstrated by the attempts made to bring men to justice following the civil war of 1264–5 by identifying which households they had belonged to at the time of the troubles.[14] It is also interesting to note the harshness with which Edward II treated the followers of his opponents in the aftermath of the rebellion of 1321–2. The Meaux chronicle of Yorkshire records that the wives, sons and *familiares* of the men who had risen against the king were stripped of their lands and goods.[15] Membership of a magnate household therefore constituted a substantial commitment, one not to be entered into lightly, particularly during times of political turmoil.

One way that lords could recruit men into their households or affinities in the late thirteenth century was by granting robes. 'Livery – the issue of cloth, or clothing, to members of the household – was a practice at least as old as the middle of the twelfth century';[16] but it would appear that the granting of livery to members of the wider affinity was a slightly more recent development. The larger the body of men that one could put into the field bearing one's clothing,

---

[10] G.A. Holmes, *The Estates of the Higher Nobility in Fourteenth-Century England* (Cambridge, 1957), p. 83.

[11] J.M.W. Bean, *From Lord to Patron: Lordship in Late Medieval England* (Manchester, 1989), p. 234; D. Crouch, 'Debate: Bastard Feudalism Revised', *Past and Present*, cxxxi (1991), p. 176.

[12] See, for example, C.M. Woolgar, *The Great Household in Late Medieval England* (London, 1999).

[13] M.W. Labarge, *A Baronial Household of the Thirteenth Century* (London, 1965), p. 53.

[14] See, for example, *Calendar of Inquisitions Miscellaneous (Chancery)*, 8 vols (London, 1916–2003), i, no. 936.

[15] *Melsa*, ii, p. 343. See also Holmes, *Estates of the Higher Nobility*, p. 59.

[16] Woolgar, *The Great Household*, p. 9.

the greater one's prestige was likely to be among one's fellow soldiers. In this sense livery offered a more flexible symbol of association than retaining by fee or annuity; and it enabled a lord to extend his circle of followers with relative ease.[17] The thirteenth-century chronicler Matthew Paris noted that when Henry III's brother Richard, earl of Cornwall, set out on crusade in 1250, he was attended by a large retinue of forty knights splendidly adorned in new garments, all alike.[18] According to another chronicle, the *Brut*, the earls who witnessed the coronation of Edward I in 1274 were each joined by 100 knights arrayed in their arms.[19] The evidence of surviving wardrobe accounts shows that lords were at pains to ensure that their retainers were dressed in clothes and colours appropriate to their status.[20] This may have been reflected in the clothes that knights and sergeants wore on the battlefield.[21] Livery could also indicate one's allegiance to a political cause. For example, in 1321 the opponents of Edward II and the Despensers chose to show their unity by sporting a common uniform.[22]

Although the granting of livery was a widespread phenomenon by the late thirteenth century, only members of the royal family and the leading bishops, earls, barons and bannerets possessed the resources to exploit its potential to the full. A list has survived of the members of Edward of Caernarfon's *familia* in 1301, the year that he led an army in western Scotland. This shows that the prince's household at that time contained three bannerets, six knights and fifty-eight *valletti et servientes*.[23] When he became king the size of his retinue increased considerably. During Edward II's fifth regnal year (1311–12) there were around thirty-six knights within the royal household, but not all of these were retained at the same time.[24] John de Hastings reportedly led 160 men-at-

---

[17] Bean, *From Lord to Patron*, pp. 21–2.

[18] *Chronica Majora*, v, p. 97. For a discussion of the retinue that Richard led to Germany for his coronation in 1257, see N. Denholm-Young, *Richard of Cornwall* (Oxford, 1947), pp. 90–1.

[19] *The Brut, or the Chronicles of England*, ed. F.W.D. Brie, 2 vols, Early English Text Society, cxxxi, cxxxvi (London, 1906–8), i, p. 179.

[20] F. Lachaud, 'Dress and Social Status in England before the Sumptuary Laws', *Heraldry, Pageantry and Social Display in Medieval England*, ed. P. Coss and M. Keen (Woodbridge, 2002), pp. 120–2.

[21] One of the earliest examples of English soldiers wearing uniform dates from the Weardale campaign of 1327, when the men raised 'from the lands of Queen Isabella in Holderness' were expected to wear short cloaks 'of one suit': A.E. Prince, 'The Importance of the Campaign of 1327', *EHR*, 1 (1935), p. 302.

[22] *Scalacronica*, p. 85; *Trokelowe*, p. 109.

[23] E 101/360/17. See also: E 101/370/29; H. Johnstone, *Edward of Carnarvon, 1284–1307* (Manchester, 1946), pp. 74–6.

[24] BL, Cotton Nero C VIII, fols 90v–91r, 92r, 94r. For fluctuations in the number of household knights and bannerets during the reigns of Edward I and Edward II, see C. Given-Wilson, 'The King and the Gentry in Fourteenth-Century England', *TRHS*, 5th ser., xxxvii (1987), p. 89. For discussions of Edward II's household retainers, see M. Prestwich, 'The Unreliability of Royal Household Knights in the Early Fourteenth Century', *Fourteenth Century England II* (Woodbridge, 2002), pp. 1–11; and A. Tebbit, 'Royal Patronage and Political Allegiance: The Household Knights of Edward II, 1314–1321', *Thirteenth Century England X*, ed. M. Prestwich, R. Britnell and R. Frame (Woodbridge, 2005), pp. 197–208.

arms to the siege of Caerlaverock in 1300 on behalf of the bishop of Durham;[25] but this should not be taken as representative of the size of the bishop's household, for many of these men were probably brought into his pay for the duration of the campaign and then dismissed. Of roughly equal status were the earls. J.R. Maddicott has shown that Thomas of Lancaster had a core of around twenty-five to fifty knightly retainers,[26] with the size of his household tending to fluctuate according to political circumstances. The earl of Lincoln also seems, from his expenditure on robes, to have retained around twenty-five knights.[27] In 1300 he took eight household knights (*familiares*) with him on his journey to the papal court.[28] Even lords of sub-comital status could sometimes rely on fairly large numbers of retainers. John de Vescy had no fewer than seventeen knightly followers in 1280. We know this because the said household knights (*familiaribus militibus*), along with their lord, had committed a trespass in Sherwood Forest.[29] It is unlikely that many other men of Vescy's status could call on the services of so many knights.[30]

At its full extent a war *comitiva* might contain men who were only loosely associated with their lord. Yet at the heart of the retinue it was still common for the leader to be accompanied by his kinsmen and close friends, a phenomenon dating back to the early Middle Ages.[31] As Michael Prestwich has noted, 'family and neighbourhood connections were probably as important [to the formation of magnate retinues in the thirteenth and fourteenth centuries] as formal contracts'.[32] His point is supported by an abundance of evidence in contemporary records of family members serving alongside one another in the king's armies. When John de Eyville set out for Wales in 1282, for example, he was accompanied by two of his kinsmen, Gocelyn and Thomas de Eyville.[33] Similarly, three members of the Zouche family – Philip, Aymer and William – accompanied Alan la Zouche to Scotland in 1306.[34] Service by members of the same family in close proximity to one another must have instilled a special esprit de corps within a large number

25 *Siege of Caerlaverock*, p. 23.

26 Maddicott, *Thomas of Lancaster*, p. 45.

27 Prestwich, *Plantagenet England*, p. 375.

28 *CCR, 1296–1302*, p. 370. For examples of the strength of comital retinues in slightly later and earlier periods, see M. Cherry, 'The Courtenay Earls of Devon: The Formation and Disintegration of a Late Medieval Aristocratic Affinity', *Southern History*, i (1979), pp. 72–3, and G.G. Simpson, 'The *Familia* of Roger de Quincy, Earl of Winchester and Constable of Scotland', *Essays on the Nobility of Medieval Scotland*, ed. K.J. Stringer (Edinburgh, 1985), p. 121.

29 *CCR, 1279–88*, p. 19.

30 For additional examples of household lists and accounts, see *A Roll of the Household Expenses of Richard de Swinfield, bishop of Hereford, during part of the years 1289 and 1290*, ed. J. Webb, 2 vols, Camden Society 1st ser., lix, lxii (1854–5), i, pp. 194–7; and *Household Accounts from Medieval England*, ed. C.M. Woolgar, 2 parts, Records of Social and Economic History, new ser., xvii–xviii (Oxford, 1992–3), ii, no. 25.

31 S.S. Evans, *The Lords of Battle: Image and Reality of the* Comitatus *in Dark-Age Britain* (Woodbridge, 1997), p. 34.

32 Prestwich, *Plantagenet England*, p. 382.

33 C 47/2/7, m. 8; C 67/8, m. 5.

34 C 67/16, m. 8.

of retinues. Yet, by placing them collectively in harm's way, it might also court disaster for the aristocratic houses concerned. According to the chronicler Pierre de Langtoft, John de Segrave was captured alongside his brother and son during their service in Scotland in 1303;[35] and later, of four brothers from the Neville family who were active north of the border during the reign of Edward II, one was killed and the other three were taken prisoner for ransoms.[36]

As integral as such bonds were to the process of recruitment, lords of high social standing could not rely on the service of their kinsmen and friends alone. During the reign of Edward I, it became increasingly common for lords to draw up indentures for service in peace and war to supplement their usual forces.[37] Contracts had been employed to recruit soldiers for the Lord Edward's crusade of 1270–2,[38] but they do not seem to have been used to any great extent during Edward I's wars in Wales. One exception was an indenture drawn up between Edmund de Mortimer and Peter de Mauley in 1287 for service against Rhys ap Maredudd.[39] This contract is unusual in that it lists the values of the horses in Mauley's retinue, with the provision that Mortimer was to compensate Mauley for any mounts that he lost during his service in the army. There is no indication that the link thus created was intended to last beyond the duration of the campaign. By contrast, most indentures of the 1290s and 1300s were drawn up with a view to long-term service. In effect, they seem to have been envisaged as a way of extending the *familia* rather than as a radical departure from it.[40] An indenture composed between Aymer de Valence and Thomas de Berkeley, dated 2 July 1297, stipulates that Berkeley was to serve with Valence 'in peace and in war, in England, in Wales and in Scotland' (*en pes come en guerre, en Engleterre, en Gales e en Escoce*).[41] Oddly, no mention is made of service overseas, despite the fact that Berkeley had his horse appraised in Valence's retinue for service in Flanders just a few weeks later, on 17 August.[42] It is also interesting that the terms of the indenture state that Berkeley was to be entitled to *bouche*

---

[35] *Langtoft*, p. 410.

[36] *Northern Petitions*, no. 132.

[37] On the link between Edward's wars and the development of the contract system, see N.B. Lewis, 'The Organisation of Indentured Retinues in Fourteenth-Century England', *TRHS*, 4th ser., xxvii (1945), p. 31.

[38] H.G. Richardson and G.O. Sayles, *The Governance of Mediaeval England from the Conquest to Magna Carta* (Edinburgh, 1963), pp. 463–5.

[39] N.B. Lewis, 'An Early Indenture of Military Service, 27 July 1287', *BIHR*, xiii (1935), pp. 85–9; *CCR, 1279–88*, p. 486.

[40] See Bean, *From Lord to Patron*, pp. 129, 143; and *idem*, '"Bachelor" and "Retainer"', pp. 125–6. For additional comment on the continuity in lord–follower relations represented in, and facilitated by, such indentures, see S.L. Waugh, 'Tenure to Contract: Lordship and Clientage in Thirteenth-Century England', *EHR*, ci (1986), p. 839; and D. Crouch, *The Beaumont Twins: The Roots and Branches of Power in the Twelfth Century* (Cambridge, 1986), p. 101. Not all indentures for service in peace and war were composed between lords and their men. For discussion of an indenture drawn up in 1298 between two knights of equal status, see K.B. McFarlane, 'An Indenture of Agreement between Two English Knights for Mutual Aid and Counsel in Peace and War, 5 December 1298', *BIHR*, xxxviii (1965), pp. 200–10.

[41] 'Private Indentures for Life Service in Peace and War 1278–1476', ed. M. Jones and S. Walker, *Camden Miscellany XXXII*, Camden Society, 5th ser., iii (1994), no. 4.

[42] E 101/6/28, m. 2i.

a court, as well as an annual fee and robes, all elements traditionally associated with full membership of a magnate household.[43]

The Valence–Berkeley indenture for service in peace and war is one of five to have survived dating from 1297. This is the largest number of extant indentures drawn up for any single year during the reign of Edward I. Although the Valence–Berkeley contract makes no mention of service overseas, the remainder do. In fact, most of these agreements were probably composed with the forthcoming campaign to Flanders in mind. The indenture drafted between John de Grey of Rotherfield and Robert de Tothale stipulates that the latter was to serve with the former 'in the king's army overseas or in any other place where it might please the said John'.[44] Another compact, involving John Bluet and William Martel, refers to service 'in the war between the kings of England and France'.[45] Some of the indentures dating from 1297 were probably conceived as a quick-fix solution to a short-term problem, namely the need to recruit large numbers of men for an unpopular campaign at a time when more traditional methods of inducement, such as the granting away of lands, were no longer feasible.[46] Other agreements drawn up in less fraught circumstances might formalise service bonds that had existed *de facto* for some years. Nicholas de Hastings had served in Ralph Fitz William's retinue in Scotland on five separate occasions by the time that an indenture was drawn up between the two men in 1311.[47] In other instances the need for such contracts might be circumvented completely by the granting of annuities in return for military service. In 1300 Hugh de Neville granted to John Filiol 100 shillings and two robes yearly 'for his service in the war of Scotland' (*por soun aler en la Gwere de Eskose*).[48]

To summarise, then, members of the aristocracy in late thirteenth- and early fourteenth-century England could employ a number of techniques to recruit men into their retinues. Most earls, barons and bannerets sought in the first instance to activate personal bonds with their kinsmen and household retainers. In doing so they continued a tradition dating back to the early Middle Ages. Nevertheless, by the reign of Edward I most lords endeavoured to supplement their *familiae* by recruiting additional men with whom their links might be less strong. These men could be merged with the main corpus of retainers whenever the lord was summoned to arms by the king. The members of this wider affinity might simply be kitted out in their lord's livery for a short spell of service before being dismissed; yet it was increasingly common for military

---

43 'Private Indentures for Life Service', no. 4.

44 *Ibid.*, no. 6: '*in exercitu domini regis ad transfretando mare vel alio quoque loco quod dicto domino Johanne placuerit*'.

45 *Ibid.*, no. 7: '*en la guerre mue par entre le Rey de Engletere et le Rey de Fraunce*'.

46 For evidence of the difficulties facing one lord, the earl of Arundel, in 1297, see *Documents Illustrating the Crisis of 1297–98 in England*, ed. M. Prestwich, Camden Society 4th ser., xxiv (1980), no. 132.

47 'Private Indentures for Life Service', no. 19. For Hastings' service with Fitz William, see: 1300 (C 67/14, m. 12); 1301 (C 67/14, m. 4); 1306 (C 67/16, m. 12); 1309 (*CDS*, v, p. 449); 1310 (C 71/4, m. 10).

48 DL 25, no. 1318. These men did set out together to Scotland in 1300: *Liber Quotidianus*, p. 216.

leaders to formalise their relations with such men in indentures for service and by the granting of annuities. Be that as it may, the significance of indentures as a recruitment aid at this time should not be exaggerated, for relatively few have survived from the pre-Bannockburn era. In most cases, of the various ties of service, it seems likely that those of kinship and friendship remained the most important.

Tapping the Gentry Pool

Having looked at some of the methods by which lords sought to recruit soldiers into their retinues during the reigns of Edward I and Edward II, we must now consider how successful lords were at ensuring the repeated service of their men. After all, there was little purpose in issuing livery, composing indentures and granting annuities if it could not provide the lord with a loyal body of warriors willing to serve with him from one campaign to the next. Such ties of service, not to mention the more obvious bonds associated with membership of the *familia* or kinship group, ought to have ensured some stability in retinue composition; yet until very recently the general impression arising from the extant evidence has been that this was not, in fact, the case. Studies of the affinities of particular fourteenth-century magnates, such as those by Kenneth Fowler and Simon Walker on the retainers of Henry of Grosmont and John of Gaunt respectively, have indicated that retinue composition tended to shift markedly between campaigns.[49] Moreover, detailed analyses into retaining patterns within specific counties (most notably that by Nigel Saul for Gloucestershire)[50] have produced similar results. Indeed, taking a sweeping view across all of the later medieval period, Michael Prestwich quite recently summarised the state of research thus: 'analyses of retinues from that of William Marshal in the early thirteenth century to that of John Talbot in the fifteenth all point to similar conclusions, and suggest that apart from a small core, there was surprisingly little continuity of [retinue] membership from year to year'.[51]

A great deal of research lies behind such conclusions. They cannot, therefore, be put aside. Nevertheless, an alternative reading of the evidence has recently begun to emerge that offers a more nuanced interpretation of retinue composition and stability. Leading the way in this respect has been Andrew Ayton. His study of the English army at Crécy (1346) has shown that several lords in Edward III's host were accompanied by large numbers of men with whom they had connec-

---

[49] K. Fowler, *The King's Lieutenant: Henry of Grosmont, First Duke of Lancaster, 1310–1361* (London, 1969), pp. 182–3 and appendix III; Walker, *The Lancastrian Affinity*, p. 50. See also: D.S. Green, 'Politics and Service with Edward the Black Prince', *The Age of Edward III*, ed. J.S. Bothwell (York, 2001), pp. 58–9; C. Carpenter, 'The Beauchamp Affinity: A Study of Bastard Feudalism at Work', *EHR*, xcv (1980), pp. 519–20; S. Stewart, 'Simon de Montfort and his Followers, June 1263', *EHR*, cxix (2004), pp. 967–8.

[50] Saul, *Knights and Esquires*, p. 83. It should be noted, however, that Saul did perceive an element of stability in the length of time that *some* knights spent in the service of the Berkeley family: *ibid.*, 94–5.

[51] Prestwich, *'Miles in Armis Strenuus'*, p. 217.

tions from previous campaigns.[52] Ayton's analysis centred primarily on the retinue of the earl of Northampton; but he found similar trends within a number of other companies, including those led by the earl of Warwick, Bartholomew de Burgherssh and Hugh le Despenser. Ayton, trusting in the findings of Prestwich, Saul and others, chose not to speculate about the possibility that similar levels of continuity may have been customary within military retinues in earlier and later periods. However, studies carried out by others scholars have shown that such stability in retinue membership was not confined to the 1330s and 1340s. Adrian Bell, in his examination of the personnel taking part in the naval expeditions of 1387 and 1388, found that of the knights and esquires serving in the earl of Arundel's army in 1387, the larger part chose to accompany the same retinue leader, if he was present, in the following year. The significance of this point is hardly negated by the fact that many soldiers continued to serve in 1388 despite the absence of their previous leader.[53] Finally, and of particular relevance to this study, Andrew Spencer has recently noted (in an analysis carried out independently of, and contemporaneously with, the analysis conducted below) that the earls of the reign of Edward I could rely on the service of large numbers of men who followed them to war on more than one occasion. Seventy-two per cent of the men in the earl of Lincoln's retinue in 1307, for example, had served with him in Scotland in the previous year. Overall, over 40 per cent of the men who served with the earl at one point or another gave 'multiple service' in his war *comitiva*.[54]

Given the conflicting opinions on this issue, the time now seems ripe to consider the composition of the retinues led to war by men of *all* ranks during the reigns of Edward I and Edward II. As we have seen, the records for military service which might facilitate such a study are particularly voluminous for the period between the Welsh war of 1277 and the Bannockburn campaign of 1314. It would be impractical to attempt to examine the retinues of all men who led soldiers to war in the stated period. A single military summons list, such as that issued by Edward II in the aftermath of Bannockburn,[55] might contain the names of in excess of 300 men. This gives some idea as to how large a number of lords led retinues to war throughout the four decades under consideration. Consequently, it is necessary to narrow our focus. For this purpose, a sample of retinue leaders has been selected based on the lords named on the Falkirk horse inventories of 1298. The benefits of these inventories as a basis for such a sample have been outlined in chapter 3. Of the 150 or so lords who appear with armed companies on these horse inventories, the retinues of fifty, or a third, have been singled out for closer analysis. A number of factors were taken

---

52 Ayton, 'The English Army at Crécy', pp. 204–15. Ayton, in a separate article, has observed similar levels of stability in the composition of the retinue of Thomas Ughtred, Edward III's sub-marshal at Crécy: *idem*, 'Sir Thomas Ughtred', p. 123.

53 Bell, *War and the Soldier*, pp. 98–9.

54 A. Spencer, 'The Comital Military Retinue in the Reign of Edward I', *Historical Research* (forthcoming 2009). I am grateful to Andrew Spencer for allowing me to consult this article in advance of its publication.

55 *Parl. Writs*, II, ii, pp. 427–30.

into account when deciding which leaders to include in the sample and which to leave out, including: the size of the company with each lord at Falkirk, as shown on the horse inventories; the number of men known to have served with the same lords across all campaigns; and the nature and extent of each leader's connections, familial or otherwise, with other retinue leaders.

A list of the fifty lords selected in this way can be found in the appendix.[56] Chief in terms of social seniority was Edward I's nephew, Thomas, earl of Lancaster. There were forty-five men in his retinue on the Falkirk campaign. In total, we have information on some ninety men who followed him to war at one point or another in the years between his first appearance in the records for military service, in 1297, and 1314. This is despite the fact that he did not serve with Edward II in Scotland in 1310–11 nor at Bannockburn. There is also a wealth of information on the men-at-arms who served on various occasions with his father, Edmund Crouchback, and his brother, Henry.[57] Aymer de Valence, the only other man of comital status (as the heir to an earldom) whose retinue is listed on the horse inventories for the Falkirk expedition, was joined by forty-nine men-at-arms in Scotland in 1298.[58] Approximately 400 individuals can be traced in his service for all campaigns, up to and including the expedition that he led to Scotland in 1315.[59] Most of the lords within our sample, however, led retinues containing far fewer men than the numbers discussed so far. The household retainer Edward Charles and the northern lord John Fitz Reginald each led four *valletti* at Falkirk.[60] Not a great deal separates lords such as these from others who have been left out of the sample. In a few instances the retinues of the father and son have been considered as one. This is for one of two reasons: either they served in close proximity to one another on a number of campaigns or their careers overlapped around the time of the Falkirk expedition. Hugh le Despenser senior and his grasping son, Hugh le Despenser junior, have been included among this group. It is often difficult to distinguish between their respective retainers and military followers.[61]

The lords within our sample were, in general, remarkably active campaigners. Eighteen can be traced in the records for military service on ten or more occasions. Henry de Beaumont fought in seventeen hosts between 1296 and the Scottish campaign of Edward III in 1335;[62] and the crowning moment of his

---

56 Only the sample leaders' surnames are used in most subsequent footnotes.

57 *Scotland in 1298*, pp. 179–81.

58 *Ibid.*, pp. 216–18.

59 For the service in 1315, see E 101/15/6.

60 *Scotland in 1298*, pp. 195, 207.

61 Nigel Saul has made a similar point in 'The Despensers and the Downfall of Edward II', *EHR*, xcix (1984), p. 6. The other fathers and sons whose retinues will be considered as one are: Peter (d. 1303) and John (d. 1344) de Chavent; Nicholas de Meynill senior (d. 1299) and junior (d. 1322); Alan Plukenet senior (d. 1298) and junior; Fulk Fitz Waryn senior (d. 1315) and junior (d. 1336) and Robert de Haustede senior (d. 1321) and junior (d. 1330).

62 1296 (E 101/5/23, m. 3); 1297 (E 101/6/37, m. 7); 1298 (*Scotland in 1298*, p. 172); 1300 (E 101/8/23, m. 2); 1301 (E 101/9/24, m. 1); 1303 (E 101/612/11, m. 1); 1306 (E 101/13/16, fol. 2r); 1308 (*Rotuli Scotiae*, i, pp. 57–9); 1309 (*CDS*, v, p. 447); 1310 (C 71/4, m. 11); 1314 (C 71/6, m. 3); 1319 (E 101/378/4, fol. 31r); 1322 (*CPR, 1321–24*, p. 185); 1327 (C 71/11, m. 6); 1332 (*Scalacronica*, pp. 108–9); 1333 (C 71/13, m. 1); 1335 (C 71/15, m. 17). For a

military career came in 1332, when he led the Disinherited to victory at Dupplin Moor. Furthermore, Bartholomew de Badlesmere,[63] Robert de Clifford,[64] one or other of the Despensers[65] and Aymer de Valence[66] can each be traced in at least a dozen different armies, almost invariably with identifiable men-at-arms in their service. The frequency with which these men served in the king's armies, with fully or at least partially documented companies of named soldiers, means that it is possible to trace the changing composition of their retinues over a number of years and campaigns. For example, nineteen of the lords in our sample took part in one or both of the Welsh wars of 1277 and 1282–3. Only eight of these men (including Walter de Beauchamp, Eustace de Hacche and William de Leyburn)[67] led retinues on either of those occasions, but this enables an investigation of continuity of membership in some retinues between the Welsh wars and the later Scottish campaigns. Moreover, most of our lords led retinues to Scotland on a near-annual basis in the years following the victory at Falkirk. Several, in fact, continued to perform their duties as retinue leaders beyond 1314.[68]

Before consulting the records for military service for insights into the recruitment patterns of the fifty lords in our sample, we must consider the nature and reliability of the evidence. In a thorough exposition of the documentary materials available to prosopographers of fourteenth-century military service,

summary of his military activities, see S. Cameron and A. Ross, 'The Treaty of Edinburgh and the Disinherited (1328–1332), *History*, lxxxiv (1999), pp. 251–2.

[63] For his military service up to and including the Bannockburn campaign, see p. 54, n. 154 and p. 57, n. 179. He also served in 1315 (E 101/376/7, fol. 60r) and 1319 (E 101/378/4, fol. 19v).

[64] 1294 (C 67/10, m. 4); 1296 (E 101/5/23, m. 1i); 1297 (E 101/6/30, m. 1); 1298 (*Scotland in 1298*, p. 196); 1300 (E 101/8/23, m. 5); 1301 (C 67/14, m. 2); 1302 (C 67/15, m. 15); 1303 (E 101/612/11, m. 2); 1306 (E 101/612/15, m. 1); 1307 (E 101/14/15, m. 9); 1309 (*CDS*, v, p. 448); 1310 (E 101/374/5, fols 76r–v); 1314 (C 71/6, m. 1).

[65] 1294 (C 67/10, m. 6); 1296 (E 101/5/23, m. 1i); 1297 (C 67/12, m. 7); 1298 (*Scotland in 1298*, p. 187); 1300 (C 67/14, m. 10); 1301 (C 67/14, m. 5); 1303 (C 67/15, m. 14); 1306 (C 67/16, m. 11); 1307 (*CDS*, v, p. 445); 1308 (*Rotuli Scotiae*, i, p. 55); 1314 (C 71/6, m. 3); 1319 (E 101/378/4, fol. 19v); 1322 (BL, Stowe MS 553, fols 61r–v).

[66] For his service between 1297 and the winter of 1311–12, see p. 41, n. 60. He also led troops of men to war in 1314 (C 71/6, m. 5); 1315 (E 101/15/6, m. 1); 1319 (C 71/10, m. 5); 1322 (BL, Stowe MS 553, fol. 56r); and 1324–5 (*CPR, 1321–24*, p. 427).

[67] Beauchamp (E 101/4/1, m. 1); Hacche (C 47/2/6, m. 2); Leyburn (E 101/3/12; C 47/2/5, m. 2).

[68] Ten of the lords in our sample served at the siege of Berwick in 1319: Badlesmere (E 101/378/4, fol. 19v); Beaumont (E 101/378/4, fol. 31r); Despenser (E 101/378/4, fol. 19v); Haustede junior (C 71/10, m. 4); Lancaster (C 71/10, m. 4); Lovel (C 71/10, m. 7); Mohaut (E 101/378/4, fol. 28v); Meynill junior (C 71/10, m. 9); Mortimer of Chirk (E 101/378/4, fol. 19r); Valence (C 71/10, m. 5). No fewer than seven of the retinue leaders in our sample served in Scotland in 1322, not including those who made proffers at the feudal muster but for whom no evidence of service in that year survives: Beauchamp of Somerset (*CPR, 1321–24*, p. 184); Beaumont (*CPR, 1321–24*, p. 185); the Despensers (BL, Stowe MS 553, fols 61r–v); Haustede junior (BL, Stowe MS 553, fol. 60r); Lovel (BL, Stowe MS 553, fol. 60v); Mohaut (*CPR, 1321–24*, p. 198); Valence (BL, Stowe MS 553, fol. 56r). Finally, three of our lords can be traced in armies raised during the early years of the reign of Edward III: Beaumont (see above, p. 121, n. 62); Fitz Waryn junior in 1327 and 1333 (C 71/11, m. 5; C 71/13, m. 1); and Lovel in 1327 (C 71/11, m. 6).

Andrew Ayton has highlighted some of the pitfalls of working with sources such as pay-rolls and enrolled letters of protection.[69] There is no need to summarise all of Ayton's findings here, but it is worthwhile reiterating some of his main points and linking them to the evidence available for our fifty leaders.

One of the main obstacles to a full understanding of recruitment practices in late thirteenth- and early fourteenth-century England is that two of the sources on which we are most reliant for names of men-at-arms, letters of protection and of attorney, regularly reveal the identities of only a third or fewer of the soldiers in any given *comitiva*. For example, of the eleven men listed in the company of William de Cantilupe on the household horse inventory for the Scottish campaign of 1300, only three appear with enrolled letters of protection for service in his retinue in that year.[70] Given that 'protections, together with enrolled appointments of attornies, are very much the staple diet of the student of Edwardian armies',[71] the incompleteness of the data provided by such sources is a major problem. Furthermore, letters of protection and of attorney were 'statements of intent [of service], rather than firm evidence of performance'.[72] We cannot therefore always be certain that the men who appear on the Scottish rolls and supplementary patent rolls with enrolled letters of protection actually went to war. Although for this earlier period there also survive enrolled letters of respite of debts (which record the names of men whose debts to the king were postponed for the duration of their service in his armies),[73] it remains the case that there are very large gaps in the evidence. This problem is exacerbated by the tendency of many earls and bannerets to serve in the armies of Edward I and Edward II without Crown pay. Such men as these, and their retinues, do not appear on the extant horse inventories or the few surviving pay-rolls. The upshot of all of this is that the evidence for retinue composition is patchy and uneven. Lords might appear with well-documented groups of men-at-arms for some campaigns, but with only partially recorded companies for others.[74] It should also be borne in mind that the size of some leaders' retinues increased dramatically during their careers, meaning that large numbers of men in their later retinues must not have served with them on previous occasions.[75]

---

[69] Ayton, *Knights and Warhorses*, chapter 5.

[70] E 101/8/23, m. 2; C 67/14, m. 11.

[71] Ayton, *Knights and Warhorses*, p. 157.

[72] *Ibid.*, p. 157. See also J.S. Critchley, 'The Early History of the Writ of Judicial Protection', *BIHR*, xlv (1972), pp. 198–9.

[73] Letters of respite of debts add very little to the information provided by letters of protection but are for some campaigns at least as valuable as letters of attorney. On the supplementary patent roll for the year 1300, for example, there are 125 letters of respite of debts compared with 736 letters of protection and just forty-four letters of attorney: C 67/14, mm. 8–14.

[74] For example, Thomas de Furnivall is recorded with ten men (including his sub-leader Henry de Pinkeney) on the *forinsec* horse inventory for the army of 1298. In 1296 we have the name of just one man who took out a letter of attorney for service in Furnivall's retinue; and in 1300 we have the names of only two men with enrolled letters of protection for service with the same lord: *Scotland in 1298*, pp. 211, 222; C 67/11, m. 4; C 67/14, m. 9.

[75] The retinues of Bartholomew de Badlesmere and Henry de Beaumont supply evidence of this kind of increase in strength. From Badlesmere's retinues we know the identities of one

Overall, the evidence provided by the records for military service is distorted in such a way as to suggest that retinue membership was less stable than was probably the case. Bearing this in mind, the figures given in the remainder of this chapter are general indicators of recruitment trends rather than precise statistics. Nevertheless, these figures have their uses, and they can be relied upon for two reasons. Firstly, they provide as accurate an insight into the shifting patterns of retinue recruitment as the sources will allow. Secondly, as minimum figures, they err on the side of caution.

Of the military campaigns that took place between the Welsh war of 1277 and Bannockburn, the parameters set for this study, the Falkirk campaign of 1298 was the only one (for obvious reasons) on which all fifty of the leaders in the sample were present and served with fully documented retinues. Continuity data for all fifty companies put into the field on that occasion can be found in the appendix, but some of the main points arising from this evidence can be summarised here. Of the 647 knights and *valletti* who appear on the Falkirk horse inventories in the retinues of the said lords, a total of 289, or 45 per cent, can be traced in the service of the same men on at least one other campaign between 1277 and 1314. In addition to this, 169, or 26 per cent, served within the same retinue on two other occasions or more. This suggests a fairly high level of continuity, particularly given that some of these retinues are poorly documented and bring the overall average down. John de Havering, the justice of Wales who played a major role in putting down the Welsh rebellion of 1294–5, was present at Falkirk with a retinue of twenty-five men, but little evidence survives of his followers from other campaigns.[76] By contrast, nineteen of the sample retinues at Falkirk reveal continuity levels of 60 per cent or higher. All four of the sergeants with Edward Charles – John de Boxstede, Roger de Aston, William de Shoreham and Thomas de Harlesdon – had followed him to Flanders in the previous year. Two of these men, Boxstede and Harlesdon, joined his company on a further, third occasion.[77] Other modestly sized retinues at Falkirk that display high levels of continuity include those of Hugh Pointz (four out of five men with him on other

man who took out a letter of protection for service in Gascony in 1294 (*Rôles Gascons*, iii, p. 101), one who had a protection enrolled for service in Flanders (C 67/12, m. 1), four who appear on the household horse inventory for the army of 1298 (*Scotland in 1298*, p. 190), and then only five men in total who took out protections for the Scottish campaigns of 1301 (C 67/14, m. 2), 1303 (C 67/15, mm. 7, 13), 1306 (C 67/16, m. 13) and 1310 (C 71/4, m. 13). By contrast, some fifty men appear in Badlesmere's sub-retinue for the Bannockburn campaign: C 71/6, mm. 1, 5; C 81/1727, m. 18. For Beaumont we have the names of one military follower in 1296 (E 101/5/23, m. 3), five in 1297 (E 101/6/37, m. 7), five in 1298 (*Scotland in 1298*, p. 172), six in 1300 (E 101/8/23, m. 2), seven in 1301 (E 101/9/24, m. 1), six in 1303 (E 101/612/11, m. 1) and two in 1306 (E 101/13/16, fol. 19r). He seems to have led much larger companies to war in 1309 and 1314 (*CDS*, v, pp. 447–9; C 71/6, mm. 3, 4). Similar points concerning the distortion in the evidence caused by increases in retinue strength or the need to create a retinue from scratch, have been made by Andrew Ayton in his study of the English army on the Crécy campaign, 'The English Army at Crécy', pp. 211–13.

[76] *Ann. Wigorn.*, p. 522; *Scotland in 1298*, pp. 228–9; E 101/5/18, m. 1; SC 1/27, no. 24.

[77] *Scotland in 1298*, p. 195; E 101/6/37, m. 7; E 101/5/23, m. 1i; E 101/612/11, m. 6.

campaigns),[78] William le Brun (seven out of eight men)[79] and John Botetourt (eleven out of sixteen men).[80] Although it is not possible to enter into detail on all of these retinues, the service continuity of the men with Robert de Mohaut in 1298 can be taken as reasonably representative, as shown in table 4.1.

Table 4.1: Service given with Robert de Mohaut by the men in his retinue in 1298[81]

Name of soldier	Campaigns served with Mohaut
John de Bracebridge (K)	1297, 1298, 1301, 1303, 1307, 1310
Roger de Bilney (K)	1297, 1298, 1301, 1303, 1310
Nicholas de Mohaut (S)	1298, 1301, 1303
William de Bilney (S)	1298, 1300, 1301, 1303
Ralph de Kerdiff (S)	1298
Robert Botevilleyn (S)	1298, 1301, 1303
Thomas Fattinge (S)	1297, 1298, 1300, 1301, 1303
Richard Strech (S)	1298, 1300, 1301, 1303, 1310
Adam Place (S)	1298
Adam de Werington (S)	1298
Nicholas de Lalleford (S)	1298
Bartholomew de Morley (S)	1298
William de Bibington (S)	1298
John de la Mare (S)	1298, 1300, 1301
Geoffrey de Bracebridge (S)	1298

K = knight
S = sergeant

The core element within the Mohaut retinue was even more stable than is indicated in table 4.1, as a number of the men-at-arms with Robert de Mohaut in Scotland in 1298 – including Roger de Bilney, John de Bracebridge and Bartholomew de Morley – had taken out letters of protection with his older brother, Roger, in the mid-1290s.[82] The presence of a group of men who had served together in the recent past must have added to the feeling of mutual trust within the Mohaut retinue at the battle of Falkirk.

---

[78] This includes two men, his son Nicholas and Isambert de St Blimund, who were with him on a further three campaigns, in 1294–5 (C 67/10, m. 7), 1297 (E 101/6/19, m. 1) and 1300 (C 67/14, m. 9).

[79] Of these men, four were with him in 1297 and 1300, namely John de Roches, Peter de Roches, Reginald de la Forde and Hugh de Godeshulle: *Scotland in 1298*, p. 176; E 101/6/37, m. 1i; E 101/8/23, m. 4.

[80] His kinsman William Botetourt was with him on six additional occasions. For most of this service, see above, p. 94, n. 173. He also rode to Scotland in 1301 (C 67/14, m. 6) and 1306 (E 101/612/15, m. 3).

[81] 1297 (C 67/12, m. 2, 7); 1298 (*Scotland in 1298*, p. 209); 1300 (*Documents and Records of Scotland*, p. 231); 1301 (E 101/9/23, m. 2); 1303 (C 67/15, mm. 8, 12; E 101/612/8, m. 1); 1307 (*CDS*, v, pp. 445–6); 1310 (C 71/4, mm. 6, 12).

[82] *Rôles Gascons*, iii, pp. 121, 298.

The same can be said for a large number of other retinues in Edward I's army in 1298. Particularly high levels of continuity can be detected in the *comitivae* of the thirty-two lords within our sample who had led companies to the Low Countries in the previous year. Of the 387 men-at-arms who served in the retinues of these thirty-two leaders in Flanders in 1297, 172 (44 per cent) subsequently followed the same lords north of the border to confront William Wallace's army at Falkirk. One of the lords who served in both of these armies was the future earl of Pembroke, Aymer de Valence. His retinue in Flanders in 1297 consisted of fifty-four soldiers (including those who appear with enrolled letters of protection or attorney). Of these men, twenty-seven (50 per cent) went on to serve with him in Scotland in the following year.[83] Moreover, of the soldiers who were present on both of these occasions, thirteen, or around a half, appear in his retinue on at least one other campaign. Among these individuals were some of Valence's most frequent followers, such as Walter de Gacelyn and John de la Ryvere.[84] The steward Walter de Beauchamp led a similarly large retinue on the Flanders campaign.[85] Comparison of the composition of his retinue in 1297 with that at Falkirk reveals similar trends to those already noted for Aymer de Valence. Of the thirty-four men who were with Beauchamp and his son in the Low Countries, seventeen (50 per cent) followed Beauchamp senior to Scotland a few months later;[86] and eleven saw service with the same lord on more than just these two expeditions. No fewer than eight of these men-at-arms had accompanied Beauchamp to Scotland in 1296;[87] and a minimum of three – Roger de la Mare, John Paynot and William le Skirmissour – had been connected to him since the Welsh war of 1294–5.[88] Therefore, even though the Falkirk campaign took place at an early stage in the Scottish wars, many retinue leaders were already able to rely on a core of followers who had seen service with them during the wars in Wales and France.

There is no agreed standard against which stability in retinue membership can be tested, with historians probably differing in the criteria that they set in this respect. Nevertheless, given that around 50 per cent of the men in our sample from 1298 served with their retinue leader from that year on at least one other occasion, and that around 25 per cent did so on a third occasion (if not more), it seems that there was greater stability in retinue composition in the late thirteenth and early fourteenth centuries than has sometimes been assumed. Yet, what if the levels of retinue stability for the Flanders and Falkirk expeditions were exceptional? How can we be sure that such high levels of continuity were

---

[83] For his retinues in 1297 and 1298, see E 101/6/28, m. 2i and *Scotland in 1298*, pp. 216–18 respectively.

[84] Gacelyn: 1297 (E 101/6/28, m. 2i); 1298 (*Scotland in 1298*, p. 216); 1299 (Phillips, *Aymer de Valence*, appendix 2); 1300 (C 67/14, m. 10); 1302 (Phillips, *Aymer de Valence*, appendix 2); 1303 (C 67/15, m. 7); 1311 (C 71/5, m. 4). For de la Ryvere's service, most of which he performed in Valence's retinue, see above, p. 24, n. 108.

[85] E 101/6/37, m. 1ii.

[86] For his retinue at Falkirk, see *Scotland in 1298*, pp. 183–4.

[87] E 101/5/23, m. 2.

[88] *CCW*, p. 48.

normal throughout the four decades under investigation? Evidently, a wider survey of the evidence is required.

The army that Edward I led to Scotland in 1296 was one of the most successful to be conducted out of England in the thirteenth century. The campaign began with the sack and capture of Berwick by Edward's soldiers and culminated in the victory of the earl Warenne over the Scottish feudal army at Dunbar. Of the fifty lords in our sample, twenty served north of the border in 1296 with companies of named soldiers. Table 4.2 shows what proportion of the said soldiers served with their leader from 1296 on other occasions between 1277 and 1314. The table also reveals the frequency with which the men who gave repeated service with their leaders from 1296 went to war in the retinues of the said lords.

Table 4.2: Retinue continuity for sample leaders in Scotland, 1296 (1277–1314)

Leader	Number of men with leader:		% continuity	Times served with leader other than in 1296:						
	In 1296	In 1296 (who also served in another year)		1	2	3	4	5	6	7
Audley	3	2	66	1	1	–	–	–	–	–
J. Beauchamp	3	1	33	–	–	1	–	–	–	–
W. Beauchamp	10	8	80	1	1	–	4	2	–	–
Beaumont	1	1	100	–	–	–	1	–	–	–
Brun	2	1	50	1	–	–	–	–	–	–
Charles	3	1	33	–	1	–	–	–	–	–
Chavent	9	4	44	–	2	–	1	1	–	–
Clifford	14	8	57	3	3	1	–	–	–	1
Courtenay	2	2	100	1	–	1	–	–	–	–
Despenser	26	12	46	6	2	2	–	1	–	1
Fitz Payn	7	5	71	–	2	1	1	–	1	–
Fitz Waryn	11	1	9	1	–	–	–	–	–	–
Furnivall	1	1	100	–	1	–	–	–	–	–
H. Mortimer	1	1	100	1	–	–	–	–	–	–
Plukenet	13	5	38	2	1	2	–	–	–	–
Scales	4	4	100	–	1	–	1	2	–	–
Tony	1	1	100	–	1	–	–	–	–	–
Tregoz	1	0	0	–	–	–	–	–	–	–
Tuchet	2	0	0	–	–	–	–	–	–	–
Welles	8	3	38	–	–	1	–	1	1	–
Total	122	61	50	17	16	9	8	7	2	2

The figures for the Berwick–Dunbar campaign of 1296, like those for the Falkirk expedition of 1298, suggest that lords who led armed companies during the opening stages of the Scottish war could rely, in general, on fairly high levels of continuity in retinue personnel. In 1296 some of these lords appear to have been establishing new service connections rather than tapping into old ones. Of the seven men who are named on the horse inventory for 1296 in the retinue of Robert Fitz Payn, no fewer than five later gave service with him in

the Low Countries or on expeditions to Scotland;[89] yet, not one of these men can
be traced in his service during the earlier, Welsh wars. This may be the result
of unbalanced documentary survival. Fitz Payn's retinues are well documented
from 1296; but for the expeditions to Wales we have the names of just three men
who were with him in 1277 and a further three from 1282.[90] Indeed, some of the
more fully documented companies in 1296 *do* reveal continuity in membership
from previous campaigns. For example, Hugh le Despenser senior and Nicholas
de Audley could call on the service of five men and two men respectively who
had accompanied them to Wales in 1294–5.[91] Yet irrespective of *when* such
service bonds were established, the most striking point to emerge from this
cross-section of retinues is the large proportion of men who gave service with
their lords from 1296 on two additional campaigns. Of the 122 named individuals
in our sample from the Berwick–Dunbar campaign, forty-four, or 36 per cent,
fall into this category. This compares with only 26 per cent of the men-at-arms
from our sample in 1298 who served with their leaders from that year on two or
more additional military ventures. Among these forty-four individuals, in 1296,
were two soldiers, Thomas de Monteny and John de Haudlo[92] (in the retinues
of Robert de Clifford and Hugh le Despenser senior respectively), who served
with their lords from the Berwick–Dunbar campaign on seven other occasions.[93]
Adam de Welles could count on the service of Thomas de Brumwych in no
fewer than six additional hosts.[94]

   The similarity of the evidence for continuity in retinue personnel from the
campaigns of 1296, 1297 and 1298 is unlikely to be a coincidence. In each

---

[89] In addition to 1296, John de Cary was with Fitz Payn in Flanders in 1297 (E 101/6/19, m.
1) as well as in Scotland in 1298 (*Scotland in 1298*, p. 171), 1300 (*Documents and Records of
Scotland*, p. 221), 1303 (C 67/15, m. 6), 1306 (C 67/16, m. 4) and 1310 (C 71/4, m. 13). John
de Derneford could be found in Fitz Payn's retinue in 1297 (E 101/6/19, m. 1), 1298 (*Scotland
in 1298*, p. 171) and 1310 (C 71/4, m. 13). For Geoffrey de Harden's service with the same
lord, see: 1297 (E 101/6/19, m. 1); 1298 (*Scotland in 1298*, p. 171); 1300 (*Documents and
Records of Scotland*, p. 221); 1303 (BL, Additional MS 8835, fol. 46v). For Geoffrey de la
Linde's additional service with Fitz Payn, see: 1297 (E 101/6/19, m. 1) and 1298 (*Scotland in
1298*, p. 171). Finally, Simon de Ralegh served with Fitz Payn again in 1297 (E 101/6/19, m.
1) and 1298 (*Scotland in 1298*, p. 171). For the service of these men in 1296, see E 101/5/23,
m. 2.

[90] *Parl. Writs*, i, pp. 202, 229.

[91] Despenser: John de Haudlo, John Hastang, Robert de Stanegrave, Henry le Tyes and
Theobald de St George (C 67/10, mm. 5d, 6). Audley: John de Everus and Robert de Meynill
(*CCW*, p. 46).

[92] Haudlo (or 'Handlo') was one of the few men, along with Hugh le Despenser senior,
who remained loyal to Edward II around the time of the Boulogne agreement of 1308: R.M.
Haines, *King Edward II: Edward of Caernarfon, His Life, His Reign and Its Aftermath*
(Montreal, 2003), p. 69. See also Saul, 'The Despensers and the Downfall of Edward II', pp.
6–7.

[93] Monteny: 1296–1311 (see above, p. 94, nn. 174–5). He also served with Clifford in 1314:
C 71/6, m. 1. Haudlo: 1294 (C 67/10, m. 6); 1296 (E 101/5/23, m. 1i); 1297 (C 67/12, m. 3d);
1298 (*Scotland in 1298*, p. 187); 1300 (C 47/1/6, m. 3); 1303 (*CVCR*, p. 82); 1306 (C 67/16,
m. 6); 1314 (C 71/6, m. 3).

[94] 1296 (E 101/5/23, m. 1i); 1297 (E 101/6/37, m. 4); 1300 (E 101/8/23, m. 4); 1301 (E
101/9/24, m. 1); 1303–4 (BL, Additional MS 8835, fol. 49r); 1306 (C 67/16, m. 11); 1310
(C 71/4, m. 11).

of these years we find roughly the same levels of retinue stability, albeit with apparently wide divergence between retinues. The expeditions of Edward I's later years supply the best opportunity to analyse the issue of retinue stability in detail, for this is the period for which the documentary materials are most complete. Indeed, horse inventories of varying size have survived for all of the campaigns (except those to Gascony) between 1296 and 1307. This is fortunate as horse inventories, unlike letters of protection, of attorney and of respite of debts, usually indicate the status of each man-at-arms: *miles* or *vallettus*. Taking five of these horse inventories, for the successive campaigns of 1297 (Flanders), 1298, 1300, 1301 and 1303–4 (Scotland), it is possible to compare the loyalty shown by lords' knightly followers with that displayed by their sergeants. Of the fifty lords and retinues in our sample, eleven are represented on each of the said horse inventories. As most of the horse inventories of these years list the names of the king's *familiares*, this group of retinue leaders is dominated by Edward's household retainers. In 1300, William de Leyburn, Robert de Scales, Adam de Welles and Henry de Beaumont received fees and robes as household bannerets, while Thomas de Bykenore and Robert de Haustede were among the king's knights.[95] Nicholas de Malemains, Richard Lovel and Robert de Tony were connected to the royal household in other years. The group also includes two household clerks, John de Drokensford and John de Benstede. Despite their clerical status, these men led some of the largest retinues on campaign during these years. Table 4.3 presents the continuity data for the knights (K) and sergeants (S) who served in the retinues of these eleven lords between 1297 and 1303. The data are presented on a campaign-by-campaign basis so as to provide an impression of retinue stability as it may have been discerned at the time.

These figures offer a relatively precise insight into levels of retinue stability. They suggest that lords could usually rely on the service of around 50 per cent of the knights whom they had led to war on the most recent expedition (the lower figure for continuity between 1301 and 1303 appears to have been exceptional). In the case of the lords' sergeants, this level of continuity drops to 35–40 per cent. To interpret these figures correctly, a couple of factors must be taken into consideration. Firstly, large retinues often contained a number of smaller sub-units; and in such instances the bachelors rather than the sergeants would have acted as the secondary recruiters. This is illustrated by the composition of the earl Warenne's retinue during the war of Saint-Sardos (1324–5). Of the lesser men-at-arms in the earl's extended retinue, no fewer than eighty were recruited by his (mainly knightly) sub-leaders.[96] This means that we cannot always be sure that the sergeants in any given retinue had been recruited by the company leader directly. Moreover, when a lord went on campaign, most of his regular followers could be found among his sergeants. Thus, taking the five expeditions as whole, of the sergeants with the keeper of the wardrobe, John de Drokensford: eight were named in his retinue twice; seven served with him on three occasions; two (John de Flambard and William de Fauconberg) were

95 *Liber Quotidianus*, pp. 188–95, 310–13, 324–6.
96 E 101/17/31.

Table 4.3: Service continuity in selected retinues, by rank (1297–1303)[97]

Leader	Retinue continuity from campaign to campaign*							
	1297–8		1298–1300		1300–1		1301–3	
	K	S	K	S	K	S	K	S
Beaumont	1/1	3/4	1/1	3/4	1/1	2/5	0/1	2/6
Benstede	2/2	2/5	–	–	2/2	3/9	1/2	4/10
Bykenore	–	2/3	–	1/3	–	2/2	–	3/3
Drokensford	1/3	6/25	3/3	10/21	3/6	7/21	2/3	9/20
Haustede	–	2/4	–	1/3	–	1/2	–	1/3
Leyburn	1/4	7/18	1/3	4/12	3/6	4/15	2/3	5/12
Lovel	–	2/3	–	2/5	–	4/5	–	4/8
Malemains	–	2/6	–	0/3	–	2/2	–	1/4
Scales	0/1	3/8	0/1	1/6	0/1	2/6	0/3	2/14
Tony	2/2	2/12	1/2	3/14	1/2	4/8	0/3	1/15
Welles	0/1	7/13	1/3	3/11	1/4	3/11	1/2	3/10
Total	7/14	38/101	7/13	28/82	11/22	34/86	6/17	35/105
(% by rank)	(50%)	(38%)	(54%)	(34%)	(50%)	(40%)	(35%)	(33%)

* Clerks not included. Benstede's retinue on the 1300 inventory contains just one named man, a clerk, so his figures for 1300–1 are carried over from 1298.

connected to his *comitiva* four times; and one (Thomas de Burghunt) was named in his retinue for all five campaigns.[98] To what extent Drokensford, as keeper of the wardrobe, actually led these men is open to question (his own horse was not always appraised); but the example of the cofferer Ralph de Manton, who was killed while serving as an armoured warrior in Scotland in 1303,[99] should remind us that household officials did not always allow their clerical duties to get in the way of martial pursuits. Drokensford's inclusion on the Falkirk roll of arms probably reflects his soldierly credentials.[100] Similar levels of stability can be detected in the retinue of John de Benstede (another household clerk),[101]

---

[97] Sources: Flanders in 1297–8 (E 101/6/19, 28, 37), and Scotland in 1298 (*Scotland in 1298*, pp. 160–237), 1300 (E 101/8/23), 1301 (E 101/9/23, 24) and 1303–4 (E 101/612/7, 8, 9, 11).

[98] For Drokensford's retinues on these campaigns, see: E 101/6/37, mm. 2i–ii; *Scotland in 1298*, pp. 174–5; E 101/8/23, mm. 3–4, 7d; *Liber Quotidianus*, pp. 202–3; E 101/9/24, mm. 1d, 3, 4; and E 101/612/11, m. 5.

[99] Prestwich, *Armies and Warfare*, p. 170.

[100] *Rolls of Arms, Edward I*, i, p. 414. Unfortunately, a short biographical article on Drokensford does not reveal a great deal about his activities in Scotland, other than that he spent a lot of time there during the 1290s and was temporarily appointed as treasurer of Scotland following Hugh de Cressingham's death in battle in 1297: N.G. Brett-James, 'John de Drokensford, bishop of Bath and Wells', *Transactions of the London and Middlesex Archaeological Society*, x (1951), p. 286.

[101] One sergeant, Alexander de Norton, was with Benstede on all four campaigns for which his men-at-arms are listed. Two others, Richard de Dunmowe and John de Aulton, are named three times: E 101/6/37, m. 2iii; *Scotland in 1298*, p. 177; E 101/9/24, m. 2; E 101/612/11, m. 3. In 1296 Benstede had been appointed, along with the earl of March, to estimate the number of men slain at the battle of Dunbar: C.L. Kingsford, 'John de Benstede and his Missions for Edward I', *Essays in History presented to Reginald Lane Poole*, ed. H.W.C. Davis (Oxford, 1927), p. 335.

as well as in the companies of lesser lords such as Richard Lovel and Thomas de Bykenore.[102] Company leaders did not lack strong connections with their *valletti*. On the contrary, among the sergeants in any lord's retinue there could usually be found a substantial core of loyal followers.

The figures in table 4.3 for the service of lords' knights are particularly worthy of our attention, revealing as they do that the more established members of the gentry (the kind of men perhaps generally inclined to pursue their own interests) were not averse to giving repeated service under the same banner. One or two examples will suffice to demonstrate this point. Of the six knights who were in William de Leyburn's retinue on the Caerlaverock campaign of 1300, two had served with him in Flanders in 1297, one had been in his company at Falkirk, three joined his retinue in Scotland in 1301 and three served with him north of the border in 1303.[103] Moreover, the cluster of six knights in Leyburn's retinue in 1300 represented his most successful recruitment effort of this stage of the wars. His companies usually contained no more than three or four knights. Consequently, of the knights in Leyburn's retinue, there was a high proportion who served with him repeatedly. One knight, Fulk Peyforer, rode under his banner on all five expeditions between 1297 and 1303; and another, John de Champayne, joined Leyburn's company in 1300, 1301 and 1303.[104] Stable recruitment patterns can be detected in other retinues. Adam de la Forde and William de Chabenore served with Robert de Tony in Flanders in 1297 and then followed him to Scotland a few months later.[105] Of the knights in Adam de Welles' retinue in 1303, one, Thomas de St Loe, had served with him in 1300 and 1301, and another, John de Caltoft, had joined his company at Falkirk.[106] One exception to this general stability in retinue membership was the *comitiva* of Robert de Scales. He recruited a new knight or set of knights for almost every campaign. Of the knights who served with him during these years, only one, John de Vaux, did so more than once: in 1298 and 1301. Vaux had previously joined Scales' company as a sergeant, in Flanders in 1297.[107]

Although table 4.3 provides a detailed insight into continuity patterns at the height of Edward I's wars, it does not account for the many instances when men left lords' service between 1297 and 1303 only to rejoin their retinues in later armies. Service connections might span several decades; but this is not always immediately manifest in the records for military service. One of the men in Robert de Clifford's retinue at Falkirk was a *vallettus* by the name of Thomas

---

[102] William de Punchardon served with the former, and John de Bykenore served with the latter, in all five armies. Punchardon: 1297 (E 101/6/37, m. 4); 1298 (*Scotland in 1298*, p. 179); 1300 (E 101/8/23, m. 1); 1301 (E 101/9/24, m. 2); 1303 (E 101/612/11, m. 1). John de Bykenore: 1297 (E 101/6/37, m. 4); 1298 (*Scotland in 1298*, p. 162); 1300 (E 101/8/23, m. 4); 1301 (E 101/9/24, m. 2); 1303 (E 101/612/11, m. 3).

[103] E 101/6/37, m. 4; *Scotland in 1298*, p. 194; E 101/8/23, m. 4; E 101/9/23, m. 3; E 101/612/11, m. 5d.

[104] For their service, see the sources listed in note 103.

[105] E 101/6/37, m. 4; *Scotland in 1298*, p. 164.

[106] 1298 (*Scotland in 1298*, p. 172); 1300 (E 101/8/23, m. 4); 1301 (E 101/9/24, m. 1); 1303 (E 101/612/11, m. 2).

[107] *Scotland in 1298*, p. 170; E 101/9/24, m. 4; E 101/6/37, m. 2i.

de Hauteclou.[108] He possibly served with Clifford on some of the campaigns that followed, but he appears next to have joined the same lord's retinue on the Scottish March in the winter of 1311–12.[109] Sometimes, only consultation of non-military sources reveals the durability of relations between lords and their military followers. Roger de la Mare served with Walter de Beauchamp on six occasions between 1294 and 1301;[110] but it would seem, from the evidence of a commission of oyer and terminer issued in Worcestershire in 1284, that the two men had known one another for at least a decade by the time of the great Welsh rebellion.[111] William Malherbe appears to have served in Richard Lovel's war *comitiva* on only one occasion, in 1314,[112] but these men may have been friends. Lovel had requested, five years previously, that Malherbe be granted a weekly market in Somerset.[113] Ties between lords and individuals who served in their retinues only infrequently or occasionally can sometimes be detected in heraldic records. Of the knights who served with William de Leyburn between the Welsh war of 1277 and his death in 1310, six bore heraldic charges that were similar to, or incorporated aspects of, the Leyburn coat of arms: *azure, six lions rampant argent*. It seems likely that at least some of these Kentish landholders[114] (Leyburn's main estates lay in Kent also), or their ancestors, had adapted the Leyburn design. Yet each of these knights – Thomas de Sandwich,[115] Nicholas Pessun,[116] Richard de Rokesley,[117] John le Sauvage,[118] Roger de Tilmanston[119] and William de Detling[120] – could be found in Leyburn's campaign retinue on no more than one occasion.

Having established that men-at-arms who appear to have served with their lords on only one or two occasions often had more lasting connections to them, we can now turn our attention to soldiers who served in their lords' retinues more frequently. Consideration of this group of men raises an obvious question: where did retinue leaders draw their most reliable military followers from? Ties of kinship, tenure, locality and service were among the most important.

---

[108] *Scotland in 1298*, p. 197.

[109] E 101/14/15, m. 3.

[110] 1294 (see above, p. 126, n. 88); 1296 (E 101/5/23, m. 2); 1297 (E 101/6/37, m. 1ii); 1298 (*Scotland in 1298*, p. 183); 1300 (*Liber Quotidianus*, p. 174); 1301 (E 101/9/24, m. 2).

[111] *CPR, 1281–92*, p. 144.

[112] C 71/6, m. 3.

[113] *Cal. Ch. Rolls*, iii, p. 128.

[114] For the connections of these men (their names are given a little lower down in the main text) with Kent, see *Rolls of Arms, Edward I*, ii, pp. 141, 339, 368, 380, 381 and 416.

[115] *Rolls of Arms, Edward I*, ii, p. 380; E 101/13/7, m. 2 (1306). (He bore *or, on a chief azure three lions rampant argent*).

[116] *Rolls of Arms, Edward I*, ii, p. 339; *Parl. Writs*, i, p. 203 (1277). (He bore *ermine, on a fess azure three lions rampant argent*).

[117] *Rolls of Arms, Edward I*, ii, p. 368; E 101/8/23, m. 4 (1300). (He bore *azure, a fess gules between six lions rampant argent*).

[118] *Rolls of Arms, Edward I*, ii, p. 381; E 101/6/37, m. 4 (1297). (He bore *ermine, on a chief azure three lions rampant argent*).

[119] *Rolls of Arms, Edward I*, ii, p. 416; C 47/2/5, m. 2 (1282–3). (He bore *gules, six lions rampant with forked tails argent*).

[120] *Rolls of Arms, Edward I*, ii, p. 141; *Scotland in 1298*, p. 194 (1298). (He bore *sable, six lions rampant argent*).

Taking the first of these, there is evidence that the lords in our sample relied quite heavily on the service of their relatives, be they relatives by blood or marriage. In 1275 a union was proposed between John, son of Henry de Hastings, and Isabella, daughter of William de Valence, to strengthen the kinship ties that already existed between these families (John and Isabella were within the third and fourth degrees of kindred) and to overcome an enmity that had arisen during the civil war of 1264–5.[121] This kinship bond was still being exploited by William de Valence's son, Aymer, a generation later. Although not one member of the Hastings family was in Valence's retinue at Falkirk, John de Hastings junior served with Valence in Scotland on several occasions during the reign of Edward II: in 1311, 1314, 1315, 1319 and 1322.[122] Moreover, a glance through any series of military retinues in the late thirteenth and early fourteenth centuries would reveal a number of knights and sergeants who shared their surnames with their leaders. A lord's blood relatives could usually be relied upon to give frequent service within his *comitiva*. William de Leyburn's son Thomas, for example, appears in his father's retinue on four occasions between 1298 and 1306.[123] In like manner, Philip de Welles followed his brother Adam to war on four expeditions during the late 1290s and early 1300s.[124]

The importance of kinship connections to retinue composition can also be analysed in another way: by considering the familial bonds between men in the retinue who were not related to their lord. As we have seen, of the men-at-arms in our sample of retinues from the Falkirk campaign, a minimum of 45 per cent served with their leader from that year on at least one other occasion between 1277 and 1314. If we consider continuity of service within the family, this figure rises. For example, four of the soldiers listed in Ralph Pipard's company in 1298 – Adam le Mareschal, Simon Barry, John de Scalebroke and George Giffard – seem to have followed him to war on just that one occasion; yet, each of these men shared his surname with another soldier in Pipard's retinue in 1298 who served with the same lord on at least one other campaign.[125] Analysis of

[121] *Calendar of Entries in the Papal Registers Relating to Great Britain and Ireland: Papal Letters,* ed. W.H. Bliss *et al.,* 20 vols, vols i–xiv (London, 1893–1960), vols xv–xx (Dublin, 1978–2005), i, p. 450.

[122] 1311 (C 71/5, m. 4); 1314 (C 71/6, m. 3); 1315 (E 101/15/6, m. 1); 1319 (C 71/10, m. 5); 1322 (*CPR, 1321–24,* p. 186).

[123] 1298 (*Scotland in 1298,* p. 194); 1300 (C 67/14, m. 9); 1303–4 (BL, Additional MS 8835, fol. 56r); 1306 (E 101/13/7, m. 2).

[124] 1296 (E 101/5/23, m. 1i); 1297 (BL, Additional MS 7965, fol. 64v); 1298 (*Scotland in 1298,* p. 172); 1300 (E 101/8/23, m. 4).

[125] *Scotland in 1298,* pp. 220–1. Ralph le Mareschal and William de Scalebroke served with Pipard in 1294–5 (C 67/10, m. 3), and John Giffard and Robert Barry were in the same lord's retinue in 1300 (C 47/1/6, m. 3). A similar phenomenon can be found in the retinue of Aymer de Valence. William de Acton, Peter de Paris, Richard Pauncefot, Roger de Sakeville and Hugh le Taillour were with Valence on the Falkirk campaign only (*Scotland in 1298,* pp. 216–18). However, the following men with the same surnames were with Valence in other years: Walter de Acton and Gilbert de Paris in 1297 (E 101/6/28, m. 2i); a Walter Pauncefot in 1306 (C 67/16, m. 13); a Richard de Sakeville in 1315 (E 101/15/6, m. 1); a Thomas de Sakeville in 1301 and 1303 (E 101/9/24, m. 1d; E 101/612/10, m. 1); and Robert and William le Taillour in 1297 and 1301 respectively (E 101/6/28, m. 2i; E 101/9/24, m. 1d).

the composition of Robert de Clifford's retinues for all campaigns reveals the presence of no fewer then twenty-two kinship groups.[126] Taking one of these, the Harcla family, we find that three of its members served in Clifford's retinue on separate occasions: John de Harcla in Scotland in 1296; William de Harcla at Falkirk; and Andrew de Harcla, the man who later became earl of Carlisle, in 1311.[127] Although not one of these men seems to have served with Clifford on more than one occasion, the family was represented in his retinue on a minimum of three campaigns to Scotland. Clifford could also count on repeated service by different members of the Penreth family. Robert de Penreth served in his campaign retinue in 1300; John de Penreth in 1303, 1306, 1307 and 1310; and a third member of the family, Andrew, in 1311.[128] The composition of Clifford's retinues was by no means exceptional in this respect. Of the individuals who served in Thomas of Lancaster's *comitiva* during the period under investigation, fifteen shared their surnames with at least one other Lancastrian follower.[129] Consideration of Aymer de Valence's military retinues reveals a startling fifty-one similar connections.[130]

Some historians have perceived a decline in the importance of tenurial ties to the composition of war retinues by the late thirteenth century.[131] Nevertheless, there is evidence to suggest that such bonds retained much of their vitality.[132] Of the men who appear in Henry de Beaumont's inquisition *post mortem*, dating from 1340, as his tenants in Lincolnshire, it would seem that five may have served in the same lord's retinue in or before 1314.[133] Included among these was a certain William Marmyon, possibly the individual of that name who had

---

[126] The families of Hellebek, Multon, Redman, Penreth, Engleys, Harcla, Vepont, Monteny, Stirkeland, Lancaster, Kirkebride, Latimer, Rossegill, Louther, Sheffeld, Boys, Haustede, Leyburn, Joneby, Mauneby, Swyneburne and Ellesfeld.

[127] E 101/5/23, m. 1i; *Scotland in 1298*, p. 197; C 71/4, m. 4. For a discussion of Andrew de Harcla's career, see J. Mason, 'Sir Andrew de Harcla, Earl of Carlisle', *Transactions of the Cumberland and Westmorland Antiquarian and Archaeological Society*, new ser., xxix (1929), pp. 98–137.

[128] Robert: E 101/8/23, m. 5. John: 1303 (E 101/612/11, m. 2); 1306 (C 67/16, m. 13); 1307 (E 101/14/15, m. 9); 1310 (*Rotuli Scotiae*, i, p. 89). Andrew: E 101/14/15, m. 3.

[129] Gacelyn, St Maur, Legh, Swynnerton, Waldeshef, Dacre, Holland, Lughtburghe, Limesey, Botiller, Grandison, Metham, Segrave, St Martin and Trussell.

[130] For example, Reginald de Paveley served in Valence's retinue in 1301 and 1314 (see above, p. 109, n. 262). He was also proffered by Valence in Scotland in 1322 (C 47/5/10, m. 1iii). Richard de Paveley served with the same lord in 1315 (E 101/15/6, m. 1). Finally, Walter de Paveley served with Valence during the war of Saint-Sardos in 1324–5 (*CPR, 1321–24*, p. 427).

[131] See, for example, H. Ridgeway, 'William de Valence and his *Familiares*, 1247–72', *Historical Research*, lxv (1992), p. 241.

[132] It is interesting to note, for example, that following the conquest of Wales in 1282–3 many lords granted lands to their followers in the newly won territories. These lands were to be held by military service: R.R. Davies, 'Colonial Wales', *Past and Present*, lxv (1974), pp. 5–6. See also Morgan, *War and Society*, p. 19; and Maddicott, *Simon de Montfort*, pp. 61–2.

[133] For the inquisition *post mortem*, see *CIPM*, viii, no. 271.

served with Beaumont in Scotland in 1308, 1309, 1310 and 1314.[134] It is impossible to know whether the men named in 1340 as Beaumont's tenants were his earlier military followers (they may have been their descendants). Nor can we be sure that these men had held land from Beaumont in the 1300s: it could be that they had been granted their estates at some later date. More convincingly, Robert de Clifford's inquisition *post mortem* from 1314, the year of his death at Bannockburn, shows that seventeen of the individuals named in his campaign retinues had been either his tenants or relatives of his tenants.[135]

It is possible that Beaumont and Clifford had granted lands to the soldiers named in their inquisitions *post mortem* as reward for, or in anticipation of, the performance of military service. William de Leyburn's grant of a manor in Kent to Fulk Peyforer in 1297 seems to fall into the latter category.[136] Peyforer first gave military service with Leyburn on the Flanders campaign of 1297–8 and, as we have seen, continued to serve with him on a regular basis thereafter.[137] On the other hand, the sum of 40 pounds in rent granted by Roger de Mortimer of Wigmore to Richard de Harley in November 1314 may have been intended as a gift.[138] Harley had served with Mortimer of Wigmore's uncle, Roger de Mortimer of Chirk, in 1306 and 1310, and he had taken out a letter of protection for service with Roger de Mortimer of Wigmore himself earlier in 1314.[139]

Indentures for life service in peace and war, in some respects, provide the most valuable insights into relations between lords and their military followers; but, as we saw earlier in this chapter, relatively few indentures were drawn up during the pre-Bannockburn era. The earliest surviving military contract between the Crown and one of its English subjects dates from 1316–17. This is an indenture of war between Edward II and William la Zouche, by which Zouche agreed to give military service for one year with thirty men-at-arms.[140] It may be that few lords went to the trouble of employing similar contracts in their own relationships until the Crown began to use the indenture system more regularly. Nevertheless, the few indentures relating to the lords in our sample indicate that where used, such contracts could be very effective in guaranteeing the repeated service of a core of soldiers. J.M.W. Bean has drawn attention to an indenture, now lost but dating from 16 July 1297, involving Robert de Tony and Adam

---

[134] 1308 (*Rotuli Scotiae*, i, p. 59); 1309 (*CDS*, v, p. 449); 1310 (C 71/4, m. 11); 1314 (C 71/6, m. 3). The other families were St Loe, Bayouse, Doune and Darcy.

[135] *CIPM*, v, no. 533. Thomas de Hellebek, Andrew de Harcla, Richard de Musgrave, Robert de Askeby, Robert le Engleys, the Tailleboys family, Thomas de Multon of Gilsland, John de Harcla, the Coupland family, the Helton family, Thomas de Hauteclou, the Engayne family, the Swyneburne family, the Mauleverer family, John de Penreth, John le Engleys and the Monteny family.

[136] *A Descriptive Catalogue of Ancient Deeds in the Public Record Office*, 6 vols (London, 1890–1915), iii, p. 160.

[137] See above, p. 131, n. 104.

[138] C 143/106/2.

[139] C 67/16, m. 4; C 71/4, m. 13; C 71/6, m. 1. See also I. Mortimer, *The Greatest Traitor: The Life of Sir Roger Mortimer, 1st Earl of March, Ruler of England, 1327–1330* (London, 2003), p. 66.

[140] N.B. Lewis, 'An Early-Fourteenth Century Contract for Military Service', *BIHR*, xx (1943–5), pp. 111–18.

de la Forde as the contracting parties. For his part, Bean noted, Tony agreed to give de la Forde '5 pounds a year, together with a robe and a saddle, for life, presumably, in the light of that date, for services that involved participation in the king's wars'.[141] That Bean was almost certainly correct in his assessment of the purpose of the contract is demonstrated by de la Forde's service in Tony's retinue on four occasions between 1297 and 1301.[142] One other contract, this time extant, involving the men in our sample is that between Aymer de Valence and John Darcy, dated 29 November 1309.[143] Darcy had served in Valence's retinue in 1306 and must have impressed his lord on that occasion to earn the now earl of Pembroke's 'sustenaunce et robes', as it is described in the terms of the indenture.[144] He later served with Valence in Scotland in 1314, 1315, 1319 and 1322; and he was proffered on the earl's behalf at the feudal muster at Tweedmouth in 1310.[145]

By the late 1290s, lords were beginning to realise, in increasingly large numbers, that indentures for life service in peace and war could be a valuable weapon in their artillery, enabling them to bind soldiers to their service. As we have seen, in essence indentured retainers were not very different from the group of men more traditionally charged with the task of forming the core of the campaign retinue: *household* retainers. Both indentured retainers and their household equivalents were bound to their lords by ties of service, and both were expected to accompany their leaders on military expeditions whenever called on to do so. In this respect the military obligations owed by the lord's *familiares* appear to have retained some of their former significance. Geoffrey de Langley, one of Edmund Crouchback's household followers, gave service in his lord's retinue in Wales in 1282 and Gascony in 1295.[146] Geoffrey's son Edmund, possibly named after the old earl, later followed Thomas of Lancaster to Flanders in 1297 and to Scotland in 1298 and 1301.[147] Another household functionary who knew how to turn his hand to soldiering was John de Cam. A steward in the Mortimer household in 1284,[148] he can be traced either preparing for or serving in war with Roger de Mortimer of Chirk on seven occasions between 1294 and 1319.[149]

It can be notoriously difficult to pin down other, less formal types of connection. J.R. Maddicott traced the link between Robert Fitz Nigel and Thomas of

---

[141] Bean, *From Lord to Patron*, pp. 47–8.

[142] See above, p. 90, n. 146 and p. 131, n. 105.

[143] 'Private Indentures for Life Service', no. 15.

[144] C 67/16, m. 13; 'Private Indentures for Life Service', no. 15.

[145] 1310 (*Parl. Writs*, II, ii, p. 401); 1314 (C 71/6, m. 5); 1315 (E 101/15/6, m. 1); 1319 (C 71/10, m. 5); 1322 (*CPR, 1321–24*, p. 186).

[146] 1282 (C 67/8, m. 5d); 1295 (*Rôles Gascons*, iii, p. 296). For evidence of Langley's activities as a member of Lancaster's *familia*, see *Trivet*, p. 330. See also W.E. Rhodes, 'Edmund, Earl of Lancaster', *EHR*, x (1895), p. 228; 'Account of the Expenses of John of Brabant and Thomas and Henry of Lancaster, AD 1292–3', ed. J. Burtt, *Camden Miscellany II*, Camden Society 1st ser., lv (1853), xv, p. 10.

[147] 1297 (C 67/12, m. 3); 1298 (*Scotland in 1298*, p. 179); 1301 (C 67/14, m. 5).

[148] *Ancient Deeds*, iii, p. 439.

[149] 1294 (*Rôles Gascons*, iii, p. 167); 1300 (E 101/8/23, m. 6); 1301 (E 101/9/23, m. 2); 1306 (C 67/16, m. 8); 1310 (C 71/4, m. 13); 1314 (C 71/6, m. 1); 1319 (C 71/10, m. 3).

Lancaster back to 1302, when Fitz Nigel witnessed one of the earl's charters.[150] However, a roll of household expenses of Thomas and Henry of Lancaster dating from 1297 records payments for two saddles with the arms of Robert Fitz Nigel.[151] This suggests that the connection went back still further. The nature of the bond between these men is not at all clear. It was, at least, long-lasting, for Fitz Nigel later joined Lancaster's retinue in Scotland in 1303, 1306 and 1319, as well as at the first Dunstable tournament (1309).[152] Fitz Nigel had served in the war of 1282 and so must have been at least a decade older than his more illustrious associate. Perhaps he passed on some of his experience to Lancaster on one of their early military ventures together. The nature of various other long-term connections can be equally difficult to determine. William de Scalebroke followed Ralph Pipard to Wales in 1295 and to Scotland in 1298 and 1300, but all that we know of their relationship, other than this, is that Scalebroke witnessed one of Pipard's land grants in 1301.[153] The knight Ralph le Bygod served in Peter de Chavent's retinue in 1297 and 1298; and he later accompanied the same lord overseas in the summer of 1301 on what may have been a diplomatic mission.[154] Unfortunately, it is probably now impossible to discern whether the ties between these men were ever formalised within the household or through indentures for life service.

Up to this point, our analysis has focused primarily on the period between the outbreak of war in Scotland in 1296 and the death of Edward I in 1307. There is good reason for this, for the voluminous documentary materials of these years supply the perfect opportunity to analyse the issue of stability in retinue membership in detail. Be that as it may, comparison of retinue composition in these years with that for earlier and later campaigns may assist our investigation. Do magnate retinues reveal a high rate of turnover in membership between the 1280s and the French and Scottish wars of the 1290s, or was there some continuity in personnel throughout the period?

Of the fifty lords in our sample, nine, or around a fifth, served as retinue leaders during the second Welsh war, of 1282–3; but we lack the names of the two sergeants who were with Walter de Beauchamp. Taking the remaining eight fully documented retinues, which appear on the extant horse inventories for Edward I's army in 1282, how much stability was there in retinue composition between this campaign and the expeditions of the 1290s and 1300s? Despite the twelve-year gap between the conquest of Wales and the hectic military schedule of the mid-1290s (the intervening Welsh campaign of 1287 was a fairly low-key affair, from which relatively little evidence of named soldiers survives), we find some evidence of continuity in personnel within half of the said retinues.

---

[150] Maddicott, *Thomas of Lancaster*, p. 61, n. 5.
[151] C 47/3/28, m. 3.
[152] 1303 (C 67/15, m. 13); 1306 (C 67/16, m. 10); 1309 (A. Tomkinson, 'Retinues at the Tournament of Dunstable, 1309', *EHR*, lxxiv (1959), p. 74); 1319 (Maddicott, *Thomas of Lancaster*, p. 61, n. 5).
[153] C 67/10, m. 3; *Scotland in 1298*, p. 220; *Documents and Records of Scotland*, p. 222; *Ancient Deeds*, ii, p. 163.
[154] E 101/6/37, m. 1i; *Scotland in 1298*, p. 168; *CPR, 1292–1301*, p. 601.

Of the nineteen men with Ralph Basset of Drayton in 1282, for example, three later served with him in Wales in 1294–5.[155] Of these three men, one, Robert de Shelton, also served with Basset in Gascony in 1296 and Scotland in 1298.[156] In addition, there was some continuity of personnel in the retinues of Peter de Chavent (two from six soldiers serving with him in 1282 joined his retinue in Flanders or at Falkirk),[157] William de Leyburn (two from nine men served under his banner in the 1290s)[158] and Thomas de Bykenore, who was accompanied by his kinsman John in 1282 and 1298.[159] Although the majority of the men-at-arms with our eight retinue leaders did not serve with the same lords on later campaigns, soldiers with the same surnames (probably their descendants) sometimes did. In 1282 Hugh Pointz was followed to war by a man named Richard Caus.[160] Fifteen years later, on the Flemish campaign, a William Caus could be found in his retinue.[161] In another example, the Ralph de Pipe in the *comitiva* of Ralph Basset of Drayton in 1282 was perhaps the father, uncle or older brother of the Thomas de Pipe who served under another Ralph Basset twenty-four years later.[162]

Turning our attention from the Welsh wars of Edward I to the early campaigns of the reign of his son, what levels of stability can be detected? In these years the military reputation of the English sunk to an all-time low, but can the new king's failures be linked in any way to changes in the composition of the military community since the more successful days of Dunbar and Falkirk? Several of the lords in our sample, such as Ralph Pipard (d. 1303), Hugh Bardolf (d. 1304) and Robert de Tony (d. 1309), predeceased the defeat at Bannockburn in 1314. One or two other prominent figures, such as Thomas of Lancaster, did not take part in that campaign for political reasons. One suspects that this must have had a detrimental effect on Edward II's preparations for the expedition. Furthermore, careful analysis of the retinues of the ten men in our sample who served as leaders in 1314 gives the impression that there was a lack of collective experience within some of the retinues. Of the sixty named men with the Despensers in 1314, only eleven (18 per cent) can be found in their service in previous hosts.[163] Similarly, only 19 per cent (five from twenty-seven) of

---

[155] C 47/2/7, m. 4; C 67/10, m. 6. (John de Bodeham, John de Clinton and Robert de Shelton).

[156] *Rôles Gascons*, iii, p. 324; *Scotland in 1298*, p. 224.

[157] Peter Doleyns: C 47/2/7, m. 12; *Scotland in 1298*, p. 168. Canadus de Staney: C 47/2/7, m. 12; E 101/6/37, m. 1i.

[158] William de Iffeld: 1282 (C 47/2/5, m. 2); 1297 (E 101/6/37, m. 4); 1298 (*Scotland in 1298*, p. 194). Peter de Ros: 1282 (C 47/2/5, m. 2); 1297 (E 101/6/37, m. 4); 1303 (E 101/612/11, m. 5d).

[159] C 47/2/6, m. 6; *Scotland in 1298*, p. 162.

[160] C 47/2/7, m. 1.

[161] E 101/6/19, m. 1.

[162] C 47/2/5, m. 2; C 67/16, m. 5.

[163] Ralph de Cammoys: 1297 (C 67/12, m. 3d); 1298 (*Scotland in 1298*, p. 188); 1300 (C 67/14, m. 10); 1303 (C 67/15, m. 14); 1306 (C 67/16, m. 11); 1307 (*CDS*, v, p. 445); 1308 (*Rotuli Scotiae*, i, p. 55). John de Ratingden: 1294 (C 67/10, m. 6); 1297 (C 67/12, m. 3d); 1298 (*Scotland in 1298*, p. 187); 1303 (*CVCR*, p. 81); 1306 (C 67/16, m. 5); 1307 (C 67/7, m. 1). John de Haudlo: see above, p. 128, n. 93. Walter Haket: 1297 (C 67/12, m. 3d); 1298

the men with Henry de Beaumont appear to have accompanied him on earlier campaigns.[164] Yet, before conclusions are drawn from these figures about the reasons for the English defeat, it should be noted that by 1314 neither of the Despensers had given military service for several years. Moreover, Henry de Beaumont led a much larger retinue to Scotland in that year than he had on previous campaigns. If we consider, too, that the Bannockburn campaign is relatively poorly documented (there is little evidence for the names of soldiers other than enrolled letters of protection), it is clear that there is a danger of underestimating the size of the stable element within Edward II's army. Turning our attention to other retinues at Bannockburn, for which the pre-1314 documentary materials are more complete, we are, in fact, given a slightly different impression of retinue stability. Of the seventy-six men who had letters of protection or attorney enrolled for service in the earl of Pembroke's retinue in 1314, no fewer than twenty (26 per cent) had served with him before the Bannockburn campaign.[165] The same applies to seven of the thirteen soldiers (54 per cent) who took out letters of protection or attorney in the same year with Robert de Clifford.[166]

Overall, then, it seems that there were proportionally more first-time warriors in Edward II's army in 1314 than there had been in Edward I's armies in the late 1290s and early 1300s, but perhaps not so large a proportion as to have seriously influenced the outcome of the battle. We might be inclined to read greater significance into the apparently large number of men-at-arms making their first appearance in war at Bannockburn were it not for the survival of more complete evidence relating to an English army that served in Scotland just three years previously, in 1310–11. On that occasion Edward's incursion into Scotland did not culminate in a battle, but his inability to defeat Bruce and his followers gave the Scots free rein to wreak havoc in the northern counties of England during the two or three years that followed.[167] The evidence relating to the nine lords from

(*Scotland in 1298*, p. 187); 1300 (C 67/14, m. 10). John Russel: 1296 (E 101/5/23, m. 1i); 1298 (*Scotland in 1298*, p. 187). John Joce: 1296 (E 101/5/23, m. 1i); 1297 (C 67/12, m. 3d); 1298 (*Scotland in 1298*, p. 188). Martin de Fishacre: 1306 (C 67/16, m. 9). Richard de Everley: 1298 (*Scotland in 1298*, p. 188); 1300 (C 67/14, m. 10). Richard de Chastillon: 1306 (C 67/16, m. 8). Robert de Bologne: 1300 (C 67/14, m. 10). Nicholas de Alneto: 1306 (C 67/16, m. 11). For the service of these men in Scotland in 1314, see C 71/6, mm. 1–5.

164 Richard le Breton: 1311 (C 71/5, m. 5). Henry de Percy: 1309 (*CDS*, v, p. 448). John de Eure: 1308 (*Rotuli Scotiae*, i, p. 58); 1311 (C 71/4, m. 5). Roger de Haudlo: 1301 (E 101/9/24, m. 1); 1303 (E 101/612/11, m. 1); 1308 (*Rotuli Scotiae*, i, p. 59). William Marmyon: 1308, 1309 and 1310 (see above, p. 135, n. 134). For the service of these men in Scotland in 1314, see C 71/6, mm. 3, 4.

165 Eight of these men – Maurice de Berkeley, Robert de Berkeley, Richard Wyriott, John de la Ryvere, John de Gacelyn, Thomas de Gurnay, William de Wauton and Roger de Ingepenne – had ridden with him on the Falkirk campaign: *Scotland in 1298*, pp. 216–18; C 67/13, m. 7. For the service of these men in Scotland in 1314, see C 71/6, mm. 1, 3, 5, 8.

166 Most of these soldiers, including Richard de Huddleston (C 67/16, m. 8; C 71/6, m. 1) and Nicholas and Robert de Leyburn (C 67/16, m. 13; C 71/6, m. 1), had joined Clifford's retinue since 1306.

167 For a fuller account of this campaign and the men who served on it, see Simpkin, 'The English Army and the Scottish Campaign of 1310–1311', pp. 14–39. For evidence of the

our sample who served with named followers on this campaign, Edward II's first as king, suggests that the stable element in lords' retinues during the early part of the new reign was far from negligible (see table 4.4).

Table 4.4: Retinue continuity for sample leaders in Scotland, 1310–11 (1277–1314)

Leader	Number of men with leader:		% continuity	Times served with leader other than in 1310						
	In 1310	In 1310 (who also served in other year)		1	2	3	4	5	6	7
Badlesmere	1	0	0	–	–	–	–	–	–	–
Beaumont	13	3	23	1	1	1	–	–	–	–
Botetourt	7	2	29	1	1	–	–	–	–	–
Clifford	47	24	51	11	5	4	2	1	–	1
Fitz Payn	11	6	55	3	1	1	–	–	1	–
Lovel	2	2	100	–	–	–	1	–	1	–
Mohaut	14	4	29	–	1	–	2	1	–	–
R. Mortimer	9	6	66	1	–	2	2	1	–	–
Welles	1	1	100	–	–	–	–	–	1	–
Total	105	48	46	17	9	8	7	3	3	1

Note: This table does not include data on men proffered by the lords at the feudal muster.

The sample for the 1310 campaign is not very large. Even so, it is interesting to note that a minimum of three of the men with Henry de Beaumont in that year and five of those with Robert de Clifford served with the same lords in 1314.[168] Indeed, recent research has shown that around 100 of the men in all retinues in 1310, and around thirty of the company leaders, took out letters of protection four years later.[169] This adds to the impression that the English defeat at Bannockburn was probably not due to an excessive number of inexperienced soldiers serving in that year. Looking backwards from 1310 to previous campaigns, we find that three of the soldiers with Robert de Mohaut had served with him at Falkirk;[170] and the same number of men in Roger de Mortimer of Chirk's retinue had taken out letters of protection for service in his *comitiva* in Gascony in 1294.[171] This was before Mortimer pulled out of that expedition to deal with the rebellion in Wales. If all of the retinues in Edward II's early armies contained a similar number of veterans, as they probably did, then it would be

damage caused by Scottish raids into northern England following the departure of Edward II's army, see McNamee, *Wars of the Bruces*, pp. 53–7.
[168] Beaumont: Breton, Eure and Marmyon (see above, p. 139, n. 164). Clifford: Nicholas and Robert de Leyburn (see above, p. 139, n. 166); Thomas de Monteny (see above, p. 94, n. 175 and p. 128, n. 93); John Mauleverer (*CCW*, p. 351; C 71/6, m. 1); and William de Penyngton (*Rotuli Scotiae*, i, p. 89; C 71/6, m. 1).
[169] Simpkin, 'The English Army and the Scottish Campaign of 1310–1311', p. 28.
[170] Roger de Bilney, John de Bracebridge and Richard Strech (see above, p. 125 table 4.1 and n. 81).
[171] John de Cam (see above, p. 136, n. 149), Hugh Godard (see above p. 104, n. 237 and *Rôles Gascons*, iii, p. 167) and John de Mortimer (*Rôles Gascons*, iii, p. 167; C 71/4, m. 13).

difficult to attribute Edward's failures north of the border to a lack of experienced personnel. Indeed, although Henry de Beaumont and the Despensers seem to have been building or rebuilding their retinues around the time of the Bannockburn campaign, they led very experienced retinues to Scotland later in the reign.[172]

In the late thirteenth and early fourteenth centuries, then, there was far greater stability in retinue composition than has generally been perceived. In his detailed study of the English army at Crécy, Andrew Ayton raised the question of whether high levels of 'stability and continuity of personnel' may have been 'one of the fundamental ways in which Edward III's armies differed from those of his predecessors, an important aspect of the transformation of English armies during the 1330s and 1340s'.[173] The analysis in this chapter indicates, however, that the armies of Edward III did not differ from earlier armies in this respect (this point, as we have seen, is supported by Andrew Spencer's work on levels of continuity within comital retinues during the reign of Edward I).[174] The concept of an English military revolution, taking place during the 1330s and 1340s, remains very much alive, but its characteristics must be sought elsewhere.

Loyal Service, Shifting Allegiances

Our analysis of retinue composition in English armies during the period between Edward I's Welsh wars and the battle of Bannockburn has so far been dominated by a survey of lords' ties to their military followers. It is now necessary to alter our viewpoint and to examine in more detail the range of service connections enjoyed by the gentry who staffed these retinues. In chapter 3 we saw how many of the men-at-arms who served on the Falkirk campaign of 1298, knights and sergeants alike, had careers spanning twenty years or more. Consideration of the

---

[172] Of the twenty-two men who had letters of protection enrolled for service with Henry de Beaumont in 1319, nine (41 per cent) had fought alongside him at Bannockburn or earlier. These men were: William de Bokminster, in 1309 (*CDS*, v, p. 448); Robert le Breton, in 1314 (C 71/6, m. 3); Peter de Saltmarsh, John de Lymbury, Thomas de Gaveley and Philip and Norman Darcy, each in 1314 (C 71/6, m. 3); Thomas Gray, in 1311 (C 71/5, m. 5); and William le Mareschal in 1297 (E 101/6/37, m. 7); 1298 (*Scotland in 1298*, p. 172); 1300 (E 101/8/23, m. 2); 1301 (E 101/9/24, m. 1); 1303 (E 101/612/11, m. 1). For the service of these men in 1319, see C 71/10, m. 4. For additional evidence of the relationship between Beaumont and Thomas Gray, see *Scalacronica*, p. 75. No fewer than fourteen of the men-at-arms who headed north of the border with the Despensers in 1322 had been connected to them since Bannockburn or earlier. These men were: Ralph de Cammoys, Richard de Chastillon, Martin de Fishacre, John de Haudlo, John Joce and John de Ratingden (see above p. 138, n. 163); Ralph Basset, in 1300 (C 67/14, m. 10) and 1301 (C 67/14, m. 5); Thomas Chaunterel, in 1314 (C 71/6, m. 3); Ralph de Gorges, in 1304 (C 67/15, m. 2), 1306 (C 67/16, m. 12) and 1309 (Tomkinson, 'Retinues at Dunstable', p. 76); Simon de Lyndeseye, in 1314 (C 71/6, m. 5); Richard de Mascy, in 1314 (C 71/6, m. 3); Robert de Stanegrave, in 1294 (C 67/10, m. 5d) and 1296 (E 101/5/23, m. 1i); Robert de Torkesey, in 1314 (C 71/6, m. 3); and Philip de Verley, in 1310 (*Parl. Writs*, II, ii, p. 402). For the service of these men in Scotland in 1322, see *CPR, 1321–24*, pp. 186–9; and BL, Stowe MS 553, fols 61r–v.

[173] Ayton, 'The English Army at Crécy', p. 204.

[174] Spencer, 'The Comital Military Retinue in the Reign of Edward I'.

personal ties that brought so many men into the king's armies holds the key to a fuller understanding of the recruitment process; and this inevitably requires the interpretation of hundreds of career profiles. A summary of the military allegiances of all the men-at-arms who went to war during the stated period lies beyond the scope of this study. Nevertheless, our fifty sample retinues (taken from the horse inventories for the Falkirk campaign) provide ample opportunity to reconstruct a proportion of these ties, providing as they do the names of 647 mounted soldiers. Not all of these individuals can be identified with absolute certainty. There were many, too, whose military careers appear to have been fairly short-lived. Yet this group contains a sufficiently large number of soldiers, who were regularly active during the wars in Wales, France and Scotland, to enable answers to be provided to a number of key questions. How many of these 647 men, for instance, remained with the same lords throughout their military careers? What proportion, on the other hand, seems to have changed their allegiance on a regular basis? And in those instances when soldiers *do* appear to have switched lords, what factors, now often difficult to discern, may have influenced their decisions?

Since the publication of K.B. McFarlane's seminal studies on 'bastard feudalism' and the late-medieval nobility, many discussions about the military service of the aristocracy have been coloured by his conclusions. His assessment of the gentry during the Wars of the Roses as men who 'turned their coats as often and with the same chequered success as their betters', and his belief that the fourteenth-century soldier 'seemed more anxious to see service than to care whether it was always under the same banner', have left a firm imprint on subsequent historiography.[175] Nor was he alone in his negative interpretation of the evidence. Helen Cam had earlier expressed the opinion that the aristocracy of the later Middle Ages were an altogether less faithful and dependable group than their forebears of the eleventh and twelfth centuries. In her opinion, the 'parasitic institution' of 'bastard feudalism' was 'far removed ... from the atmosphere of responsibility, loyalty and faith which had characterised the relationship of lord and vassal in the earlier Middle Ages'.[176] McFarlane and Cam were writing primarily about the late fourteenth and fifteenth centuries, when the system of contracting for military service had taken deeper root within English society. Notwithstanding that, their views have been widely accepted and applied to earlier periods. 'The evidence', a fairly recent summary of research on retinue personnel in medieval English armies has noted, 'suggests that there was a floating population of men willing to take service with whoever offered them the best terms'.[177] For J.M.W. Bean, 'the society of late medieval England was one in which loyalty to a lord, even if nurtured by generations of family tradition, was subject to erosion'.[178]

---

[175] K.B. McFarlane, 'The Wars of the Roses', *England in the Fifteenth Century: Collected Essays* (London, 1981), p. 248; *idem*, 'Bastard Feudalism', p. 176.

[176] H.M. Cam, 'The Decline and Fall of English Feudalism', *History*, xxv (1940), p. 225.

[177] Prestwich, *'Miles in Armis Strenuus'*, p. 217. See also Saul, *Knights and Esquires*, p. 98.

[178] Bean, *From Lord to Patron*, p. 188.

There can be no denying that such statements contain a large element of truth. Indeed, the faithlessness detected by modern historians was often only too evident to contemporaries. One song on the reign of Edward II depicted the knights of that unhappy time as debased and lamentably arrayed; and it characterised the squires as deceitful men who could not be trusted.[179] When we also consider the well-documented and widely condemned betrayals by their retainers of the earl of Gloucester at Bannockburn and Thomas of Lancaster at Boroughbridge, it is evident that not all soldiers active under the first two Edwards were unreservedly devoted to their lords.[180] Nevertheless, if men-at-arms did often move from one retinue to another and sometimes, in difficult circumstances, abandoned their lords to their miserable fates, it is not clear whether such actions were all that common. It would be a mistake to presume, moreover, that men who changed retinue always did so without the consent of their usual lord. Edward II shared his retainers and placed them at the service of his favourite and possible brother-in-arms, Piers Gaveston.[181] Nor was he alone in such actions. As Michael Hicks has noted, 'feed men were often retained by more than one lord. As early as 1297, in his indenture with the earl of Norfolk, John Segrave was allowed to serve under other lords when the earl himself was not on campaign.'[182] In like manner, Thomas of Lancaster's wardrobe account for 1318–19 reveals that 'two robes were made up' for his retainer Robert de Holland 'of the liveries of Hugh de Audley and Bartholomew de Badlesmere'.[183] Evidently, the military community was not fragmented by rigid boundaries between different lords and their followers.

As Christine Carpenter has perceived, 'impressionistic surveys confined to a small number of the gentry are not enough' when studying the personal networks, military or otherwise, of the active men of this age.[184] Our sample of 647 soldiers from the Falkirk campaign makes it possible to push beyond such limits and to conduct an analysis that is 'both comprehensive and systematic'.[185]

---

179 *Thomas Wright's Political Songs*, pp. 335–6.
180 See above, pp. 10–11 and *Thomas Wright's Political Songs*, pp. 270–1. For further comment on lordship bonds and the rebellion of 1322, see O. de Ville, 'Jocelyn Deyville: Brigand, Or Man of his Time?', *Northern History*, xxxv (1999), p. 45; C. Valente, *The Theory and Practice of Revolt in Medieval England* (Aldershot, 2003), pp. 149–53.
181 J.S. Hamilton, *Piers Gaveston, Earl of Cornwall 1307–1312: Politics and Patronage in the Reign of Edward II* (Detroit, Mich., 1988), pp. 102, and 167, n. 100. At least ten of the men from Gaveston's campaign retinues in 1306 and 1310 were members of Edward's household, or joined it after Gaveston's death. These men were: Edmund Bacon, John Howard, John de Charlton, John de la Beche, Robert de Sapy, Humphrey de Littlebury, Thomas de Chaucombe, Warin de Lisle, John Knokyn and Robert de Kendal. For their service with Gaveston, see E 101/13/7, m. 1; *Rotuli Scotiae*, i, p. 89; C 71/4, mm. 4–13. For their service in Edward II's household, see E 101/369/11, fol. 107r; BL, Cotton Nero C VIII, fols 36r, 42r, 90v–92r; E 101/376/7, fol. 54v. For additional comment on the relationship between Edward and Gaveston, see P. Chaplais, *Piers Gaveston: Edward II's Adoptive Brother* (Oxford, 1994), pp. 20–2.
182 Hicks, *Bastard Feudalism*, p. 88.
183 Maddicott, 'Thomas of Lancaster and Sir Robert Holland', p. 465.
184 C. Carpenter, 'Gentry and Community', p. 369.
185 *Ibid.*

In an attempt to provide as subtle an interpretation of the military bonds of these individuals as possible, the career profile of each soldier has been placed into one of several categories. At one extreme are men-at-arms who can be shown to have remained in the service of the same lord throughout their military careers, and at the other are those who changed allegiance at some stage for no obvious reason. Between these two extremes is a third group consisting of individuals who served in the retinue of more than one lord, but whose change of *comitiva* can be explained by one of a variety of stimuli, such as the death of their retinue leader, links to another man from the same family or region as the lord with whom they usually served, the absence of their usual leader from a particular campaign or membership of a sub-retinue which might see them move between different companies while remaining part of the same 'primary group'. Dividing the profiles of hundreds of men-at-arms into these categories is a difficult exercise, yet the resulting data are likely to provide a more accurate insight into patterns of service than a facile division into those who appear to have remained loyal and those who did not (see table 4.5).

Table 4.5: Allegiances of sample men-at-arms from the army of 1298 (1277–1314)

	Knights	Sergeants
Served one lord only	37	311
Changed lord according to:		
regional factors	5	28
familial factors	6	8
death of leader	12	23
non-service of leader	6	13
as part of sub-retinue	3	22
combination of above	6	6
other explanation	3	2
Change of lord unexplained	35	84
Total	113	497

Difficulties of identification mean that it has been necessary to exclude thirty-seven of the sergeants in our sample from table 4.5. It should also be noted that the category headed 'served one lord only' contains many individuals who can be traced on campaign within a retinue on no more than one occasion. Five of the knights and 193 of the sergeants fall into this category. If we leave these soldiers out of our calculations, we find the following. Of the 108 knights who served within a magnate retinue on more than one expedition, thirty-two (30 per cent) served with the same lord, as far as we can tell, throughout their military careers. The same applies to 118 of the equivalent 304 sergeants (39 per cent). Thus, it would appear that around a third of the men-at-arms in Edward I's army in 1298 served under the same banner on every other occasion that they gave military service. Admittedly, this figure might be lower if the records at our disposal were more complete. Nevertheless, it would seem that the proportion of men-at-arms who had no desire, or need, to move from service with one lord to the retinue of another was far from negligible. A sizeable number of these men, particularly the sergeants, can be traced in the records for military service in the years up to and including the Bannockburn campaign on no more than two or three occasions. However, there were many other men-at-arms, of both ranks, who stayed with the same lord on four, five or more expeditions. Hugh Godard, a knight of Roger de Mortimer of Chirk, prepared to go to war under his lord's banner on six occasions between 1294 and 1310.[186] Robert de Dutton and Thomas de Cirencester, knights of John de Benstede and Hugh de Courtenay respectively, each followed their lord to war on no fewer than four expeditions.[187] Similar examples of loyal service can be found within the body of sergeants. Alan de Sumborn and Hamo Bygod each served in four different hosts with Alan Plukenet senior or junior.[188] Neither seems ever to have left the Plukenet retinue to seek service elsewhere. Robert de Suthwold followed Thomas de Verdon to war an equal number of times.[189] Such men as these may have been among their lords' household or indentured retainers, but it is generally impossible to demonstrate this with firm evidence from the sources.

It would be a mistake to contrast too sharply the stable with the unstable elements within lords' retinues. Relations that seem to have been steady for long periods might suddenly deteriorate for reasons that are now difficult to discern. For example, members of the Berkeley family served in the retinue of Aymer de Valence on numerous occasions, including at the battles of Falkirk and Bannockburn, before attacking his manor of Painswick in 1318.[190] At the other extreme, many of the soldiers who have been placed, in table 4.5, into the category 'changes unexplained' actually displayed a great deal of continuity in their service. Thomas de Coudray can be located in three different groups of retinues between 1297 and 1314, but he gave repeated service in each. He was with Hugh le Despenser or his sub-leader John ap Adam in 1297, 1298 and 1307, with John de St John in 1294, 1299, 1300 and 1301 and with either Ralph de Monthermer or Gilbert de Clare (earls of Gloucester at different times each) in 1303, 1306 and 1314.[191] From one perspective he may appear to have been one of K.B. McFarlane's prototype freelances, 'going abroad in the "comitiva" of now this commander and now that'.[192] But if we think of Coudray's service

---

[186] See above, p. 104, n. 237 and p. 140 n. 171. He took out a letter of protection independently for service in Scotland in 1314.

[187] Dutton: 1297 (E 101/6/37, m. 2iii); 1298 (*Scotland in 1298*, p. 177); 1301 (E 101/9/24, m. 2); 1303 (E 101/612/11, m. 3). Cirencester: 1296 (E 101/5/23, m. 1ii); 1298 (*Scotland in 1298*, p. 208); 1300 (*Rolls of Arms, Edward I*, i, p. 454); 1304 (*Documents and Records of Scotland*, p. 272).

[188] E 101/5/23, m. 1ii; E 101/6/37, m. 1i; *Scotland in 1298*, p. 190; C 67/14, m. 11; *Documents and Records of Scotland*, p. 218; E 101/9/24, m. 1d.

[189] 1297 (E 101/6/37, m. 6i); 1298 (*Scotland in 1298*, p. 173); 1300 (C 67/14, m. 10); 1301 (E 101/9/24, m. 1).

[190] *Scotland in 1298*, pp. 216–17; C 71/6, mm. 1, 5; M. Prestwich, *The Three Edwards: War and State in England 1272–1377* (London, 1980), p. 145.

[191] For his military service, see above, p. 24, n. 108.

[192] McFarlane, 'Bastard Feudalism', p. 176.

in another way, it is clear that he operated within fairly well-defined parameters. Henry de Glastingbury has also been placed, for the purposes of our analysis, into this 'unstable' category. He joined the retinue of John de Mohun in 1303.[193] But he also served with one or other of the Lancaster brothers, Thomas and Henry, or their father, Edmund, in four other hosts; and he joined the retinue of one of Thomas of Lancaster's tenants, Payn de Tibetot, in Scotland in 1306.[194] Thus there was no clear dichotomy between loyal soldiers, on the one hand, and those who changed their allegiance frequently, on the other. The reality of most men-at-arms' service at this time was a good deal more complex than that.

Bearing this in mind, it is the third group in table 4.5, representing the individuals who switched retinues but who did so due to altered circumstances or within the parameters of identifiable social networks, that best reflects the experiences of the average man-at-arms of this period. It is also this group that, by taking into account lords' deaths and non-service, most accurately conforms to the diachronic approach, according to which all forms of network analysis should ideally operate.[195] The impact of deaths and non-service on soldiers' choice of lords shall be considered in due course. However, it was perfectly possible for men to join the companies of other military leaders while their usual lords were still alive, without this in any way reflecting disloyalty. This was evidently the case in instances when soldiers served under a relative of their usual retinue leader. Two of the knights and three of the sergeants listed in Thomas of Lancaster's company on the household horse inventory for the Falkirk campaign can be found on other occasions in the campaign retinue of his younger brother Henry.[196] Not all of these men have been included in the section of table 4.5 headed 'familial factors' as some had additional retinue connections in other years. Similarly, the household steward Walter de Beauchamp made good use of his relationship with his older brother William, earl of Warwick. Although only two of the men in Walter de Beauchamp's company at Falkirk – the knight William le Blount and his probable relation, the *vallettus* Walter le

---

193 C 67/15, m. 8.

194 He served with Edmund, Thomas or Henry of Lancaster in: 1295 (C 67/10, m. 3); 1297 (C 67/12, m. 3); 1298 (*Scotland in 1298*, p. 179); 1300 (C 67/14, m. 10). For his service with Tibetot, see E 101/13/7, m. 1. For Tibetot's tenurial links with Lancaster, see *CIPM*, v, no. 519.

195 *Network Analysis: Studies in Human Interaction*, ed. J. Boissevain and J.C. Mitchell (The Hague, 1973), p. xi. Studies by David Crouch on the tenants and retainers of the twelfth-century earls of Warwick, David Green on the affinity of the Black Prince and Simon Walker on the followers of John of Gaunt have each shown that generational changes or long spells between campaigns sometimes undermined bonds which, viewed from a short-term perspective, could be quite stable: D. Crouch, 'The Local Influence of the earls of Warwick, 1088–1242: A Study in Decline and Resourcefulness', *Midland History*, xxi (1996), pp. 11–12; Green, 'Politics and Service with Edward the Black Prince', p. 59; Walker, *The Lancastrian Affinity*, p. 50.

196 Knights: Henry de Glastingbury (see above, n. 194); Nicholas de St Maur (*Scotland in 1298*, p. 179, C 67/7, m. 3). Sergeants: William de Lughtburghe (*Scotland in 1298*, p. 180; C 67/16, m. 6); Adam de Skelton (for his service in 1298, 1300, 1303 and 1306, see p. 110, n. 265); Roger de Bray (C 67/12, m. 3; *Scotland in 1298*, p. 181; C 67/14, m. 10; C 67/14, m. 3; C 67/16, m. 10).

Blount – had previously accompanied the earl to war,[197] analysis of the affinities of the two brothers for all campaigns reveals that there were ten families or individuals with allegiances to both siblings.[198] Almost all of these men had served in the earl's retinue before finding service with the steward.

If fraternal and other familial bonds provided one connecting thread along which retainers and military followers might manoeuvre, it was not the only one. Membership of a regional network of soldiers might enable men-at-arms to shift between lords holding lands in the same part of the country while remaining part of a self-contained military pool. Identifying connections of this kind is not a straightforward task, but the change of retinue of around five of the knights and twenty-eight of the sergeants from our sample can be explained by such regional determinants.

In his analysis of the campaign retinues of Thomas Ughtred, sub-marshal of Edward III's army at Crécy, Andrew Ayton identified 'the existence of a distinctive, Yorkshire-based regional military community'.[199] His point is borne out by the proximity in the nave of York Minster of a large number of the heraldic shields of the families of that county. These shields were erected at the time of Edward I's Scottish wars.[200] One man who seems to have been a member of this regional military community was the sergeant Simon de Blakeshale. He found service in the company of William de Ryther at Falkirk and of Ryther's fellow Yorkshireman Robert de Mauley in Scotland in 1306.[201] Looking across to the other side of the Pennines we find that Richard de Kirkebride served on separate occasions with Robert de Clifford and John de Lancaster, two of his fellow landholders from the northwest.[202] The strong regional ties of some men-at-arms from the northern counties of England were matched, in a few instances, by the local connections of soldiers from the south. A few of the sergeants from

---

[197] William: 1294–5 and 1297 with the earl (C 67/10, m. 5; E 101/6/37, m. 6i) and 1298 with the steward (*Scotland in 1298*, p. 183). Walter: 1294–5 with the earl (C 67/10, m. 5); 1297 and 1298 with Walter de Beauchamp and his son (E 101/6/37, m. 1ii; *Scotland in 1298*, p. 184).

[198] For the Blount family, see note 197 above. Andrew Astley, John and Owain Brompton, Roger Cheney, Fulk Fitz Waryn, Nicholas Harpur, William Saltmarsh and John and Robert de Sapy each served with the earl in Wales in 1294–5 (SC 1/26, nos 86, 87, 92, 96, 97, 98 and 100, catalogued in *Ancient Correspondence Concerning Wales*; C 67/10, mm. 2, 5). Gilbert Heton and William St Mareys each had a horse appraised with the earl for service in Flanders in 1297 and probably went on to serve in the Low Countries with the earl's son, Guy (E 101/6/37, m. 6i). Roger Cheney was with Walter de Beauchamp as well as with the earl in Wales in 1294–5 (C 67/10, m. 7). Walter Astley, Geoffrey Fitz Waryn and Richard Harpur served with Walter de Beauchamp and his son in Flanders in 1297 (E 101/6/37, m. 1ii). Walter Brompton, Geoffrey Fitz Waryn, Richard Harpur, John Saltmarsh and John St Mareys were with Walter de Beauchamp on the Falkirk campaign (*Scotland in 1298*, p. 184; C 67/13, m. 8). Gilbert Heton served under Walter de Beauchamp in 1300 (E 101/8/23, m. 2). John Sapy could be found in Walter de Beauchamp's retinue in Scotland in 1301–2 (E 101/9/24, m. 2).

[199] Ayton, 'Sir Thomas Ughtred', pp. 124–5.

[200] S. Brown, *'Our Magnificent Fabrick'. York Minster: An Architectural History* c. *1220– 1500* (Swindon, 2003), p. 129 and appendix 2.

[201] *Scotland in 1298*, p. 226; E 101/13/16, fol. 20v.

[202] *Scotland in 1298*, p. 196; E 101/612/15, m. 1d.

our sample moved between retinues of different lords possessing estates in the southeast. Robert de Echingham (of Sussex) could be found in the *comitivae* of four men with landed interests in Kent or Sussex in the years leading up to and including the Bannockburn campaign: those of the household banneret William de Leyburn (1297); his (Robert's) brother William de Echingham (1298); and the earl of Gloucester and Bartholomew de Badlesmere jointly (1314).[203] Similarly, Edmund de St Leger had links to three Kentish lords. He served with William de Leyburn on three occasions and Stephen de Burgherssh and the earl of Gloucester once each.[204] The presence of such regional networks suggests that soldiers might serve in the retinues of a variety of lords without necessarily undermining the cohesion or effectiveness of royal hosts.

It must also be borne in mind, when considering the stability of soldiers' military allegiances, that the largest campaign retinues usually comprised a number of sub-units. These 'primary groups', to use modern parlance, are not easy to trace in the records for military service that date from this era as written subcontracts were not yet in use or have not survived. But it seems that the leaders of such groups, rather than the main retinue leaders, had the first call on their men's service. For example, one of Robert Fitz Payn's knights at Falkirk, Ingelram de Berenger, and two of his sergeants had been to Flanders a year previously in the retinue of John de Berewyk.[205] It is almost certain that these sergeants, Michael Criketot and Frarius de Ameney, were associates of Berenger rather than of Berewyk or Fitz Payn. As such, the sergeants did not really switch retinues between campaigns, as they may appear to have done, but remained with their group leader (Berenger) on both expeditions. Similarly, the sergeants Warin de St Maur and Robert de Strode served alongside the knight Nicholas de St Maur in Robert Fitz Payn's retinue in Flanders in 1297, but in the following year they followed St Maur, who appears to have been their group leader, into the retinue of Thomas, earl of Lancaster for the Falkirk campaign.[206] The significance of such sub-units is indicated far more clearly in sources relating to armies raised later in the Middle Ages. Anne Curry has noted that the duke of Clarence's retinue on the Agincourt campaign of 1415 contained seventy sub-units, the majority of which were recruited by the duke's esquires.[207] The size, structure and composition of military retinues changed a great deal over the century separating Bannockburn from Agincourt, but the

---

[203] For his service with Leyburn in 1297 and with Gloucester and Badlesmere in 1314, see above, p. 30, nn. 155–6. He was with his brother, William, on the Falkirk campaign (*Scotland in 1298*, p. 213). His other lords, the Despensers, had links to the earl of Gloucester through the marriage of Despenser junior to the young earl's sister, Eleanor. Despenser junior also held Swanscombe manor in Kent. For Echingham's military service with the Despensers, see 1303 (C 67/15, m. 9); 1306 (C 67/16, m. 10); and *CPR, 1301–07*, p. 443. For Despenser junior's marriage and landholding, see *Rolls of Arms, Edward I*, ii, pp. 140–1.

[204] He served with Leyburn in 1297 (E 101/6/37, m. 4), 1298 (*Scotland in 1298*, p. 194) and 1300 (E 101/8/23, m. 4). See also his service with Burgherssh in 1306 (C 67/16, m. 6) and with the earl in 1314 (C 81/1727, m. 11).

[205] C 67/12, m. 1; E 101/6/28, mm. 2i–2ii; *Scotland in 1298*, p. 171.

[206] E 101/6/19, m. 1; *Scotland in 1298*, pp. 179–80.

[207] Curry, *Agincourt*, p. 63.

germ of many later developments, like subcontracting, can be traced back at least as far as the armies of Edward I.

There were a number of reasons, then, why soldiers might switch retinues while their former or usual lord was still alive. But what happened to a lord's men following his death, or when he did not take part in a campaign? Did they serve regardless of his absence? If not, with whom did they serve instead? From the reign of Edward I, the most famous example of non-service was the decision of Roger le Bygod, earl of Norfolk (in his capacity as marshal of England), not to follow the king to Flanders in 1297. This led to Edward's angry claim that the earl would either go to Flanders or hang, and the earl's famous rejoinder that he would neither go nor hang.[208] How did the men who had served with the earl on previous military ventures respond to his stubborn resistance? We cannot, of course, be sure that Bygod's former followers would have gone with him to Flanders even if he *had* served there. Nevertheless, it is interesting to note that of the men who had served under the earl of Norfolk on previous military ventures, no fewer than thirteen appear to have joined the king in the Low Countries. Most notably, all three knightly members of the Berkeley family who were active at this time, Thomas and his sons Thomas junior and Maurice – at least two of whom were with Bygod in Wales during 1294–5[209] – began their association with Aymer de Valence in that year.[210] This may have constituted a major drain on the earl of Norfolk's military resources. Yet we should also remember that the earl may not have been averse to these men serving in Flanders in his absence. It should be recalled that an indenture drawn up between Bygod and John de Segrave in the summer of 1297 had allowed the latter to serve under other lords if the former did not go on campaign.

The absence of a lord on a short-term basis inevitably caused far less disruption than his death. When the Marcher lord Roger de Mortimer died during the Welsh war of 1282, there were reports of disturbances and unrest among his tenants.[211] In a society that depended so heavily on the 'vertical' relations between lords and their followers, the death of a lord could lead to the erosion of his retinue and to subtle shifts in the recruitment networks of the regions in which he had operated. The household steward Walter de Beauchamp's death

---

[208] Prestwich, *The Three Edwards*, p. 28.

[209] C 47/2/10, m. 8.

[210] E 101/6/28, m. 2i. The other ten men who had served with the earl of Norfolk before 1297 yet went to Flanders without him were: John ap Adam (Bygod 1277, *CPR, 1272–81*, p. 217; 1287, *CPR 1281–92*, p. 273; 1294, C 67/10, m. 7; 1296, *CCW*, p. 71; 1297, C 67/12, m. 9d); Ralph le Bygod (Bygod 1282, C 67/8, m. 7; 1297, E 101/6/37, m. 1i); William de Boyton (Bygod 1294, C 67/10, m. 6; 1296, C 67/11, m. 2; 1297, E 101/6/37, m. 6i); Richard le Keu (Bygod 1287, *CPR, 1281–92*, p. 274; 1297, C 67/12, m. 3d); John de Knoville (Bygod 1294, C 67/10, m. 6; 1297, E 101/6/37, m. 4); Hugh and Nicholas Pointz (Bygod 1294, C 47/2/10, m. 8; 1296, C 67/11, m. 6; 1297, BL, Additional MS 7965, fol. 69r); Thomas de Scales (Bygod 1296, C 67/11, m. 4; 1297, E 101/6/19, m. 2); John de Sotebroke (Bygod 1287, *CPR, 1281–92*, p. 273; 1294 C 67/10, m. 7; 1297, E 101/6/37, m. 1ii); Nicholas de Stotevillle (Bygod 1283, SC 1/9, no. 83; 1297, C 67/12, m. 9d). For information on some of these men and their relationship with the earl of Norfolk, see M. Morris, *The Bigod Earls of Norfolk in the Thirteenth Century* (Woodbridge, 2005), pp. 138–53.

[211] *Ancient Correspondence Concerning Wales*, p. 131.

in 1303 deprived the king of one of his most faithful supporters. Some stability may have been maintained by the fact that two of Beauchamp's former soldiers, the knight Simon le Chamberleyn and the sergeant Geoffrey Fitz Waryn, later served under Aymer de Valence (albeit, as far as we can tell, eight years apart from one another).[212] However, his other former followers joined the companies of different lords. The experienced campaigner Stephen de la More went on to serve with the earl of Gloucester on Edward II's campaign of 1310–11;[213] and it is perhaps indicative of the high social standing that Beauchamp had enjoyed that some of his soldiers gravitated towards men of comital status. Beauchamp's younger son, William, seems to have found service with Robert Fitz Payn, a banneret who by the campaign of 1310 had replaced William's father as steward of the royal household.[214] Ties of tenure and kinship, too, might determine soldiers' decisions when looking to attach themselves to new lords. Ralph le Botiller, a sergeant of Nicholas de Audley, seems, following his lord's death in 1299, to have served under Audley's younger brother, Hugh, on the Bannockburn campaign.[215] In 1310 Nicholas Pointz found service in Scotland with his tenurial lord Gilbert de Clare, earl of Gloucester.[216] This was two years after the demise of Nicholas' father and former retinue leader, Hugh.[217]

Far from consisting of a shifting mass of men who switched retinues at will or, at the other extreme, a happy fellowship of loyal soldiers, the military community was characterised, as one would expect, by something in between these extremes. There was, of course, a significant degree of mobility and fluidity; but the movements that did take place usually involved subtle shifts within familial or regional networks. They might also be necessitated by changes within the composition of the military community caused by deaths or non-service. Only rarely do soldiers appear to have displayed no continuity in their choice of lord and retinue. Such individuals did exist but, just like those who stayed with one lord for six or seven campaigns without ever entering the service of another man, they were the exception. For most knights and sergeants it made sense to remain in the service of retinue leaders whom they knew personally and had campaigned with in the past; but there was no expectation, for the most part, that men-at-arms would stay with the same lords throughout their careers.

---

212 Chamberleyn in 1314 (C 71/6, m. 1); Fitz Waryn in 1306 (C 67/16, m. 13).
213 C 71/4, m. 10.
214 C 47/5/7, m. 1; C 71/4, m. 13.
215 C 71/6, m. 1.
216 C 71/4, m. 10. For evidence of the tenurial connection between Pointz and the earl, see *CIPM*, v, no. 346.
217 Nicholas had served in his father's retinue on the Falkirk campaign as well as on other occasions: *Scotland in 1298*, p. 215.

5

Feudal Service and the Pre-Contract Army

A prosopographical analysis of the military service given by the English gentry
and nobility during the wars of Edward I and his son can add a great deal to
our knowledge of the mounted armoured forces of this period. The foregoing
chapters have demonstrated the frequency with which members of the aristocracy gave military service, their connections to other members of the military
community and the methods by which they were recruited. If, as is commonly
perceived, Edward I inherited a far from glorious military legacy from his father,
then by the end of his reign he would appear to have fashioned a well-trained
military elite, hardened by years of regular campaigning and strengthened by
a sense of group solidarity that was reflected in the wide dissemination of new
and increasingly complex coats of arms. Yet, as we have seen, the armies of this
period were not universally successful; there was no continuous spell of victorious campaigning such as that which earned the armies of Edward III a glowing
reputation during the 1340s and 1350s. The gradual process of conquest was
punctuated by significant reversals both in Wales and Scotland. In Gascony the
English were usually on the defensive. Why, then, were the armies of this period,
despite their obvious and significant triumphs, generally less successful than the
forces raised later in the fourteenth century? And how can a study of the men-
at-arms of this period assist our investigation?

*

There were a number of characteristics that made the armies of Edward III
different from those of his father's and grandfather's reigns. The importance of
some of these – including the employment of mixed retinues containing men-
at-arms and archers in equal numbers, and the widespread use of indentures
of war – cannot be explored in a study of the mounted forces of the reigns of
Edward I and Edward II for the simple reason that they did not yet exist or (in
the case of indentures) were not yet widely used. These were new innovations
of the 1330s and 1340s that can only be understood through an analysis of the
armies raised during those years.[1] However, two additional and closely related
developments that have long been seen as fundamental to the transformation
from the pre-contract armies of the years before Bannockburn to the contract
armies of the later fourteenth century are the increased prevalence of paid mili-

---

[1] For such a discussion, see Ayton, *Knights and Warhorses*, chapter 1.

tary service and the concomitant abandonment of obligatory feudal service:[2] the system by which military service was given in return for lands held in chief. These changes *can*, to some extent, be examined in a study of aristocratic military service before 1314. J.E. Morris believed that this transformation gained momentum during the Welsh wars of Edward I, noting that that king attempted to 'substitute paid for feudal service ... just because the formal feudal service was unsatisfactory'.[3] Looking at the situation from the perspective of the mid-fourteenth century, Andrew Ayton has more recently summarised these developments thus: 'in broad brush-stroke terms, the feudal host, based upon the compulsory, unpaid provision of companies of men-at-arms by tenants-in-chief in fulfilment of their military obligations, had been superseded by contract armies, consisting of paid volunteers'.[4]

The general inclination of historians writing since J.E. Morris has been to follow him in perceiving this change as a symptom of the inadequacies of feudal military service. K.B. McFarlane, in his work on 'bastard feudalism', expressed the opinion that the days of the fee-based method of raising mounted forces[5] were numbered 'when the need was felt for an army more efficient and more durable than the feudal host'.[6] Bryce Lyon, whose work on *fiefes-rentes* (cash fees given in return for military service, but with regard to feudal homage and tenure) seemed to provide evidence of a missing link between the feudal and wholly paid phases in military history, affirmed that 'feudalism' was 'no longer ... equal to supplying the forces needed for the more extensive, frequent, and distant campaigns of Edward I'.[7] The simplicity of such explanations, and the conviction with which they have been expressed, might have sealed the argument were it not for a number of awkward facts that do not accord with this theory of feudal military service's gradual and inevitable demise. Work carried out separately by J.O. Prestwich and Marjorie Chibnall has demonstrated that armies of the eleventh and twelfth centuries already comprised a combination of

---

2   Susan Reynolds has skilfully deconstructed the concept of 'feudalism' and shown it to be flawed: *Fiefs and Vassals: The Medieval Evidence Reinterpreted* (Oxford, 1994). However, the term 'feudal service' still seems the most appropriate way of describing the military service rendered by tenants-in-chief in return for the lands, predominantly knights' fees, that they held in chief. Indeed, Michael Prestwich has noted that the term 'feudal' 'can be used with some precision in relation to military service': *Armies and Warfare*, p. 57.

3   Morris, *Welsh Wars*, p. 36.

4   Ayton, 'English Armies in the Fourteenth Century', p. 22.

5   A few footmen might be recruited (by tenants-in-chief holding their lands by sergeanty tenure), but they were very much in a minority. Almost all the soldiers recruited by means of the feudal summons served on horseback. For a discussion of the foot element, see E.G. Kimball, *Serjeanty Tenure in Medieval England* (London, 1936), pp. 70–1.

6   McFarlane, 'Bastard Feudalism', p. 162. For similar views, see, for example, A.L. Poole, *Obligations of Society in the XII and XIII Centuries* (Oxford, 1946), p. 39; F.M. Powicke, *The Thirteenth Century, 1216–1307*, 2nd edition (Oxford, 1962), p. 543; and J.M.W. Bean, *The Decline of English Feudalism, 1215–1540* (Manchester, 1968), pp. 5–6.

7   B.D. Lyon, 'The Feudal Antecedent of the Indenture System', *Speculum*, xxix (1954), p. 504; *idem, From Fief to Indenture: The Transition from Feudal to Non-Feudal Contract in Western Europe* (Cambridge, Mass., 1957), pp. 198–232.

'paid' and 'feudal' soldiers,[8] much as was the case under Edward I. The feudal host had never formed the sole platform upon which the kings of England had built their military strength. Moreover, far from abandoning this traditional method of recruiting men-at-arms and attempting to replace it with wholly paid service, Edward I and his son, as both Michael Powicke and Michael Prestwich have shown, continued to call out the feudal host on a regular basis.[9] The composition of the mounted armoured forces of the late thirteenth and early fourteenth centuries, partly paid, partly voluntary unpaid and partly feudal,[10] was essentially conservative. There was no revolution in recruitment or organisation in this period.[11]

On coming to the throne, Edward I demonstrated his strong links to previous reigns by issuing feudal summonses for the majority of his campaigns: not only for the Welsh wars of 1277 and 1282–3 but also for expeditions to Scotland in 1300, 1303 and 1306. He even tried to call out the feudal host, abortively, for a continental campaign in 1294.[12] Historians have accounted for the king's persistent use of feudal military service in a number of ways, the most common explanation being that he was forced to rely on this method of raising mounted forces due to the baronage's reluctance to accept Crown pay.[13] Yet Edward's continued use of this kind of summons should come as no surprise when we consider that the mounted soldiers produced by calling out the feudal levy regularly constituted around a quarter of the total number of men-at-arms.[14] Furthermore, feudal service was the form of military obligation to which Edward had become most accustomed as a young man. During the civil war of the 1260s, in which Edward had played a full part, Henry III had issued a feudal summons more than once to deal with his domestic enemies. This form of summons had been used, for example, before the siege of Northampton in 1264 and in order to confront the rebels who were holding out at Kenilworth castle two years

---

[8] J.O. Prestwich, 'War and Finance in the Anglo-Norman State', *TRHS*, 5th ser., iv (1954), pp. 42–3; M. Chibnall, 'Mercenaries and the *Familia Regis* under Henry I', *History*, new ser., lxii (1977), pp. 15–23. For comment on the performance of feudal military service during the eleventh and twelfth centuries, see F.M. Stenton, *The First Century of English Feudalism, 1066–1166* (Oxford, 1932), pp. 176–7.

[9] Powicke, *Military Obligation*, p. 97; M. Prestwich, 'Cavalry Service in Early Fourteenth-Century England', *War and Government in the Middle Ages: Essays in Honour of J.O. Prestwich*, ed. J. Gillingham and J.C. Holt (Woodbridge, 1984), p. 148.

[10] Prestwich, *War, Politics and Finance*, p. 91.

[11] See N. Housley, 'European Warfare, *c.* 1200–1320', *Medieval Warfare: A History*, ed. M. Keen (Oxford, 1999), p. 114.

[12] See H.M. Chew, *The English Ecclesiastical Tenants-in-Chief and Knight Service, especially in the Thirteenth and Fourteenth Centuries* (London, 1932), p. 71.

[13] Morris, *Welsh Wars*, p. 158; Prestwich, *Armies and Warfare*, pp. 73–4. The main exceptions to this rule have been the interpretations of Helena Chew and Michael Powicke. Each of these historians has argued that Edward favoured feudal service for practical, military reasons: Chew, *Ecclesiastical Tenants-in-Chief*, p. 71; Powicke, 'The General Obligation to Cavalry Service', p. 832.

[14] M. Prestwich, 'Money and Mercenaries in English Medieval Armies', *England and Germany in the High Middle Ages*, ed. A. Haverkamp and H. Vollrath (Oxford, 1996), p. 133.

later.[15] In fact, Henry could reputedly memorise and recite 250 of the realm's tenancies-in-chief by name,[16] but whether he did this with military or financial objectives in mind is far from clear. Either way, on coming to the throne Edward would have been well acquainted with the uses to which this form of military obligation could be put. His son, in turn, raised the feudal levy for most of the armies that he marched north of the border. Edward II issued feudal summonses in 1310, 1314 and 1322. He attempted to do so, as well, for some abortive campaigns, such as that of 1309.[17] Feudal military service was becoming more rather than less common in the years leading up to Bannockburn, and Edward II felt no need to dispense with it even following the events of 1314.

The aim of this chapter is not to study feudal military service in general. Rather, it is to better understand the nature of the pre-contract armies of the reigns of the first two Edwards by focusing on the men who discharged this type of obligation. As we have seen, the mounted armoured forces of this period contained a mixture of paid, voluntary unpaid and feudal elements. In this they differed markedly from the wholly paid levies of men-at-arms in the armies of Edward III. Of the three types of aristocratic warrior in the armies of Edward I and Edward II ('paid', 'voluntary unpaid' and 'feudal'), those serving for Crown pay are the least likely to be of value to our investigation, for two reasons. Firstly, by receiving the king's wages they had the most in common with the men-at-arms of the reign of Edward III. Secondly, the manner of their service within the armies, in retinues of varying strength, is well known and immediately obvious from the extant source materials. The body of men-at-arms serving gratuitously would furnish a more interesting focus for analysis if it were not for the fact that their names are not, for the most part, recorded in the records for military service. How their military service may have differed from that given by 'paid' warriors, whether they retained greater independence or freedom of action, will probably never be known. It is, therefore, the remaining men-at-arms, those serving in fulfilment of feudal obligations, who constitute the most interesting group. Little is currently known about how these men performed their military service, whether in retinues or separately from other mounted troops,[18] and no attempt has hitherto been made to carry out a prosopographical analysis of this body of soldiers as a whole. Yet the names of hundreds of these men survive on proffer rolls: the documents, drawn up at feudal musters, recording the names of men-at-arms who performed obligatory service on behalf of tenants-in-chief. Moreover, given that feudal military service has received such a bad press from historians, a better understanding of 'feudal' men-at-arms and feudal military

---

[15] *Documents of the Baronial Movement*, pp. 181–3; *Royal and Other Historical Letters Illustrative of the Reign of Henry III*, ed. W.W. Shirley, 2 vols (London, 1862–6), ii, pp. 300–2; *Ann. Dunstaple*, p. 229; *Ann. Waverley*, p. 370.

[16] J.S. Critchley, 'Summonses to Military Service early in the Reign of Henry III', *EHR*, lxxxvi (1971), p. 80.

[17] Powicke, *Military Obligation*, p. 162, note A.

[18] See: Prestwich, *War, Politics and Finance*, p. 82; *idem*, 'Cavalry Service', pp. 150–1, *idem*, *Armies and Warfare*, p. 73.

service generally may shed some light on why Edward III deemed it necessary to carry out a series of military reforms during the 1330s and 1340s.

Who Was the 'Feudal' Soldier?

Our investigation will ultimately lead us to consider how mounted armoured warriors performing feudal service were integrated into the armies of Edward I and Edward II alongside those serving for pay or gratuitously. In some respects this part of the inquiry will constitute an extension of the discussion in chapter 4, for once again the aim will be to analyse the ties between aristocratic soldiers, and to consider how their connections to one another, their personal networks, influenced military organisation at a higher level. As a prelude to this, it is first necessary to establish the identities of the men-at-arms who performed feudal military service and to determine what, if anything, set them apart from other mounted soldiers. This raises a number of questions. For example, did the patterns of service of soldiers proffered by tenants-in-chief in fulfilment of their feudal obligations differ in any way from those given by other kinds of mounted warrior? Did they serve as frequently, were they as professional, as men-at-arms in receipt of Crown pay? Indeed, were there *any* distinguishing characteristics of what may be termed, for the sake of convenience, the 'feudal' soldier? If not, how may this affect the way that we perceive the mounted armoured element of early Edwardian forces?

One of the main drawbacks with previous studies of feudal military service is that relatively little attempt has been made to look at this subject, as with other forms of military obligation, from the perspectives of the soldiers themselves. Fundamental questions relating to the identities of these men, their relationship to the tenants-in-chief, and their experience of military service in a more general sense, have not been considered in sufficient detail. An obvious reason for this is that prior to the reign of Edward I the detailed records for military service, on which such studies must be based, do not exist in sufficient quantity or depth. Although such records have survived for the late thirteenth and early fourteenth centuries, historians who have worked on feudal military service in this period, most notably Helena Chew and Michael Prestwich,[19] have focused more on the functions of the Crown and the tenants-in-chief than on those of the soldiers who performed the service. The studies carried out by Chew and Prestwich are tremendously valuable, not least because they have demonstrated the continued vitality of feudal military service within late thirteenth- and early fourteenth-century England. The aim of what follows is not to challenge this existing body of work, but to add to it by placing men-at-arms rather than their tenurial lords at the centre of our investigation.

Seven feudal musters took place between the Welsh wars of Edward I and the battle of Bannockburn. The proffer roll for the army of 1314, which is no longer extant, was probably lost in the aftermath of the defeat at Bannockburn.

---

[19] Chew, *Ecclesiastical Tenants-in-Chief*, *passim*; Prestwich, 'Cavalry Service', *passim*.

However, proffer rolls of varying degrees of completeness have survived for the armies of 1277, 1282, 1300, 1303, 1306 and 1310.[20] Unfortunately, as Prestwich has noted, 'those for 1303 are probably incomplete and those for 1306 little more than fragmentary'.[21] In total, the extant proffer rolls for the stated period contain the names of around 2,000 mounted armoured warriors (that is, actual individuals rather than names, exclusive of tenants-in-chief who do not appear to have performed the service in person). In chapter 3 it was estimated that an aggregate of around 8,000 individual men-at-arms went to war between 1272 and 1314.[22] Due account must be taken of the fact that this figure of 8,000 is an approximate total, and that, owing to the nature of the sources, the margin of error may be quite large. Nevertheless, comparison of this total with the figure of 2,000 'feudal' soldiers suggests that as many as one in four men-at-arms may have served in the Crown's armies, at one point or another, in fulfilment of feudal obligations. Indeed, the proportion of 'feudal' soldiers may have been much larger than this as surviving proffer rolls, even ones that appear to be complete, do not provide a full record of the men-at-arms performing feudal service. J.E. Morris suggested that during Edward I's Welsh wars, tenants-in-chief, such as Maurice de Berkeley, who proffered the service of two or three knights but not one *serviens* probably had 'troopers two or three times more in number than the knights'.[23] Moreover, Michael Prestwich has observed that 'magnates did not always trouble to have their quotas enrolled'.[24] Consequently, before an attempt is made to examine the military service performed by 'feudal' soldiers, it is necessary to establish how incomplete the proffer rolls are and to gain some idea of how many names may be missing.

At first glance, the methods by which feudal service was recorded seem clear. The marshal, constable or captain of the army would note down the names of the tenants-in-chief, along with the size of their quotas and the names of the men-at-arms being proffered.[25] Once the campaign was over, the rolls would be sent into the chancery and exchequer. Usually, the king would request to see the rolls at some subsequent stage, with the intention of ascertaining who had done their service and who had not.[26] In truth, however, the picture was more complicated than this. When several armies were serving simultaneously in different theatres of war, the responsibility for recording the performance of feudal service

---

[20] The proffer rolls can be found at: 1277 (*Parl. Writs*, i, pp. 197–213); 1282 (*ibid.*, pp. 228–43); 1300 (*Documents and Records of Scotland*, pp. 209–31); 1303 (E 101/612/10; E 101/612/29); 1306 (C 47/5/7); 1310 (*Parl. Writs*, II, ii, pp. 401–8). One slightly later proffer roll, for 1322, can be found at C 47/5/10.

[21] Prestwich, 'Cavalry Service', p. 148.

[22] See above, p. 68.

[23] Morris, *Welsh Wars*, p. 65.

[24] Prestwich, 'Cavalry Service', p. 148. See also *idem, War, Politics and Finance*, pp. 79–80.

[25] In 1300, for example, this duty was performed by the earl of Hereford as constable of England (*Documents and Records of Scotland*, p. 209). The heading on one of the proffer rolls for 1303 shows that the responsibility for supervising the muster in that year lay with Aymer de Valence as 'cheveteyn de lost': E 101/612/10.

[26] See, for example, *CCR, 1272–79*, p. 484.

might fall, as we have seen, on more than one regional army captain.[27] A letter from Robert de Chandos to the chancellor, dated *c.* 1285, shows, incidentally, that his service in the army in Wales three years previously had been recorded on the rolls of Roger de Mortimer senior, the captain at Montgomery, as well as on those of the earl Marshal.[28] Sometimes the marshal, constable or captain would provide written confirmation in the form of certificates to verify that feudal service had been performed. For example, in 1322 the constable, Henry de Beaumont, and the marshal, Thomas, earl of Norfolk, certified that Eleanor de Parles had proffered 'her service at Newcastle upon Tyne on 4 August for a quarter of a knights' fee for her lands in Northamptonshire, the said service being performed by Walter de Watford with a barded horse'.[29] Although Parles' quota was also recorded on the proffer roll for the army in Scotland in that year,[30] in other instances such certificates or indentures might be the only proof that obligations had been met. The scutage and related rolls are replete with references to indentures delivered in to chancery verifying that tenants-in-chief had discharged their feudal service,[31] as well as with instances when it was stated that *a* (usually the chancellor or a campaign commander) testified that *b* had met his obligations.[32] Even the king might be called on to testify in the absence of other records. Edward I recalled, in 1305, that William de Breouse had fulfilled his feudal obligations two years previously despite the fact that his name was not recorded on the marshal's register.[33] In 1306 Roger de Somerville relied on letters of Prince Edward to confirm that he had performed his feudal service in Scotland, where he had stayed, he claimed, in the *comitiva* of Henry de Percy.[34]

It seems, then, that many more men-at-arms performed feudal service than is apparent from the extant proffer rolls. Fortunately, it is possible to ascertain how incomplete the proffer rolls are by drawing not only on the information contained within them but also on the scutage rolls, supplementary close rolls and the rolls recording fines made in lieu of the performance of field service.[35] The scutage rolls and supplementary close rolls are particularly valuable because they reveal the names of tenants-in-chief who were allowed to levy scutage (a cash payment owed by 'feudal' tenants who had not given military service) from their sub-tenants in recognition of the fact they had discharged their feudal

---

[27] See: *CDS*, ii, no. 1397; *CCR, 1307–13*, p. 12.

[28] *Ancient Correspondence Concerning Wales*, p. 114.

[29] BL, Additional Charter 21506: '*son service devant nos a Noef Chastel sur Tyne le iiii jour du mois daust pur la quarte partie de un fee de chivaler pur ses terres en le conte de Norhampton fessant per Wauter de Watford ove un chival couvert*'.

[30] C 47/5/10, m. 1iii.

[31] See, for example, *CVCR* (supplementary close rolls), p. 108 (Henry de Grey), and p. 109 (Payn de Tibetot).

[32] *Ibid.* (scutage rolls), pp. 365–73.

[33] *CCW*, p. 253.

[34] *Parl. Roll.*, ii, p. 386.

[35] Data from the scutage rolls and supplementary close rolls can be found in *CVCR*. Most of the fines can be found in The National Archive, class E 370: Lord Treasurer's Remembrancer, Miscellanea rolls.

obligations.[36] These rolls distinguish between, on the one hand, tenants-in-chief who had supplied men-at-arms, and on the other, those who had made fines. Numerous petitions were sent to Edward I by tenants-in-chief protesting that they were being charged with scutage, particularly for the armies in Wales in 1282 and Scotland in 1306,[37] even though they had performed their service. This may have been linked to a general dispute arising from the Crown's attempts to turn scutage into a general tax.[38] This controversy reached its peak at the parliament of February 1292. There the tenants-in-chief 'complained that those who, by themselves or their predecessors, had already discharged their obligations, were now, nevertheless, being frequently and grievously distrained to pay scutage on the fees which they held of the king'.[39] However, in the majority of cases tenants-in-chief seem to have been wrongfully charged with scutage for no greater reason than that their service had not been recorded, or had not been noticed among the records of the exchequer. As we have seen, many men-at-arms gave feudal service during these years without registering their names at the muster.

The scale of these problems, and how much they have led to an underestimation of the size of the mounted armoured forces raised through feudal summonses, remains to be worked out. Table 5.1 provides data for all six campaigns between 1277 and 1314 for which proffer rolls have survived. It shows what proportion of the male lay tenants-in-chief who were summoned individually in 1277, 1282, 1300, 1303, 1306 and 1310 proffered their contingent of men-at-arms or made fines, as well as how many individuals made proffers or fines on each of the said campaigns despite not having been summoned directly.

Table 5.1: Numbers of male lay tenants-in-chief who proffered feudal service[40]

	1277	1282	1300	1303	1306	1310
Summoned in person	179	165	107	100	81	138
Made proffers (on roll)	88	42	41	23	14	53
Paid fine	11	15	2	4	13	3
Not summoned in person						
Made proffers (on roll)	144	77	117	83	36	80
Paid fine	39	42	3	14	22	0

[36] See Morris, *Welsh Wars*, pp. 108–9.
[37] *Ancient Correspondence Concerning Wales*, pp. 132–3; *Parl. Roll.*, ii, pp. 386–8.
[38] H.M. Chew, 'Scutage under Edward I', *EHR*, xxxvii (1922), p. 324.
[39] *Ibid.*, p. 324.
[40] For the summonses, see: *Parl. Writs*, i, pp. 193–5, 225–6, 327–8, 366–7, 377; *ibid.*, II, ii, pp. 394–6. For the fines, see: *CFR*, i, pp. 85–7; E 370/1/13, mm. 1–6, 11. Many fines for the 1277 and 1282 campaigns can be found on the proffer rolls for those years. A few fines can be found on the proffer roll for 1300. The figure given for the individually summoned men who made proffers in 1310 is a little higher than that given by Michael Powicke: 'Edward II and Military Obligation', *Speculum*, xxxi (1956), p. 117.

These figures demonstrate that the obligation to provide mounted soldiers in return for lands held in chief affected many more landholders than the 100 or so magnates who were summoned in person. The obligation to provide the service due (*servicium debitum*) for lands held in chief evidently had very deep roots within landed society. If, by the late thirteenth century, feudal service had no future as a system of raising an effective mounted force, it seems remarkable that so many individuals should have been willing to provide men-at-arms without being directly ordered to do so by the king. Presumably the many landholders who made proffers despite not having been summoned by name were responding to the sheriffs' summonses, which were issued in county assemblies. But precisely how the Crown was able to enforce the service of these men, and why some individuals responded to the summonses while others apparently did not, is less clear. Whatever the reasons for this widespread response to the feudal summons (whether the motive lay in the threat of coercion or in a benevolent desire to contribute to the war effort), the fact that so many lesser landholders were willing and able to provide mounted armoured warriors for service in the king's armies attests to the existence of a vast web of service connections within Edwardian England that could be activated, it would seem, at any time.

However, a different feature of the figures presented in table 5.1 provides a less positive impression of feudal military service during the reigns of the first two Edwards. Of the tenants-in-chief who were summoned by name, generally only a quarter to a half, and in some years even fewer, appear on the extant proffer rolls. J.S. Critchley has commented on a similar phenomenon in the reign of Henry III, noting that 'not every individual who received [an individual summons] served, and conversely not everyone who served had received one'.[41] Does this suggest that magnates were beginning to ignore such summonses, deeming feudal service to be less important than service given for Crown pay or gratuitously? Here we must return to the thorny problem of the incompleteness of the records for the performance of feudal military service. We have seen, from Michael Prestwich's observations, that not all tenants-in-chief who tendered feudal service are named on the surviving proffer rolls. An examination of the scutage rolls and supplementary close rolls for the armies raised between 1277 and 1310 supports this point. It reveals that many tenants-in-chief sent their units of men-at-arms to the armies but did not (as far as we can tell) register the names of their men with the supervisors of the musters. Table 5.2 reveals the extent of this practice and demonstrates how incomplete the proffer rolls are.

[41] Critchley, 'Summonses to Military Service', p. 85.

Table 5.2: Tenants-in-chief who proffered service but are not on the proffer rolls[42]

	1277	1282	1300	1303	1306	1310
Summoned individually	n/d	32	14	29	14	21
Not summoned individually	n/d	37	25	37	57	4
Total	n/d	69	39	66	71	25

Key: n/d = no data

Besides forcing us to modify the figures presented in table 5.1, showing that more of the tenants-in-chief who were summoned by name performed their service than would appear to have done so at first glance, table 5.2 demonstrates how incomplete the surviving proffer rolls are. Fortunately, an attempt can be made to calculate the number of men-at-arms whose names are missing. For Edward II's campaign to Scotland in 1310–11, a total of 133 tenants-in-chief proffered the service of forty-two knights and 477 *servientes*.[43] This means that the average proffer in that year consisted of 3.9 mounted warriors of all ranks. If this mean average is applied to the figures presented in table 5.2, it would appear that we are missing the names of no fewer than 269, 152, 257, 277 and 98 'feudal' soldiers from 1282, 1300, 1303, 1306 and 1310 respectively. These figures are, of course, very imprecise; but they indicate that the system of obtaining mounted armoured warriors through the calling out of the *servicium debitum* was a significant feature of aristocratic military service. Therefore, an analysis of the men who were recruited in this way, and of the means by which they were integrated into the mounted forces as a whole, can potentially enhance our understanding of military organisation in the pre-Bannockburn era.

It is clear that any prosopographical analysis of the men who performed feudal service during this period must necessarily be incomplete. This should be borne in mind throughout the following discussion. Before commencing an investigation of the knights and sergeants who registered their service as men-at-arms at feudal musters, a little should first be said about the landholders responsible for recruiting these soldiers: the tenants-in-chief.[44] In his work on feudal military service in an earlier period, J.H. Round described the tenant-in-chief of eleventh- and twelfth-century England as the ' "middleman" of the feudal system'.[45] This continued to be the case through to the early fourteenth century. Indeed, male lay tenants-in-chief, as members of the landed warrior class, often took an active part in the king's military campaigns, albeit not always as 'feudal' warriors. Many tenants-in-chief, particularly in 1277 and 1282, fulfilled their

---

[42] For service not on the proffer rolls, see *CVCR* (supplementary close rolls and scutage rolls), *passim*.

[43] Simpkin, 'The English Army and the Scottish Campaign of 1310–1311', pp. 16–17.

[44] For a prosopographical analysis of the service performed by baronial tenants-in-chief between 1210 and 1322, see I.J. Sanders, *Feudal Military Service in England: A Study of the Constitutional and Military Powers of the* Barones *in Medieval England* (Oxford, 1956), pp. 136–60.

[45] J.H. Round, *Feudal England: Historical Studies on the XIth and XIIth Centuries* (London, 1895), p. 248.

feudal obligations by serving in person.[46] Forty-three proffered themselves on more than one campaign, and one tenant-in-chief, Thomas de Scales, registered his name as a man-at-arms at four feudal musters in Scotland between 1300 and 1310.[47] Although the majority of landholders, especially during the Scottish wars, preferred to discharge their feudal obligations through substitutes (men sent to the feudal muster on their behalf), the greater part nevertheless served in the king's armies in person, whether for Crown pay or gratuitously. Of the 107 male lay tenants-in-chief who received a feudal summons in 1300, seventy-five (70 per cent) served in Edward I's army in that year, the majority as retinue leaders. Three years later 100 tenants-in-chief were summoned by name. Of these, seventy-eight (78 per cent) can be shown to have performed military service in person, irrespective of whether that was for Crown pay, gratuitously or in fulfilment of their feudal obligations. It would seem, therefore, that there was nothing to prevent large numbers of male lay tenants-in-chief from leading their 'feudal' contingents in person.

Previous research suggests, however, that tenants-in-chief seldom made proffers on more than one campaign. In his analysis of the feudal musters of 1300, 1310 and 1322, Michael Prestwich found that 'there was surprisingly little continuity in the body of tenants-in-chief who responded to the feudal summonses by sending troops'.[48] Might such discontinuity have undermined the effectiveness of feudal summonses as a method of raising soldiers? Moreover, were there similar levels of instability in the body of tenants-in-chief making proffers between 1277 and 1310? A total of some 237 tenants-in-chief, or 203 if we discount females and ecclesiastics (we shall consider the obligations met by ecclesiastical tenants-in-chief in due course), appear on the surviving proffer rolls as tendering feudal military service on more than one expedition between 1277 and 1310. Of these 203 male lay tenants-in-chief, 127 proffered their service twice during the stated period; fifty did so on three occasions; twenty on four occasions; four on five occasions; and just two in all six years. An additional 252 male lay tenants-in-chief made proffers (as far as the evidence shows) on no more than one occasion. But around 130 of these individuals can be tentatively linked to other members of the same family who appear as tenants-in-chief, on the proffer rolls, in other years.[49] Moreover, the majority of the men named as tenants-in-chief on just one occasion appear on the proffer rolls of 1277 or 1310, the years that form the parameters of our analysis. It should be remembered, finally, that the extant proffer rolls offer no more than a partial insight into the full corpus of landholders who made proffers. Continuity rates would be consid-

---

[46] This had been the normal trend during the reign of Henry III. On the Welsh campaign of 1231, '128 tenants-in-chief served in person with the main army at Painscastle, and fifty-eight others sent knights and sergeants to perform their service': Walker, 'Anglo-Welsh Wars', p. 274.

[47] 1300 (*Documents and Records of Scotland*, p. 216); 1303 (E 101/612/29, m. 1); 1306 (C 47/5/7, m. 1); 1310 (*Parl. Writs*, II, ii, p. 407).

[48] Prestwich, 'Cavalry Service', p. 149.

[49] Oliver de Dynaunt, for example, appears only to have made a proffer in 1277, but his son Joyce later acknowledged his family's service in 1300, following Oliver's death: *Parl. Writs*, i, p. 203; *Documents and Records of Scotland*, p. 212.

erably higher if this analysis included tenants-in-chief who are recorded in other sources, such as the scutage rolls, as having proffered their service.

Overall, then, there seems little reason to doubt that summonses to tenants-in-chief gave the king access to a reliable supply of manpower for his wars. As for the knights and *servientes* who made up the quotas of these tenants-in-chief, the greater part appear in their 'feudal' contingents, as recorded on the proffer rolls, on no more than one occasion. This suggests that the connections between tenants-in-chief and the men proffered on their behalf were not very strong. Perhaps this was a source of organisational weakness. The reasons for this general discontinuity are not difficult to find. An inquest in 1293 into the lands of Henry de la Pomeray shows that some fifty free tenants (*libere tenentes*) held land from him by military service (*per servicium militare*) in his manor of Tregony in Cornwall alone.[50] The pool from which tenants-in-chief could draw men to fulfil their feudal obligations was, therefore, very large.

Despite this there was some continuity. For example, at least eight of the knights and thirteen of the sergeants who were proffered at the feudal muster in Wales in 1277 were employed by the same tenants-in-chief five years later. Some ecclesiastical tenants-in-chief, in particular, repeatedly drew on the same body of soldiers to discharge their feudal service. The abbot of St Albans appears to have used one of the knights and three of the sergeants whom he proffered in the first Welsh war (1277) to represent him at the feudal muster in 1282.[51] It was not only ecclesiastics, however, who repeatedly drew on the same individuals to perform their feudal service. Between 1277 and 1310 at least forty male lay tenants-in-chief proffered men-at-arms whom they had employed as part of their 'feudal' contingents on previous occasions. The knights Ralph de Trehampton and William le Vavasur could be found in the 'feudal' contingent of the earl of Lincoln in both of the first two Welsh wars of Edward I's reign.[52] In like manner, the Doddingseles family sent or led the sergeants Clement de la More and John de Wygenhale to more than one muster: the former in 1300 and 1303, the latter in those years as well as in 1310.[53] Even when the same soldiers were not re-employed by tenants-in-chief, members of the same family might be. In 1294, for the abortive feudal muster for the Gascon campaign, the abbot of Ramsey tried to force William de Haningfeld to give feudal service on his behalf in the way that his ancestors had done.[54] This demonstrates that tenants-in-chief were sometimes keen to maintain traditions of feudal service over succeeding generations. In instances of familial continuity the proffered men were often related to their lords, but not always. For example, a Simon de Coleford was one of the

---

[50] *Liber Feodorum. The Book of Fees commonly called Testa de Nevill*, 3 vols (London, 1920–31), ii, pp. 1316–19.
[51] The knight Stephen de Cheynduit (but the Cheynduit junior who served in 1282 may have been the son of the knight of that name who had fought for the abbot in 1277), and the sergeants John de Linlegh, John le Mareschal and John de Russepot: *Parl. Writs*, i, pp. 198, 228.
[52] *Ibid.*, i, pp. 199, 229.
[53] *Documents and Records of Scotland*, p. 216; E 101/612/29, m. 1; *Parl. Writs*, II, ii, p. 403.
[54] *Select Pleas in Manorial and Other Seignorial Courts*, i, p. 78.

men proffered on behalf of Hugh de Courtenay in 1300, but an Alexander de Coleford performed the service for him six years later.[55] Two members of the Bakepuz family, John and Reginald, were proffered as members of Nicholas de Meppershall's 'feudal' contingent in separate years.[56]

In fact, although tenants-in-chief may not, in general, have used the same men repeatedly to discharge their feudal obligations, many of the men-at-arms who registered their service at the feudal musters were connected, in different capacities in other years, to the men by whom they had been proffered. This is an important point as it suggests that the military ties between tenants-in-chief and the soldiers serving in their 'feudal' contingents were sometimes very strong. Once again, a few examples must suffice to support this observation.

Thomas Paynel, who gave feudal service on behalf of John de St John in Wales in 1282, could be found in the same lord's retinue, or that of St John's son, in a non-feudal capacity in 1294 (Gascony), 1299, 1300, 1301, 1303 and 1306 (all Scotland).[57] In another example, on 14 July 1303, at a muster taken at Edinburgh, Thomas de Wokyndon registered his feudal service as a knight on behalf of the tenant-in-chief Henry de Grey.[58] Although Wokyndon does not appear to have served as part of the same lord's 'feudal' contingent on any other occasion, he had letters of protection enrolled for service in Grey's war *comitiva* on three additional campaigns: in 1298, 1300 and 1306.[59] Finally, in 1310 John Darcy and Simon de Cokefeld were proffered at the feudal muster by Aymer de Valence and Payn de Tibetot respectively.[60] Both Darcy and Cokefeld had joined the retinues of the same lords on previous expeditions.[61] Indeed, no fewer than sixteen of the knights who registered their service at the feudal muster in 1300, and twelve of the equivalent knights in 1310, had additional service ties, in other years, to the tenants-in-chief by whom they were proffered. In other instances, connections between tenants-in-chief and their 'feudal' soldiers may be less immediately obvious in the extant sources. Richard de Mascy gave feudal service on behalf of Ralph de Cammoys in Scotland in 1310.[62] Four years later he served in the retinue of Cammoys' lord, Hugh le Despenser, on

---

[55] *Documents and Records of Scotland*, p. 225; C 47/5/7, m. 1.

[56] *Parl. Writs*, i, pp. 204, 234.

[57] 1282 (*ibid.*, i, p. 231; E 101/4/1, m. 10); 1294 (*Rôles Gascons*, iii, p. 167); 1299–1300 (E 101/8/26, m. 1); 1301 (C 67/14, m. 4); 1303 (C 67/15, m. 7d); 1306 (E 101/612/15, m. 1); temp. Edward II (E 101/17/32).

[58] E 101/612/10, m. 1.

[59] 1298 (C 67/13, m. 6d); 1300 (C 67/14, m. 10); 1306 (C 67/16, m. 13). He also had a letter of protection enrolled for service with Grey in Scotland in 1303: C 67/15, m. 14.

[60] *Parl. Writs*, II, ii, pp. 401, 405.

[61] Darcy: see above, p. 136. Cokefeld: 1303 (E 101/612/11, m. 2d); 1306 (E 101/13/7, m. 1). All four of the knights sent to the muster by Thomas of Lancaster had served with him either in Scotland in 1306 or at the Dunstable tournament of 1309: Peter de Limesey and William Trussell junior in 1306 (C 67/16, mm. 9, 4d); Roger de Swynnerton and John de Twyford in 1309 (Tomkinson, 'Retinues at Dunstable', pp. 74–5). For details of Thomas of Lancaster's proffer in 1310, see *Parl. Writs*, II, ii, p. 406.

[62] *Parl. Writs*, II, ii, p. 403.

the Bannockburn campaign.[63] There seems to have been a three-way connection between these men, with Mascy's links to Cammoys almost certainly accounting for his presence in Despenser's retinue in Scotland in 1314.

The fact that 'feudal' soldiers sometimes served on other campaigns for Crown wages, and, as J.E. Morris noted in his study of the Welsh wars of Edward I,[64] entered pay once their feudal service had been discharged, has been recognised for a long time. Possibly bearing these points in mind, Michael Prestwich has observed quite recently that 'there is nothing to suggest that those who performed [feudal] service under Edward or his son were incompetent or ill-equipped, apart from a small lunatic fringe'.[65] An examination of the careers of many ordinary men-at-arms who performed feudal military service during these years supports this impression.

Of the *servientes* proffered at the feudal musters in Wales in 1277 and Scotland in 1310, the majority have proved difficult to trace in the records for other campaigns. This suggests that these men were fairly obscure individuals. An analysis of the men-at-arms who gave feudal service in other years, however, shows that this was by no means universally the case. Of the forty or so knights proffered at the feudal muster in Scotland in 1300, thirty-five served in other armies in non-feudal capacities. There is insufficient space to discuss each individual case here, but the example of Robert Peverel may be taken as representative. He was proffered by Walter de Langton at the feudal muster of 1300.[66] Prior to this he had had letters of protection enrolled for service in armies north of the border in 1296, 1298 and 1299, and he appears to have fought as a retinue leader in Flanders in 1297.[67] In each of these years – 1296, 1297, 1298 and 1299 – no feudal summons had been issued. This means that when he was proffered by Walter de Langton in 1300, Peverel had experience of giving non-obligatory service in more than one theatre of war. Turning our attention to men of lesser status, it would seem that, although reconstructing the careers of sergeants can be very difficult, around a half of the *valletti* proffered by tenants-in-chief in 1300 served on other campaigns in non-feudal capacities. Geoffrey de Briggeford, for example, registered his name as one of four sergeants performing the service of two knights' fees on behalf of Edmund Deyncurt.[68] Two years previously he had served for Crown pay in Scotland in the *comitiva* of Eustace de Hacche, and he went on to serve in Hacche's paid retinue once again in 1301.[69]

---

[63] C 71/6, m. 3. Cammoys was later named as one of the corrupt justices appointed to office by the Despensers during their spell in charge of the government in the mid-1320s. In 1326 he was given responsibility for the defence of Hampshire as preparations were made to repel the anticipated invasion by Isabella and Mortimer: N. Fryde, *The Tyranny and Fall of Edward II 1321–1326* (Cambridge, 1979), pp. 47–8, 183. See also Saul, 'The Despensers and the Downfall of Edward II', pp. 6–8.

[64] Morris, *Welsh Wars*, p. 132.

[65] Prestwich, *Armies and Warfare*, p. 73.

[66] *Documents and Records of Scotland*, p. 210.

[67] 1296 (C 67/11, m. 4); 1297 (C 67/12, m. 3d); 1298 (C 67/13, m. 7); 1299 (C 67/14, m. 15).

[68] *Documents and Records of Scotland*, p. 215.

[69] 1298 (*Scotland in 1298*, p. 192); 1301 (E 101/9/24, m. 3). He also served for pay in the

As with Peverel and many other 'feudal' men-at-arms, Briggeford seems to have been a perfectly competent soldier. Aristocratic warriors who gave feudal service were sometimes, in fact, among the most exalted warriors of their day. Ten of the knights proffered at the feudal muster in Wales in 1277 had taken part in the Lord Edward's crusade to the Holy Land a few years previously.[70] Moreover, Giles de Argentein, one of the reputed paragons of chivalry, fought as a sergeant in the feudal levy of 1300 and registered his service as a knight, on behalf of Piers Gaveston, earl of Cornwall, at Tweedmouth in 1310.[71]

Distinctions between 'feudal' and other types of mounted soldier, therefore, have little merit.[72] This may appear to be a fairly trivial point, but it also raises a number of interesting questions that are of direct relevance to the issue of military organisation in the pre-Bannockburn era. For instance, if mounted soldiers serving in fulfilment of feudal obligations were often experienced soldiers, might it not be the case that they were recruited and integrated into the armies in the same way as other men-at-arms? Furthermore, if they *were* recruited and organised into the armies via the same processes as all other mounted soldiers, might this not mean that the continued use of the feudal summons by Edward I and Edward II actually had a minimal impact on the way that the mounted part of these armies functioned in the field? The remainder of this chapter will seek to answer these questions.

Structure and Organisation: An Intricate Fusion of Elements[73]

In any study of medieval armies the most important question is also invariably the most difficult to answer, namely how were these hosts organised in the field? This question takes on added complexity prior to the reign of Edward III. During the era of pre-contract armies, mounted armoured forces, as we have seen, contained a mixture of paid, voluntary unpaid and feudal elements. Although horse inventories and the few surviving pay-rolls provide information on the paid part of many campaign retinues, there remains a great deal of confusion about how men-at-arms not in receipt of the king's wages (particularly those serving in fulfilment of feudal obligations) were combined with those serving for Crown pay. The leading scholar in this field, Michael Prestwich, has on more than one occasion highlighted the prevailing uncertainty surrounding the issue of the organisation of the feudal host.[74] In one of his most recent observations

---

retinue of Hacche's sub-leader William de Hardreshull in Flanders in 1297: BL, Additional MS 7965, fol. 73v.

[70] Ralph de Wodeburg, Thomas Lercedekne, Peter de Chaluns, John de Gurnay, William de Wodeburg, Thomas Boter, Thomas du Pyn, Walter de Cambhou, Robert Martin and Ralph de Cotun: Lloyd, *English Society and the Crusade*, appendix 4.

[71] *Documents and Records of Scotland*, p. 212; *Parl. Writs*, II, ii, p. 403.

[72] For a similar view relating to an earlier period, see S.D.B. Brown, 'Military Service and Monetary Reward in the Eleventh and Twelfth Centuries', *History*, lxxiv (1989), pp. 22, 34.

[73] This section develops observations made by the author in a recently published article: Simpkin, 'The English Army and the Scottish Campaign of 1310–1311', pp. 28–39.

[74] Prestwich, *War, Politics and Finance*, p. 82; *idem*, 'Cavalry Service', pp. 150–1.

on this subject he commented that 'the sources do not normally reveal whether those performing feudal service were formed up together as a single body in the army, or whether, once they had registered their service with the marshal or officials responsible for keeping the record, they were dispersed among the army'.[75] This constitutes an unfortunate gap in knowledge. Unless we know more about how men-at-arms were arranged within the king's armies during their spells of obligatory service, we cannot provide an accurate assessment of how effective feudal military service was.

This is not, of course, to suggest that historians have made no observations on this subject. In her work on ecclesiastical tenants-in-chief, Helena Chew wrote at length about the provision of feudal military service in English armies between the eleventh and early fourteenth centuries. She noted that 'when the muster was complete the [feudal] contingents were apportioned among the various captains and commanding officers'.[76] In support of this observation, Chew relied primarily on the evidence of chronicles and bishops' registers. She drew attention, for example, to the fact that in 1282 the group of eight men-at-arms supplied by the bishop of Hereford served as a group under the command of Roger de Mortimer senior at the castle of Builth.[77] Writing a few decades later, N.B. Lewis added to the historiography on this subject in his study of the feudal summons of 1327 (the last such summons to be issued until Richard II's campaign to Scotland in 1385).[78] This paper's primary contribution was its analysis of a written contract drawn up between the archbishop of York and Robert de Constable of Flamborough for the provision of feudal military service. Lewis observed that this agreement proved 'that the written contract, which had for so long been used to embody undertakings for non-feudal service, had also been adopted to engage troops to fulfil the feudal obligation before the system was finally abandoned'.[79] More recently, Michael Prestwich has returned to the issue previously examined (but not definitively) by Helena Chew, namely how men-at-arms carried out their feudal service following the muster. Although noting that the 'feudal' contingents raised for the campaign against Robert Bruce in 1306 seem to have performed their feudal service together as a group,[80] he has been inclined to believe that men discharging such obligations were generally distributed among the retinues.[81]

---

[75] Prestwich, *Armies and Warfare*, p. 73.

[76] Chew, *Ecclesiastical Tenants-in-Chief*, p. 94.

[77] *Ibid.*, p. 94.

[78] N.B. Lewis, 'The Summons of the English Feudal Levy, 5 April 1327', *Essays in Medieval History Presented to Bertie Wilkinson*, ed. T.A. Sandquist and M.R. Powicke (Toronto, 1969), pp. 236–49. On the importance of the campaign of 1327 as a turning-point in the king's relationship with his barons, see S. Painter, *Studies in the History of the English Feudal Barony* (Baltimore, Md., 1943), p. 45. For the summons of 1385, see: N.B. Lewis, 'The Last Medieval Summons of the English Feudal Levy, 13 June 1385', *EHR*, lxxiii (1958), pp. 1–26; J.J.N. Palmer, 'The Last Summons of the Feudal Army in England (1385)', *EHR*, lxxxiii (1968), pp. 771–5; and N.B. Lewis, 'The Feudal Summons of 1385', *EHR*, c (1985), pp. 729–43.

[79] Lewis, 'The Summons of the English Feudal Levy', p. 242.

[80] Prestwich, *Armies and Warfare*, p. 73.

[81] Prestwich, *War, Politics and Finance*, p. 82; *idem*, 'Cavalry Service', p. 150.

Despite the progress that has been made in this field of research, a great deal remains to be done. The studies of Chew, Lewis, Prestwich and others have clarified a number of key points relating to the provision of feudal military service in early Edwardian England. However, the crucial issue of how aristocratic warriors performed this kind of service remains a matter for debate.

One explanation for this lack of certainty is that the sources that have hitherto been used to shed light on this subject – mainly chronicles, ecclesiastical records and comments written on proffer rolls (as opposed to names of men recorded on proffer rolls) – tend to be of limited value. Monastic chroniclers were generally either unaware of the more intricate matters of military organisation or deemed them too commonplace to be worth recording. There are some exceptions to this rule and these will be considered in due course. Bishops' registers can be of some value and will be incorporated into the analysis a little later, but they tend to be concerned more with matters of pay and recruitment before the musters than with what happened afterwards. Comments made on the proffer rolls can be of greater assistance. A note on the proffer roll of 1277 suggests that Baldwin Wake, who was a member of the household of the earl of Gloucester (*de familia Comitis Gloucestriae*), performed part of his feudal service in that year in the retinue of the said earl.[82] In like manner, the proffer rolls for the army that served in Wales in 1282 state both that Robert de Sevans gave his feudal service in the *comitiva* of John le Mareschal and that John de Vaux, who recognised the service of one knights' fee for his lands in Suffolk, was in the company of the earl marshal by the king's licence (*in comitiva Comitis Marescalliae de licencia Regis*).[83] These comments make it clear that men-at-arms sometimes performed their feudal service in the retinues of other men. However, it is difficult to be sure, from the proffer rolls alone, whether these examples were representative. If they *were* representative, then why was the king's licence sometimes required to allow soldiers to give feudal service in the companies of other campaign leaders? An additional problem is that such comments do not reveal whether men-at-arms were dispersed among the retinues by the marshal, constable, or captain at the muster, or had made arrangements to serve in the retinues of other tenants-in-chief beforehand.

Drawing on evidence relating to Henry III's Welsh campaign of 1257, when the knights proffered on behalf of the abbot of St Albans were sent to serve in one part of the army and the abbot's sergeants dispatched to another, Michael Powicke has suggested that the key organisational decisions were made at the muster. There, he observed, 'the constable and marshal would draw up horse and foot according to whatever tactical grouping might at the time be in favour'.[84]

---

[82] *Parl. Writs*, i, p. 200; Morris, *Welsh Wars*, p. 70; M. Altschul, *A Baronial Family in Medieval England: The Clares, 1217–1314* (Baltimore, Md., 1965), pp. 138–9. The note reads, in full: '*de familia Comitis Gloucestriae. Et supplicat Regi quod possit facere servicium in ii quarentena.*'

[83] *Parl. Writs*, i, pp. 232, 233.

[84] Powicke, *Military Obligation*, p. 34. For further discussion of the organisation of the abbot's 'feudal' contingent in 1257, and similar examples dating from Henry III's Welsh wars, see Walker, 'Anglo-Welsh Wars', pp. 40–1, 178–9; and below p. 178.

The account on which this assertion was based, that of the monastic chronicler Matthew Paris,[85] has often been cited by historians because it is one of the very few contemporary comments to cast any light on what happened at feudal musters. It should be remembered, however, that Paris' account relates to the organisation of just one 'feudal' contingent. Consequently, it would be dangerous to presume that all groups of proffered men were split up in this way. Although the muster may have been the ideal place to group retinues of various sizes into larger units and battles, it is unlikely that the internal structure of the companies was interfered with at that point unless this was felt to be absolutely necessary. Secondly, it must be remembered that on many expeditions there was more than one muster and that men and units arrived and departed from the army at different times. 'A medieval army,' as F.M. Powicke once noted, 'was a fluctuating thing.'[86] Therefore, to find out more about how men-at-arms performing feudal service were integrated into the armies alongside those serving for pay or gratuitously, it is not enough to rely solely on odd snippets in chronicles or monastic registers.

One obvious yet under-utilised source of information for the structure and composition of the mounted part of early Edwardian armies is the heraldic rolls of arms. Of particular value in this respect are the occasional rolls which record the names of men present on particular campaigns. As we saw in chapter 2, Michael Prestwich has used some of these occasional rolls to good effect, demonstrating, by comparing the names found on these rolls with those found in pay accounts and on proffer rolls, that large numbers of bannerets in the armies of Edward I served gratuitously. Might these armorials also be of some value for our investigation into the knights and *servientes* performing obligatory feudal service?

Two occasional rolls that provide some insights into the way that soldiers discharged their feudal service are the Caerlaverock roll and the Galloway roll, both of which were compiled in 1300. Each of these armorials appears to have been drawn up shortly after the events that it commemorates.[87] In the instance of the Caerlaverock roll, this means the siege, by English forces under Edward I, of Caerlaverock castle in southwestern Scotland in July 1300.[88] The martial event to which the Galloway roll relates is a skirmish between English and Scottish forces at the river Cree, to the west of Caerlaverock, which took place just a month after the said siege.[89] The Caerlaverock roll is, in fact, a heraldic poem rather than a roll of arms in the usual sense of the term. It records the names and arms of 106 knights in Edward I's army, all but six of whom were knights

---

85   *Chronica Majora*, vi, p. 374.
86   Powicke, *The Thirteenth Century*, p. 411.
87   See the summaries in *Rolls of Arms, Edward I*, i, pp. 433, 446.
88   For discussion of the Caerlaverock roll, see: N. Denholm-Young, *The Song of Carlaverock and the Parliamentary Roll of Arms as found in Cott. MS. Calig. A. XVIII in the British Museum* (1962); *Rolls of Arms, Edward I*, i, pp. 432–3. For the contents of the Caerlaverock roll, see *Rolls of Arms, Edward I*, i, pp. 434–44, and *The Siege of Caerlaverock, passim*.
89   Denholm-Young, 'The Galloway Roll', p. 132; *idem*, *Country Gentry*, pp. 151–2; *Rolls of Arms, Edward I*, i, pp. 445–6. For the contents of the Galloway roll, see *Rolls of Arms, Edward I*, i, pp. 447–68.

banneret.[90] The Galloway roll is at first glance a more conventional roll of arms, recording 261 coats of arms, including a few flawed entries, in blazon (the technical language of heraldry). Yet in some respects this roll of arms is one of the most innovative to have survived. Not only is it the first extant occasional roll to record the names and arms of large numbers of knights bachelor as well as of bannerets, but it is also the first to group men-at-arms into the retinues in which they served.[91] As such, it is a source of great value to prosopographers of military service.

Given that it records the names of just six men below the status of knight banneret, and that very few bannerets gave feudal service in person during the war in Scotland, the Caerlaverock roll is of relatively limited value to our investigation. However, in one of the apparently eye-witness accounts towards the end of the poem, the herald-minstrel notes that the Basset brothers (*li frere Basset*) were present alongside the Berkeley brothers (*li bon frere de Berkelee*), Maurice and Thomas junior, during the siege of Caerlaverock castle.[92] This is a matter of some interest because, on turning our attention to the proffer roll for the army of 1300, we find that Thomas de Berkeley senior (who does not appear to have served in person) had proffered the service of Edmund and John Basset, along with one other knight, at the feudal muster on 2 July.[93] The connection between the two sets of brothers is also highlighted by the Galloway roll. The Basset brothers are listed on that armorial just a little below the names of the Berkeley brothers and alongside the third knight proffered in fulfilment of Berkeley senior's feudal obligations, Thomas de Gurnay.[94] The Galloway roll also records the name of one other knight who seems to have been serving in the Berkeley retinue, William de Wauton.[95] He, like the Berkeley brothers, does not appear to have received Crown pay. Overall, the evidence suggests that the Basset brothers were in the Berkeley retinue throughout their feudal service, including at the siege of Caerlaverock, and that they were joined in the *comitiva* by other soldiers who had not (as far as we can tell) registered their names at the feudal muster.

The Berkeley retinue in 1300, then, seems to have consisted of two sets of men-at-arms: one kind serving gratuitously, the other in fulfilment of feudal obligations.[96] Fortunately, the innovative structure of the Galloway roll – the division of the knights listed on the armorial into retinues – means that it is possible to trace additional instances of 'feudal' soldiers serving alongside other mounted armoured warriors, not performing feudal service, within the army's constituent companies.

---

90 Denholm-Young, 'The Galloway Roll', p. 131.
91 *Ibid.*, p. 131.
92 *Rolls of Arms, Edward I*, i, p. 443.
93 *Documents and Records of Scotland*, p. 221.
94 *Rolls of Arms, Edward I*, i, p. 468.
95 *Ibid.*, p. 468.
96 R.F. Walker has noted that some of the tenants-in-chief who made proffers on Henry III's Welsh campaign of 1245 'produced extra knights "de gratia"': Walker, 'Anglo-Welsh Wars', p. 56.

On 29 June 1300 Hugh de Vere (a younger son of the earl of Oxford), who in addition to being a tenant-in-chief was also a retinue leader in Edward I's army in Scotland, proffered the service of one knight, John de Hulles, at the feudal muster.[97] Sixteen days previously, on 13 June, Hulles had had a letter of protection enrolled for service in Vere's war *comitiva*.[98] This suggests, but does not prove, that he was in Vere's retinue while performing his feudal service. What is more, Hulles also appears on the Galloway roll, dating from around 8 August, just four places below Hugh de Vere and in close proximity to five other knights – Alphonse de Vere, Robert Fitz Nigel, Arnold de Monteny, John de Rivers and Simon de Crey – who had had letters of protection enrolled on 13 June for service in Vere's retinue in Scotland.[99] Not one of these five additional knights was proffered by Vere on 29 June at the feudal muster (Hulles is the only soldier named in Vere's proffer). As Vere does not appear in the wardrobe accounts for this campaign in receipt of Crown pay, it seems that he and the knights in his retinue, except for Hulles, were serving gratuitously. Therefore, the Vere retinue in 1300, like the Berkeley retinue, seems to have comprised a mixture of feudal and voluntary unpaid elements. Yet what is particularly interesting in this example is that Hulles had been attached to the retinue since before the muster (he had had a protection enrolled on 13 June), and that his preparations in the build-up to the campaign, the legal precautions that he took, were no different from those of the other men-at-arms in Vere's retinue. Indeed, Hulles seems to have been a member of Vere's personal network of comrades in arms. He served with Vere again, in a non-feudal capacity, in Scotland in the following year.[100]

The only detail missing from John de Hulles' service record in 1300 is any evidence linking him to Hugh de Vere's retinue from 29 June 1300, the day on which he was proffered at the muster, to 8 August, the date around which he appears with Vere on the Galloway roll. This is a little unfortunate as the intervening thirty-eight-day period was, one suspects, the time during which he performed his feudal service. Nevertheless, some tenants-in-chief in 1300 made their proffers a little later in the summer. In such instances, the Galloway roll can provide us with a more accurate and trustworthy insight into how and where soldiers performed their feudal service.

William de Leyburn was a household banneret and one of Edward I's most trusted and respected soldiers. The author of the Caerlaverock poem described him as a 'valiant man, without but and without if'.[101] On 14 July 1300 Leyburn proffered two knights – Fulk Peyforer and Henry de Leyburn – at the feudal muster for the lands that he held in chief in Kent.[102] This was just twenty-four days before the skirmish at the river Cree, which the Galloway roll commemorates. Both Peyforer and Henry de Leyburn should therefore have been about halfway through their spells of feudal service (such spells usually lasted for

---

[97]   *Documents and Records of Scotland*, p. 216.
[98]   C 67/14, m. 12.
[99]   *Rolls of Arms, Edward I*, i, p. 456; C 67/14, m. 12.
[100] C 67/14, m. 4.
[101] *Rolls of Arms, Edward I*, i, p. 440: '*vaillans homs sanz mes e sanz si*'.
[102] *Documents and Records of Scotland*, p. 228.

forty days, as did this one) by the time the English army arrived at the Cree estuary on 8 August. Bearing this in mind, it is very telling to find both prof-fered men, Peyforer and Henry de Leyburn, listed next to three of William de Leyburn's other bachelors – Simon de Leyburn, William de Creye and John de Champayne – on the Galloway roll.[103] This strongly suggests that the two 'feudal' knights remained within the retinue throughout their obligatory stint. Moreover, as William de Leyburn and his men were in receipt of Crown pay,[104] it would seem that this retinue contained a mixture of paid and feudal compo-nents. There is, however, one piece of evidence that complicates this issue. When William de Leyburn and his men entered pay on 8 July, six days before he made his proffer at the feudal muster, he was paid not for three knights – the aforesaid Simon de Leyburn, William de Creye and John de Champayne – but for five.[105] Consultation of the horse inventory for this campaign shows that the two additional knights in Leyburn's paid retinue receiving Crown pay from 8 July were Fulk Peyforer and Henry de Leyburn.[106] These were the men who seem, from the evidence of the proffer roll, to have begun their spell of feudal service just six days later.

This raises a number of questions. Was Leyburn fraudulently receiving pay for his two 'feudal' soldiers during the time that they should have been performing obligatory service? Did Peyforer and Henry de Leyburn give two spells of paid service (the first for just a few days between 8 July and 14 July, the second from the beginning of September), sandwiching a spell of feudal service in between? Or did soldiers not necessarily commence their periods of feudal service on the day that they registered their names at the muster? Perhaps Leyburn's 'feudal' knights postponed their obligatory stints until later in the campaign. Whichever of these is the correct answer, it is clear that the distinction between paid, volun-tary unpaid and feudal service was blurred at the edges, and that many retinues (we will have reason to look at some more in a moment) incorporated two, or perhaps even all three, of these elements.

It may assist our investigation of the retinue-level organisation of early Edwardian armies if the search is now broadened out beyond the rolls of arms. Indeed, as valuable a source as the Galloway roll may be, there is a limit to what armorials can reveal about the composition of mounted retinues in the armies of Edward I and Edward II. Not one of the extant occasional rolls of arms of this period records the name of a single man of sub-knightly status. Yet of the soldiers who registered their service at feudal musters during the Scottish wars, it was often the case that around 90 per cent were *servientes* rather than knights. As we have seen, of the 519 men who proffered their service at the muster at Tweed-mouth in the autumn of 1310, 477 (91 per cent) were of sub-knightly status. An equally significant problem is that it is not possible to date the heraldic rolls of arms precisely. Although, for example, the Galloway roll commemorates events that took place on 8 August 1300, we cannot be certain (however likely it may

---

103 *Rolls of Arms, Edward I*, i, p. 463.
104 *Liber Quotidianus*, p. 195.
105 *Ibid.*, p. 195.
106 E 101/8/23, m. 4.

be) that the armorial reflects the composition of the English army on that day. The herald-minstrel may have incorporated materials drawn up at the muster or at some other, later stage in the campaign. Consequently, if we wish to arrive at a fuller understanding of the organisation and structure of pre-contract armies, a more wide-ranging prosopographical analysis is required.

The most logical place to begin is with the male lay tenants-in-chief. Many of these men, as was noted earlier, not only made proffers at feudal musters but also went on to serve in the same armies as retinue leaders. The examples of the retinues of the bannerets Hugh de Vere and William de Leyburn in Scotland in 1300, mentioned above, suggest that when a lay tenant-in-chief made a proffer and then led a retinue on the same expedition, the men whom he had proffered remained in his company during their feudal service.[107] Looking beyond the heraldic rolls of arms, we find that, in all years when the feudal summons was issued, there tends to be some overlap between the men named in the 'feudal' contingents of the tenants-in-chief and those who served within their wider *comitivae*. One or two examples drawn from the records for military service will illustrate this point.

Of the eight men proffered on 1 July 1277 by the earl of Lincoln at the feudal muster for Edward I's first Welsh war, four – the *serviens* Aymer de Bruy-curt, and the knights, Ralph de Trehampton, William le Vavasur and Robert de Kirketon – also had letters of protection enrolled for service in his campaign retinue in that year.[108] Three of these men (the one possible exception being Kirketon) had been in Lincoln's retinue, if the dates of their protections can be trusted, since the earliest operations of the war during the previous winter, when the earl had led six knights and twenty-three sergeants in his capacity as captain of the garrisons at Whitchurch and Montgomery on the Welsh March.[109] It seems unlikely that these men would have left the earl's retinue, in which they had been serving for several months, during their forty days of feudal service in the summer. In fact, of the three proffered men who had had protections enrolled with the earl of Lincoln on 24 January 1277, two (Bruycurt and Trehampton) had additional protections enrolled for service in his retinue on 19 July in that year, just eighteen days into their spell of feudal service.[110]

Similarly, all four men proffered by the household knight Richard Lovel (for the lands that he held in chief in Somerset) in Scotland on 2 June 1303 had had their horses appraised in his retinue just a few weeks previously, on 18 May.[111] This, once again, raises a number of questions. Did Lovel continue to accept Crown pay fraudulently for these men once their feudal service had begun? Moreover, did the four sergeants – Hugh de Sturgeun, Michael de Wemmes,

---

[107] This was not a novel phenomenon of the late thirteenth century. There is evidence, for example, that tenants-in-chief had led their own 'feudal' contingents in Henry I's army at the battle of Tinchebrai in 1106: C.W. Hollister, *The Military Organization of Norman England* (Oxford, 1965), p. 89.

[108] *Parl. Writs*, i, p. 199; *CPR, 1272–81*, pp. 189, 190, 221.

[109] *Ibid.*; and see also E 101/3/12.

[110] *CPR, 1272–81*, p. 221.

[111] E 101/612/29, m. 2; E 101/612/11, m. 1.

Elias de la Forde and John Vyvian – remain within Lovel's retinue once they had registered their names on 2 June at the feudal muster? We can be fairly sure that they *did* remain in his retinue during their obligatory stint, not least because three of the same sergeants (Sturgeun, Wemmes and de la Forde) had long-term connections to Richard Lovel, having previously served in his retinue in Scotland for Crown pay. Sturgeun could be found in Lovel's *comitiva* on the Falkirk campaign of 1298, as well as on the Scottish campaigns of 1300 and 1301.[112] Elias de la Forde and Michael de Wemmes, meanwhile, had served in Lovel's retinue on the expeditions of 1300 and 1301 respectively.[113]

Male lay tenants-in-chief did not always serve on royal campaigns as retinue leaders. In some instances, therefore, there was no choice but for men-at-arms to ride with a different lord from the one by whom they had been proffered. This situation might arise if a tenant-in-chief was too old to give military service in person, or if he did not wish to take part in an expedition for political reasons. In 1310–11 the opposition to Edward II was so widespread, due to the favouritism that he was showing towards the Gascon parvenu Piers Gaveston, that only two leading earls besides Gaveston (who had been made earl of Cornwall) followed the king to Scotland.[114] Nevertheless, by issuing the traditional feudal summons, the king was able to ensure that those who remained at home – predominantly the Ordainers, a committee appointed 'with full power to reform the state of the realm and the royal household'[115] – at least sent a few men-at-arms to the feudal muster. One of the Ordainers was Aymer de Valence, earl of Pembroke. Interestingly, the single knight sent by Valence to the muster, his indentured retainer John Darcy, had a letter of protection enrolled for service in Scotland in 1310 in the company of another Ordainer, Gilbert de Clare, earl of Gloucester.[116] As we have seen, Gloucester, unlike Valence, ignored his responsibilities as an Ordainer and followed the king north of the border. Darcy's appearance in Gilbert de Clare's retinue in 1310 suggests, therefore, that Pembroke and Gloucester, two of the earls most favourably disposed towards the king, had come to an agreement for the provision of Pembroke's feudal service in that year, by which Clare agreed to lead Valence's men on the campaign. Further plausibility is added to this theory by the fact that Gilbert Pecche, who had served with Valence in 1301 and 1306, had a letter of protection enrolled for service in the earl of Gloucester's campaign retinue in 1310.[117]

The presence of Valence's feudal contingent in the earl of Gloucester's retinue in 1310 supports the point made in chapter 4 that men sometimes moved from the company of one lord to service with another because their usual lord was not

---

[112]　1298 (*Scotland in 1298*, p. 179); 1300 (E 101/8/23, m. 7d); 1301 (E 101/9/24, m. 2).

[113]　Forde; 1300 (E 101/8/23, m. 7d; *Documents and Records of Scotland*, p. 220); Wemmes; 1301 (E 101/9/24, m. 2).

[114]　The additional earls were Warenne and Gloucester: *Vita Edwardi Secundi*, pp. 21–3.

[115]　*Plantagenet England*, p. 182.

[116]　C 71/4, m. 10; *Parl. Writs*, II, ii, p. 401.

[117]　For his service with Valence, see: E 101/9/24, m. 1d; E 101/13/16, fol. 5v. For his letter of protection in the service of the earl of Gloucester in 1310, see C 71/4, m. 10.

on campaign. In this respect, soldiers serving in fulfilment of feudal obligations were no different from mounted men-at-arms serving for Crown pay or gratuitously. Yet sometimes, even when a tenant-in-chief *was* serving on a campaign, the men proffered on his behalf might have connections, in the same year, to other retinue leaders.

On 24 January 1277 Peter de Chaluns and Robert de Dynaunt had letters of protection enrolled for service in Wales in the company of Oliver de Dynaunt, a landholder from the southwest of England.[118] Later in the summer, on 1 July, the same two knights, among others, were proffered at the feudal muster on behalf of Edmund, earl of Cornwall.[119] The earl, like Dynaunt, held extensive estates in the southwest and the two men were probably acquainted.[120] What, then, should be concluded from the fact that two of the knights in the earl's 'feudal' contingent in the summer had apparently been serving under Dynaunt since the previous winter? Given that the earl of Cornwall gave service in person in 1277, in part-fulfilment of his feudal obligations,[121] it seems likely that some if not all of the men proffered by the earl served in *his* retinue rather than with Dynaunt. Nevertheless, Dynaunt had possibly contracted, earlier in the year, to supply some knights to the earl. He may even, upon the earl's arrival in the summer, have led these men into Edmund of Cornwall's retinue. There is no evidence of this, but Dynaunt may, of course, have been serving within the earl's *comitiva* gratuitously. What is clear from the evidence of the enrolled letters of protection is that Peter de Chaluns and Robert de Dynaunt had been serving in the army for several months prior to being proffered at the feudal muster, and that Oliver Dynaunt and the earl of Cornwall, lords from the same region of England, appear to have reached some kind of agreement in connection with the service of these two men.

Although Oliver de Dynaunt and the earl of Cornwall shared a common regional identity, there is no evidence (although the incompleteness of the sources has to be borne in mind) that Dynaunt ever served in the earl's campaign retinue. Thus it is possible that the appearance in Dynaunt's retinue in 1277 of two knights who later served on the same campaign with the earl of Cornwall was merely a coincidence. Sometimes, however, when the men proffered by a tenant-in-chief served in the retinue of a different lord from the same county or region, it can be proven that the same tenant-in-chief and lord had given military service together on previous expeditions. In such instances as these, not only can the existence of a personal tie between the tenant-in-chief and the retinue leader be proven beyond doubt, but the processes by which the 'feudal' soldiers were recruited and organised within the retinues can usually be established with a high degree of certainty.

As we have seen, on 14 July 1300 the banneret William de Leyburn proffered

---

[118] *CPR, 1272–81*, p. 189.

[119] *Parl. Writs*, i, p. 198.

[120] A Walter de Dynaunt is named in the earl of Cornwall's estate accounts, dating from the 1290s: *Ministers' Accounts of the Earldom of Cornwall, 1296–1297*, ed. L.M. Midgley, 2 vols, Camden Society 3rd ser., lxvi, lxviii (1942–5), ii, p. 231.

[121] *CPR, 1272–81*, p. 217.

the service of two knights at a feudal muster in Scotland. Interestingly, yet one might be inclined to presume coincidentally, the next two tenants-in-chief listed on the proffer roll, Nicholas de Kiryel and John le Sauvage, made proffers, like Leyburn, for lands that they held in chief in Kent.[122] Perhaps these three men were friends and neighbours, deciding to ride together to Scotland. That the appearance of these men next to one another on the proffer roll was not, actually, a coincidence is suggested by the fact that both Kiryel and Sauvage had served in Leyburn's *comitiva* in Flanders just three years previously.[123] Leyburn, of course, served as a retinue leader on the Scottish campaign of 1300 but it cannot be proved that Kiryel and Savage were present and made their proffers in person as neither had letters of protection enrolled or horses appraised for this expedition. If they did not serve in person, then what happened to the men in their 'feudal' contingents? The answer, at least in Kiryel's case, is that they served in William de Leyburn's company. We know this because the two sergeants proffered on Kiryel's behalf, Peter Pycard and Edmund de St Leger, had had their horses appraised in Leyburn's retinue on 8 July, six days before they registered their names with the constable at the feudal muster.[124] Given what has been noted about the men proffered by Leyburn in 1300, it would seem that Leyburn's retinue in that year comprised a mixture of his own 'paid' and 'feudal' soldiers, as well as of another landholder's 'feudal' soldiers. Although Kiryel, Sauvage and Sauvage's men do not appear in the extant records for military service for the Caerlaverock campaign, it may be that they, too, served in Leyburn's retinue gratuitously.

Some tenants-in-chief, like the earl of Cornwall and William de Leyburn, were distinguished magnates who frequently led retinues on campaign. Other tenants-in-chief, however, such as Nicholas de Kiryel and John le Sauvage, were men of lesser status who sometimes, if not always, served in the retinues of other lords.[125] In 1300, Kiryel and Sauvage may, as sub-leaders, have led their 'feudal' contingents into William de Leyburn's retinue; but the extant sources do not show this. Nevertheless, there is evidence to suggest that lesser tenants-in-chief did sometimes act as sub-recruiters for more prominent lords, and that, when they did so, the men in their 'feudal' units would follow them into magnates' campaign retinues.

For example, on 4 July 1300 seven men had letters of protection enrolled for service in Scotland in the *comitiva* of Guy de Beauchamp, earl of Warwick.[126] Ten days later, on 14 July, one of these men, John de Mohun, proffered the service of four knights and three sergeants for the service of four knights' fees in Somerset (he failed to fill his quota slightly).[127] Of the seven men proffered by Mohun on 14 July, two – the knight Andrew Luterel and the sergeant Roger de Arundel – had had letters of protection enrolled on 4 July, like Mohun,

122 *Documents and Records of Scotland*, p. 228.
123 E 101/6/37, m. 4.
124 E 101/8/23, m. 4.
125 See Powicke, 'Edward II and Military Obligation', p. 118.
126 C 67/14, m. 9.
127 *Documents and Records of Scotland*, p. 227.

for service in the earl of Warwick's retinue. It seems likely, therefore, that Mohun was leading his 'feudal' contingent as a sub-unit within Guy de Beauchamp's much larger company. In like manner, a little over ten years later, on 17 September 1310, Nicholas Pointz, a banneret from the southwest of England, proffered the service of two *servientes* at the feudal muster for Edward II's campaign to Scotland.[128] We know that Pointz was riding in the earl of Gloucester's company in that year because he had two letters of protection enrolled for service with the earl: one on 8 September and the other on 21 September.[129] It would seem, moreover, that Pointz was leading the aforesaid *servientes* within the earl's retinue, as one of the men proffered on his behalf, Raymond Harang, had a letter of protection enrolled for service with the earl of Gloucester in the same year, on 6 October.[130]

Feudal military service, then, was perfectly compatible with the process of sub-recruitment, which (as was discussed in chapter 4) was fundamental to the formation of many of the largest campaign retinues, particularly those led by men of comital status. In fact, once the veneer of compartmentalisation presented by the Crown records is removed, revealing the intricate reality of retinue recruitment and organisation at ground level, the differences between 'paid', 'voluntary unpaid' and 'feudal' men-at-arms, and therefore between paid, gratuitous and feudal service, begin to melt away.

If it is remembered that male lay tenants-in-chief were, in general, frequent campaigners, this should come as no surprise. To such men as these, it mattered little whether the summons was for paid or feudal service: the basic objective, to recruit men-at-arms and lead them on campaign, was the same. The situation facing female and ecclesiastical tenants-in-chief, on the other hand, was rather different. When a woman or a clergyman received a summons from the king ordering them to send their *servicium debitum* to a forthcoming muster in Wales or Scotland, they could not simply gather together a few comrades in arms, relatives or tenants and lead them on campaign. With one or two notable exceptions (the chief one being Antony Bek, bishop of Durham),[131] female and ecclesiastical tenants-in-chief never went on campaign in person. Certainly, they moved in roughly the same social circles as their male lay counterparts; but the process of recruiting a group of men-at-arms in fulfilment of their feudal obligations may for such individuals have been much more difficult than for the warrior tenants-in-chief. How, then, *did* they recruit soldiers to fulfil their feudal obligations? More importantly, how did these soldiers discharge their service?

The body of female tenants-in-chief during this period was not very large. Moreover, the extant evidence suggests that, when summoned to supply a group of men-at-arms to serve in the king's army, they did not concern themselves

---

128 *Parl. Writs*, II, ii, p. 403.

129 C71/4, m. 10. Pointz held land from the earl, in Dorset, by service of two knights' fees: *CIPM*, v, no. 346.

130 C71/4, m. 10. Harang held one knight's fee (jointly with two other men) from Nicholas Pointz in Dorset: *CIPM*, v, no. 346.

131 See C.M. Fraser, *A History of Antony Bek, bishop of Durham, 1283–1311* (Oxford, 1957), p. 69.

too much with the task of finding soldiers to discharge their military obligations, but simply passed on the responsibility to male relatives, who knew more
about where to find the required number of soldiers. There may, naturally, have
been a few women who preferred to deal with such issues by themselves; but it
made sense for their brothers, cousins or sons to take on the job of recruitment
whenever possible.

On 31 May 1303, Roger de Wellesford, a *serviens*, registered his name at
the feudal muster in Scotland on behalf of Cecily de Beauchamp, who owed
the service of half a knight's fee.[132] Turning to the main horse inventory for
the same campaign, it is found that on 18 May 1303 a Roger de Wellesford,
presumably the same man, had had his horse appraised as one of two *socii* in
the retinue of Robert de Beauchamp.[133] This was probably the same Robert de
Beauchamp as the one described in a writ dated 11 November 1302 as the son
of Cecily de Beauchamp.[134] Indeed, this writ records that Robert de Beauchamp
had performed feudal service on his mother's behalf in the army in Scotland in
1300. It would seem, therefore, that this Robert de Beauchamp took responsibility for discharging his mother's military obligations on each occasion that she
was summoned by the king. As for Roger de Wellesford, proffered on behalf of
Cecily de Beauchamp in 1303, the fact that he had had his horse appraised as
an associate of her son Robert, just a couple of weeks before the feudal muster,
suggests that he performed his obligatory service within her son's campaign
retinue.

A couple of weeks after Cecily de Beauchamp had made her proffer, another
female tenant-in-chief, the countess of Pembroke, proffered the service of two
knights and five *servientes* at the feudal muster in Edinburgh.[135] She probably
did not need to worry too much about meeting her obligations in that year as
her son Aymer de Valence, the future earl of Pembroke, was the captain responsible for taking the muster (he is described in the heading on the proffer roll
as '*cheveteyn de lost*').[136] Given that Aymer was with the army in Scotland, it
seems likely that he recruited and led his mother's 'feudal' contingent. In fact,
it can be shown that Warin Martin, one of the two knights proffered by the
countess, served in Aymer de Valence's retinue on the same expedition. The
wardrobe book for the campaign of 1303–4, where details of reimbursements
for horse losses are recorded, states that Martin had lost his mount while serving
in Valence's retinue. As compensation for this loss, he received the sizeable
sum of 40 marks.[137] Unfortunately, there is no full list of Aymer de Valence's
retinue on the extant horse inventories for this campaign,[138] but it is likely that

---

132 E 101/612/29, m. 1.
133 E 101/612/11, m. 1.
134 *CCR, 1296–1302*, p. 567.
135 E 101/612/10, m. 1.
136 *Ibid.*, m. 1.
137 BL, Additional MS 8835, fol. 46v.
138 Six knights are listed in Valence's retinue on an unusual document which records the
names of some of the elite soldiers who were with Edward I in Scotland in 1304. Warin
Martin is one of the knights named in Valence's retinue: *Documents and Records of Scotland*,
p. 269.

the other men proffered by his mother at the feudal muster served in his retinue in 1303–4.

If most female tenants-in-chief fulfilled their military obligations by charging their male relatives with the responsibility for recruiting soldiers and leading them to the muster, as Cecily de Beauchamp and the countess of Pembroke appear to have done, in practice the gender of the tenant-in-chief probably had no bearing whatsoever on how the service was performed. But did ecclesiastical tenants-in-chief find it as easy as their female lay counterparts to find friends, relatives or neighbours from among the warrior aristocracy willing to discharge their feudal service?

The seminal study on the subject of English ecclesiastical tenants-in-chief, by Helena Chew, was published during the 1930s.[139] Although Chew's work ranged widely, she was not in a position to take advantage of the extensive records for military service surviving from the reigns of Edward I and his son. Consequently, her work on the feudal military service supplied by ecclesiastical tenants-in-chief was not, and could not have been, definitive. Indeed, authoritative conclusions about various aspects of this form of military obligation will continue, no doubt, to prove elusive. Nevertheless, by consulting the records for military service, and by comparing the names of the knights and sergeants proffered on behalf of ecclesiastical tenants-in-chief with those found on horse inventories, Scottish rolls and other 'record' sources, it is possible to add to the current state of knowledge by demonstrating how men-at-arms proffered by ecclesiastical tenants-in-chief were integrated into the mounted forces.

One of Chew's most significant contributions to the debate about feudal military service was her assertion that the Crown continued to seek field service, as a matter of priority, through to 1327, when it issued the final feudal summons for fifty-nine years. She noted that, 'as late as the fourteenth century the Crown was able on occasion to insist on the render of corporal service'.[140] Chew's examination of how feudal military service was carried out was restricted, to a large extent, to the evidence supplied by sources such as bishops' registers, monastic cartularies and chronicles. Sources such as these do not, in general, say a great deal about the performance of feudal military service.[141] There are, of course, some notable exceptions. For example, Matthew Paris' account of the muster in Wales in 1257, already referred to, shows that the two knights and eight sergeants in the abbot of St Albans' 'feudal' contingent were separated, the former being sent to serve under Thomas de Gresley and Henry de Percy in the rearguard, and the latter joining the constable and other nobles in the vanguard.[142] According to a later compilation from the same monastic house,

---

[139] Chew, *Ecclesiastical Tenants-in-Chief*.

[140] *Ibid.*, p. 54, n. 1.

[141] For some exceptions to this rule, see *Chronica Majora*, vi, p. 374; *Gesta Abbatum Monasterii Sancti Albani, a Thoma Walsingham, Regnante Ricardo Secundo, ejusdem Ecclesiae Praecentore, compilata*, ed. H.T. Riley, 3 vols, Rolls Ser., xxviii 4 (London, 1867–9), i, p. 435; *Registrum Malmesburiense: The Register of Malmesbury Abbey*, ed. J.S. Brewer, 2 vols, Rolls Ser., lxxii (London, 1879–80), ii, pp. 404–5. However, even these accounts are, on the whole, infuriatingly imprecise.

[142] *Chronica Majora*, vi, p. 374.

the men proffered in the abbot's name in 1277 stayed together as a group during their service in Edward I's army in Wales. We are told that the one knight and four *armigeri* proffered by the abbot were well armed and served for a total of eight weeks, partly for Crown pay.[143] However, this account, unlike Matthew Paris' earlier narrative, does not reveal how, or by whom, the abbot's men were led during their feudal service. Records preserved in the register of Malmesbury Abbey are even less informative. They reveal the names of the men who had performed feudal service in Scotland on the abbot's behalf, but they are much less forthcoming, typically, about how these individuals had discharged the service.[144]

The only way to move this subject forward is to accept that there are limits to the kind of information that such sources can yield and to consider the identities of the mounted armoured warriors who were proffered on behalf of ecclesiastical tenants-in-chief. A prosopographical analysis of these soldiers, utilising the records for military service and incorporating, where possible, evidence supplied by bishops' registers, cannot, of course, restore a complete picture of how men proffered by ecclesiastical tenants-in-chief discharged their service. Yet it may enable some of the details to be sketched in, from which a fairly clear image may begin to appear.

Both Helena Chew and N.B. Lewis have uncovered a number of agreements, involving ecclesiastical tenants-in-chief, for the provision of feudal military service. Only one of these covenants survives in the form of a written contract.[145] The others can be traced, nevertheless, in the payments sections of bishops' registers. One of the earliest examples of such an agreement, discovered by Chew, involved William Wykewane, archbishop of York, and John de Eyville, a prominent knight. Eyville received 100 pounds to cover the expenses that he had incurred while conducting the archbishop's 'feudal' contingent to the muster for the Welsh war of 1282–3 (*ad expensas suas pro servitio nostro faciendo in Wallia*).[146] Yet it is not clear from this small detail whether Eyville had actually led the archbishop's service on the campaign, or whether he had simply recruited the required number of men, accompanied them to the muster and then left them at the disposal of the marshal or constable.

This is where the records for military service can be of some assistance. The extant proffer rolls for Edward I's second Welsh war show that John de Eyville was one of four knights (there were also two *servientes*) who registered their names on behalf of the archbishop of York at the feudal muster on 2 August

---

[143] *Gesta Abbatum Monasterii Sancti Albani*, i, p. 435: '*per quadraginta dies ad sumptus proprios, et ulterius ad Regis stipendia, moram traxissent.*'

[144] *The Register of Malmesbury Abbey*, ii, pp. 404–5.

[145] See Lewis, 'The Summons of the English Feudal Levy', p. 242.

[146] Chew, *Ecclesiastical Tenants-in-Chief*, p. 156, n. 2; *The Register of William Wickwane, Lord Archbishop of York 1279–1285*, ed. W. Brown, Surtees Society, cxiv (1907), no. 839. For evidence of (non-military) service by another member of the Eyville family on behalf of an archbishop of York, see *The Register of Thomas of Corbridge, Lord Archbishop of York, 1300–1304*, ed. W. Brown with introduction by A. Hamilton Thompson, 2 vols, Surtees Society, cxxxviii, cxli, (1925–8), ii, no. 949.

1282.[147] Eyville also appears on the main horse inventory for this expedition as the leader of a paid retinue, consisting of six knights (including Eyville) and ten *valletti*.[148] Intriguingly, four of the five men (not including the sixth, Eyville himself) who gave feudal service on behalf of the archbishop of York from 2 August appear in Eyville's retinue on the horse inventory (the fifth man, John de Meaux, had a letter of protection enrolled for service with Eyville on this campaign).[149] In fact, Eyville and the men in his paid retinue had had their horses appraised on 17 July, two weeks before the feudal muster. Eyville makes his first appearance on the main pay-roll, accordingly, on the following day; but he was paid only 10 shillings per day, whereas the full cost of daily wages for the men in his retinue (as shown on the horse inventory) would have been more than double that amount.[150] It is possible that the archbishop's men were performing feudal service from 18 July, two weeks before they stepped forward at the feudal muster to discharge his service. This would partly explain the small sum that was paid to Eyville daily. Alternatively, it may be that the entries on the pay-roll are not completely accurate, and that the clerks had simply summarised the payment details.[151] Either way, the horse inventory shows that the archbishop's men were incorporated, from 17 July, within Eyville's larger *comitiva*, containing non-feudal elements, where they almost certainly remained throughout their spell of obligatory service. Eyville's retinue disappears from the pay-roll between 2 August and 10 September, this being the most likely period (given the date of the proffer) when feudal service was performed.[152] From 11 September, Eyville was paid for a retinue comprising three knights (four if we count Eyville himself) and seven sergeants.[153] This was roughly the size of his retinue on 17 July, as shown on the horse inventory, minus the five additional 'feudal' men-at-arms. It seems, then, that the three knights (excluding Eyville himself) and two sergeants proffered on the archbishop of York's behalf served in Eyville's retinue alongside his non-'feudal' soldiers for a total of around eight weeks, between 17 July and 10 September, the first two weeks of this service being for Crown pay.

This would provide a neat explanation, but it is not clear that this is precisely what happened. Firstly, if John de Eyville's retinue consisted, between 2 August and 10 September, partly of men serving for Crown pay and partly of men serving in fulfilment of feudal obligations, then why are there no details for the paid part of his retinue during that period? Moreover, all retinues, whether serving for Crown pay, gratuitously or in fulfilment of feudal obligations, tended to lose a few men-at-arms as campaigns progressed. We cannot be sure that

---

[147] *Parl. Writs*, i, p. 228.

[148] C 47/2/7, mm. 8–9.

[149] C 67/8, m. 5.

[150] E 101/4/1, m. 3.

[151] Andrew Ayton's work on *vadia guerre* accounts dating from the reign of Edward III has shown that we must now always take such pay accounts at face value: Ayton, *Knights and Warhorses*, pp. 138–55.

[152] Cf. R.F. Walker, 'William de Valence and the Army of West Wales, 1282–1283', *WHR*, xviii (1997), p. 415.

[153] E 101/4/1, m. 6.

the men who departed from Eyville's retinue after 10 September were, in fact, the three knights (excluding Eyville) and two sergeants in the archbishop of York's 'feudal' contingent. Finally, it should be noted that two of the men named in Eyville's paid company on 17 July – the knight Robert de Balliol and the sergeant Thomas de Ryhull – were later proffered on behalf of the bishop of Durham at the feudal muster on 2 August, the same day that the archbishop of York made his proffer.[154] Given that the proffer rolls for 1282, as for other partly 'feudal' campaigns, do not yield details of the proffers made by all tenants-in-chief, it may well be the case that each of the knights and sergeants named in Eyville's paid retinue on 17 July gave feudal military service from 2 August to 10 September.

One thing that can, at least, be said with some certainty is that the archbishop of York's 'feudal' contingent served in John de Eyville's retinue, alongside other men-at-arms (some of whom may have been in receipt of Crown pay at the time), during their spell of obligatory service. This was not at all unusual. Many campaign retinues during this period, it is now apparent, were amalgams of paid, voluntary unpaid and feudal elements. What is more, the archbishop of York was not the only ecclesiastical tenant-in-chief who seems to have contracted with John de Eyville for his feudal service in the build-up to the Welsh war of 1282. As we have seen, two of the soldiers proffered on behalf of the bishop of Durham, who made his proffer immediately after the archbishop of York on 2 August, appear in Eyville's paid retinue on the main horse inventory on 17 July. This is unlikely to be a coincidence. Although there does not seem to be any surviving evidence of an agreement dating from 1282 for the provision of the bishop of Durham's feudal service, it would appear that John de Eyville had contracted with the bishop, as well as with the archbishop of York, in that year.

He did not, however, contract for all of the bishop's feudal service. In fact, of the sixteen men (four knights and twelve *servientes*) in the bishop of Durham's 'feudal' contingent in 1282,[155] no fewer than seven – the knights Robert de Twenge and John Fitz Marmaduke, and the sergeants Thomas Stanlow, John de Wyville, William Fitz William, Robert Fitz William and John de Bothwick – served in 1282 in the retinue of the Yorkshire banneret William le Latimer. Six of these men appear on the main horse inventory on a separate membrane (containing the names of seven additional men) attached, by contemporary stitching, to Latimer's retinue.[156] The seventh man, Robert de Twenge, had a letter of protection enrolled for this campaign with Marmaduke de Twenge,[157] a knight named on the horse inventory in Latimer's retinue. No date is entered on the horse inventory beside the names of Latimer and his men, but the main pay-roll shows that Latimer's retinue first entered pay on 11 June. On that date he had four knights and sixteen sergeants in his service; and he still had the same number of men with him by the end of July when he was in the vicinity of

154 *Parl. Writs*, i, p. 228; C 47/2/7, mm. 8–9.
155 *Parl. Writs*, i, p. 228.
156 C 47/2/7, mm. 4, 6.
157 C 67/8, m. 5d.

Rhuddlan[158] If we exclude the thirteen men, including six of the seven 'feudal' soldiers, named on the separate, attached membrane, this is the number of men listed in Latimer's retinue on the horse inventory. This suggests that the men proffered by the bishop of Durham did not join Latimer's retinue until they had registered their service at the feudal muster on 2 August. Nevertheless, the appearance of the bishop's 'feudal' soldiers on the horse inventory with appraised mounts means that they must have served for Crown pay in Latimer's retinue at some point during the campaign. Perhaps they remained within his retinue once their spell of feudal service was over. Alternatively, it may be (as perhaps in the example of John de Eyville's retinue) that the pay-roll cannot be trusted and that the bishop's soldiers were receiving Crown pay in Latimer's retinue before 2 August.

Whatever the explanation, the presence of some of the bishop of Durham's 'feudal' contingent in William le Latimer's paid retinue in 1282 emphasises the point that feudal service was not separate from, or incompatible with, other forms of military service.[159] Military recruitment in the late thirteenth and early fourteenth centuries was a complex business; but careful analysis of the identities of the men who served in the king's armies, and of their connections with other soldiers, can make the intricate organisational details more comprehensible. Indeed what we find, upon doing this, is that the key players in the recruitment of mounted armoured warriors, whatever the form of summons issued, were the retinue leaders. Once the facade of feudal service as something fundamentally different from other forms of military service is stripped away, it becomes clear that all retinues, even those containing feudal elements, were raised in the same way. In this respect, the identity of the tenant-in-chief nominally making the proffer, whether a member of the laity or an ecclesiastic, seems to have made little or no difference to how the service was performed.

One final example, relating to the military service supplied by an ecclesiastical tenant-in-chief during the war in Scotland, may help to illustrate this point. In 1300, for the campaign that resulted in the siege of Caerlaverock castle, Richard de Swinfield, the bishop of Hereford, made an agreement with a local knight, William de Grandison, for the performance of his military service. An entry in the bishop's register shows that Grandison had been paid 120 marks for performing the service.[160] It also records that the bishop's service had been proffered on 29 June; and this accords with what we find on the extant proffer roll for the 1300 campaign.[161] The bishop's quota of five knights' fees was discharged by one knight and nine sergeants. Although William de Grandison, unlike John de Eyville in the example noted above from 1282, did not register his name at the feudal muster in 1300 in person, he was leading the bishop's 'feudal'

[158] E 101/4/1, mm. 2, 3.

[159] For discussion of a similar example dating from 1282 (concerning the feudal military service provided by the abbot of Winchcombe), see D. Simpkin, 'The English Aristocracy at War, 1272–1314', PhD thesis, University of Hull, 2006.

[160] *Registrum Ricardi de Swinfield, Episcopi Herefordensis, AD MCCLXXXIII–MCCCXVII*, ed. W.W. Capes, Canterbury and York Society, vi (1909), pp. 375–6.

[161] *Documents and Records of Scotland*, p. 214.

contingent on the campaign. We know this because the single knight proffered on behalf of the bishop, Thomas de Bermingham, appears on the Galloway roll (apparently dating from around 8 August) just two places below Grandison and immediately below another knight, Nicholas de Valers, who was serving with Grandison in Scotland in 1300.[162] Moreover, Bermingham entered pay in Grandison's retinue on 11 August immediately after his spell of feudal service was over, which suggests that he had been in the retinue all along.[163] What is particularly significant in this example, however, is that it can be demonstrated that Bermingham and two of the sergeants – Walter de Cadington and John de Dun – proffered on behalf of the bishop of Hereford in 1300 served in Scotland in other years in Grandison's retinue. All three men went on to serve with Grandison in 1301,[164] and Bermingham, at least, served in the same retinue in 1304.[165] In essence, then, the bishop of Hereford's 'feudal' contingent in 1300 was not really *his* group of men-at-arms at all, but Grandison's retinue placed temporarily in the bishop's service.

The End of an Era

The examples discussed in this chapter and in chapter 4 demonstrate that the processes of military recruitment in early Edwardian England were determined by soldiers' connections to one another and to their lords. Once this is acknowledged, it is clear that all retinues in the armies of Edward I and Edward II were assembled in much the same way, irrespective of the kind of summons issued. Consequently, the concept of a military community, or at least of interlocking military communities, seems apposite, not least as it reminds us that armies of this period were, primarily, social organisms.

Although pre-contract armies consisted of a combination of paid, voluntary unpaid and feudal elements, it is doubtful whether the average mounted armoured warrior serving within the campaign retinues would have recognised such distinctions. Certainly, to an earl or banneret charged with the responsibility of gathering a retinue and leading it on campaign, there would have been a significant difference between military service given for Crown pay and gratuitous service. For such men as these, service without the king's wages could lead to financial difficulties. Other soldiers, however, serving in the retinues of these earls and bannerets, were probably scarcely affected by the variations in their lords' service to the king. Most knights bachelor and *valletti* would have received similar amounts of pay (2 shillings a day for the former and 1 shilling a day for the latter) from their retinue leader, regardless of whether their lord was serving for Crown pay or gratuitously. Moreover, given that the men proffered at feudal musters by male lay tenants-in-chief were often seasoned campaigners,

---

162 *Rolls of Arms, Edward I*, i, p. 455. For Valers' service with Grandison, see *Liber Quotidianus*, p. 199.
163 *Liber Quotidianus*, p. 199.
164 E 101/9/23, m. 2.
165 *Documents and Records of Scotland*, p. 270.

who on other occasions served for Crown pay, and that ecclesiastical tenants-in-chief frequently raised paid, hired troops, it seems likely that the majority of soldiers serving in fulfilment of feudal obligations received pay, either from their retinue leader directly or via a non-serving tenant-in-chief.

If, then, obligatory military service, like paid and gratuitous service, was performed within the retinues, and the soldiers recruited to discharge this form of obligation were recruited in the same way as other mounted warriors, why, after 1327, was feudal military service abandoned by Edward III? By way of a postscript to this chapter, it may be worth, very briefly, considering this important question.

Let us first accept that there was nothing inherently dysfunctional about feudal military service. This chapter has shown that soldiers serving obligatorily often, if not always, discharged their military service in the same way as other aristocratic warriors: in the campaign retinues. Next, let us consider the changing attitude of the aristocracy towards paid service from the later years of the reign of Edward I onwards. Already, by the early years of the Scottish wars, there is evidence that the king's campaigns were creating financial difficulties for the gentry and nobility. In 1297 Richard Fitz Alan, earl of Arundel complained to Edward I of the impoverishment that he had suffered and continued to suffer as a consequence of his service in the king's wars, and of the difficulties that he was now facing in trying to recruit a group of men to serve under him in Flanders.[166] In the following year, shortly after receiving a summons to a muster at York, Richard de Baskerville wrote to the chancellor with a similar message. He begged to be excused from the muster, stating that he could not find a single man willing to ride with him to Scotland due to a lack of money (*ne pus trover nul homme en tut mun pays qe me voyle nule chevisance fere pro la defaute de deners qe il y a en pays pur quoix … vos prier e requer si vos plest pur vostre graunt curteysie qe de ceste chose dever nostre seignur le Ray me voylez aver escuse*).[167]

Given these circumstances of financial hardship, any attempt by the king to force his magnates and lesser landholders to give military service without pay is likely to have been treated with some dismay. We know, thanks to the work of Michael Prestwich, that a large proportion of earls and bannerets *did* serve without Crown pay during these years, even when they were not required to do so in fulfilment of feudal obligations. It seems unlikely, however, that this kind of service was always given willingly and without some accompanying distress. Indeed, it should be remembered that such service was still, strictly speaking, obligatory (as a consequence of the homage that all subjects owed to the king), even if it was not feudal.

Moreover, although the established view is that 'it was aristocratic, rather than governmental, conservatism that meant that feudal service continued to be demanded for so long',[168] this opinion tallies neither with what we know about the aristocracy's financial difficulties at this time, nor with contemporary narra-

---

[166] *Documents Illustrating the Crisis of 1297–98*, no.132.
[167] SC 1/26, no.74.
[168] Prestwich, *Armies and Warfare*, pp. 73–4.

tive accounts. The chronicle of the Abbey of Bury St Edmunds refers to discussions held during the parliament at York in 1300. On that occasion Edward I seems to have clashed with some of his barons, who claimed that they did not owe military service in Scotland.[169] The war in Scotland had, by that stage, been in progress for four years, but the 1300 campaign was the first time that the king had issued a feudal summons for an expedition north of the border. The king, facing financial difficulties of his own, no doubt saw the advantages of such a summons. However, it would seem that by this time the aristocracy were already cooling towards all forms of unpaid military service. Edward II's failures in Scotland are likely to have led to increased calls, particularly after 1314, for Crown pay to be made more widely available. The change in attitude was such, as Andrew Ayton has noted, that 'by the 1330s the attraction of voluntary, unpaid service appears very largely to have disappeared'.[170]

By the time that Edward III carried out his military reforms, then, feudal military service had become a liability not because the service provided in this way was inferior to service for Crown pay, but due to the fact that the heavy period of campaigning between 1294 and 1327 had made unpaid service extremely unpopular with large sections of the aristocracy. Moreover, once the focus of the king's attention had shifted from Scotland to France, the chances of successfully enforcing feudal service on the king's campaigns were very slim. As A.E. Prince has noted, the requirements of overseas campaigns 'dealt the coup de grâce to the feudal method of enlistment'.[171]

---

[169] *Bury St Edmunds*, p. 156.
[170] Ayton, *Knights and Warhorses*, p. 142.
[171] A.E. Prince, 'The Payment of Army Wages in Edward III's Reign', *Speculum*, xix (1944), p. 152.

Conclusion

In the years between the accession of Edward I and the battle of Bannockburn, the English aristocracy served in expeditionary forces to Wales (1277–95), Gascony (1294–8), Flanders (1297–8) and Scotland (1296–1314). Moreover, during part of the same period, garrisons were maintained, at the expense of the exchequer, throughout the newly conquered territories within the British Isles as well as in the Crown's threatened enclaves in southwestern France. Fortunately, the names of thousands of men-at-arms who served on these campaigns and in these garrisons have survived. The aim of this book has been to reconstruct the military careers of these men, their connections to one another, the means by which they were recruited and the way that they performed their service in the king's armies. In essence, this has amounted to an investigation of mounted armoured warriors' experience of, and commitment to, the calling of arms, both as individuals and as members of groups.

The process of recruitment worked on three different but parallel levels: those of the individual soldier, the retinues within which he served, and the armies as a whole. The initial movement towards raising an army came from the king. Prior to 1277, there had been no campaign against an external enemy for two decades. Even after 1277, the first two-thirds of Edward I's reign saw little campaigning, other than the war of 1282–3, on an exceptionally large scale. All of this changed, however, following the outbreak of war with France in 1294 and the beginning of the long-drawn-out conflict with the Scots two years later. The years between 1294 and 1314 saw large numbers of warriors from among the landed classes taking up arms for the first time. The mobilisation effort affected large numbers of men in all counties, not only on the Marches of Wales and Scotland. Indeed, an examination of the extant rolls of arms, comparing the names found in these sources with those documented in the records for military service, indicates that at least four-fifths of the knights bachelor alive at this time served in the king's armies at one point or another. In truth, given that the source materials are incomplete, it seems that scarcely any landholding families within England failed to contribute soldiers. Driving this mobilisation process forward, in the first instance, was Edward I. His forceful personality, willingness to innovate, and soldierly persona, ensured that most of the time, and on most campaigns, he achieved the response from the gentry and nobility that he desired. However, shifting political circumstances, twinned with financial difficulties, meant that Edward's plans did not always run smoothly. By the late 1290s the Crown's military demands were outstripping its resources, so much so that when the tide turned in favour of the Scots, early in the reign of Edward II, an effective response could no longer be mounted.

By issuing military summonses, the king set the mobilisation process in motion. Yet it is only when we look further down the military hierarchy, to the retinue leaders in the counties and the knights and sergeants in their retinues that the intricate details of raising an army come more fully into view. Following receipt of the king's summons, most earls, bannerets and lords of lesser status were able to draw on the services of soldiers whom they knew personally and had served with on previous expeditions. The impression hitherto portrayed in the historiography, that the campaign retinues of this period lacked stability in membership, can no longer be maintained without significant qualification. The military contracts known as indentures of war were not yet in use, but the underlying ties between lords and their followers were no different, nor less strong, in this period than they were to prove during the early stages of Edward III's French war. To staff their retinues, lords activated ties of kinship, friendship and locality, as well as formal bonds arising from the *familia* or more novel forms of association such as annuities and indentures for life service in peace and war. Yet they did not recruit their men within a social vacuum. Soldiers might have ties to several lords within a particular county or region; still others might shift their allegiance between different members of the same lordship family. Lords' connections to other lords meant, in effect, that men-at-arms might move from retinue to retinue without any show of disloyalty towards their previous retinue leader, or threat to the cohesiveness of the king's armies.

The key to evaluating the success of the Crown's recruitment initiatives, and the fine details of retinue stability, is the individual man-at-arms. In this respect, 'military service prosopography' can unlock a number of secrets relating to the structure and composition of early Edwardian armies. In fact, the individual soldier is a valuable unit of investigation in his own right. Although soldiers' motives for joining the king's armies can rarely be ascertained, it is possible, by identifying the number of times that they served in royal hosts, and their relative commitment to soldiering *vis-à-vis* other forms of public service, to distinguish between bellicose warriors, on the one hand, and reluctant soldiers, on the other. Of course, not every mounted armoured warrior who appears in the extant service records for only one or two campaigns necessarily served merely on those occasions, and so our evaluation of the aristocracy's commitment to soldiering will always be a sizeable underestimate. Bearing this in mind, the frequency with which members of the gentry and nobility took part in campaigns to Wales, France and Scotland, and the length of their careers in arms, as indicated in this study, were remarkable. Moreover, although soldiers' attitudes towards war can seldom be detected in written forms of communication, except occasionally in petitions, some idea can be obtained, through an exploration of heraldic dissemination, of the impact that the wars of Edward I and his son had on the mentality of the landed elites. To what extent abstract notions of chivalry played a part in this process is difficult to discern. Far more recognisable is the thread connecting the heavy campaigning demands of these years to the widening of the armigerous elite. As families took up knighthood for the first time, in response to the distraint process or as a consequence of other, less obvious stimuli, they entered a world in which membership of the warrior elite, of the upper strata of the military community, gained visual expression in the form of heraldic coats of arms. Yet what is particularly striking, and perhaps best testifies to the martial overtones of heraldic dissemination in early Edwardian England, is the fact that large numbers of these new knightly families appear to have adapted their heraldic designs from those of their military leaders. In this way, coats of arms provide a window into a world in which martial display and martial reality were once again becoming intertwined.

Of the individuals who served in the king's armies, those responsible for leading these forces, or their constituent retinues, fulfilled the most important function. For the most part, the men who occupied positions of military command during the reigns of the first two Edwards were drawn from the upper echelons of the aristocracy: the earls and bannerets. At this stage there were relatively few parvenus rising meteorically from obscurity to leadership of the king's forces, and with the possible exception of Andrew de Harcla certainly not any to bear comparison with the likes of Robert Knolles and Hugh de Calveley, commanders, of lowly origins, in France during the 1370s. Accessing the inner world of decision-making from which appointments to captaincies and constableships stemmed is a most difficult task. If formal minutes were kept of the discussions, involving the king and his council, that must have taken place on this subject, they have not survived. Nevertheless, it is clear, from the appointments that were made, that both Edward I and Edward II placed their trust in a fairly small number of commanders. Leading members of the military community such as the earl Warenne, Aymer de Valence, and John de St John were repeatedly trusted with the command of large forces. The correspondence between such men as these and the king provides rare and valuable insights into broader issues of military organisation and campaign strategy. They reveal, in particular, that Edward I exercised a large measure of control over his commanders in the field, at least within the British Isles. Matters of campaign-planning and strategy appear to have been the preserve, for the most part, of the king himself. Yet, in other respects, in terms of the disciplinary rights that they enjoyed and the duties that they were expected to discharge, the king's captains wielded considerable independent authority. Moreover, consideration of these responsibilities – ranging from the power to capture and garrison castles to more mundane duties, like the granting of compensation for horse losses – highlights, better than most kinds of evidence, the realities of life on campaign and the nature of the king's commanders' relationship with their men.

Looking at the issue of military organisation from the perspective of the king and his captains, however, should not detract attention from the fact that the armies of this period can only really be understood through examination of the personal connections between soldiers at ground level. Once the armies of Edward I and Edward II had assembled at the muster, the king or his commanding officers could take over. Yet before this, from the moment when the military summonses were issued, up to the muster, the key organisational role was played by retinue leaders in the localities. In this respect, the pre-contract armies of the years before the battle of Bannockburn differed little from the forces raised during the 1330s and 1340s. It is true, of course, that the armies of Edward III were wholly paid, whereas the mounted part of the armies of Edward I comprised a mixture of paid, voluntary unpaid and feudal elements. Nevertheless, in practice, soldiers serving in fulfilment of feudal obligations seem to have discharged their service in much the same way as soldiers serving for Crown pay or gratuitously. As such, and despite appearances to the contrary, the principles of military recruitment in the armies of Edward I and Edward II were not so different from those in the armies of Edward III. The type of soldier being recruited, and the formal mechanisms governing the process of recruitment, may have changed a great deal by the 1330s, but the underlying reality, of lords in the counties recruiting their kinsmen, friends, tenants and neighbours, was the same.

Indeed, many elements of continuity across the dividing line of Bannockburn, or perhaps more accurately of 1327, can be detected. The military reforms implemented during the 1330s and 1340s, which probably amounted to an Edwardian military revolution of sorts, facilitated, or were facilitated by, transformations in the social composition of the military community, in the mechanisms employed to aid the processes of recruitment, and in the much wider availability than hitherto of Crown pay. Yet when Edward III and his advisers carried out these reforms they were building, as has been acknowledged,[1] on firm foundations laid during the reign of Edward I. Between 1272 and 1314 the English aristocracy, in its widest sense, became familiarised with the grinding demands of near-annual campaigning in the king's armies. By the time that Edward I's grandson came to the throne, they were consequently well prepared to deal with anything that might be required of them.

---

[1]   See, for example, Ayton, 'Sir Thomas Ughtred', pp. 111–12.

Appendix

Continuity in retinue personnel for 50 sample lords from the Falkirk campaign of 1298 (1277–1314)*

Leader	Number of men with leader:		% continuity	Times served with leader other than in 1298:						
	In 1298	In 1298 (who also served in other year)		1	2	3	4	5	6	7
Audley	15	2	13	1	1	–	–	–	–	–
Badlesmere	4	1	25	–	1	–	–	–	–	–
Bardolf	14	6	43	2	2	1	1	–	–	–
Basset	11	3	27	2	–	1	–	–	–	–
J. Beauchamp	11	7	64	4	1	2	–	–	–	–
W. Beauchamp	25	16	64	6	2	2	4	2	–	–
Beaumont	5	4	80	–	1	1	2	–	–	–
Benstede	14	9	64	2	5	2	–	–	–	–
Botetourt	16	11	69	7	2	1	–	1	–	–
Brun	8	7	88	3	4	–	–	–	–	–
Bykenore	3	2	66	1	–	–	–	1	–	–
Cantilupe	11	2	18	1	–	1	–	–	–	–
Charles	4	4	100	2	2	–	–	–	–	–
Chavent	16	12	75	7	3	1	–	1	–	–
Clifford	34	18	53	5	7	1	2	1	1	1
Courtenay	11	5	45	2	1	2	–	–	–	–
Despenser	49	18	37	6	3	5	–	1	1	2
Drokensford	25	14	56	4	4	5	1	–	–	–
Echingham	5	3	60	3	–	–	–	–	–	–
Fitz Payn	19	8	42	3	2	1	1	–	1	–
Fitz Reginald	4	0	0	–	–	–	–	–	–	–
Fitz Waryn	5	3	60	3	–	–	–	–	–	–
Furnivall	10	3	30	2	1	–	–	–	–	–
Grandison	9	1	11	–	1	–	–	–	–	–
Hacche	12	8	66	3	2	3	–	–	–	–
Haustede	3	2	66	1	–	1	–	–	–	–
Havering	25	2	8	2	–	–	–	–	–	–
Kyngeston	3	0	0	–	–	–	–	–	–	–
Lancaster	45	14	31	7	3	4	–	–	–	–
Leyburn	15	9	60	2	2	1	1	3	–	–
Lovel	5	2	40	–	–	1	–	–	1	–
Malemains	3	2	66	2	–	–	–	–	–	–
Mauley	4	1	25	1	–	–	–	–	–	–
Meynill	7	2	29	1	–	1	–	–	–	–

Mohaut	15	8	53	–	3	1	3	1	–	–
Montacute	9	1	11	1	–	–	–	–	–	–
H. Mortimer	9	0	0	–	–	–	–	–	–	–
R. Mortimer	20	11	55	3	4	1	1	1	1	–
Pichard	2	0	0	–	–	–	–	–	–	–
Pipard	20	5	25	4	1	–	–	–	–	–
Plukenet	4	4	100	–	1	3	–	–	–	–
Pointz	5	4	80	–	2	2	–	–	–	–
Ryther	8	1	13	1	–	–	–	–	–	–
Scales	7	3	43	–	–	–	1	2	–	–
Tony	17	10	59	5	4	1	–	–	–	–
Tregoz	12	1	8	1	–	–	–	–	–	–
Tuchet	4	3	75	1	1	1	–	–	–	–
Valence	49	27	55	16	6	1	2	–	2	–
Verdon	2	2	100	1	–	1	–	–	–	–
Welles	14	8	57	2	4	1	–	1	–	–
Total	647	289	45	120	76	49	19	15	7	3

* The full names of the 50 leaders in the sample are as follows: Nicholas de Audley, Bartholomew de Badlesmere, Hugh Bardolf, Ralph Basset of Drayton, John de Beauchamp of Somerset, Walter de Beauchamp, Henry de Beaumont, John de Benstede, John Botetourt, William le Brun, Thomas de Bykenore, William de Cantilupe, Edward Charles, Peter/John de Chavent, Robert de Clifford, Hugh de Courtenay, Hugh le Despenser senior/junior, John de Drokensford, William de Echingham, Robert Fitz Payn, John Fitz Reginald, Fulk Fitz Waryn, Thomas de Furnivall, William de Grandison, Eustace de Hacche, Robert de Haustede senior/junior, John de Havering, John de Kyngeston, Thomas of Lancaster, William de Leyburn, Richard Lovel, Nicholas de Malemains, Edmund de Mauley, Nicholas de Meynill senior/junior, Robert de Mohaut, Simon de Montacute, Hugh de Mortimer, Roger de Mortimer of Chirk, Miles Pichard, Ralph Pipard, Alan Plukenet senior/junior, Hugh Pointz, William de Ryther, Robert de Scales, Robert de Tony, John Tregoz, William Tuchet, Aymer de Valence, Thomas de Verdon and Adam de Welles.

Bibliography

Manuscript Sources

The National Archives, Kew
Chancery
C 47 Chancery Miscellanea
C 54 Close Rolls
C 66 Patent Rolls
C 67 Supplementary Patent Rolls
C 71 Scottish Rolls
C 77 Welsh Rolls
C 81 Warrants for the Great Seal
C 143 Inquisitions *ad quod damnum*

Duchy of Lancaster
DL 25 Deeds, Series L

Exchequer
E 39 Treasury of Receipt: Scottish Documents
E 101 King's Remembrancer: Accounts Various
E 159 K.R.: Memoranda Rolls
E 198 K.R.: Records Relating to Feudal Tenure and Distraint of Knighthood
E 370 Lord Treasurer's Remembrancer: Miscellaneous Rolls
E 372 L.T.R.: Pipe Rolls
E 403 Exchequer of Receipt: Issue Rolls

Special Collections
SC 1 Ancient Correspondence
SC 8 Ancient Petitions

The British Library, London
Additional Manuscripts
Additional MS 7965 (Wardrobe book, 25 Edward I)
Additional MS 7966a (Wardrobe book, 29 Edward I)
Additional MS 8835 (Wardrobe book, 32 Edward I)
Additional MS 7967 (Wardrobe accounts for Aquitaine, 17–19 Edward II)

Additional Charters
Additional Charter 21506 (Certificate of knight service, 16 Edward II)

Cotton Manuscripts
Cotton Nero C VIII (Wardrobe book, 4 Edward II)

Stowe Manuscripts
Stowe MS 553 (Wardrobe book, 15–17 Edward II)

Stowe Charters
Stowe Charter 622 (Will of Sir Fulk de Penebrigg, 1325)

The Bodleian Library, Oxford
Tanner MS, 197 (Wardrobe book, 4 Edward II)

Printed Primary Sources and Reference Works

'Account of the Expenses of John of Brabant and Thomas and Henry of Lancaster, AD 1292–3', ed. J. Burtt, *Camden Miscellany II*, Camden Society 1st ser., lv (1853)

Ancient Petitions Relating to Northumberland, ed. C.M. Fraser, Surtees Society, clxxvi (1966)

Annales Cestrienses; or, Chronicle of the Abbey of St. Werburg, at Chester, ed. R.C. Christie, The Record Society for the Publication of Original Documents Relating to Lancashire and Cheshire, xiv (1886)

'Annales Londonienses', *Chronicles of the Reigns of Edward I and Edward II*, ed. W Stubbs, 2 vols, Rolls Ser., lxxvi (London, 1882–3), i

'Annales Monasterii de Waverleia (AD 1–1291)', *Annales Monastici*, ed. H.R. Luard, 5 vols, Rolls Ser., xxxvi (London, 1864–9), ii

'Annales Monasterii de Wintonia, 519–1277', *Annales Monastici*, ed. H.R. Luard, 5 vols, Rolls Ser., xxxvi (London, 1864–9), ii

'Annales Prioratus de Dunstaplia (AD 1–1297)', *Annales Monastici*, ed. H.R. Luard, 5 vols, Rolls Ser., xxxvi (London, 1864–9), iii

'Annales Prioratus de Wigornia (AD 1–1377)', *Annales Monastici*, ed. H.R. Luard, 5 vols, Rolls Ser., xxxvi (London, 1864–9), iv

The Anonimalle Chronicle 1307–1334, From Brotherton Collection MS 29, ed. W.R. Childs and J. Taylor, The Yorkshire Archaeological Society Record Ser., cxlvii (1991)

Aspilogia II: Rolls of Arms, Henry III, ed. A.R. Wagner, Harleian Society, cxiii, cxiv (1961–2)

Aspilogia III: Rolls of Arms, Edward I (1272–1307), ed. G.J. Brault, 2 vols (Woodbridge, 1997)

Bartholomaei de Cotton, Historia Anglicana (AD 449–1298), ed. H.R. Luard, Rolls Ser., xvi (London, 1859)

Book of Prests of the King's Wardrobe for 1294–5, ed. E.B. Fryde (Oxford, 1962)

The Brut, or the Chronicles of England, ed. F.W.D. Brie, 2 vols, Early English Text Society, cxxxi, cxxxvi (London, 1906–8)

Brut y Tywysogyon or The Chronicle of the Princes, Peniarth MS 20 Version, trans. T. Jones (Cardiff, 1952)

Calendar of Ancient Correspondence Concerning Wales, ed. J.G. Edwards (Cardiff, 1935)

Calendar of Ancient Petitions Relating to Wales (Thirteenth to Sixteenth Century), ed. W. Rees (Cardiff, 1975)

Calendar of Chancery Warrants, 1244–1326 (London, 1927)

Calendar of the Charter Rolls, 6 vols (London, 1903–27)

Calendar of Close Rolls

Calendar of Documents Relating to Scotland., ed. J. Bain, 4 vols (Edinburgh, 1881–8); v, ed. G.G. Simpson and J.D. Galbraith (Edinburgh, 1986)

Calendar of Entries in the Papal Registers Relating to Great Britain and Ireland: Papal Letters, ed. W.H. Bliss *et al.*, 20 vols, vols i–xiv (London, 1893–1960), vols xv–xx (Dublin, 1978–2005)

Calendar of Fine Rolls, 22 vols (London, 1911–62)

Calendar of Inquisitions Miscellaneous (Chancery), 8 vols (London, 1916–2003)

Calendar of Inquisitions Post Mortem and other Analogous Documents, 23 vols (London, 1904–2004)

Calendar of the Liberate Rolls, 6 vols (London, 1916–64)

Calendar of Patent Rolls

Calendar of Various Chancery Rolls. Supplementary Close Rolls. Welsh Rolls. Scutage Rolls. (AD 1277–1326) (London, 1912)

Christine de Pizan, *The Book of Deeds of Arms and of Chivalry*, trans. S. Willard and ed. C.C. Willard (Philadelphia, Pa., 1999)

Chronica Monasterii de Melsa, a Fundatione usque ad Annum 1396, Auctore Thoma de Burton, Abbate. Accedit Continuatio ad Annum 1406 a Monacho quodam ipsius Domus, ed. E.A. Bond, 3 vols, Rolls Ser., xliii (London, 1866–8)

The Chronicle of Bury St Edmunds, 1212–1301, ed. A. Gransden (London, 1964)

The Chronicle of Walter of Guisborough, ed. H. Rothwell, Camden Society 3rd ser., lxxxix (1957)

The Chronicle of William de Rishanger of the Barons' Wars, ed. J.O. Halliwell, Camden Society 1st ser., xv (1840)

Chronicon de Lanercost, MCCI–MCCCXLVI, ed. J. Stevenson (Edinburgh, 1839)

'Chronicon vulgo dictum Chronicon Thomae Wykes, 1066–1289', *Annales Monastici*, ed. H.R. Luard, 5 vols, Rolls Ser., xxxvi (London, 1864–9), iv

Chronique de Jean le Bel, ed. J. Viard and E. Déprez, 2 vols (Paris, 1904–5)

The Complete Peerage, by G.E. Cockayne, revised and edited by V. Gibbs, H.A. Doubleday, Lord Howard de Walden and G.H. White, 13 vols (London, 1910–59)

The Controversy between Sir Richard Scrope and Sir Robert Grosvenor in the Court of Chivalry, AD MCCCLXXXV–MCCCXC, ed. N.H. Nicolas, 2 vols (London, 1832)

A Descriptive Catalogue of Ancient Deeds in the Public Record Office, 6 vols (London, 1890–1915)

The Devonshire Lay Subsidy of 1332, ed. A.M. Erskine, Devon and Cornwall Record Society, new ser., xiv (1969)

Documents of the Baronial Movement of Reform and Rebellion 1258–1267, selected by R.F. Treharne and edited by I.J. Sanders (Oxford, 1973)

Documents Illustrating the Crisis of 1297–98 in England, ed. M. Prestwich, Camden Society 4th ser., xxiv (1980)

Documents Illustrative of English History in the Thirteenth and Fourteenth Centuries, ed. H. Cole (London, 1844)

Documents Illustrative of the History of Scotland from the Death of King Alexander the Third to the Accession of Robert Bruce MCCLXXXVI–MCCCVI, ed. J. Stevenson, 2 vols (Edinburgh, 1870)

Documents and Records Illustrating the History of Scotland and the Transactions between the Crowns of Scotland and England, ed. F. Palgrave (London, 1837)

The Dorset Lay Subsidy Roll of 1327, ed. A.R. Rumble, Dorset Record Society, vi (1980)

Eight Thirteenth-Century Rolls of Arms in French and Anglo-Norman Blazon, ed. G.J. Brault (London, 1973)

Ellis, R.H., *Catalogue of Seals in the Public Record Office: Personal Seals*, 2 vols (London, 1978–81)

English Mediaeval Rolls of Arms: Volume I, *1244–1334*, ed. R.W. Mitchell (Peebles, 1983)

Flores Historiarum, ed. H.R. Luard, 3 vols, Rolls Ser., xcv (London, 1890)

Foedera, Conventiones, Litterae etc, ed. T. Rymer, revised edition by A. Clarke, F. Holbrooke and J. Caley, 4 vols in 7 parts (Record Commission, 1816–69)

Gesta Abbatum Monasterii Sancti Albani, a Thoma Walsingham, Regnante Ricardo Secundo, ejusdem Ecclesiae Praecentore, compilata, ed. H.T. Riley, 3 vols, Rolls Ser., xxviii 4 (London, 1867–9)

'Gesta Edwardi de Carnarvon, Auctore Canonico Bridlingtoniensi, cum Continuatione ad AD

1377', *Chronicles of the Reigns of Edward I and Edward II*, ed. W. Stubbs, 2 vols, Rolls Ser., lxxvi (London, 1882–3), ii

Giraldi Cambrensis Itinerarium Kambriae, et Descriptio Kambriae, ed. J.F. Dimock, Rolls Ser., xxi 6 (London, 1868)

Gray, Sir Thomas, *Scalacronica 1272–1363*, ed. A. King, Surtees Society, ccix (2005)

Gray Birch, W. de, *Catalogue of Seals in the Department of Manuscripts in the British Museum*, 6 vols (London, 1887–1900)

Historical and Municipal Documents of Ireland AD 1172–1320, ed. J.T. Gilbert, Rolls Ser., liii (London, 1870)

Historical Papers and Letters from the Northern Registers, ed. J. Raine, Rolls Ser., lxi (London, 1873)

Household Accounts from Medieval England, ed. C.M. Woolgar, 2 parts, Records of Social and Economic History new ser., xvii–xviii (Oxford, 1992–3)

Inquisitions and Assessments Relating to Feudal Aids, 1284–1431, 6 vols (London, 1899–1920)

Johannis de Fordun Chronica Gentis Scotorum, ed. W.F. Skene, The Historians of Scotland Ser., i (Edinburgh, 1871)

Johannis de Trokelowe et Henrici de Blaneforde, Monachorum S. Albani, necnon quorundam Anonymorum, Chronica et Annales, ed. H.T. Riley, Rolls Ser., xxviii 3 (London, 1866)

John Barbour, *The Bruce*, ed. A.A.M. Duncan (Edinburgh, 1997)

Knights of Edward I, ed. C. Moor, 5 vols, Harleian Society, lxxx–lxxxiv (1929–32)

Liber Feodorum. The Book of Fees commonly called Testa de Nevill, 3 vols (London, 1920–31)

Liber Quotidianus Contrarotulatoris Garderobae, 1299–1300, ed. J. Topham *et al.* (London, 1787)

A Lincolnshire Assize Roll for 1298, ed. W.S. Thomson, Lincoln Record Society, xxxvi (1944)

List of Sheriffs for England and Wales, From the Earliest Times to AD 1831, PRO Lists and Indexes, ix (London, 1893)

Littere Wallie, ed. J.G. Edwards (Cardiff, 1940)

Matthaei Parisiensis, Monachi Sancti Albani, Chronica Majora, ed. H.R. Luard, 7 vols, Rolls Ser., lvii (London, 1872–83)

Memorando de Parliamento, or, Records of the Parliament holden at Westminster on the Twenty-Eighth Day of February, in the Thirty-Third Year of the Reign of King Edward the First (AD 1305), ed. F.W. Maitland, Rolls Ser., xcviii (London, 1893)

Ministers' Accounts of the Earldom of Cornwall, 1296–1297, ed. L.M. Midgley, 2 vols, Camden Society 3rd ser., lxvi, lxviii (1942–5)

Monumenta Juridica: The Black Book of the Admiralty, ed. T. Twiss, 4 vols, Rolls Ser., lv (London, 1871–6)

Nicholai Triveti, de Ordine Frat. Praedicatorum, Annales (AD MCXXXVI–MCCCVII), ed. T. Hog, English Historical Society (London, 1845)

Northern Petitions Illustrative of Life in Berwick, Cumbria and Durham in the Fourteenth Century, ed. C.M. Fraser, Surtees Society, cxciv (1981)

The Northumberland Lay Subsidy Roll of 1296, ed. C.M. Fraser (Newcastle upon Tyne, 1968)

'Notes and Communications', *SHR*, xxiv (1927), pp. 325–8

Ordonnances des Roys de France de la Troisième Race, ed. D.F. Secousse *et al.*, 21 vols (Paris, 1723–1849, reprinted 1967–8)

The Original Chronicle of Andrew of Wyntoun, ed. F.J. Amours, 6 vols, The Scottish Text Society, l–lxiii (Edinburgh, 1903–14)

The Parliament Rolls of Medieval England, 1275–1504, ed. C. Given-Wilson *et al.*, 16 vols (London, 2005)

Parliamentary Writs and Writs of Military Summons, ed. F. Palgrave, 2 vols in 4 parts (London, 1827–34)

Pierre de Langtoft, le règne d'Édouard 1er, ed. J.C. Thiolier (Créteil, 1989)

Placita de Quo Warranto temporibus Edw. I. II. and III. in Curia Receptae Scaccarii Westm. asservata., ed . W. Illingworth (Record Commission, 1818)

'A Plea Roll of Edward I's Army in Scotland, 1296', ed. C.J. Neville, *Miscellany XI*, Scottish History Society, 5th ser., iii (1990), pp. 7–133

Polychronicon Ranulphi Higden Monachi Cestrensis, ed. C. Babington and J.R. Lumby, 9 vols, Rolls Ser., xli (London, 1865–86)

'Private Indentures for Life Service in Peace and War 1278–1476', ed. M. Jones and S.K. Walker, *Camden Miscellany XXXII*, Camden Society 5th ser., iii (1994), pp. 1–190

Records of Antony Bek, Bishop and Patriarch 1283–1311, ed. C.M. Fraser, Surtees Society, clxii (1953)

The Register of Thomas of Corbridge, Lord Archbishop of York, 1300–1304, ed. W. Brown with introduction by A. Hamilton Thompson, 2 vols, Surtees Society, cxxxviii, cxli (1925–8)

The Register of William Wickwane, Lord Archbishop of York 1279–1285, ed. W. Brown, Surtees Society, cxiv (1907)

Registrum Malmesburiense: The Register of Malmesbury Abbey, ed. J.S. Brewer, 2 vols, Rolls Ser., lxxii (London, 1879–80)

Registrum Ricardi de Swinfield, Episcopi Herefordensis, AD MCCLXXXIII–MCCCXVII, ed. W.W. Capes, Canterbury and York Society, vi (1909)

Return of the Name of Every Member of the Lower House of the Parliaments of England, Scotland and Ireland, 1213–1874 (London, 1878)

Rôles Gascons 1242–1307, ed. F. Michel, C. Bémont, and Y. Renouard, 5 vols (Paris, 1885–1962)

The Roll of Arms of the Princes, Barons, and Knights who attended King Edward I. to the Siege of Caerlaverock, in 1300, ed. T. Wright (London, 1864)

A Roll of the Household Expenses of Richard de Swinfield, bishop of Hereford, during part of the years 1289 and 1290, ed. J. Webb, 2 vols, Camden Society 1st ser., lix, lxii (1854–5)

Rolls of Arms of the Reigns of Henry III and Edward III, ed. N.H. Nicolas (London, 1829)

Rotuli Hundredorum temp. Hen. III. and Edw. I. in Turr' Lond' et in Curia Receptae Scaccarii Westm. asservati, 2 vols, ed. W. Illingworth and J. Caley (Record Commission, 1812–18)

Rotuli Scotiae in Turri Londinensi et in Domo Capitulari Westmonasteriensi asservati, ed. D. MacPherson, J. Caley, W. Illingworth and T.H. Horne, 2 vols (Record Commission, 1814–19)

Royal and Other Historical Letters Illustrative of the Reign of Henry III, ed. W.W. Shirley, 2 vols (London, 1862–6)

Scotichronicon by Walter Bower, ed. D.E.R. Watt *et al.*, 9 vols (Aberdeen and Edinburgh, 1987–98)

Scotland in 1298: Documents Relating to the Campaign of Edward I in that Year, ed. H. Gough (London, 1888)

Select Cases before the King's Council, 1243–1482, ed. I.S. Leadam and J.F. Baldwin, Selden Society, xxxv (1918)

Select Cases in the Court of King's Bench under Edward I, ed. G.O. Sayles, 3 vols, Selden Society, lv–lviii (1936–9)

Select Pleas in Manorial and Other Seignorial Courts: Volume I, *Reigns of Henry III and Edward I*, ed. F.W. Maitland, Selden Society, ii (1888)

The Song of Lewes, ed. C.L. Kingsford (Oxford, 1890)

South Lancashire in the Reign of Edward II, ed. G.H. Tupling, Chetham Society 3rd ser., i (1949)

The Statutes of the Realm, 1101–1713, ed. A. Luders *et al.* (Record Commission, 1810–28)

The Tax Roll for Devon 31 Edward I, ed. T.M. Whale, *Transactions of the Devonshire Association for the Advancement of Science, Literature and Art*, xxxi (1899), pp. 376–429

Testamenta Vetusta: Being Illustrations from Wills, of Manners, Customs, etc, as well as of the Descents and Possessions of many Distinguished Families, ed. N.H. Nicolas, 2 vols (London, 1826)

Thomas Wright's Political Songs of England: From the Reign of John to that of Edward II, ed. P. Coss (Cambridge, 1996)

The Tree of Battles of Honoré Bonet, ed. G.W. Coopland (Liverpool, 1949)

Vita Edwardi Secundi, ed. W.R. Childs (Oxford, 2005)

Willelmi Rishanger, quondam Monachi S. Albani, et quorundam Anonymorum, Chronica et Annales, Regnantibus Henrico Tertio et Edwardo Primo, ed. H.T. Riley, Rolls Ser., xxviii 2 (London, 1865)

Wills and Inventories Illustrative of the History, Manners, Language and Statistics, etc., of the Northern Counties of England from the Eleventh Century Downwards, Part 1, ed. J. Raine, Surtees Society, ii (1835)

Yorkshire Lay Subsidy being a Fifteenth, collected 30 Edward I (1301), ed. W. Brown, The Yorkshire Archaeological Society Record Ser., xxi (1987)

Secondary Sources

Abels, R.P., *Lordship and Military Obligation in Anglo-Saxon England* (London, 1988)

Ailes, A., 'The Knight, Heraldry and Armour: The Role of Recognition and the Origins of Heraldry', *Medieval Knighthood IV*, ed. C. Harper-Bill and R. Harvey (Woodbridge, 1992), pp. 1–21

——, 'Up in Arms: The Rise of the Armigerous *Vallettus*, c. 1300', *The Coat of Arms*, new ser., xii (1997), pp. 10–16

Alexander, J., and P. Binski, eds., *Age of Chivalry: Art in Plantagenet England 1200–1400* (London, 1987)

Altschul, M., *A Baronial Family in Medieval England: The Clares, 1217–1314* (Baltimore, Md., 1965)

Armitage-Smith, S., *John of Gaunt. King of Castile and Leon, Duke of Aquitaine and Lancaster, Earl of Derby, Lincoln and Leicester, Seneschal of England* (London, 1964)

Ayton, A., 'English Armies in the Fourteenth Century', *Arms, Armies and Fortifications in the Hundred Years War*, ed. A. Curry and M. Hughes (Woodbridge, 1994), pp. 21–38

——, *Knights and Warhorses: Military Service and the English Aristocracy under Edward III* (Woodbridge, 1994)

——, 'Knights, Esquires and Military Service: The Evidence of the Armorial Cases before the Court of Chivalry', *The Medieval Military Revolution: State, Society and Military Change in Medieval and Early Modern Europe*, ed. A. Ayton and J.L. Price (London, 1995), pp. 81–104

——, 'Edward III and the English Aristocracy at the Beginning of the Hundred Years War', *Armies, Chivalry and Warfare in Medieval Britain and France* (Stamford, 1998), pp. 173–206

——, 'Sir Thomas Ughtred and the Edwardian Military Revolution', *The Age of Edward III*, ed. J.S. Bothwell (York, 2001), pp. 107–32

——, 'The English Army at Crécy', A. Ayton and P. Preston, *The Battle of Crécy, 1346* (Woodbridge, 2005), pp. 159–251

Barker, J.R.V., *The Tournament in England, 1100–1400* (Woodbridge, 1986)

Barrow, G.W.S., *Robert Bruce and the Community of the Realm of Scotland*, 3rd edition (Edinburgh, 1988)

Bartlett, R., *The Making of Europe: Conquest, Colonization and Cultural Change 950–1350* (London, 1993)

Bean, J.M.W., *The Decline of English Feudalism, 1215–1540* (Manchester, 1968)

——, '"Bachelor" and "Retainer"', *Medievalia et Humanistica: Studies in Medieval and Renaissance Culture*, new ser., iii (London, 1972), pp. 117–31

——, *From Lord to Patron: Lordship in Late Medieval England* (Manchester, 1989)

Bedell, J., 'Memory and Proof of Age in England 1272–1327', *Past and Present*, clxii (1999), pp. 3–27

Beebe, B., 'The English Baronage and the Crusade of 1270', *BIHR*, xlviii (1975), pp. 127–48

Bell, A.R., *War and the Soldier in the Fourteenth Century* (Woodbridge, 2004)

Bennett, M., 'The Status of the Squire: The Northern Evidence', *The Ideals and Practice of Medieval Knighthood I*, ed. C. Harper-Bill and R. Harvey (Woodbridge, 1986), pp. 1–11

Bennett, M.J., *Community, Class and Careerism: Cheshire and Lancashire Society in the Age of* Sir Gawain and the Green Knight (Cambridge, 1983)

——, 'Careerism in Late Medieval England', *People, Politics and Community in the Later Middle Ages*, ed. J. Rosenthal and C. Richmond (Gloucester, 1987), pp. 19–39

Boissevain, J., and J.C. Mitchell, eds, *Network Analysis: Studies in Human Interaction* (The Hague, 1973)

Bothwell, J.S., *Edward III and the English Peerage: Royal Patronage, Social Mobility and Political Control in Fourteenth-Century England* (Woodbridge, 2004)

Boyle, M.L., 'Early History of the Wardens of the Marches of England towards Scotland, 1296–1377', MA thesis, University of Hull, 1980

Brault, G.J., 'A French Source of the Lord Marshal's Roll (1295–6)', *The Antiquaries Journal*, lxxiii (1993), pp. 27–36

Breslow, B., 'The English Sheriff during the Reign of King Edward I', PhD thesis, University of Ohio, 1968

Brett-James, 'John de Drokensford, bishop of Bath and Wells', *Transactions of the London and Middlesex Archaeological Society*, x (1951), pp. 281–301

Brown, M., 'War, Allegiance and Community in the Anglo-Scottish Marches: Teviotdale in the Fourteenth Century', *Northern History*, xli (2004), pp. 211–38

——, '*Scoti Anglicati*: Scots in Plantagenet Allegiance during the Fourteenth Century', *England and Scotland in the Fourteenth Century: New Perspectives*, ed. A. King and M. Penman (Woodbridge, 2007), pp. 94–115

Brown, S., *'Our Magnificent Fabrick'. York Minster: An Architectural History* c. *1220–1500* (Swindon, 2003)

Brown, S.D.B., 'Military Service and Monetary Reward in the Eleventh and Twelfth Centuries', *History*, lxxiv (1989), pp. 20–38

Bullock-Davies, C., *Menestrellorum Multitudo: Minstrels at a Royal Feast* (Cardiff, 1978)

Cam, H.M., 'Studies in the Hundred Rolls: Some Aspects of Thirteenth-Century Administration', *Oxford Studies in Social and Legal History*, ed. P. Vinogradoff, vi (Oxford, 1921)

——, *The Hundred and the Hundred Rolls: An Outline of Local Government in Medieval England* (London, 1930)

——, 'The Decline and Fall of English Feudalism', *History*, xxv (1940), pp. 216–33

Cameron, S., and A. Ross, 'The Treaty of Edinburgh and the Disinherited (1328–1332)', *History*, lxxxiv (1999), pp. 237–56

Carpenter, C., 'The Beauchamp Affinity: A Study of Bastard Feudalism at Work', *EHR*, xcv (1980), pp. 514–32

——, *Locality and Polity. A Study of Warwickshire Landed Society, 1401–1499* (Cambridge, 1992)

——, 'Gentry and Community in Medieval England', *Journal of British Studies*, xxxiii (1994), pp. 340–80

Carpenter, D.A., 'Was there a Crisis of the Knightly Class in the Thirteenth Century? The Oxfordshire Evidence', *EHR*, xcv (1980), pp. 721–52

——, 'The Beginnings of Parliament', *The Reign of Henry III* (London, 1996), pp. 381–408

Carr, A.D., 'An Aristocracy in Decline: The Native Welsh Lords after the Edwardian Conquest', *WHR*, v (1970), pp. 103–29

Chaplais, P., *Piers Gaveston: Edward II's Adoptive Brother* (Oxford, 1994)

Cherry, J., 'Heraldry as Decoration in the Thirteenth Century', *England in the Thirteenth Century*, ed. W.M. Ormrod (Stamford, 1991), pp. 123–34

Cherry, M., 'The Courtenay Earls of Devon: The Formation and Disintegration of a Late Medieval Aristocratic Affinity', *Southern History*, i (1979), pp. 71–97

Chew, H.M., 'Scutage under Edward I', *EHR*, xxxvii (1922), pp. 321–36

——, *The English Ecclesiastical Tenants-in-Chief and Knight Service, especially in the Thirteenth and Fourteenth Centuries* (London, 1932)

Chibnall, M., 'Mercenaries and the *Familia Regis* under Henry I', *History*, new ser., lxii (1977), pp. 15–23

Clayton, M., *Catalogue of Rubbings of Brasses and Incised Slabs* (London, 1979)

Coales, J., ed., *The Earliest English Brasses: Patronage, Style and Workshops 1270–1350* (London, 1987)

Contamine, P., *War in the Middle Ages* (Oxford, 1984)

Coss, P., 'Sir Geoffrey de Langley and the Crisis of the Knightly Class in Thirteenth- Century England', *Past and Present*, lxviii (1975), pp. 3–37

——, *Lordship, Knighthood and Locality: A Study in English Society c. 1180-c. 1280* (Cambridge, 1991)

——, *The Knight in Medieval England, 1000–1400* (Stroud, 1993)

——, 'Knights, Esquires and the Origins of Social Gradation in England', *TRHS*, 6th ser., v (1995), pp. 155–78

——, 'Knighthood, Heraldry and Social Exclusion in Edwardian England', *Heraldry, Pageantry and Social Display in Medieval England*, ed. P. Coss and M. Keen (Woodbridge, 2002), pp. 39–68

——, *The Origins of the English Gentry* (Cambridge, 2003)

Critchley, J.S., 'Military Organisation in England, 1154–1254', PhD thesis, University of Nottingham, 1968

——, 'Summonses to Military Service Early in the Reign of Henry III', *EHR*, lxxxvi (1971), pp. 79–95

——, 'The Early History of the Writ of Judicial Protection', *BIHR*, xlv (1972), pp. 196–213

Crouch, D., *The Beaumont Twins: The Roots and Branches of Power in the Twelfth Century* (Cambridge, 1986)

——, 'Debate: Bastard Feudalism Revised', *Past and Present*, cxxxi (1991), pp. 165–77

——, *The Image of Aristocracy in Britain, 1000–1300* (London, 1992)

——, 'From Stenton to McFarlane: Models of Societies of the Twelfth and Thirteenth Centuries', *TRHS*, 6th ser., v (1995), pp. 179–200

——, 'The Local Influence of the Earls of Warwick, 1088–1242: A Study in Decline and Resourcefulness', *Midland History*, xxi (1996), pp. 1–22

——, 'The Historian, Lineage and Heraldry, 1050–1250', *Heraldry, Pageantry and Social Display in Medieval England*, ed. P. Coss and M. Keen (Woodbridge, 2002), pp. 17–37

——, *The Birth of Nobility: Constructing Aristocracy in England and France 900–1300* (Harlow, 2005)

Curry, A., *Agincourt: A New History* (Stroud, 2005)

Davies, R.R., 'Colonial Wales', *Past and Present*, lxv (1974), pp. 3–23

——, *Lordship and Society in the March of Wales, 1282–1400* (Oxford, 1978)

——, *Conquest, Coexistence, and Change: Wales 1063–1415* (Oxford, 1987)

Denholm-Young, N., *Richard of Cornwall* (Oxford, 1947)

——, *The Song of Carlaverock and the Parliamentary Roll of Arms as found in Cott. MS. Calig. A XVIII in the British Museum* (1962)

——, *History and Heraldry 1254 to 1310: A Study of the Historical Value of the Rolls of Arms* (Oxford, 1965)

——, *The Country Gentry in the Fourteenth Century, with Special Reference to the Heraldic Rolls of Arms* (Oxford, 1969)

——, 'Feudal Society in the Thirteenth Century: The Knights', *Collected Papers of N. Denholm-Young* (Cardiff, 1969), pp. 83–94

——, 'The Galloway Roll', *Collected Papers of N. Denholm-Young* (Cardiff, 1969), pp. 131–2

Duby, G., 'Youth in Aristocratic Society: Northwestern France in the Twelfth Century', *The Chivalrous Society* (London, 1977), pp. 112–22

Edwards, J.G., 'The Personnel of the Commons in Parliament under Edward I and Edward II', *Essays in Medieval History Presented to T.F. Tout*, ed. A.G. Little and F.M. Powicke (Manchester, 1925), pp. 197–214

Evans, S.S., *The Lords of Battle: Image and Reality of the* Comitatus *in Dark-Age Britain* (Woodbridge, 1997)

Faulkner, K., 'The Transformation of Knighthood in Early Thirteenth-Century England', *EHR*, cxi (1996), pp. 1–23

Fleming, D.F., 'Landholding by *Milites* in Domesday Book: A Revision', *Anglo-Norman Studies XIII*, ed. M. Chibnall (Woodbridge, 1991), pp. 83–98

Fowler, K., *The King's Lieutenant: Henry of Grosmont, First Duke of Lancaster, 1310–1361* (London, 1969)

Frame, R., 'Military Service in the Lordship of Ireland 1290–1360: Institutions and Society on the Anglo-Gaelic Frontier', *Medieval Frontier Societies*, ed. R. Bartlett and A. MacKay (Oxford, 1989), pp. 101–26

France, J., *Western Warfare in the Age of the Crusades, 1000–1300* (London, 1999)

Fraser, C.M., *A History of Antony Bek, bishop of Durham, 1283–1311* (Oxford, 1957)

Fryde, N., *The Tyranny and Fall of Edward II 1321–1326* (Cambridge, 1979)

Given-Wilson, C., *The Royal Household and the King's Affinity: Service, Politics and Finance in England 1360–1413* (London, 1986)

——, *The English Nobility in the Late Middle Ages: The Fourteenth-Century Political Community* (London, 1987)

——, 'The King and the Gentry in Fourteenth-Century England', *TRHS*, 5th ser., xxxvii (1987), pp. 87–102

Gorski, R., 'A Methodological Holy Grail: Nominal Record Linkage in a Medieval Context', *Medieval Prosopography*, xvii (1996), pp. 145–79

——, *The Fourteenth-Century Sheriff: English Local Administration in the Late Middle Ages* (Woodbridge, 2003)

Green, D.S., 'Politics and Service with Edward the Black Prince', *The Age of Edward III*, ed. J.S. Bothwell (Woodbridge, 2001), pp. 53–68

Haines, R.M., *King Edward II: Edward of Caernarfon, His Life, His Reign, and Its Aftermath, 1284–1330* (Montreal, 2003)

Hamilton, J.S., *Piers Gaveston, Earl of Cornwall 1307–1312: Politics and Patronage in the Reign of Edward II* (Detroit, Mich., 1988)

Harding, A., 'The Origins and Early History of the Keeper of the Peace', *TRHS*, 5th ser., x (1960), pp. 85–109

——, *England in the Thirteenth Century* (Cambridge, 1993)

Harriss, G.L., *King, Parliament, and Public Finance in Medieval England to 1369* (Oxford, 1975)

Hartland, B., 'The Household Knights of Edward I in Ireland', *Historical Research*, lxxvii (2004), pp. 161–77

Harvey, P.D.A. and A. McGuiness, *A Guide to British Medieval Seals* (London, 1996)

Harvey, S., 'The Knight and the Knight's Fee in England', *Past and Present*, il (1970), pp. 3–43

Haskell, M., 'Breaking the Stalemate: The Scottish Campaign of Edward I, 1303–4', *Thirteenth Century England VII*, ed. M. Prestwich, R. Britnell and R. Frame (Woodbridge, 1999), pp. 223–41

Heslop, T.A., 'English Seals in the Thirteenth and Fourteenth Centuries', *Age of Chivalry: Art in Plantagenet England 1200–1400*, ed. J. Alexander and P. Binski (London, 1987), pp. 114–17

Hicks, M., *Bastard Feudalism* (London, 1995)

Hilton, R.H., *A Medieval Society: The West Midlands at the End of the Thirteenth Century* (London, 1966)

Hollister, C.W., *The Military Organization of Norman England* (Oxford, 1965)

Holmes, G.A., *The Estates of the Higher Nobility in Fourteenth-Century England* (Cambridge, 1957)

Housley, N., 'European Warfare, c. 1200–1320', *Medieval Warfare: A History*, ed. M. Keen (Oxford, 1999), pp. 113–35

Howarth, S.J.P., 'King, Government and Community in Cumberland and Westmorland c. 1200–c. 1400', PhD thesis, University of Liverpool, 1988

Hunnisett, R.F., *The Medieval Coroner* (Cambridge, 1961)

Hunter Blair, C.H., 'Northern Knights at Falkirk, 1298', *Archaeologia Aeliana, or Miscellaneous Tracts Relating to Antiquity*, ed. C.H. Hunter Blair, 4th ser., xxv (1947), pp. 68–114

Illsley, J.S., 'Parliamentary Elections in the Reign of Edward I', *BIHR*, xlix (1976), pp. 24–40

Ingamells, R.L., 'The Household Knights of Edward I', 2 vols, PhD thesis, University of Durham, 1992

Jewell, H.M., *English Local Administration in the Middle Ages* (Newton Abbot, 1972)

——, 'Local Administration and Administrators in Yorkshire, 1258–1348', *Northern History*, xvi (1980), pp. 1–19

Johnstone, H., *Edward of Carnarvon, 1284–1307* (Manchester, 1946)

Jones, M., 'An Indenture between Robert, Lord Mohaut, and Sir John de Bracebridge for Life Service in Peace and War, 1310', *Journal of the Society of Archivists*, iv (1972), pp. 384–94

Juřica, A.R.J., 'The Knights of Edward I: An Investigation of the Social Significance of Knightly Rank in the Period 1272–1307 based on a Study of the Knights of Somerset', PhD thesis, University of Birmingham, 1976

Kaeuper, R.W., *War, Justice and Public Order: England and France in the Later Middle Ages* (Oxford, 1988)

Keen, M., *Chivalry* (London, 1984)

——, 'English Military Experience and the Court of Chivalry: the Case of Grey v. Hastings', *Guerre et Société en France, en Angleterre et en Bourgogne XIVe–XVe siècle*, ed. P. Contamine, C. Giry-Deloison and M. Keen (Lille, 1992), pp. 123–42

——, 'Richard II's Ordinances of War of 1385', *Rulers and Ruled in Late Medieval England: Essays presented to Gerald Harriss*, ed. R.E. Archer and S. Walker (London, 1995), pp. 33–48

——, 'Heraldry and Hierarchy: Esquires and Gentlemen', *Orders and Hierarchies in Late Medieval and Renaissance Europe*, ed. J. Denton (London, 1999), pp. 94–108

——, *Origins of the English Gentleman: Heraldry, Chivalry and Gentility in Medieval England, c. 1300-c. 1500* (Stroud, 2002)

Kimball, E.G., *Serjeanty Tenure in Medieval England* (London, 1936)

King, A., 'Englishmen, Scots and Marchers: National and Local Identities in Thomas Gray's *Scalacronica*', *Northern History*, xxxvi (2000), pp. 217–31

——, 'War, Politics and Landed Society in Northumberland, *c.* 1296-*c.* 1408', PhD thesis, University of Durham, 2001

——, '"According to the Custom used in French and Scottish Wars": Prisoners and Casualties on the Scottish Marches in the Fourteenth Century', *Journal of Medieval History*, xxviii (2002), pp. 263–90

——, '"Pur Salvation du Roiaume": Military Service and Obligation in Fourteenth-Century Northumberland', *Fourteenth Century England II*, ed. C. Given-Wilson (Woodbridge, 2002), pp. 13–31

Kingsford, C.L., 'On Some Ancient Deeds belonging to Lord de L'Isle and Dudley', *Archaeologia, or Miscellaneous Tracts Relating to Antiquity*, lxv (1914), pp. 251–68

——, 'John de Benstede and his Missions for Edward I', *Essays in History presented to Reginald Lane Poole*, ed. H.W.C. Davis (Oxford, 1927), pp. 332–59

Labarge, M.W., *A Baronial Household of the Thirteenth Century* (London, 1965)

Lachaud, F., 'Dress and Social Status in England before the Sumptuary Laws', *Heraldry, Pageantry and Social Display in Medieval England*, ed. P. Coss and M. Keen (Woodbridge, 2002), pp. 105–23

Lawrance, H., *Heraldry from Military Monuments before 1350 in England and Wales*, Harleian Society, xcviii (1946)

Lewis, N.B., 'An Early Indenture of Military Service, 27 July 1287', *BIHR*, xiii (1935), pp. 85–9

——, 'An Early Fourteenth-Century Contract for Military Service', *BIHR*, xx (1943–5), pp. 111–18

——, 'The Organisation of Indentured Retinues in Fourteenth-Century England', *TRHS*, xxvii (1945), pp. 29–39

——, 'The English Forces in Flanders, August–November 1297', *Studies in Medieval History Presented to F.M. Powicke*, ed. R.W. Hunt, W.A. Pantin and R.W. Southern (Oxford, 1948), pp. 310–18

——, 'The Last Medieval Summons of the English Feudal Levy, 13 June 1385', *EHR*, lxxiii (1958), pp. 1–26

——, 'The Recruitment and Organization of a Contract Army, May to November 1337', *BIHR*, xxxvii (1964), pp. 1–19

——, 'The Summons of the English Feudal Levy, 5 April 1327', *Essays in Medieval History Presented to Bertie Wilkinson*, ed. T.A. Sandquist and M.R. Powicke (Toronto, 1969), pp. 236–49

——, 'The Feudal Summons of 1385', *EHR*, c (1985), pp. 729–43

Lloyd, S., *English Society and the Crusade 1216–1307* (Oxford, 1988)

Lubimenko, I., *Jean de Bretagne, Comte de Richmond: sa vie et son activité en Angleterre, en Éscosse et en France (1266–1334)* (Paris, 1908)

Lyon, B.D., 'The Feudal Antecedent of the Indenture System', *Speculum*, xxix (1954), pp. 503–11

——, *From Fief to Indenture: The Transition from Feudal to Non-Feudal Contract in Western Europe* (Cambridge, Mass., 1957)

McFarlane, K.B., 'Bastard Feudalism', *BIHR*, xx (1943–5), pp. 161–80

——, 'An Indenture of Agreement between Two English Knights for Mutual Aid and Counsel in Peace and War, 5 December 1298', *BIHR*, xxxviii (1965), pp. 200–10

——, *The Nobility of Later Medieval England* (Oxford, 1973)

——, 'The Wars of the Roses', *England in the Fifteenth Century: Collected Essays* (London, 1981), pp. 231–61

McNamee, C.J., 'William Wallace's Invasion of Northern England in 1297', *Northern History*, xxvi (1990), pp. 40–58

——, *The Wars of the Bruces: Scotland, England and Ireland 1306–1328* (East Linton, 1997)

Maddicott, J.R., *Thomas of Lancaster 1307–1322: A Study in the Reign of Edward II* (Oxford, 1970)

——, 'Thomas of Lancaster and Sir Robert Holland: A Study in Noble Patronage', *EHR*, lxxxvi (1971), pp. 449–72

——, 'The County Community and the Making of Public Opinion in Fourteenth-Century England', *TRHS*, 5th ser., xxviii (1978), pp. 27–43

——, 'Edward I and the Lessons of Baronial Reform: Local Government, 1258–80', *Thirteenth Century England I*, ed., P.R. Coss and S.D. Lloyd (Woodbridge, 1986), pp. 1–30

——, 'The Crusade Taxation of 1268–1270 and the Development of Parliament', *Thirteenth Century England II*, ed., P.R. Coss and S.D. Lloyd (Woodbridge, 1988), pp. 93–117

——, *Simon de Montfort* (Cambridge, 1994)

Mason, J., 'Sir Andrew de Harcla, Earl of Carlisle', *Transactions of the Cumberland and Westmorland Antiquarian and Archaeological Society*, new ser., xxix (1929), pp. 98–137

Morgan, P., *War and Society in Medieval Cheshire, 1277–1403* (Manchester, 1987)

——, 'Making the English Gentry', *Thirteenth Century England V*, ed. P.R. Coss and S.D. Lloyd (Woodbridge, 1995), pp. 21–8

Morillo, S., *Warfare under the Anglo-Norman Kings, 1066–1135* (Woodbridge, 1994)

Morris, J.E., *The Welsh Wars of Edward I* (Oxford, 1901)

——, 'Cumberland and Westmorland Military Levies in the Time of Edward I and Edward II', *Transactions of the Cumberland and Westmorland Antiquarian and Archaeological Society*, new ser., iii (1903), pp. 307–27

——, *Bannockburn* (Cambridge, 1914)

Morris, M., *The Bigod Earls of Norfolk in the Thirteenth Century* (Woodbridge, 2005)

Morris, W.A., *The Medieval English Sheriff to 1300* (Manchester, 1927)

Mortimer, I., *The Greatest Traitor: The Life of Sir Roger Mortimer, 1st Earl of March, 1327–1330* (London, 2003)

Musson, A.J., 'Sub-Keepers and Constables: The Role of Local Officials in Keeping the Peace in Fourteenth-Century England', *EHR*, cxvii (2002), pp. 1–24

Nicholson, H., *Medieval Warfare: Theory and Practice of War in Europe 300–1500* (Basingstoke, 2004)

Norton, R., 'The Arms of Eustace Hatch and Others', *The Coat of Arms*, new ser., v (1982), pp. 18–19

Orme, N., *From Childhood to Chivalry: The Education of the English Kings and Aristocracy 1066–1530* (London, 1984)

Ormrod, W.M., 'The Domestic Response to the Hundred Years War', *Arms, Armies and Fortifications in the Hundred Years War*, ed. A. Curry and M. Hughes (Woodbridge, 1994), pp. 83–101

Painter, S., *Studies in the History of the English Feudal Barony* (Baltimore, Md., 1943)

Palmer, J.J.N., 'The Last Summons of the Feudal Army in England (1385)', *EHR*, lxxxiii (1968), pp. 771–5

Pasquet, D., *An Essay on the Origins of the House of Commons* (London, 1964)

Payne, A., 'Medieval Heraldry', *Age of Chivalry: Art in Plantagenet England 1200–1400*, ed. J. Alexander and P. Binski (London, 1987), pp. 55–9

Phillips, J.R.S., *Aymer de Valence, Earl of Pembroke 1307–1324: Baronial Politics in the Reign of Edward II* (Oxford, 1972)

Poole, A.L., *Obligations of Society in the XII and XIII Centuries* (Oxford, 1946)

Powicke, F.M., *The Thirteenth Century, 1216–1307*, 2nd edition (Oxford, 1962)

Powicke, M.R., 'Distraint of Knighthood and Military Obligation under Henry III', *Speculum*, xxv (1950), pp. 457–70

——, 'The General Obligation to Cavalry Service under Edward I', *Speculum*, xxviii (1953), pp. 814–33

——, 'Edward II and Military Obligation', *Speculum*, xxxi (1956), pp. 92–119

——, *Military Obligation in Medieval England: A Study in Liberty and Duty* (Oxford, 1962)

Prestwich, J.O., 'War and Finance in the Anglo-Norman State', *TRHS*, 5th ser., iv (1954), pp. 19–43

Prestwich, M., *War, Politics and Finance under Edward I* (London, 1972)

——, *The Three Edwards: War and State in England 1272–1377* (London, 1980)

——, 'Cavalry Service in Early Fourteenth-Century England', *War and Government in the Middle Ages: Essays in Honour of J.O. Prestwich*, ed. J. Gillingham and J.C. Holt (Woodbridge, 1984), pp. 147–58

——, 'Colonial Scotland: The English in Scotland under Edward I', *Scotland and England 1286–1815*, ed. R.A. Mason (Edinburgh, 1987), pp. 6–17

——, *Edward I* (London, 1988)

——, *English Politics in the Thirteenth Century* (London, 1990)

——, '*Miles in Armis Strenuus:* The Knight at War', *TRHS*, 6th ser., v (1995), pp. 201–20

——, 'Money and Mercenaries in English Medieval Armies', *England and Germany in the High Middle Ages*, ed. A. Haverkamp and H. Vollrath (Oxford, 1996), pp. 129–50

——, *Armies and Warfare in the Middle Ages: The English Experience* (London, 1996)

——, 'The Unreliability of Royal Household Knights in the Early Fourteenth Century', *Fourteenth Century England II*, ed. C. Given-Wilson (Woodbridge, 2002), pp. 1–11

——, *Plantagenet England, 1225–1360* (Oxford, 2005)

Prince, A.E., 'The Importance of the Campaign of 1327', *EHR*, l (1935), pp. 299–302

——, 'The Payment of Army Wages in Edward III's Reign', *Speculum*, xix (1944), pp. 137–60

Putnam, B.H., 'The Transformation of the Keepers of the Peace into the Justices of the Peace, 1327–1380', *TRHS*, 4th ser., xii (1929), pp. 19–48

Reid, R.R., 'The Office of the Warden of the Marches; Its Origin and Early History', *EHR*, xxxii (1917), pp. 479–96

Reynolds, S., *Fiefs and Vassals: The Medieval Evidence Reinterpreted* (Oxford, 1994)

Rhodes, W.E., 'Edmund, Earl of Lancaster', *EHR*, x (1895), part 1, pp. 19–40, part 2, pp. 209–37

Richardson, H.G., and G.O. Sayles, *The Governance of Mediaeval England from the Conquest to Magna Carta* (Edinburgh, 1963)

Ridgeway, H., 'William de Valence and his *Familiares*, 1247–72', *Historical Research*, lxv (1992), pp. 239–57

Rogers, C.J., '"As if a New Sun had Arisen": England's Fourteenth-Century RMA', *The*

Dynamics of Military Revolution 1300–2050, ed. M. Knox and W. Murray (Cambridge, 2001), pp. 15–34

Rosenthal, J.T., *Old Age in Late Medieval England* (Philadelphia, Pa., 1996)

Round, J.H., *Feudal England: Historical Studies on the XIth and XIIth Centuries* (London, 1895)

Royston Fairbank, F., 'The Last Earl of Warenne and Surrey, and the Distribution of his Possessions', *Yorkshire Archaeological Journal*, xix (1907), pp. 193–264

Rushworth, A., and R. Carlton, *Thirlwall Castle: History of a Northumberland Border Stronghold*, Northumberland National Park Documentary Survey (Hexham, 2001)

Sanders, I.J., *Feudal Military Service in England: A Study of the Constitutional and Military Powers of the Barones in Medieval England* (Oxford, 1956)

Saul, N., *Knights and Esquires: The Gloucestershire Gentry in the Fourteenth Century* (Oxford, 1981)

——, 'The Social Status of Chaucer's Franklin: A Reconsideration', *Medium Aevum*, lii (1983), pp. 10–26

——, 'The Despensers and the Downfall of Edward II', *EHR*, xcix (1984), pp. 1–33

——, *Scenes from Provincial Life: Knightly Families in Sussex 1280–1400* (Oxford, 1986)

——, ed. *Age of Chivalry: Art and Society in Late Medieval England* (London, 1992)

Sayles, G.O., 'Parliamentary Representation in 1294, 1295 and 1307', *The English Parliament in the Middle Ages*, ed., H.G. Richardson and G.O. Sayles (London, 1981), XI, pp. 110–15

Scammell, J., 'The Formation of the English Social Structure: Freedom, Knights, and Gentry, 1066–1300', *Speculum*, lxviii (1993), pp. 591–618

Shahar, S., *Growing Old in the Middle Ages: 'Winter Clothes Us in Shadow and Pain'* (London, 1997)

Simpkin, D., 'The English Aristocracy at War, 1272–1314', PhD thesis, University of Hull, 2006

——, 'The English Army and the Scottish Campaign of 1310–1311', *England and Scotland in the Fourteenth Century: New Perspectives*, ed. A. King and M. Penman (Woodbridge, 2007), pp. 14–39

Simpson, G.G., 'The *Familia* of Roger de Quincy, Earl of Winchester and Constable of Scotland', *Essays on the Nobility of Medieval Scotland*, ed. K.J. Stringer (Edinburgh, 1985), pp. 102–30

Smith, L.B., 'The Death of Llywelyn ap Gruffydd: The Narratives Reconsidered', *WHR*, xi (1982), pp. 200–13

Smith, P.W., 'A Study of the Lists of Military and Parliamentary Summons in the Reign of Edward I: The Families of Lists and their Significance', 2 parts, PhD thesis, University of Iowa, 1967

Spencer, A., 'The Comital Military Retinue in the Reign of Edward I', *Historical Research* (forthcoming, 2009)

Stenton, F.M., *The First Century of English Feudalism, 1066–1166* (Oxford, 1932)

Stewart, S., 'Simon de Montfort and his Followers, June 1263', *EHR*, cxix (2004), pp. 965–9

Suppe, F.C., *Military Institutions on the Welsh Marches: Shropshire, AD 1066–1300* (Woodbridge, 1994)

Sutherland, D.W., *Quo Warranto Proceedings in the Reign of Edward I 1278–1294* (Oxford, 1963)

Tebbit, A., 'Royal Patronage and Political Allegiance: The Household Knights of Edward II, 1314–1321', *Thirteenth Century England X*, ed. M. Prestwich, R. Britnell and R. Frame (Woodbridge, 2005), pp. 197–208

Tomkinson, A., 'Retinues at the Tournament of Dunstable, 1309', *EHR*, lxxiv (1959), pp. 70–89

Tout, T.F., 'The *Communitas Bacheleriae Angliae*', *EHR*, xvii (1902), pp. 89–95

——, *Chapters in the Administrative History of Mediaeval England, The Wardrobe, the Chamber and the Small Seals*, 6 vols (Manchester, 1920–33)

Tuck, A., *Crown and Nobility, 1272–1461: Political Conflict in Late Medieval England* (Oxford, 1985)

Vale, M.G.A., 'The Gascon Nobility and the Anglo-French War 1294–98', *War and Government in the Middle Ages: Essays in Honour of J.O. Prestwich*, ed. J. Gillingham and J.C. Holt (Woodbridge, 1984), pp. 134–46

——, *The Angevin Legacy and the Hundred Years War, 1250–1340* (Oxford, 1990)

Valente, C., *The Theory and Practice of Revolt in Medieval England* (Aldershot, 2003)

Verbruggen, J.F., *The Art of Warfare in Western Europe during the Middle Ages: From the Eighth Century to 1340*, 2nd edition (Woodbridge, 1997)

Verduyn, A., 'The Selection and Appointment of Justices of the Peace in 1338', *Historical Research*, lxviii (1995), pp. 1–25

Ville, O. de, 'Jocelyn Deyville: Brigand, or Man of his Time?', *Northern History*, xxxv (1999), pp. 27–49

Wagner, A.R., *Historic Heraldry of Britain* (London, 1939)

——, *Heralds and Heraldry in the Middle Ages: An Inquiry into the Growth of the Armorial Function of Heralds*, 2nd edition (Oxford, 1956)

Walker, R.F., 'The Anglo-Welsh Wars, 1217–1267 with Special Reference to English Military Developments', DPhil thesis, University of Oxford, 1954

——, 'William de Valence and the Army of West Wales, 1282–1283', *WHR*, xviii (1997), pp. 407–29

Walker, S., *The Lancastrian Affinity 1361–1399* (Oxford, 1990)

Ward, J.C., *The Essex Gentry and the County Community in the Fourteenth Century* (Chelmsford, 1991)

Watson, F.J., *Under the Hammer: Edward I and Scotland, 1286–1306* (East Linton, 1998)

Waugh, S.L., 'Reluctant Knights and Jurors: Respites, Exemptions, and Public Obligations in the Reign of Henry III', *Speculum*, lviii (1983), pp. 937–86

——, 'Tenure to Contract: Lordship and Clientage in Thirteenth-Century England', *EHR*, ci (1986), pp. 811–39

——, 'The Third Century of English Feudalism', *Thirteenth Century England VII*, ed. M. Prestwich, R. Britnell and R. Frame (Woodbridge, 1999), pp. 47–59

Woolgar, C.M., *The Great Household in Late Medieval England* (London, 1999)

Index

Warfare in History

The Battle of Hastings: Sources and Interpretations, *edited and introduced by Stephen Morillo*

Infantry Warfare in the Early Fourteenth Century: Discipline, Tactics, and Technology, *Kelly DeVries*

The Art of Warfare in Western Europe during the Middle Ages, from the Eighth Century to 1340 (second edition), *J.F. Verbruggen*

Knights and Peasants: The Hundred Years War in the French Countryside, *Nicholas Wright*

Society at War: The Experience of England and France during the Hundred Years War, *edited by Christopher Allmand*

The Circle of War in the Middle Ages: Essays on Medieval Military and Naval History, *edited by Donald J. Kagay and L.J. Andrew Villalon*

The Anglo-Scots Wars, 1513–1550: A Military History, *Gervase Phillips*

The Norwegian Invasion of England in 1066, *Kelly DeVries*

The Wars of Edward III: Sources and Interpretations, *edited by Clifford J. Rogers*

The Battle of Agincourt: Sources and Interpretations, *Anne Curry*

War Cruel and Sharp: English Strategy under Edward III, 1327–1360, *Clifford J. Rogers*

The Normans and their Adversaries at War: Essays in Memory of C. Warren Hollister, *edited by Richard P. Abels and Bernard S. Bachrach*

The Battle of the Golden Spurs (Courtrai, 11 July 1302): A Contribution to the History of Flanders' War of Liberation, 1297–1305, *J.F. Verbruggen*

War at Sea in the Middle Ages and the Renaissance, *edited by John B. Hattendorf and Richard W. Unger*

Swein Forkbeard's Invasions and the Danish Conquest of England, 991–1017, *Ian Howard*

Religion and the conduct of war, c.300–1215, *David S. Bachrach*

Warfare in Medieval Brabant, 1356–1406, *Sergio Boffa*

Renaissance Military Memoirs: War, History and Identity, 1450–1600, *Yuval Harari*

The Place of War in English History, 1066–1214, *J.O. Prestwich, edited by Michael Prestwich*

War and the Soldier in the Fourteenth Century, *Adrian R. Bell*

German War Planning, 1891–1914: Sources and Interpretations, *Terence Zuber*

The Battle of Crécy, 1346, *Andrew Ayton and Sir Philip Preston*

The Battle of Yorktown, 1781: A Reassessment, *John D. Grainger*

Special Operations in the Age of Chivalry, 1100–1550, *Yuval Noah Harari*

Women, Crusading and the Holy Land in Historical Narrative, *Natasha R. Hodgson*